Christianity and Plurality

Christianity and Plurality

Classic and Contemporary Readings

Edited by

Richard J. Plantinga

BLACKWELL Publishers

Copyright © Blackwell Publishers Ltd 1999
Editorial matter and organization copyright © Richard J. Plantinga 1999

First published 1999

2 4 6 8 10 9 7 5 3 1

Blackwell Publishers Ltd
108 Cowley Road
Oxford OX4 1JF
UK

Blackwell Publishers Inc.
350 Main Street
Malden, Massachusetts 02148
USA

British Library Cataloguing in Publication Data
A CIP catalogue record for this book is available from the British Library.

Library of Congress Cataloging-in-Publication Data
Christianity and plurality : classic and contemporary readings /
edited by Richard J. Plantinga.
    p.   cm.
    Includes bibliographical references (p.   ) and index.
    ISBN 0–631–20914–X (alk. paper). — ISBN 0–631–20915–8 (alk.
paper)
    1. Christianity and other religions.   2. Religious pluralism-
Christianity.   I. Plantinga, Richard J.
    BR127.C47415 1999
    261.2—dc21   98–52528
                                                                        CIP

Contents

Contents

Acknowledgments

Like many undertakings in life, this project was not accomplished by one person thinking and working alone. While one person was central to its vision and completion, several people have assisted with the project in some fashion. I therefore wish to take this opportunity to recognize their contributions and express my gratitude.

Blackwell Publishers and my editor, Alex Wright, have been professional and generous in their handling of this project from beginning to end. I wish to acknowledge their helpful suggestions and assistance.

I also wish to express my gratitude to my colleagues in the Department of Religion and Theology at Calvin College. Fellow faculty members heard me out on the plan of the book and read segments of it that I wrote. My students over the years in "Christianity and the World's Religions" helped me plan and develop this book – most often without their knowledge. Lastly, the department's administrative assistant, Pat Sturgeon, provided kind, capable, and invaluable assistance.

As always, to my family – to my wife and best friend, Joan, and to our children, Carrie, Kristie, and Matthew – I would like to express my gratitude for their support, patience, and willingness to excuse my absences of body and mind from our home and hearth. The wisdom contained in the old Frisian proverb well expresses the generosity of their individual dispositions and the grace of their collective posture toward me: "Sin en wille kinn' folle tille" (roughly: "A little fun and an outlook bright can help to make a task seem light"). To them I dedicate this volume.

The editor and publishers wish to thank the following for permission to reproduce material:

Justin Martyr, *Early Christian Fathers* (ed. Cyril C. Richardson) (Library of Christian Classics) (Westminster Press, Philadelphia, 1943. Used by permission of Westminster John Knox Press).

St Augustine, *The City of God* (trans. H. Bettenson) (Penguin Books, Harmondsworth, 1972).

Acknowledgments

"The Athanasian Creed" reprinted from *Ecumenical Creeds and Reformed Confessions*. pp. 9–10, © 1988 CRC Publications, Grand Rapids, MI 49560. I–800–333–8300. All rights reserved. Used by Permission.

Thomas Aquinas, *Summa Theologiae. A Concise Translation* (ed. Timothy McDermott) (Eyres and Spottiswoode, London, 1989).

Boniface VIII, *The Papal Encyclicals In Their Historical Context* (ed. Anne Freemantle) (G. P. Putnam & Sons, New York, 1956).

Martin Luther, *Martin Luther: Selections From His Writings* (ed. John Dillenberger) (Doubleday & Company Inc., Garden City, NY, 1961).

John Calvin, *Institutes of the Christian Religion* (ed. J. T. McNeill; trans. F. L. Battles) (Library of Christian Classics) (Westminster Press, Philadelphia, 1960. Used by permission of Westminster John Knox Press).

Herbert of Cherbury, *Attitudes Towards Other Religions: Some Christian Interpretations* (ed. Owen C. Thomas) (Harper & Row, New York, 1969).

G. E. Lessing, *Nathan the Wise* (trans. B. Q. Morgan) (Frederick Ungar Publishing, New York, 1955).

Friedrich Schleiermacher, *The Christian Faith*, vol. I (eds H. R. Mackintosh and J. S. Stewart) (Harper & Row, New York, 1963).

Ernest Troeltsch, *Attitudes Towards Other Religions: Some Christian Interpretations* (ed. Owen C. Thomas) (Harper & Row, New York, 1969).

Karl Barth, *Church Dogmatics: The Doctrine of the Word of God*, vol. I/2 (trans. G. T. Thomson and H. Knight; ed. G. W. Bromily and T. F. Torrance) (T. & T. Clark Ltd, Edinburgh, 1956).

Hendrik Kraemer, *Why Christianity of All Religions* (trans. Hubert Hoskins) (Westminster Press, Philadelphia, © 1962 The Westminster Press. Used by permission of Westminster John Knox Press).

Joachim Wach, *Understanding and Believing: Essays by Joachim Wach* (ed. Joseph Kitagawa) (Harper & Row, New York, 1968).

Paul Tillich, *Christianity and the Encounter of the World Religions* (© 1963 Columbia University Press, New York, reprinted with permission of the publisher).

Karl Rahner, "Christianity and the Non-Christian Relgions" in *Theological Investigations*, vol. 5 (trans. K. -H. Krueger) (The Crossroad Publishing Co., New York, 1983).

Second Vatican Council, *The Documents of Vatican II* (Association Press/Follett Publishing Co., Chicago, 1966).

Wilfred Cantwell Smith, *Patterns of Faith Around the World* (Oneworld Publications, Oxford, 1998).

Acknowledgments

John Hick, *Christianity and Other Religions: Selected Readings* (eds J. Hick and B. Hebblethwaite) (Fortress Press, Philadelphia, 1980).

John Hick, *A John Hick Reader* (ed. Paul Badham) (Trinity Press International, Philadelphia, 1990).

Lesslie Newbigin, *The Gospel in a Pluralist Society* (© 1989 Wm. B. Eerdmans Publishing Co., Grand Rapids; Used by permission of the publisher: all rights reserved).

His Holiness John Paul II, "Crossing the Threshold of Hope" (trans. J. and M. McPhee, ed. V. Messori) (translation copyright © 1994 by Alfred A. Knopf, Inc., New York; reprinted by permission of the publisher).

Every effort has been made to trace copyright holders. The publishers apologize for any errors or omissions in the above list and would be grateful to be notified of any corrections that should be incorporated in the next edition or reprint of this book.

Introduction: Religious Pluralism
Old and New

To state that the world is religiously plural is hardly to utter a novelty, for religious pluralism is an old, established reality. One need only think of the genesis and ongoing presence of the several of the world's great religious traditions: the Hindu tradition with its origins and the Jewish tradition with its roots in the second millennium BCE; the Confucian tradition with its ancestry, the Taoist tradition with its fountainhead, and the Buddhist tradition with its source in the first millennium BCE; the Christian tradition with its beginnings in the first century CE; and the Islamic tradition with its birth in the seventh century CE. One could augment this list of old, established traditions by pointing to ancient religious traditions which are no longer ongoing or alive, such as ancient Egyptian religion, ancient Greek religion, and Manichaeism. In addition, the plethora of new religious movements which have made themselves known in the last two centuries – such as the Church of Jesus Christ of Latter-Day Saints, the International Society for Krishna Consciousness, and the New Age Movement – suggest themselves for consideration.

While in some sense, therefore, religious pluralism is nothing new, in another sense there is something novel about religious pluralism in our time. This novelty concerns not the fact of manyness, but the increasing recognition and consciousness of that fact. It might therefore be claimed that while religious pluralism is very old *objectively* speaking, it is rather new *subjectively* speaking. What are the factors that have made Westerners, to narrow the focus somewhat, newly conscious of pluralism in our time? While any attempt at exhaustiveness would be ill-advised in this introduction, it is possible to outline several key events and movements in modern history that have contributed to heightened Western consciousness of religious plurality.

It is worth recalling that it was only half a millennium ago, thanks to the discoveries made by explorers of the seas and new continents, that the Western world began to awaken in a real way to the existence of civilizations in places such as the Americas and Asia. In time, these discoveries were followed by a series of colonial and missionary ventures launched by various European peoples, including

1

the Spanish, the Portuguese, the French, the English, and the Dutch. This cluster of developments can be thought of as the "Columbus factor."

At approximately the same time that explorers were expanding Western knowledge of the globe, European Christianity was engaged in a protracted family quarrel which resulted in divorce and an augmentation of intra-Christian plurality. After these upheavals of the sixteenth century, then, in addition to the established Roman Catholic Church and the Eastern Orthodox Churches, there existed several new Christian communions. These communions included various Protestant churches inspired by reformers such as Martin Luther and John Calvin, as well as the Church of England, which came to be largely through the machinations of King Henry VIII. This series of events can be thought of as the "Reformation factor."

On top of the Columbus and Reformation developments, Christianity faced a new series of challenges as it entered the seventeenth and eighteenth centuries. Some of these provocations came from emergent modern science, inspired by the work of Copernicus, Bacon, Galileo, and Newton. One such fundamental skirmish centered on issues of knowledge and authority as regards the nature of the cosmos; for whereas the Bible and the Church affirmed a geocentric universe, science seemed able to produce evidence for a heliocentric one. What does one do when faith and reason collide, or when special revelation and natural revelation conflict? Answers to this basic question created new questions and new sets of answers, which constituted yet further challenges to Christian orthodoxy. Some sets of questions and answers took the form of heterodox modifications to orthodox Christian beliefs, while others represented outright rejections of Christian orthodoxy. Deism, that halfway house between religious belief and scientific respectability, falls into the former classification; agnosticism and atheism, the respective suspension or denial of religious belief, fall into the latter classification. This complex of conflicts can be thought of as the "Enlightenment factor."

In the last third of the nineteenth century, advances in scholarship in general and historical scholarship in particular saw the birth of a new discipline dedicated to the study of the history of religion. Founded by the expatriate German scholar Friedrich Max Müller, the new "science of religion" (*Religionswissenschaft*) made resources available for studying the great religions of the world. Müller led a team of scholars in England who were translating religious texts that became the multivolume classic *The Sacred Books of the East.* Soon handbooks, compendia, and lexicons were produced by pioneers in the new field. A century later, courses in "World Religions" were a staple of university and even many pre-university curricula. With a firm foothold in European and North American educational systems, then, it was only a matter of time before the ideas and practices of the great religious traditions of humanity permeated the consciousness of educated Westerners. This advance in human knowledge can be thought of as the "scholarship factor."

By the dawn of the twentieth century, therefore, acquaintance with the world religions was on the rise. The twentieth century would witness a dramatic increase in knowledge of, and interest in, non-Western traditions. Two world wars shook the faith of many Westerners in their own civilization and its main religious traditions, Christianity and Judaism. Many who survived the Second World War found themselves unable to believe in a loving *and* powerful God who allowed the horrors of war and the unspeakable reality of genocide – to say nothing of the absurd specter of nuclear holocaust. In addition to the traditional attempt to justify belief in God (that is, theodicy), some felt the need to justify belief in humanity (that is, anthropodicy). This shaking of the foundations can be thought of as the "Western crisis factor."

While the stars of Christianity and Judaism thus sank for some in the West, developments in other parts of the globe foretold the rise of non-Western religious stars. Especially in Asia, the nationalism fueled by the First World War came to expression as a revolt against colonialism. As Asian nations attempted to throw off the yoke of colonial rule (for example, protests against the British in India and the Dutch in Indonesia), a sense of national and indigenous religious identity manifested itself. In the process, several Asian religious traditions came to renewed self-consciousness and expression. This interplay of conflict and self-confidence can be thought of as the "Asian renewal factor."

If one adds to these developments the fact of global travel and migration – especially emigration from Asia to Europe and North America, in which it must not be forgotten that Asian immigrants entered their adopted homelands with their personal and communal identities at least partly defined by their religious beliefs and practices – the picture of a multicultural and religiously plural world in the West emerges from haziness and begins to take shape. The story could have taken an ugly turn here, for it could well have been the case that the Hindus, Muslims, Sikhs, and others who came to the West found nothing but conflict in their new, adopted countries. Although they most certainly did encounter some illegitimate prejudice and lack of civility, it turned out that the Enlightenment's legacy of tolerance and religious disestablishment, along with the decline of the mainline Western religious traditions, had prepared the ground for new seeds to grow. For at least some factions in the West, then, there was infatuation and eagerness to embrace the novel and mysterious religious traditions from Asia. The tumultuous, countercultural decade of the 1960s, for example, was of a mind to explore not only the old and venerable traditions of Asia, which appeared new to many in the West, but also a variety of new religious movements seeking to sell their wares in the emerging religious marketplace. Moreover, the development of global communications in the twentieth century fostered a sense of the planet's relative smallness and ecosystemic interdependence, such that when a certain Asian leader flexes his muscles, world leaders, as well as markets, sit up and take notice. This web of interrelationships can be thought of as the "globalization factor."

In the considerations outlined above – the Columbus factor, the Reformation factor, the Enlightenment factor, the scholarship factor, the Western crisis factor, the Asian renewal factor, and the globalization factor – one can readily see the constituent parts of the contemporary pluralist puzzle. To focus on a group of people in the West for whom religious pluralism represents a particular challenge and conundrum, the position of dedicated adherents of the mainline, Western traditions caught in the vertigo of these modern and postmodern developments must now be considered. These believers – let us say, more particularly, Christian believers, the people for whom this book will be of greatest interest – have not given up their faith and are very much committed to their religious traditions; but they often have difficulty putting biblical or theological confession ("Christianity is true and other religions are not, which spells dire eternal consequences for their adherents") together with existential or experiential confession ("Many non-Christian persons whom I know are highly moral and in their own ways devout – can their ultimate fate really be so bleak?").

This book seeks to guide those interested in, and perhaps perplexed by, what Christian thought says about the status of religious traditions other than Christianity itself. The book's title, *Christianity and Plurality: Classic and Contemporary Readings*, is intentionally ambiguous. Primarily, it seeks to draw attention to the particular problem of religious plurality or pluralism.[1] Thus, it makes available some of the key resources from the Christian tradition for thinking about this problem. In so doing, it seeks to demonstrate the wealth of material found in the tradition for thinking about the challenge of religious otherness, especially when that otherness has become manyness in a *subjectively* real way. Put slightly differently, this book is intended to help students of Christianity, who may or may not themselves confess the Christian faith, make sense of Christian claims about non-Christian religious traditions, given the challenge of religious pluralism in the twentieth century – the period on which the book concentrates – as well as in the emerging twenty-first century.

But the title of the book also seeks to reflect the perspectival and theological plurality which exists *within* the Christian tradition; it therefore draws on a variety of sources. Some are classical, some contemporary; some are Roman Catholic, some Protestant; some the mainline Christian tradition considers to be orthodox, some it judges to be rather more heterodox. In light of the many classical texts presented in this volume, the book may also be of use to students of various backgrounds who wish to acquaint themselves generally with the intellectual and theological history of Christianity. In any case, the intent is to offer a balanced and ecumenical approach.

The book is arranged in the following fashion. Owing to the intellectually demanding nature of the contemporary theological problem of religious pluralism, it is imperative that one be grounded in the main sources that fund Christian theological inquiry: the biblical text and the repository of Christian wisdom known as "tradition." The book therefore begins with an introduction to the Christian Bible and then recommends a series of biblical passages for consideration, along with a summary and brief discussion of them. It then turns to texts from the four main periods in the history of Christianity: Patristic (*c*.100–*c*.500), medieval (*c*.500–*c*.1350), Renaissance and Reformation (*c*.1350–*c*.1600), and modern and postmodern (*c*.1600 to the present).[2] Here many of the great names of the Christian tradition will be found, including Augustine, Aquinas, Luther, Calvin, Schleiermacher, Barth, and Rahner. In each case, a brief introduction to the author (where appropriate) and the text is provided. The emphasis of this book, however, falls on the reading of primary sources. Naturally, readers are free to select the readings they deem appropriate; and it hardly needs to be stated that they are encouraged to come to their own theological conclusions about what the Bible and the Christian tradition teaches – and about what they themselves can or should believe. Recommendations for further reading are found at the end of the book; some of the works referred to in the introductions to the selected texts can also be found there.

In examining the primary sources included in this book, a typology of positions – or what might be thought of as a series of ideal types – concerning Christianity's relationship to non-Christian traditions can be distilled. These will be better understood after completing the primary readings; but, as the reader will encounter the types in various places in the book, it seems wise to introduce them briefly at the outset. The positions focus on the question of salvation, which is the principal question that Christian theologians have considered in thinking about the non-Christian religious traditions and peoples of the world. Who is saved? Who is not saved? How are people saved? While there are several key doctrines to be considered in the theology of religious pluralism – including the doctrines of God and creation – those most often appealed to in Christian theology have been the doctrines of Christ and redemption.[3]

The first position can be called "exclusivism." It contends that the full light of divine revelation is uniquely given to Christianity. It thus concludes that ultimate truth is an exclusive Christian domain. It also holds that other traditions are excluded as possible paths to salvation, for salvation comes only through the atoning merit of Christ, which is made available exclusively through the Christian Church. Exclusivism is therefore a position that is self-consciously Christocentric and ecclesiocentric (from the Greek term for church: *ekklesia*). In varying degrees of purity and emphasis, it is found in several of the writings included in this book.[4]

The second position can be termed "inclusivism." This position, which is best understood as a variant of exclusivism, also holds that the full light of divine revelation is given to Christianity; but it is inclined to be more generous in recognizing the revelatory workings of God and instances of truth outside Christianity. It thus concludes that other traditions are included in God's plan of salvation for the world, although salvation must somehow finally be accomplished through the atoning work of Christ. It too, therefore, is a Christocentric, but not necessarily ecclesiocentric, position. In varying degrees of purity and emphasis, it too is found in several of the writings in this book.

The third position can be designated "pluralism." Unlike the relatively weak sense of the term "pluralism" (that is, the fact and even the consciousness that there are many religions – see note 1), the position known as "pluralism" connotes something rather stronger (that is, it is loaded with philosophico-theological assumptions and claims). Pluralism in this strong sense asserts, most often in dispute with exclusivism and on the basis of an assumed unity in the history of religion, that all intentional religious paths are ultimately efficacious, insofar as they all lead to supreme reality or the transcendent. It therefore understands the scope of salvation to be very broad; at a minimum, pluralism maintains that salvation is available in and through all traditions in which salvation is a goal. Pluralism is sometimes likened to a Copernican revolution in which, not Christ (the Earth), but God (the Sun), is central to the universe of faiths. It is therefore a position that is theocentric (from the Greek term for God, *theos*). Although variants of this position can be found in some established Asian religious and philosophical traditions, it is relatively new to the West. In varying forms, the reader will also find it in some of the writings contained in this book.

The fourth position can be described with the term "universalism." Just as inclusivism is best understood as a variant of exclusivism, so universalism can best be understood as a variant of pluralism. Universalism's chief claim is that God is revealed to all and related to all in some way. Whether or not a person is conscious of a saving relationship with the divine or wills such a relationship, salvation will come to all without qualification.[5] The reasons adduced for these claims vary among the adherents of universalism; they often focus on the doctrine of God or on particular divine attributes, such as unconditional divine love or condign divine justice cloaked with expansive divine mercy, or on the doctrine of Christ and the all-encompassing nature of the atonement. It too can be thought of as a theocentric position. The reader will sense this position in some of the readings in this book. However, when it surfaces, universalism tends to be a position not so much held as hinted at or implied, mostly for one of two reasons. First, and more weakly, its theological warrant has been judged to be at minimum ambiguous, and not clearly in accordance with Christian orthodoxy. Second, and more strongly, its theological warrant has been judged to be at maximum heretical, and clearly not in accordance with Christian orthodoxy. In either case, to openly espouse such a position was, through much of Christian history, to risk unpleasant personal consequences.

Exploring the Christian theology of religious pluralism in the present is not as personally risky as it may have been in the past. But, given the complexities of our world and time, the task is no easier than heretofore – especially given the ever growing quantity and sophistication of writings on the subject. Rather than approach exploration of this complex issue with a gloomy disposition, however, one might better regard Christian theological investigation into the matter of religious pluralism as an illuminating opportunity and an invigorating challenge. May such turn out to be the case for all readers of this book.

Notes

1   The terms "plurality" and "pluralism" are both employed in the literature on "religious pluralism." While the two are not rigorously distinguished from one another, and more often than not are used more or less interchangeably, the difference between them can be thought of in the following way: "plurality" refers to the fact of manyness, while "pluralism" refers to the fact and consciousness of manyness. Pluralism is thus the richer and more ambiguous – not to mention the more commonly used – term. Furthermore, to add one more note of clarification, and as this introduction indicates, the term "pluralism" is also used by some thinkers as a description of a definite, substantive position on or view of religious pluralism. That is, pluralism in this positional sense describes a certain philosophico-theological view of the fact, consciousness, and implications of manyness.

    The terms "plurality" and "pluralism" will be used more or less synonymously in what follows. When the need arises to distinguish between them or between the senses of the term "pluralism," that need will be met.

2   This periodization is offered for the sake of convenience and is in no way intended as

definitive. For the purposes of this book, I have judged "postmodern" developments, which can be said to have their beginning at some point in the twentieth century, to be insufficiently distinct at this juncture in time as to warrant designation as a separate historical period. Greater historical distance may well require a different verdict. In any event, it should be recognized that contemporary consciousness of, and attention to, pluralisms of various kinds is very much at the heart of the diffuse movement known by the name "postmodernism" – provided that such a centric reference (i.e. heart) does not do violence to the spirit of the movement.

3   A theology of religious pluralism which does not focus on redemption (thought of as what is to come, or human life in the future) at the expense of creation (thought of as what is, or human life in the present) is an item of great importance on the agenda of contemporary Christian theology.

4   It should be noted that exclusivism is called "particularism" by some scholars.

5   A fifth *logical*, but not *theological*, position might be termed "nihilism." Nihilism would be the claim that no one is saved from despair or evil either in this life or in the life to come. As such, it can be thought of as the diametrical opposite of universalism. The nihilist position is not found in this book; neither is it, to my knowledge, held by any Christian thinker in the history of theology.

Part I

Biblical Texts

1

The Bible and Religious Pluralism

1. The Christian Bible

Christianity is sometimes referred to as a "religion of the book." This designation arises from the fact that one of the fundamental sources which funds Christian thought and practice takes its name from a Greek word for "book" or "books," or, more accurately, "scroll" (*biblion* (singular), *biblia* (plural)). The source in question, of course, is the Bible. The Bible also goes by the name "Scripture," which is rooted in a Latin word meaning "writing" (*scriptura*). The Bible or Scripture is also referred to as the "Word of God," insofar as the human words which the text contains seek to make manifest the revelation and will – or Word – of God. Furthermore, the Word of God is itself variously referred to in the Bible: in addition to the Word spoken by God in creating the world and the prophets who speak the Word of the Lord to the people of the covenant, the prologue to the Gospel of John declares the incarnation of the Word of God in Jesus of Nazareth. Because the Bible narrates the identity of the triune God as made known by the God-man Jesus Christ, the Christian tradition often refers to the biblical text as a whole as the Word of God.

What we today call the Bible, however, was originally a series of oral traditions and written sources which were collected over a period of time and recognized in early Christian history as authoritative. That is, certain writings were declared "canonical" (from a Greek word meaning "rule" or "measuring stick": *kanon*); and this group of writings as a whole was consequently designated as the "canon." The Christians of the Patristic Period (*c.*100–*c.*500) first adopted as canonical the Hebrew Bible, or Tanak, which consisted of three parts, known as the Law, the Prophets, and the Writings. In addition to these received writings composed mainly in the Hebrew language, the early Christians added to their canon several writings composed in the Greek language, including accounts of the life and ministry of Jesus called "gospels," letters by the apostles (especially St Paul), and some other documents. In time, then, the Christian canon came to be regarded as consisting of two parts: the Hebrew Bible, which was renamed the "Old Testament"; and the gospels, letters, and a few other writings, which as a whole were accordingly called the "New Testament." There also existed a somewhat ill-defined third group of writings that did not appear in the Hebrew Tanak, but were found in its Greek translation called the "Septuagint," as well as in the Latin translation of the entire Bible called the "Vulgate." These writings are variously referred to as the "Deutero-canon" or the "Apocrypha." Roman Catholic and (with some qualification) Eastern Orthodox Christianity recognize them as authoritative; Protestant Christianity does not.

Differences in construal of the canon by different Christian traditions come linked, not surprisingly, to different conceptions of the authority of the Bible. All Christian traditions recognize the inspiration of the Bible in one way or another, as expressed in the biblical text itself – understood in a canonical context (2 Tim. 3:16). How they move from this intra-biblical claim to extra-biblical conceptions of biblical authority, whether characterizing such authority as coequal with that of tradition (as is the case in Catholicism) or as alone authoritative and even infallible (as tends to be the case in Protestantism), is a complicated theological matter perhaps best reserved for articulation by individual traditions and for ecumenical discussion.

The point to be noted at this juncture is that all Christian traditions recognize the authority of the Bible, as well as the necessity of biblical interpretation, in order to know and understand God, the world, and humanity – and *a fortiori*, in order to undertake theological work. Therefore, the sweep of the biblical text as a whole – its narration of the chief acts of creation, fall, redemption, and re-creation – must be reckoned with as the theologian seeks to make sense of particular texts which address a given issue or problem. In the case under investigation here, the issue or problem concerns religious pluralism, which might be expressed as follows. Given a particular divine revelation which makes possible a special kind of divine–human relationship culminating in salvation, how are Christians to think about the existence of a seemingly universal religiosity which takes a multiplicity of forms and which often comes to expression in seeming oblivion of the particular divine revelation recorded in the Bible?

In what follows, key biblical texts are first listed, so that they may be consulted without interposition on my part. The order of presentation follows the order in which they appear in the "minimal" biblical canon – that is, the biblical books on which all Christians agree: the Old Testament, without the deutero-canonical or apocryphal books, and the New Testament.[1] Thereafter, a summary of, and some commentary on, the texts are offered, in which a Christian and theological context of interpretation is broadly assumed. Therefore, the summary follows the "narrative" and occasionally "compositional" order of the texts – that is, the order of the events reported in the text as a whole, on occasion taking into account the time in which the particular texts were written. If, however, the reader wishes to reverse the order of the following presentation or skip the summary and interpretive reflections entirely, he or she is most free to do so.[2]

2. Biblical Texts

· *Old Testament* ·

Genesis 1–3; 6:1–8; 9:1–18; 11:1–9, 27–32; 12:1–9; 15; 17:5
Exodus 3; 19–20
Deuteronomy 4–6
Ruth
1 Kings 18
Ezra 4:1–3; 9–10:17
Nehemiah, 4:15–23; 7:61–5; 9; 10:28–39; 13:1–3, 23–7, 30–1
Esther 2–5:8; 7–8
Psalms 1, 14
Proverbs 1–4:9
Isaiah 31; 40–5; 56–7; 60
Daniel 1; 3; 6
Amos 1–3:8; 5:18–27; 9:11–15
Jonah

· *New Testament* ·

Matthew 1; 2:1–15; 5:17; 10:1–6; 21:33–46; 28
Luke 1–2:20; 3:6; 10:25–37; 14:16–24; 24:45–7
John 1; 3–6; 10:30; 12:44–50; 13:34–5; 14; 15:12; 17; 19; 20:30–1
Acts 1–2; 3:11–4:22; 8:26–11:26; 13:38–49; 14; 15; 17
Romans 1–3; 8–11
1 Corinthians 13
2 Corinthians 4:4–6
Galatians 1:1–9; 2:15–3:29
Philippians 2:1–13
Colossians 1:15–23
1 Timothy 2:1–7
1 John 3:11–4:21
Revelation 21–2

3. Summary and Commentary

The Bible does not as such contain the term "religion," which is derived from the Latin *religio*; but it does address the concept and reality of religion – understood as a relation between a person (or persons) and an objectively real, powerful other who desires observance and who offers a solution to the human predicament – albeit in a somewhat indirect, unsystematic, and thematic way.

The opening chapter of the **Old Testament** and the entire biblical narrative begin with the words: "In the beginning . . . God created the heaven and the earth." **Genesis** 1:1–2:3 seems intent on delineating a conception of God out of step with ancient Near Eastern thinking on the origin of the cosmos. The God of the Bible calls creation forth in an act without ready analogy in everyday human experience: God speaks, and it is.[3] The act of creation thus establishes an order distinct from God; creator and creation, according to the Bible, are therefore never to be confused. Created reality, Genesis 1 goes on to say, is not only differentiated from God but is differentiated internally, "of every kind" (1:11–12, 21, 24–5). Created reality is repeatedly pronounced "good" by the text, and as part of the divine intent for creation, difference and the manifold variety within creation are also declared good.

Genesis 1 goes on to relate the crowning achievement of the entire work of creation: the summoning forth of humanity, crafted in the divine image. The meaning of the image of God has been much debated by biblical interpreters and theologians. Minimally, it has to do with humanity's purpose and end – namely, to exist in relation to, and fellowship with, God. But the *imago Dei* expresses more than relationship; it involves likeness, reflection, and correspondence between creator and creature. As God has no material image in creation, humanity is called to represent God and to develop, care for, and rule creation responsibly and wisely. The image of God is borne by all human beings, and so accords all persons a basic equality and dignity before God.

Genesis 1:1–2:3 with its cosmic perspective on creation, which is complemented by the human perspective on creation articulated in Genesis 2:4–25, is therefore a key passage for understanding the Bible, Christianity, and of course, religion. It reminds the reader that all creation finds its origin in God, with the following implications: God is distinct from creation and alone worthy of worship (i.e., nothing in creation is to be worshipped); creation is good and is the arena in which human beings are to exist and flourish as embodied beings; and nothing created is incorrigibly evil. It might also be noted that God desires faithful relationship and fellowship with humanity, as well as the flourishing of all creation. These themes of particularity (faithful relationship with the one true God) and universality (divine concern with and desire for the well-being of all creation) signaled in the Bible's opening chapters return time and again in the course of its unfolding.

God created human beings with freedom and responsibility, with the intent of obedient, loving response. The biblical text relates in Genesis 3 that Adam and Eve failed God in this regard. Not respecting the boundaries laid down in creation, Adam and Eve in disobedience tried to become like God, thereby plunging humanity into sin and a strained relationship with God, with other human beings, and with the rest of created reality. Divine–human harmony became disharmonious estrangement and embarrassment. The image of God, although by no means obliterated, became tarnished and in need of restoration. Remaining faithful to the good creation, however, God continued to desire fellowship with humanity, and so promised to undo the wrong done. As evidence for this understanding, Christian thought has pointed to Genesis 3:15, which it interprets in a salvific (and even Christological) sense: redemption will come to creation in time (see Rom. 8:19–23); the fall into sin is not the last word.

The fall into sin depicted in the early chapters of Genesis seems to go on in free-fall fashion for some time, for in Genesis 6 the text notes that God is grieved, regrets having created, and ponders destroying the world (see v. 6–7). Noah finds divine favor, however, and through Noah creation is saved. After the Flood, God makes a universal covenant with creation never to punish the world in such a way again, as recorded in Genesis 9 (see v. 9–17). Interestingly, and paradigmatically, Noah, like Adam before him and others after him, is humanity's representative; God's concern with all of humanity remains abundantly clear. By Genesis 11–12, God has embarked on a plan of creational restoration by calling Abram, in order to make a great nation which is to be a light and blessing for all the earth (see Gen. 12:2–3). Through the covenant made with Abram, as recorded in Genesis 15, God's universal plan is to be accomplished through a particular people. The dialectic of universality and particularity is here evident once again. But the point to be noted at present is that Abram and his seed become humanity's new representatives (Abram is given a new name – Abraham, "ancestor of a multitude" (see Gen. 17:5)), the line from which a redeemer would come. (Instructively, the line from Abraham to Jesus is indicated in the very first verse of the New Testament in Matthew 1:1.)

As the biblical narrative continues from Genesis to **Exodus**, the reader learns of Abraham's descendants' captivity in Egypt and God's response to their cries for deliverance. Exodus 3 records God's manifestation to Moses in the form of a burning bush. One moment quietly tending sheep, the next moment Moses is charged with a momentous task: becoming the leader of the great deliverance of the Israelites from Egypt. The people are to possess a land long ago promised. After their dramatic escape from Egypt, but before possessing the new promised land, God makes a covenant with them at Mount Sinai, and reveals to them the divine will for human living. In the Decalogue (Ten Commandments) and instructions for covenant obedience, as recorded in both Exodus 19–20 and **Deuteronomy** 5–6, the Israelites are reminded that there is one, true God, revealed to Moses as Yahweh, and that Yahweh desires fidelity: Israel is to have no other gods (see Deut. 5:6–11 and 6:14; see also Deut. 4:5–8, 19). Humanity's representatives are therefore told something of universal import. The God who created, promised redemption, delivered from bondage, and gives the land is the true God, the only God deserving of praise and worship (see Deut. 6:4), the God who towers in power over all other gods; this God desires ongoing faithful relationship.

Israel's forgetfulness and tendency metaphorically to sleep around with other gods after possession of the promised land is met with warning by the prophets. Sometimes the warnings are coupled with dramatic divine rebuke in the form of manifestations of power, as in the famous Yahweh–Baal encounter on Mount Carmel recorded in **1 Kings** 18, which results in an Israelite confession of Yahweh's sole divine status (v. 39). Sometimes the warnings are linked with stern judgment of the grievous, inhuman, and divinely oblivious wrongdoings of all the nations, non-Israelite and Israelite, as in **Amos** 1–2. Too often deaf to the divine word spoken by the prophets, who warned of judgment and proclaimed divine justice along with divine mercy, the chosen people responded to such warnings foolishly, and ultimately were led into another captivity (see Amos 3:1–8; 5:18–27; 9:11–15). Lamenting folly and advocating wisdom, the **Psalms** and **Proverbs** of the Old Testament observe that fools deny or ignore the God who made the heavens and the earth, whereas the fear of Yahweh is the beginning of true knowledge and wisdom (see Ps. 1, 14; Prov. 1–4:9).

The northern and southern kingdoms, after the division of the Israelite monarchy in the tenth century BCE, fell in the eighth and sixth centuries to the Assyrians and the Babylonians, respectively. The northern kingdom never recovered its identity. The people of the southern kingdom were allowed to return home after the exile in the second half of the sixth century BCE. After the exile and return, which counts as one of the great watershed events in Old Testament history, the people of Judah were forced to ask some hard questions: If we are the chosen people and Yahweh is the sovereign God, why are the nations of the earth seemingly having their way? What are we to make of the nations? How do they figure into Yahweh's plan for the world? Different Old Testament books composed in the post-exilic period – including Ezra and Nehemiah, Ruth, Jonah, Esther, parts of Daniel, and parts of Isaiah – give seemingly diverse answers to these questions.[4] In order to get a sense of the range of the apparently disparate viewpoints, some notable cases need to be examined in order to see whether or not their presentations can be coherently synthesized.

The place to begin this investigation is with the books of **Ezra** and **Nehemiah.** The picture is a powerful one: the people slowly making their way back to their homeland with their capital city and temple in ruins. With one eye on the task at hand and the other on the lookout for would-be attackers (see Neh. 4:15–23), they begin the work of rebuilding their city, their temple, and their lives. The people, the text implies, were eager to keep outsiders at bay. In fact, the rebuilding of the walls of the city can be seen as symbolic of the desire for insulation against the non-Jewish world. Jewish identity and fidelity were therefore crucial issues. Ezra 4:1–3 indicates that even those who claim to worship God in the same way that the people of Judah do are to have no part in helping to rebuild the temple. In the context of the genealogies of those who returned from Babylon, Nehemiah 7:61–5 indicates that those unable to prove true Israelite descent are in some ways excluded from full fellowship with the house of Israel (see also Neh. 9:1–4, 13:1–3). Ezra and Nehemiah also describe the proscription against intermarriage of any kind (see Ezra 9–10:17, Neh. 13:23–7). The account of the return of the people of Judah to Jerusalem culminates in Ezra's retelling of the story of God's faithfulness to the people of Judah, followed by the people's renewed commitment to faithful covenant relationship (see Neh. 9:6–38, 10:28–39), and ends with Nehemiah's words: "Thus I cleansed them from everything foreign … Remember me, O my God, for good" (Neh. 13:30–1). The nations are thus to be kept at bay, and God is the God of Judah alone: that seems to be the central message of Ezra and Nehemiah.

The approach is rather different in the book of **Ruth.** The Moabitess Ruth refuses to take leave of her Jewish mother-in-law Naomi after Naomi decides to return to Judah from Moab. Ruth declares: "Where you go, I will go; Where you lodge, I will lodge; your people shall be my people, and your God my God" (Ruth 1:16). Ruth accompanies her mother-in-law to Bethlehem, where Naomi's kinsman Boaz generously provides for Ruth and "redeems" her, as he and Ruth marry. Their son Obed turns out to be David's grandfather, from whose line Jesus the Redeemer would come. Regarding the nations of the earth, the book of Ruth thus sketches a picture rather different from the one presented in Ezra and Nehemiah: as long as a non-Israelite embraces the God and laws of Israel, that person can be enfolded within the household of faith, even to the point where such a person – seen from the viewpoint of Christian thought – plays an important role in the history of redemption (see Matt. 1:5).

The conception of the nations of the earth in the book of **Jonah** makes an even stronger case for inclusivity than does Ruth. In apparent opposition to the view that Yahweh is the God of Israel alone, the book of Jonah relates the story of the prophet's ill-fated flight to Tarshish in order that he might avoid the task laid upon him by the word of the Lord: "Go at once to Nineveh, that great city, and cry out against it; for their wickedness has come up before me" (1:2). The text indicates that the God of the Israelites also notes and may punish the wrongdoings of nations even beyond Israel's borders. Jonah is unhappy about this state of affairs, and he therefore attempts to hide and not honor his call. After having been thrown into the sea on his journey to Tarshish, Jonah is shown mercy by God. Accordingly, he goes to Nineveh to preach, and his preaching is followed by Ninevite repentance. God's merciful response to this repentance displeases and angers the prophet, who thinks that God's typically compassionate action has rendered his prophecy of Nineveh's demise irrelevant. While he sits sulking and waiting to see what will ultimately become of the great city and its inhabitants, a bush suddenly grows up, which provides him with shade and relief from the hot sun. The bush just as quickly withers and dies, however, and Jonah laments its passing as well as his own plight. Then come the culminating and hard-hitting words of the book of Jonah, spoken by God to the prophet: "You are concerned about the bush, for which you did not labor, and which you did not grow; it came into being in a night and perished in a night. And should I not be concerned about Nineveh, that great city, in which there are more than a hundred and twenty thousand persons who do not know their right hand from their left, and also many animals?" (4:10–11). The interrogative ending of the book of Jonah makes the point that God is the creator, judge, and redeemer of all the earth, not just Israel. God is therefore more than justified in caring about all of the creation, including children and animals.

There are yet other post-exilic books which could be considered. In **Esther** a Jewess not keeping Jewish purity laws lives in a Gentile court, but her ultimate loyalty is to her people, whom she defends and saves despite personal risk (see 2–5:8; 7–8). In **Daniel**, Jews living in a Gentile world keep Jewish laws scrupulously and prosper (see 1; 3; 6). In **Isaiah**, there are indications that all the earth stands under judgment, but can turn to the one true God and be saved through the elect people of God (see 31; 40–5; 56–7; 60).

How can one reconcile the above views of the nations in the Old Testament? One must surely begin by seeing the issue against the background of creation. If the biblical idea of creation entails that God is the source of all that is, God must be understood as the God (i.e., creator and redeemer) of the entire cosmos, including all the nations. It is this idea that comes to expression in the book of Jonah. But in order to address the wrong introduced into creation by the fall into sin, God chooses a particular people who are to live a certain way and who are to be a light and example for all the earth. This truth comes to expression, one might say, in the books of Ezra and Nehemiah. Provided that they indeed live in a way that recognizes Yahweh, as revealed to the Israelites, and that honors the divine will, all are welcome in the household of faith, irrespective of tribe or tongue. This is the point of the book of Ruth. Therefore, the approaches to the nations of the earth in the books discussed above are not contrary but complementary, insofar as they express different sides of a great overall truth: God's love for the world, which would come to most profound expression in the life and ministry of Jesus of Nazareth.

The **New Testament** tells the story of the special revealed presence of the Old Testament God in human form in the person of Jesus – or what the Christian Church would later understand as the incarnation of the second person of the Holy Trinity – and the unfolding divine plan for the redemption of the world. It is quite clear that the New Testament understands the birth, life, and death of Jesus to be of world-historical, universal significance. Not only is divine love for creation expressed in the Incarnation and the Atonement, but the very nature of the Christian God is deeply revealed in the Christ-event. The God who created in the beginning and who called Abraham to be a light to the nations has now taken on human flesh and dwells among the peoples of the earth. It took the first-century Jews and the fledgling Christian Church time to understand the import of Jesus' message that neither Jews not Christians have a monopoly on God, as the investigation of specific New Testament texts will show in due course: just as the Jews were God's chosen instrument to bring light to the nations in days of old, so in the new dispensation the Church is that chosen instrument. Through the Jews came the possibility of salvation for the Gentiles; through Christianity, salvation is offered to the world, including the Jews.

The New Testament, like the Old Testament, indicates the tensions involved in addressing the issues of universality and particularity, of inclusivity and exclusivity. The Gospel of **Matthew** is instructive in this regard, as it highlights the question of the intended recipients of the message of Jesus. Much of the Gospel of Matthew seems to indicate that the newly proclaimed kingdom of heaven is a reality for Jews, but not Gentiles. It thus emphasizes the continuity of the Old Testament with the life of Jesus. Its very beginning seeks to establish Jesus' Abrahamic and Davidic lineage, in which Ruth is included, as noted above (see Matt. 1). As the new Israel, Jesus recapitulates the history of the nation, including being called out of Egypt (2:13–15) and choosing twelve disciples (10:1–4), just as Israel was delivered from Egypt and composed of twelve tribes. Jesus makes it clear that he has not come to abolish the law and the prophets, but to fulfill them (5:17). Accordingly, references throughout the Gospel of Matthew are made to Jesus' fulfillment of Old Testament prophecies. With an emphasis on the Jewishness of Jesus' message, the Gospel of Matthew relates the charge to the disciples from Jesus to minister to the lost sheep of the house of Israel, but not to the Gentiles (10:5–6). Prophetic hints about Jewish rejection of Jesus and its consequences are also recorded in Matthew, however, perhaps most notably in two places: the visit of the Magi (an event recorded only by Matthew), which intimates that those outside Israel understand who Jesus is, while those inside Israel do not (2:1–12); and the parable of the wicked tenants, through which the chief priests and Pharisees realize that Israel is being judged and the kingdom of God opened to others (21:33–46). But given the general trend, the end of Matthew's account of the life and ministry of Jesus is somewhat surprising. After the crucifixion of Jesus, the Son of God is resurrected from the dead. If the accounts of the tearing of the curtain of the temple and earthquakes were not enough to shake the disciples up, the sight of the resurrected Jesus and his seemingly shocking about-face charge to them surely must have been, for in chapter 28, the disciples, who have to this point concentrated their efforts only on Israel, are given the following charge: "Go therefore and make disciples of all nations, baptizing them in the name of the Father and of the Son and of the Holy Spirit, and teaching them to obey everything that I have commanded you. And remember, I am with you always, to the end of the age" (28:19–20). Here the Christian message is shockingly and clearly stated: the Christ-event has changed human history; from now on, all the peoples of the earth must hear and obey. The disciples must become apostles; Christianity has been given a mission mandate.

Reflection on the intertwined themes of particularity and universality also comes to penetrating expression in the Gospel of **John**, the first chapter of which begins in a cosmic fashion reminiscent of Genesis 1: "In the beginning was the Word (*logos*)." The God who created in the beginning through the Word has now become flesh. The incarnate Word, the Son, makes known the Father (1:18). But the world (*kosmos*) has failed to recognize these truths. The Gospel of John goes on to point out in an often quoted, but perhaps not always understood, passage that in spite of this cosmic blindness, the following truth obtains: "For God so loved the world that he gave his only Son, that everyone who believes in him may not perish but may have eternal life. Indeed, God did not send the Son into the world to condemn the world, but in order that the world might be saved through him" (3:16–17). The *world* beloved by God – not just the Jews – has been presented with the possibility of salvation, but it has failed to recognize the one sent to accomplish the task. It is as though the Gospel of John seeks to drive home this point about the scope of divine love and salvation in the next chapter, where Jesus' encounter with the Samaritan woman is related. Instructively, Jesus takes time to speak with her and impart to her – a Samaritan and one with whom "Jews do not share things" (4:9) – the good news: "the hour is coming when you will worship the Father neither on this mountain nor in Jerusalem. You worship what you do not know; we worship what we know, for salvation is from the Jews. But the hour is coming, and is now here, when the true worshipers will worship the Father in spirit and truth, for the Father seeks such as these to worship him" (4:21–3). The text plays a small word game here: the Father will be worshiped not *in* Jerusalem (a location) but *in* spirit and truth (a disposition), for this is what the Father wills, as shown by the Son. The fields are ready for harvest, and will be harvested by those who did not sow them (4:34–8).

Jesus' failure to teach and act in accordance with the presumed Jewish exclusivism of his day often angered the Jewish officials, who sought to limit his influence and finally to kill him. Not only did Jesus break Jewish laws and preach inclusivist heresy, he equated himself with God. What the Father wills, the Son wills; and as the Father gives life to whom he will, so does the Son (see 5:19–29). All that is required to claim this new life is belief in the Son sent by the Father (see 6:27–40; see also 12:44–50). This intimate relationship between Father and Son, which was increasingly shocking and offensive to the ears of the Jewish authorities, becomes more and more explicit in the Gospel of John, perhaps nowhere more so than in Jesus' declaration that "the Father and I are one" (10:30). This statement is expanded upon later by Jesus, when, having enjoined the disciples to love one another even as they have been loved (13:34–5; see also 15:12), he explains that he must go to prepare a place for those he loves. In responding to a question seeking clarification of the way to this place, Jesus says: "I am the way, and the truth, and the life. No one comes to the Father except through me. If you know me, you will know my Father also. From now on you do know him and have seen him" (14:6–7). When Philip asks that the Father be shown, Jesus somewhat exasperatedly responds: "'Have I been with you all this time, Philip, and you still do not know me? Whoever has seen me has seen the Father … Do you not believe that I am in the Father and the Father is in me? … Believe me that I am in the Father and the Father is in me" (14:9–11).

Sensing that his ministry was coming to a close, Jesus prepares for death, in order that those who love the Father might have life. He prays for the disciples and for those who know him, but not for the world (17:9). Subsequently, Jesus offers a prayer on behalf of the world, "so that the world may believe that you have sent me" (17:21). Obedient unto death, Jesus is arrested, humiliated, and subjected to indignities and scorn on the way to Golgotha. In a moment of biblical irony, Pilate designates Jesus "the man" (19:5), by which appellation the reader, interpreting the text in a canonical context, understands the following: the exemplary human being, the true image of God (see **2 Cor.** 4:4; Col. 1:15). After his crucifixion, Jesus is resurrected from the dead, and is manifested to his disciples so that they might believe. The author of the Gospel of John reminds the reader – instructively, the identity of the potential reader is not qualified, and the scope of readership not restricted – that Jesus' signs and acts are recorded "so that you may come to believe that Jesus is the Messiah, the Son of God, and that through believing you may have life in his name" (20:31).

The theme of the universality of the gospel, or its not-for-Jews-onlyness, is further amply expressed in the Gospel of **Luke**. The angels who announce the birth of Jesus to the shepherds proclaim a joy which will come to all people (Luke 2:10). John the Baptizer's preaching suggests that salvation will come to all the world (3:6). In the parable of the great banquet, several of those invited beg off, after which the host invites a wide array of outcasts (14:16–24). In addition to these hints at the widened scope of salvation, the Gospel of Luke also demonstrates concern and compassion for the downtrodden and outcast. The Song of Mary says that God has lifted up the lowly (1:48–53); the parable of the good Samaritan, recorded only in Luke, is also instructive in this regard (10:25–37). After the completion of his earthly ministry, in which Jesus recapitulates Adam's test and passes it, the second Adam, who is obedient unto death, bows his head on the cross and gives up his spirit. Like Matthew, Luke ends his gospel with the resurrected Christ and theme of commissioning: "Then he opened their minds to understand the scriptures, and he said to them, 'Thus it is written, that the Messiah is to suffer and to rise from the dead on the third day, and that repentance and forgiveness of sins is to be proclaimed in his name to all nations, beginning from Jerusalem'" (24:45–7). The message seems straightforward enough: though a particular event – namely, the incarnation of the Son of God – salvation has been in principle made universally available.

After the resurrection and ascension of the Son who came to proclaim divine love to all the world, it was left to the fledgling and called-out Christian Church to enact the divine mission in and to the world. The book of **Acts**, which continues the story begun in Luke,[5] relates the outpouring of the Spirit of the triune God upon the Church, with the result that devout people from every nation under heaven were able to hear of the mighty works of God in their own tongues. Peter indicates in his sermon in Acts 2 that the Spirit of God has been poured out upon all flesh, and that whoever calls on the name of the Lord will be saved (2:17–21). In answer to the question "what should we do?" (2:37) put to him by his audience, Peter replies: "'Repent, and be baptized every one of you in the name of Jesus Christ so that your sins may be forgiven; and you will receive the gift of the Holy Spirit. For the promise is for you, for your children, and for all who are far away, everyone whom the Lord our God calls to him'" (2:38–9; see 8:35–8).

The issue of particularity and universality, with which the New Testament Church had to come to terms, comes to further expression in the book of Acts. In Peter's sermon recorded in Acts 3, he reiterates the point that all the families of the earth are to be blessed through Abraham's posterity (3:25), from whom the Redeemer has finally come. After his arrest, Peter's defense includes a strong statement of particularity: "There is salvation in no one else, for there is no other name under heaven given among mortals by which we must be saved" (4:12). Peter's understanding of the widened scope of the Christian message and the necessity of spreading it (see 4:20) was fostered by a vision in which he was commanded to eat unclean food. In interpreting this dream, Peter remarks: "I truly understand that God shows no partiality, but in every nation anyone who fears him and does what is right is acceptable to him" (10:34–5).

The matter of the scope of redemption may have come slowly to Peter, the leader of the Jerusalem church; but it came readily to the special apostle to the Gentiles: Paul (see Acts 9:15; 13:47–8). In the books of Acts, the people of "the Way" (see 9:2) or "Christians" (see 11:26) are told that God has never anywhere left himself without a witness; God formerly allowed people to walk in their own ways, but the

Christ-event has now put all of humanity in a radically new situation (14:14–17). The theme of universal divine witness is clearly expressed by Paul in Acts 14:17 as well as in his Areopagus speech in Acts 17:16–34. Paul notes a universal religiosity and divine observance, including worship of an unknown god. Seizing the potential in this moment, Paul notes that what was unknown has now been revealed as the God who created the heavens and the earth and who became incarnate in Jesus of Nazareth. The times of ignorance, when people conceived of God as made of gold or silver, are over: all must repent, for judgment is coming; Jesus has been raised from the dead and will come again (a statement for which Paul was mocked by the Greeks). One of Paul's great themes is the reality of universal divine awareness, which orients people to God but which is finally incomplete: there is need for particular divine revelation through which salvation comes to be offered to Jew and Gentile alike (see Acts 13:38–49; **Col.** 1:15–20). Salvation is based not on works or obedience to the law, but on the gospel of grace and faith in Jesus Christ (see Acts 15; **Galatians** 1:1–9; 2:15–3:29).

Paul's understanding of the gospel is expressed very clearly in **Romans**, especially chapter 1. He had never been to Rome, and was writing a letter of introduction in which he spelled out his general position. In the first chapter, after his greeting to the church at Rome (1:1–7) and prayer of thanksgiving (1:8–15), Paul announces the theme of his letter: "the gospel ... is the power of God for salvation to everyone who has faith, to the Jew first and also to the Greek. For in it the righteousness of God is revealed through faith for faith; as it is written, 'The one who is righteous will live by faith'" (1:16–17). He then turns immediately to the general status of humanity before God (1:18–32). This passage on universal natural "knowledge" of God or general revelation (1:18–32) suggests two modes of such revelation: internal and external. The problem is that human beings resist acknowledging God, and still tend to get God wrong by confusing creator and creature. They therefore need something more – namely, special revelation (that is, incarnation over and above what is generally manifest in creation).

As Paul continues in Romans, after hinting at the universal moral sense in human beings, which, coupled with the universal religious sense, entails lack of excuse for humanity before God, he points out the guilt of the Jews before God (2:17–3:8) in addition to that of humanity at large. All are therefore guilty and incapable of self-justification or self-salvation (3:9–20). Paul therefore reiterates his theme – justification by grace through faith (3:21–31) – and then in chapters 9–11 raises the question of the identity of God's chosen, the elect (see especially 9:30–10:4; 10:14–18; 11; see also Acts 13:45–7). For Paul, election involves not sorting sheep and goats, but being called to service in the mission of God in the world, which involves witness, suffering, and love.

Near the end of the biblical canon, some of the most important statements regarding the status of religion are made. First of all, in **1 Timothy** 2:1–7, the two key biblical propositions concerning universality and particularity are underlined: the one true God desires the salvation of all; this God has been made known through the one mediator Jesus Christ. Secondly, Paul's homily on love recorded in **1 Corinthians** 13 emphasizes the importance of love for Christian living (see also

Phil. 2:1–13). The centrality of love for Christian theology is signaled even more powerfully in **1 John** 4:8–9, where the text says unconditionally that God *is* love (*agape*) – a text central to the biblical and Christian conception of God, and therefore central to the Christian doctrine of the Trinity as articulated by the post-apostolic Church. The canon closes on an eschatological note in the book of **Revelation**, in which the consummation of history is envisioned. Having proceeded through the acts of creation, fall, and redemption, the biblical text in Revelation envisions a new heaven and a new earth as well as the cessation of suffering and death (21:1–8). The canon closes with the words: " 'Surely I am coming soon.' Amen. Come, Lord Jesus! The grace of the Lord Jesus be with all the saints. Amen" (22:20–1).

A number of things should be noted by way of provisional conclusion at this point. First of all, according to the biblical text, there is a God who is the source of all created reality and who has been revealed in creation and history, and definitively in the incarnation. The biblical text tells this dramatic story of revelation and divine–human encounter. God is deeply and lovingly concerned with humanity inside and outside the household of faith, even to the point of humiliation (incarnation) and shameful death (atonement). The Christian tradition later expressed this biblical revelation of God in, among other teachings, its doctrine of the Trinity, in which it recognized that God is a transcendent, unified community of three loving persons who dwell in blessed, perfect fellowship and who seek to incorporate humanity into the sublime, relational harmony of the divine life.

Second, the Bible underscores that humanity is ineluctably related to this God. But in its divided and "in between" condition, humanity is not always cognizant of this relation: humans are created good, but fallen; related to God, but separated from God; sought by God, yet haunted by God; groping toward God, yet rebelling against God; fallen, but on the way to redemption. Religion is the expression of this inescapable reality. Religion, as a human attempt to address the problems of existence, is a response to divine revelation; there is thus something profoundly right about religion, for God is at work in it; but this response needs to be tempered and corrected, for humanity tends to be rebellious and to construct God in its own image, when the reverse is actually the case. Humanity is in need of regeneration, renewal – indeed, re-creation. Revelation thus functions as a corrective to religion; and religion should therefore be understood in the light of revelation, not vice versa. Religion is thus a fact, woven into the fabric of humanity and creation; the chief question about religion is thus its propriety (truth) or misdirection (falsehood).

Third, the Bible's attitude to proper religion is doxological: honor and praise are to be accorded to the God who has been revealed; human beings are to respond righteously, gratefully, and humbly in faith, hope, and love.

Fourth, the Bible's attitude to misdirected religion is on the whole condemnatory: there is one God, who has been revealed generally in creation and particularly in the Incarnation, who desires fellowship and fidelity (from the Latin word *fides*: faith), who judges infidelity or misdirected religion negatively, but who is also compassionate, forgiving, and the redeemer of the cosmos.

Fifth, reflecting pivotal emphases in the biblical text, the Bible reader's attitude to religion should not be one-sided, in that seemingly contrary truths must be recognized simultaneously. Although the Bible's verdict against misdirected religion is negative (but without being absolutely condemnatory), it must be recognized that God's concern for creation and salvific plan – the remedy for the wrong, the solution to the problem – concerns the whole cosmos. In other words, there is both a universal moment and a particular moment to be reckoned within the biblical text: there is the universal, creational scope of divine concern, extending even to divine desire for the salvation of all; and there is the particular, Christological revelation which makes knowledge of God, proper divine–human relationship, and salvation possible. These two moments might be termed the universal-creational and particular-revelational moments, respectively. The two are related in the following way: the universal divine concern for creation comes to expression in the dramatic measure of the particular, Christological revelation; and the particular, atoning revelation of God in Christ is of universal consequence, making possible the salvation of all the world.

The above overview of the Bible's attitude toward religion serves two basic purposes. First, it provides an interpretive summary of the content of a key theological resource in itself. Second, it furnishes a context for comprehending the Christian tradition's various construals of central biblical themes – the foundation on which that tradition built its theological articulations of its relationship to other traditions. It is to the task of seeking to understand those articulations that the presentation now turns.

Notes

1 This minimal canon is identical in content with the Protestant canon.
2 There are, of course, many versions of the Bible in the English language. The reader is encouraged to find a version which meets the twin criteria of excellence in translation: accuracy and readability. While several translations may meet these criteria, the New Revised Standard Version can be confidently recommended; quotations from the biblical text in what follows are taken from this version. Although this particular English version of the Bible is recommended here, it must be emphasized that it is very often the case that comparison of translations yields enlightening results; the reader is accordingly encouraged to undertake comparative examination of key passages and to employ reference works available for study of the Bible – concordances, commentaries, dictionaries, encyclopedias, and the like.
3 In interpreting Genesis 1, Christian thought sees evidence for the idea of creation out of nothing (*creatio ex nihilo*): creation, the argument goes, was called forth from nonbeing and fashioned not out of divine substance or out of some other preexisting matter; for, by definition, no such matter could exist alongside the sovereign and solely eternal God. Creation was thus fashioned out of nothing.
4 Ezra and Nehemiah are surely post-exilic; the other books noted are quite likely post-exilic, although biblical scholarship continues to debate such historical matters. The historical context of these texts is not the central point to be considered here; rather, their theological substance is at issue. To the degree, however, that historical scholarship enlightens the theology of the texts, such scholarship adds a useful dimension to the present discussion.

I am indebted to my colleague Ken Pomykala for pointing out the problem of the nations in early Second Temple Judaism and its significance for theological reflection about religion.

5 It is widely assumed in biblical scholarship that Luke and Acts share a common author.

Part II
Patristic Texts
(*c.*100–*c.*500)

2

Justin Martyr, "The First Apology"

Prior to the fourth century, Christians found themselves in a minority position in the Roman Empire, and were sometimes persecuted for their faith. In order to make converts and respond to persecution, some Christian thinkers attempted to explain Christian thought and practice, as well as to defend Christianity. Such thinkers are called "apologists."

Some of the apologists appealed to the authorities to treat Christians justly, and consequently chose a rather peaceful and bridge-building approach. Notable among this class of apologists is Justin Martyr, who was born c.100 and who lived as a pagan until his conversion to Christianity. With a keen eye for the intellectual dimension of Christianity, Justin sought to elucidate and advocate Christian positions. He became a Christian teacher at Rome, where he was martyred c.165.

Justin is known as a "Greek apologist," because he wrote in the Greek language. Beyond the matter of language, however, Justin can be thought of as a Greek apologist because of his careful pre-conversion study of Greek philosophy and his desire to make sense of the relation between Greek thought and Christian thought. In attempting to understand this relation, which he undoubtedly found in his own person with regard to his past beliefs and his present faith, he saw philosophy as a preparation for the gospel, as a gift of God, and as a valuable tool for the expression of Christian truth. This view of philosophy's relationship to Christianity became a classical way of resolving a much discussed issue in the history of Christianity – namely, the relationship of faith and reason.

In "The First Apology," which is formally a speech to the emperor, Justin tries to defend against legal and moral attacks and to demonstrate the Old Testament basis of the Christian gospel. He pleads for toleration, and simultaneously seeks to make some converts. (It should be borne in mind that at this early point in Christian history, the matter of the Christian canon was far from settled; Justin's "Apology" may well have functioned as a sort of manual for converts to Christianity.) In so doing, he attempts to link the claims of the gospel with the ideas of the time, in order to remove prejudices and find common ground. He argues that although Christianity is the truth, there is also truth in the non-Christian world. Such truth, according to Justin, can be found outside Christianity for two reasons. First, whereas Christ is *the* word (*logos*) of God made flesh, the seed of the word, or the seed of reason (*logos spermatikos*), has been spread throughout time and space. This concept represents Justin's philosophical way of expressing the idea of natural, or general, revelation. Second, paganism has borrowed truths from Israel, and it therefore resembles Christianity, which is the true heir to Israel's hope. Moreover, these borrowed teachings are a mixture of truth and error because of the corruption of wicked demons, who camouflage true Christian teachings and plant teachings similar to Christianity.

In the text which follows, brackets in the text are reprinted from the source edition. All footnotes, however, have been deleted.

The Text

Plea for a Fair Hearing

1. To the Emperor Titus Aelius Hadrianus Antoninus Pius Augustus Caesar, and to Verissimus his son, the Philosopher, and to Lucius the Philosopher, son of Caesar by nature and of Augustus by adoption, a lover of culture, and to the Sacred Senate and the whole Roman people – on behalf of men of every nation who are unjustly hated and reviled, I, Justin, son of Priscus and grandson of Bacchius, of Flavia Neapolis in Syria Palestina, being myself one of them, have drawn up this plea and petition.

2. Reason requires that those who are truly pious and philosophers should honor and cherish the truth alone, scorning merely to follow the opinions of the ancients, if they are worthless. Nor does sound reason only require that one should not follow those who do or teach what is unjust; the lover of truth ought to choose in every way, even at the cost of his own life, to speak and do what is right, though death should take him away. So do you, since you are called pious and philosophers and guardians of justice and lovers of culture, at least give us a hearing – and it will appear if you are really such. For in these pages we do not come before you with flattery, or as if making a speech to win your favor, but asking you to give judgment according to strict and exact inquiry – not, moved by prejudice or respect for superstitious men, or by irrational impulse and long-established evil rumor, giving a vote which would really be against yourselves. For we are firmly convinced that we can suffer no evil unless we are proved to be evildoers or shown to be criminals. You can kill us, but cannot do us any real harm.

3. But so that no one may think that this is an unreasonable and presumptuous utterance, we ask that the charges against us be investigated. If they are shown to be true [let us] be punished as is proper. But if nobody has proofs against us, true reason does not allow [you] to wrong innocent men because of an evil rumor – or rather [to wrong] yourselves when you decide to pass sentence on the basis of passion rather than judgment. Every honorable man will recognize this as a fair challenge, and only just, that subjects should give a straightforward account of their life and thought, and that rulers similarly should give their decision as followers of piety and philosophy, not with tyrannical violence. From this both rulers and subjects would gain. As one of the ancients said somewhere, "Unless both rulers and those they rule become lovers of wisdom cities cannot prosper." It is for us, therefore, to offer to all the opportunity of inspecting our life and teachings, lest we ourselves should bear the blame for what those who do not really know about us do in their ignorance. But it is for you, as reason demands, to give [us] a hearing and show

Source: *Early Christian Fathers*, Library of Christian Classics, 1, trans. and ed. C. C. Richardson.

yourselves good judges. For if those who learn [the truth] do not do what is right, they have no defense before God.

4.   The mere ascription of a name means nothing, good or bad, except for the actions connected with the name. Indeed as far as the name charged against us goes, we are very gracious people. But we do not think it right to ask for a pardon because of the name if we are proved to be criminals – and on the other hand, if neither the appellation of the name nor our conduct shows us to be wrongdoers, you must face the problem whether in punishing unjustly men against whom nothing is proved you will yourselves owe a penalty to justice. Neither reward nor punishment should follow from a name unless something admirable or evil can actually be shown about it. Among yourselves you do not penalize the accused before conviction; but with us you take the name as proof, although, as far as the name goes, you ought rather to punish our accusers. For we are accused of being Christians; and it is not right to hate graciousness. Again, if one of the accused denies the charge, saying he is not [a Christian], you dismiss him, as having no proof of misconduct against him; but if he confesses that he is one, you punish him because of his confession. You ought rather to investigate the life of the confessor and the renegade, so that it would appear from their actions what sort of person each is. There are those who, learning from Christ their teacher, when they are put to the test encourage others not to deny him – and similarly others whose bad conduct gives some excuse to those who like to accuse all Christians of godlessness and crime. This is entirely improper. There are those who assume the name and costume of philosophers, but do nothing worthy of their profession – as you know, men among the ancients who held and taught opposite views are included under the one name of philosophers. Some of them even taught godlessness, and those who became poets proclaim the impurity of Zeus, with his own children. And you do not restrain those among you who follow such teachings, but even offer prizes and honors to those who thus in beautiful words insult them [the gods].

5.   What can all this mean? You do not make judicial inquiries in our case, though we are bound neither to commit crimes nor to hold such godless ideas. Instead, you punish us injudicially without deliberation, driven by unreasoning passion and the whips of evil demons. The truth must be told. In old times evil demons manifested themselves, seducing women, corrupting boys, and showing terrifying sights to men – so that those who did not judge these occurrences rationally were filled with awe. Taken captive by fear and not understanding that these were evil demons, they called them gods and gave each of them the name which each of the demons had chosen for himself. When Socrates tried by true reason and with due inquiry to make these things clear and to draw men away from the demons, they, working through men who delighted in wickedness, managed to have him put to death as godless and impious, saying that he was bringing in new divinities. And now they do the same kind of thing to us. For these errors were not only condemned among the Greeks by reason, through Socrates, but among the barbarians, by Reason himself, who took form and became man and was called Jesus Christ. In obedience to him we say that the demons who do such things are not only not rightly called gods, but are in fact

evil and unholy demons, whose actions are in no way like those of men who long after virtue.

6. So, then, we are called godless. We certainly confess that we are godless with reference to beings like these who are commonly thought of as gods, but not with reference to the most true God, the Father of righteousness and temperance and the other virtues, who is untouched by evil. Him, and the Son who came from him, and taught us these things, and the army of the other good angels who follow him and are made like him, and the prophetic Spirit we worship and adore, giving honor in reason and truth, and to everyone who wishes to learn transmitting [the truth] ungrudgingly as we have been taught.

7. But someone will say, "Some [Christians] have been arrested and convicted as criminals." Many at various times, perhaps, if you examine in each case the conduct of those who are accused; but do not condemn [all] because of those previously convicted. We admit in general that just as among the Greeks those who teach what seems best to them are all listed under the name of philosophy, even though their teachings are contradictory, so the name which is now being attacked is common to those among the barbarians who are and those who appear to be wise. They are all listed as Christians. So we ask that the actions of those who are denounced to you be investigated, in order that whoever is convicted may be punished as a criminal, but not as a Christian, and that whoever is shown to be innocent may be freed, committing no crime by being a Christian. We shall not ask you, however, to punish our accusers, for they suffer enough from their own wickedness and their ignorance of the good.

8. Consider that we have said these things for your sake, since when put to trial we can deny [that we are Christians] – but we do not wish to live by telling a lie. For, longing for the life which is eternal and pure, we strive to dwell with God, the Father and Fashioner of all things. We are eager to confess, being convinced and believing that those who have shown to God by their actions that they follow him and long to dwell with him, where no evil can disturb, are able to obtain these things. It is this, in brief, that we look for, and have learned from Christ, and teach. Plato similarly said that Rhadamanthus and Minos would punish the wicked who came before them. We say that this is what will happen, but at the hands of Christ – and to the same bodies, reunited with their souls, and destined for eternal punishment, not for a five-hundred-year period only, as he said. If anyone says that this is unbelievable or impossible – at least the mistake affects us and no one else, as long as we are not convicted of any actual crime.

The Faith and Life of Christians

9. Certainly we do not honor with many sacrifices and floral garlands the objects that men have fashioned, set up in temples, and called gods. We know that they are lifeless and dead and do not represent the form of God – for we do not think of

God as having the kind of form which some claim that they imitate to be honored – but rather exhibit the names and shapes of the evil demons who have manifested themselves [to men]. You know well enough without our mentioning it how the craftsmen prepare their material, scraping and cutting and molding and beating. And often they make what they call gods out of vessels used for vile purposes, changing and transforming by art merely their appearance. We consider it not only irrational but an insult to God, whose glory and form are ineffable, to give his name to corruptible things which themselves need care. You are well aware that craftsmen in these [things] are impure and – not to go into details – given to all kinds of vice; they even corrupt their own slave girls who work along with them. What an absurdity, that dissolute men should be spoken of as fashioning or remaking gods for public veneration, and that you should appoint such people as guardians of the temples where they are set up – not considering that it is unlawful to think or speak of men as guardians of gods.

10.   But we have learned [from our tradition] that God has no need of material offerings from men, considering that he is the provider of all. We have been taught and firmly believe that he accepts only those who imitate the good things which are his – temperance and righteousness and love of mankind, and whatever else truly belongs to the God who is called by no given name. We have also been taught that in the beginning he in his goodness formed all things that are for the sake of men out of unformed matter, and if they show themselves by their actions worthy of his plan, we have learned that they will be counted worthy of dwelling with him, reigning together and made free from corruption and suffering. For as he made us in the beginning when we were not, so we hold that those who choose what is pleasing to him will, because of that choice, be counted worthy of incorruption and of fellowship [with him]. We did not bring ourselves into being – but as to following after the things that are dear to God, choosing them by the rational powers which he has given us – this is a matter of conviction and leads us to faith. We hold it to be for the good of all men that they are not prevented from learning these things, but are even urged to [consider] them. For what human laws could not do, that the Word, being divine, would have brought about, if the evil demons had not scattered abroad many false and godless accusations, with the help of the evil desire that is in every man by nature [and expresses itself] in all kinds of ways. None of this, however, matters to us.

11.   When you hear that we look for a kingdom, you rashly suppose that we mean something merely human. But we speak of a Kingdom with God, as is clear from our confessing Christ when you bring us to trial, though we know that death is the penalty for this confession. For if we looked for a human kingdom we would deny it in order to save our lives, and would try to remain in hiding in order to obtain the things we look for. But since we do not place our hopes on the present [order], we are not troubled by being put to death, since we will have to die somehow in any case.

12.   We are in fact of all men your best helpers and allies in securing good order,

convinced as we are that no wicked man, no covetous man or conspirator, or virtuous man either, can be hidden from God, and that everyone goes to eternal punishment or salvation in accordance with the character of his actions. If all men knew this, nobody would choose vice even for a little time, knowing that he was on his way to eternal punishment by fire; every man would follow the self-restrained and orderly path of virtue, so as to receive the good things that come from God and avoid his punishments. There are some who merely try to conceal their wrongdoing because of the laws and punishments which you decree, knowing that since you are only men it is possible for wrongdoers to escape you; if they learned and were convinced that our thoughts as well as our actions cannot be hidden from God they would certainly lead orderly lives, if only because of the consequences, as you must agree. But it seems as if you were afraid of having all men well-behaved, and nobody left for you to punish; this would be the conduct of public executioners, not of good rulers. Such things, we are convinced, are brought about by the evil demons, the ones who demand sacrifices and service from men who live irrationally; but we have not learned [to expect] any unreasonable conduct from you, who aim at piety and philosophy. But if like thoughtless men you prefer custom to truth, then go ahead and do what you can. Rulers who respect reputation rather than truth have as much power as brigands in a desert. The Word himself has shown that you will not succeed, and after God who begat him we know of no ruler more royal or more just than he. For just as all men try to avoid inheriting the poverty or sufferings or disgrace of their ancestors, so the sensible man will not choose whatever the Word forbids to be chosen. He foretold that all these things would happen – our Teacher, I mean, who is the Son and Apostle of God the Father and Master of all, that is, Jesus Christ, from whom we have received the name of Christians. We are sure that all the things taught by him are so, since we see that what he predicted is actually coming to pass. This is God's work, to announce something before it happens and then to show it happening as predicted. I might stop here and add no more, having made clear that we ask for what is just and true. But though I know that it is not easy to change over at once a mind which is bound down by ignorance, I am encouraged to add somewhat to persuade the lover of truth, being sure that one can dispel ignorance by putting truth against it.

13.   What sound-minded man will not admit that we are not godless, since we worship the Fashioner of the universe, declaring him, as we have been taught, to have no need of blood and libations and incense, but praising him by the word of prayer and thanksgiving for all that he has given us? We have learned that the only honor worthy of him is, not to consume by fire the things he has made for our nourishment, but to devote them to our use and those in need, in thankfulness to him sending up solemn prayers and hymns for our creation and all the means of health, for the variety of creatures and the changes of the seasons, and sending up our petitions that we may live again in incorruption through our faith in him. It is Jesus Christ who has taught us these things, having been born for this purpose and crucified under Pontius Pilate, who was procurator in Judea in the time of Tiberius Caesar. We will show that we honor him in accordance with reason, having learned

that he is the Son of the true God himself, and holding him to be in the second place and the prophetic Spirit in the third rank. It is for this that they charge us with madness, saying that we give the second place after the unchanging and ever-existing God and begetter of all things to a crucified man, not knowing the mystery involved in this, to which we ask you to give your attention as we expound it.

14.   We warn you in advance to be careful, lest the demons whom we have attacked should deceive you and prevent your completely grasping and understanding what we say. For they struggle to have you as their slaves and servants, and now by manifestations in dreams, now by magic tricks, they get hold of all who do not struggle to their utmost for their own salvation – as we do who, after being persuaded by the Word, renounced them and now follow the only unbegotten God through his Son. Those who once rejoiced in fornication now delight in continence alone; those who made use of magic arts have dedicated themselves to the good and unbegotten God; we who once took most pleasure in the means of increasing our wealth and property now bring what we have into a common fund and share with everyone in need; we who hated and killed one another and would not associate with men of different tribes because of [their different] customs, now after the manifesta-tion of Christ live together and pray for our enemies and try to persuade those who unjustly hate us, so that they, living according to the fair commands of Christ, may share with us the good hope of receiving the same things [that we will] from God, the master of all. So that this may not seem to be sophistry, I think fit before giving our demonstration to recall a few of the teachings which have come from Christ himself. It is for you then, as mighty emperors, to examine whether we have been taught and do teach these things truly. His sayings were short and concise, for he was no sophist, but his word was the power of God.

15.   About continence he said this: "Whoever looks on a woman to lust after her has already committed adultery in his heart before God." And: "If your right eye offends you, cut it out; it is better for you to enter into the Kingdom of Heaven with one eye than with two to be sent into eternal fire." And: "Whoever marries a woman who has been put away from another man commits adultery." And: "There are some who were made eunuchs by men, and some who were born eunuchs, and some who have made themselves eunuchs for the Kingdom of Heaven's sake; only not all [are able to] receive this."

And so those who make second marriages according to human law are sinners in the sight of our Teacher, and those who look on a woman to lust after her. For he condemns not only the man who commits the act of adultery, but the man who desires to commit adultery, since not only our actions but our thoughts are manifest to God. Many men and women now in their sixties and seventies who have been disciples of Christ from childhood have preserved their purity; and I am proud that I could point to such people in every nation. Then what shall we say of the uncounted multitude of those who have turned away from incontinence and learned these things? For Christ did not call the righteous or the temperate to repentance, but the ungodly and incontinent and unrighteous. So he said: "I have not come to call the righteous but sinners to repentance." For the Heavenly Father wishes the repentance of a sinner rather than his punishment.

This is what he taught on affection for all men: "If you love those who love you, what new things do you do? for even the harlots do this. But I say to you, Pray for your enemies and love those who hate you and bless those who curse you and pray for those who treat you despitefully."

That we should share with those in need and do nothing for [our] glory he said these things: "Give to everyone who asks and turn not away him who wishes to borrow. For if you lend to those from whom you hope to receive, what new thing do you do? Even the publicans do this. But as for you, do not lay up treasures for yourselves on earth, where moth and rust corrupt and thieves break in, but lay up for yourselves treasures in heaven, where neither moth nor rust corrupts. For what will it profit a man, if he should gain the whole world, but lose his own soul? Or what will he give in exchange for it? Lay up treasures therefore in the heavens, where neither moth nor rust corrupts." And: "Be kind and merciful, as your Father is kind and merciful, and makes his sun to rise on sinners and righteous and wicked. Do not worry as to what you will eat or what you will wear. Are you not better than the birds and the beasts? and God feeds them. So do not worry as to what you will eat or what you will wear, for your Heavenly Father knows that you need these things. But seek the Kingdom of Heaven, and all these things will be added to you. For where his treasure is, there is the mind of man." And: "Do not do these things to be seen of men, for otherwise you have no reward with your Father who is in heaven."

16.   About being long-suffering and servants to all and free from anger, this is what he said: "To him that smites you on one cheek turn the other also, and to him that takes away your cloak do not deny your tunic either. Whoever is angry is worthy of the fire. And whoever compels you to go one mile, follow him for two. Let your good works shine before men, that they as they see may wonder at your Father who is in heaven."

For we ought not to quarrel; he has not wished us to imitate the wicked, but rather by our patience and meekness to draw all men from shame and evil desires. This we can show in the case of many who were once on your side but have turned from the ways of violence and tyranny, overcome by observing the consistent lives of their neighbors, or noting the strange patience of their injured acquaintances, or experiencing the way they did business with them.

About not swearing at all, but always speaking the truth, this is what he commanded: "Swear not at all; but let your yea be yea and your nay nay. What is more than these is from the evil one."

That God only should be worshiped he showed us when he said: "The greatest commandment is: Thou shalt worship the Lord thy God and him only shalt thou serve with all thy heart and all thy strength, the Lord who made thee." And: "When one came to him and said, Good Teacher, he answered and said, There is none good, except only God who made all things."

Those who are found not living as he taught should know that they are not really Christians, even if his teachings are on their lips, for he said that not those who merely profess but those who also do the works will be saved. For he said this: "Not everyone who says to me, Lord, Lord, will enter into the Kingdom of Heaven, but he who does the will of my Father who is in heaven. For whoever hears me and does what I say hears him who sent me. Many will say to me, Lord, Lord, did we not eat in your name and drink and do mighty works? And then I will say to them, Depart from me, you workers of iniquity. Then there will be weeping and gnashing of teeth, when the righteous will shine as the sun, but the wicked will be sent into eternal fire. For many will come in my name clothed outwardly in sheep's clothing, but being inwardly ravening wolves; by their works you will know them. Every tree that does not bring forth good fruit is cut down and thrown into the fire."

So we ask that you too should punish those who do not live in accordance with his teachings, but merely say that they are Christians.

17.   More even than others we try to pay the taxes and assessments to those whom you appoint, as we have been taught by him. For once in his time some came to him and asked whether it were right to pay taxes to Caesar. And he answered, "Tell me, whose image is on the coin." They said, "Caesar's." And he answered them again, "Then give what is Caesar's to Caesar and what is God's to God." So we worship God only, but in other matters we gladly serve you, recognizing you as emperors and rulers of men, and praying that along with your imperial power you may also be found to have a sound mind. If you pay no attention to our prayers and our frank statements about everything, it will not injure us, since we believe, or rather are firmly convinced, that every man will suffer in eternal fire in accordance with the quality of his actions, and similarly will be required to give account for the abilities which he has received from God, as Christ told us when he said, "To whom God has given more, from him more will be required."

18.   Look at the end of each of the former emperors, how they died the common death of all; and if this were merely a departure into unconsciousness, that would be a piece of luck for the wicked. But since consciousness continues for all who have lived, and eternal punishment awaits, do not fail to be convinced and believe that these things are true. For the oracles of the dead and the revelations of innocent children, the invoking of [departed] human souls, the dream senders and guardians of the magi, and what is done by those who know about such things – all this should convince you that souls are still conscious after death. Then there are the men who are seized and torn by the spirits of the dead, whom everyone calls demon-possessed and maniacs, and the oracles so well-known among you, of Amphilochus and Dodona and Pytho, and any others of that kind, and the teaching of writers, Empedocles and Pythagoras, Plato and Socrates, and the ditch in Homer and the descent of Odysseus to visit the dead, and other stories like this. Treat us at least like these; we believe in God not less than they do, but rather more, since we look foward to receiving again our own bodies, though they be dead and buried in the earth, declaring that nothing is impossible to God.

19.   Indeed, what would seem more incredible to an observer than if we were not in the body and someone should say that from a single drop of human seed it were

possible for the form that we see to come into being, with bones and nerves and flesh? Consider this hypothesis; if you were not such as you are, born of such parents, and someone were to show you the human seed and a picture of a man, and assure you that the one could grow into the other, would you believe it before you saw it happening? No one would dare to deny [that you wouldn't]. In the same way unbelief prevails about the resurrection of the dead because you have never seen an instance of it. But as you at first would not have believed that from a little drop such beings [as men] could develop, yet you see it happening, so consider that it is possible for human bodies, dissolved and scattered in the earth like seeds, to rise again in due time by God's decree and be clothed with incorruption. I cannot imagine how any adequate concept of divine power can be held by those who say that everything returns into that from which it came and that not even God can do anything more than this. But I may remark that they would not have believed it possible for such creatures as they are to have come into being, yet they see themselves as they are, and indeed the whole world [as it is], and what they were made from. We have learned that it is better to believe things impossible to our own nature and to men than to disbelieve like others, since we know that our Teacher Jesus Christ said, "The things that are impossible with men are possible with God." And: "Fear not those who put you to death and after that can do no more, but fear him who after death is able to cast both body and soul into Gehenna." Gehenna is the place where those who live unrighteously will be punished, and those who do not believe that these things will come to pass which God has taught through Christ.

20.   Both Sybil and Hystaspes declared that there will be a destruction of corruptible things by fire. Those who are called Stoic philosophers teach that God himself will be resolved into fire, and the universe come into being again by return. We think that God, the Maker of all, is superior to changeable things. But if on some points we agree with the poets and philosophers whom you honor, and on others [teach] more completely and more worthily of God, and are the only ones who offer proof, why are we above all hated unjustly? When we say that all things have been ordered and made by God we appear to offer the teaching of Plato – in speaking of a coming destruction by fire, that of the Stoics; in declaring that the souls of the unrighteous will be punished after death, still remaining in conscious existence, and those of the virtuous, delivered from punishments, will enjoy happiness, we seem to agree with [various] poets and philosophers; in declaring that men ought not to worship the works of their hands we are saying the same things as the comedian Menander and others who have said this for they declared that the Fashioner is greater than what he has formed.

Superiority of Christianity to Paganism

21.   In saying that the Word, who is the first offspring of God, was born for us without sexual union, as Jesus Christ our Teacher, and that he was crucified and died and after rising again ascended into heaven we introduce nothing new beyond [what

you say of] those whom you call sons of Zeus. You know how many sons of Zeus the writers whom you honor speak of – Hermes, the hermeneutic Word and teacher of all; Asclepius, who was also a healer and after being struck by lightning ascended into heaven – as did Dionysus who was torn in pieces; Heracles, who to escape his torments threw himself into the fire; the Dioscuri born of Leda and Perseus of Danaë; and Bellerophon who, though of human origin, rode on the [divine] horse Pegasus. Need I mention Ariadne and those who like her are said to have been placed among the stars? and what of your deceased emperors, whom you regularly think worthy of being raised to immortality, introducing a witness who swears that he saw the cremated Caesar ascending into heaven from the funeral pyre? Nor is it necessary to remind you what kind of actions are related of each of those who are called sons of Zeus, except [to point out] that they are recorded for the benefit and instruction of students – for all consider it a fine thing to be imitators of the gods. Far be it from every sound mind to entertain such a concept of the deities as that Zeus, whom they call the ruler and begetter of all, should have been a parricide and the son of a parricide, and that moved by desire of evil and shameful pleasures he descended on Ganymede and the many women whom he seduced, and that his sons after him were guilty of similar actions. But, as we said before, it was the wicked demons who did these things. We have been taught that only those who live close to God in holiness and virtue attain to immortality, and we believe that those who live unjustly and do not reform will be punished in eternal fire.

22.   Now if God's Son, who is called Jesus, were only an ordinary man, he would be worthy because of his wisdom to be called Son of God, for all authors call God father of men and gods. When we say, as before, that he was begotten by God as the Word of God in a unique manner beyond ordinary birth, this should be no strange thing for you who speak of Hermes as the announcing word from God. If somebody objects that he was crucified, this is in common with the sons of Zeus, as you call them, who suffered, as previously listed. Since their fatal sufferings are narrated as not similar but different, so his unique passion should not seem to be any worse – indeed I will, as I have undertaken, show, as the argument proceeds, that he was better; for he is shown to be better by his actions. If we declare that he was born of a virgin, you should consider this something in common with Perseus. When we say that he healed the lame, the paralytic, and those born blind, and raised the dead, we seem to be talking about things like those said to have been done by Asclepius.

23.   In order to make this clear to you I will present the evidence that the things we say, as disciples of Christ and of the prophets who came before him, are the only truths and older than all the writers who have lived, and we ask to be accepted, not because we say the same things as they do, but because we are speaking the truth – [second] that Jesus Christ alone was really begotten as Son of God, being his Word and First-begotten and Power, and becoming man by his will he taught us these things for the reconciliation and restoration of the human race – and [third] that before he came among men as man, there was some who, on account of the already mentioned wicked demons, told through the poets as already having occurred the

myths they had invented, just as now they are responsible for the slanders and godless deeds alleged against us, of which there is neither witness nor demonstration.

24. The first point is that though we say the same as do the Greeks, we only are hated, because of the name of Christ. We do no wrong but are put to death as offenders [because of our worship, though] others everywhere worship trees and rivers, mice and cats and crocodiles and many kinds of irrational animals, and the same objects are not honored by all, but different ones in different places, so that all are impious to each other, because of not having the same objects of worship. Yet this is the one complaint you have against us, that we do not worship the same gods that you do, and do not bring libations and offerings of fat to the dead, crowns for their statues, and sacrifices. Yet, as you know well, the same beings are gods to some and wild animals to others, while still others think of them as sacred victims.

25. Secondly, out of every race of men we who once worshiped Dionysus the son of Semele and Apollo the son of Leto, who in their passion for men did things which it is disgraceful even to speak of, or who worshiped Persephone and Aphrodite, who were driven mad by [love of] Adonis and whose mysteries you celebrate, or Asclepius or some other of those who are called gods, now through Jesus Christ despise them, even at the cost of death, and have dedicated ourselves to the unbegotten and impassible God. We do not believe that he ever descended in mad passion on Antiope or others, nor on Ganymede, nor was he, receiving help through Thetis, delivered by that hundred-handed monster, nor was he, because of this, anxious that Thetis's son Achilles should destroy so many Greeks for the sake of his concubine Briseis. We pity those who believe [such stories], for which we know that the demons are responsible.

26. A third point is that after Christ's ascent into heaven the demons put forward various men who said that they were gods, and you not only did not persecute them, but thought them worthy of honors. One was a certain Simon, a Samaritan from the village of Gitta, who in the time of Claudius Caesar, through the arts of the demons who worked in him, did mighty works of magic in your imperial city of Rome and was thought to be a god. He has been honored among you as a god by a statue, which was set up on the River Tiber, between the two bridges, with this inscription in Latin, SIMONI DEO SANCTO. Almost all the Samaritans, and a few in other nations, confess this man as their first god and worship him as such, and a woman named Helena, who traveled around with him in those days, and had formerly been a public prostitute, they say was the first Concept produced from him. Then we know of a certain Menander, who was also a Samaritan, from the village of Capparetaea, who had been a disciple of Simon's, and was also possessed by the demons. He deceived many at Antioch by magic arts, and even persuaded his followers that he would never die; there are still some who believe this [as they learned] from him. Then there is a certain Marcion of Pontus, who is still teaching his converts that there is another God greater than the Fashioner. By the help of the demons he has made many in every race of men to blaspheme and to deny God the Maker of the universe, professing that there is another who is greater and has done

greater things than he. As we said, all who derive [their opinions] from these men are called Christians, just as men who do not share the same teachings with the philosophers still have in common with them the name of philosophy, thus brought into disrepute. Whether they commit the shameful deeds about which stories are told – the upsetting of the lamp, promiscuous intercourse, and the meals of human flesh, we do not know; but we are sure that they are neither persecuted nor killed by you, on account of their teachings anyway. I have compiled and have on hand a treatise against all the heresies which have arisen, which I will give you if you would like to consult it.

27.   That we may avoid all injustice and impiety, we have been taught that to expose the newly born is the work of wicked men – first of all because we observe that almost all [foundlings], boys as well as girls, are brought up for prostitution. As the ancients are said to have raised herds of oxen or goats or sheep or horses in their pastures, so now [you raise children] just for shameful purposes, and so in every nation a crowd of females and hermaphrodites and doers of unspeakable deeds are exposed as public prostitutes. You even collect pay and levies and taxes from these, whom you ought to exterminate from your civilized world. And anyone who makes use of them may in addition to [the guilt of] godless, impious, and intemperate intercourse, by chance be consorting with his own child or relative or brother. Some even prostitue their own children and wives, and others are admittedly mutilated for purposes of sodomy, and treat this as part of the mysteries of the mother of the gods – while beside each of those whom you think of as gods a serpent is depicted as a great symbol and mystery. You charge against us the actions that you commit openly and treat with honor, as if the divine light were overthrown and withdrawn – which of course does no harm to us, who refuse to do any of these things, but rather injures those who do them and then bring false witness [against us].

28.   Among us the chief of the evil demons is called the serpent and Satan and the devil, as you can learn by examining our writings. Christ has foretold that he will be cast into fire with his host and the men who follow him, [all] to be punished for endless ages. God delays doing this for the sake of the human race, for he foreknows that there are some yet to be saved by repentance, even perhaps some not yet born. In the beginning he made the race of men endowed with intelligence, able to choose the truth and do right, so that all men are without excuse before God, for they were made with the powers of reason and observation. Anyone who does not believe that God cares for these things either manages to profess that he does not exist, or makes out that he exists but approves of evil or remains [unaffected] like a stone, and that virtue and vice are not realities, but that men consider things good or bad by opinion alone; this is the height of impiety and injustice.

29.   And again [we do not expose children] lest some of them, not being picked up, should die and we thus be murderers. But to begin with, we do not marry except in order to bring up children, or else, renouncing marriage, we live in perfect continence. To show you that promiscuous intercourse is not among our mysteries – just recently one of us submitted a petition to the Prefect Felix in Alexandria, asking that a

physician be allowed to make him a eunuch, for the physicians there said they were not allowed to do this without the permission of the Prefect. When Felix would by no means agree to endorse [the petition], the young man remained single, satisfied with [the approval of] his own conscience and that of his fellow believers. I think it proper in this connection to remind you of the recent case of Antinoüs, whom everybody, through fear, hastened to worship as a god, though knowing perfectly well who he was and where he came from.

The Argument from Prophecy

30. But lest someone should argue against us, What excludes [the supposition] that this person whom you call Christ was a man, of human origin, and did these miracles you speak of by magic arts, and so appeared to be God's Son? – we will bring forward our demonstration. We do not trust in mere hearsay, but are forced to believe those who prophesied [these things] before they happened, because we actually see things that have happened and are happening as was predicted. This will, as we think, be the greatest and surest demonstration for you too.

31. There were among the Jews certain men who were prophets of God, through whom the prophetic Spirit announced in advance events that were to occur. The successive rulers of the Jews carefully preserved their prophecies, as they were spoken when they prophesied, in their own Hebrew language, [and] as arranged in books by the prophets themselves. When Ptolemy, king of Egypt, was founding a library, and set out to gather the writings of all mankind, he learned about these prophecies and sent to Herod, then king of the Jews, asking him to send him the prophetic books. King Herod sent them, written in the aforementioned Hebrew language. Since their contents were not intelligible to the Egyptians, he again sent and asked him to send men who could translate them into Greek. This was done, and the books remain in the hands of the Egyptians down to the present; the Jews everywhere have them too. But though they read them, they do not understand what they say, but consider us their enemies and opponents, putting us to death or punishing us, as you do, whenever they can, as you can realize – for in the Jewish War recently past Bar-Cochba, the leader of the revolt of the Jews, ordered Christians only to be subjected to terrible punishments, unless they would deny Jesus the Christ and blaspheme [him]. We find it predicted in the books of the prophets that Jesus our Christ would come, born of a virgin, grown to manhood, healing every sickness and every disease and raising the dead, hated and unacknowledged and crucified, dying and rising again and ascending into heaven, both really being and being called Son of God. [We find also that] men sent by him would proclaim these things to every race of mankind, and that men of the Gentiles especially would believe in him. This was prophesied over five thousands years before he appeared, then three thousand, and two thousand, and again one thousand, and once more eight hundred [years before]. For there were new prophets again and again as the generations passed.

32. Thus Moses, who was the first of the prophets, said in these very words: "The

ruler shall not depart from Judah, nor the governor from his thighs, until he come for whom it is reserved; and he shall be the expectation of the nations, binding his colt to the vine, washing his robe in the blood of the grape." You can inquire precisely and learn up to whose time the Jews had their own ruler and king. [It was] until the manifestation of Jesus Christ, our teacher and the expounder of the unrecognized prophecies, as was predicted by the divine and holy prophetic Spirit through Moses, that a ruler would not depart from the Jews until he should come for whom the Kingdom is reserved. For Judah was the forefather of the Jews, after whom they are called Jews; and after his [Christ's] appearance you began to rule over the Jews and gained control of their whole land. The saying, He shall be the expectation of the nations, is a testimony that men of every nation will look forward to his coming again, as you can clearly see and be convinced by the fact, for men of every race are looking for him who was crucified in Judea, immediately after which the land of the Jews fell to you as spoil of war. Binding his foal to the vine and washing his robe in the blood of the grape is a symbolic exhibition of the things that would happen to Christ, and his actions. For an ass's foal was standing at the entrance of a village, bound to a vine, which he then ordered his companions to bring to him; when it was brought he mounted and sat on it and entered into Jerusalem, where was the great Temple of the Jews which you afterward overthrew. After this he was crucified, so as to fulfill the rest of the prophecy. For washing his robe in the blood of the grape was predictive of the Passion which he was to suffer, cleansing by his blood those who believe on him. For the men who believe on him in whom dwells the seed of God, the Word, are what the divine Spirit through the prophet calls a garment. The blood of the grape that was spoken of was a sign that he who was to appear would have blood, though not from human seed but by divine power. The first Power after God the Father and Master of all, even [his] Son, is the Word – how he was made flesh and became a man we shall describe below. As the blood of the grape was not made by man, but by God, so it was testified, that [his] blood should not come from human seed, but from divine power, as we said before. Isaiah, another prophet, prophesying the same things in other words, said: "A star shall rise out of Jacob, and a flower will come forth from the root of Jesse, and upon his arm will the nations hope." The shining star has risen and the flower has grown from the root of Jesse – this is Christ. For he was by the power of God conceived by a virgin of the seed of Jacob, who was the father of Judah, the father of the Jews, as has been explained; Jesse was his ancestor, according to the oracle, and he was the son of Jacob and Judah by lineal succession.

33.   And again, hear how it was literally prophesied by Isaiah that he would be born of a virgin. He said, "Behold, the Virgin shall conceive and bear a son, and they will call his name, God with us." For God testified in advance through the prophetic Spirit that things which are unbelievable and thought impossible among men would happen, so that when this should occur it would not be disbelieved, but received with faith because it had been predicted. Lest some, not understanding the prophecy which has been referred to, should bring against us the reproach that we bring against the poets who say that Zeus came upon women for the sake of sexual

pleasure, we will try to explain these words clearly. For "Behold, the Virgin shall conceive" means that the Virgin would conceive without intercourse. For if she had had intercourse with anyone, she would not have been a virgin; but God's power, coming upon the Virgin, overshadowed her, and caused her to conceive while still remaining a virgin. The angel of God who was sent to this Virgin at the time brought her this good news, saying, "Behold, you will conceive in the womb by a Holy Spirit and will bear a son, and he will be called Son of the Highest and you shall call his name Jesus, for he will save his people from their sins," as those who recorded everything about our Saviour Jesus Christ have taught us. We believe them, since the prophetic Spirit through the above-mentioned Isaiah said that this would happen, as we noted before. The Spirit and the Power from God cannot rightly be thought of as anything else than the Word, who is also the First-born of God, as Moses the above-mentioned prophet testified. So this [Spirit], coming upon the Virgin and overshadowing her, made her pregnant – not by intercourse, but by [divine] power. The name Jesus in Hebrew means the same as Saviour in Greek, and so the angel said to the Virgin, "And you shall call his name Jesus, for he will save his people from their sins." Even you will agree, I think, that those who prophesied were inspired by none other than the divine Word.

34. Hear also in what part of the earth he was to be born, as another prophet, Micah, foretold. He said, "And you Bethlehem, land of Judah, are by no means the least among the rulers of Judah; for out of you will come a Ruler who will shepherd my people." This is a village in the land of the Jews, thirty-five stadia from Jerusalem, in which Jesus Christ was born, as you can learn from the census which was taken under Quirinius, who was your first procurator in Judea.

35. How the Christ after his birth was to live hidden from other men until he grew to manhood, as also happened – hear the predictions that refer to this. There is this: "A child is born to us, and a young man is given to us, and the government will be upon his shoulder" – testifying the power of the cross, which when crucified he took upon his shoulders, as will be shown more clearly as the argument proceeds. Again the same prophet Isaiah, inspired by the prophetic Spirit, said: "I have stretched out my hands over a disobedient and contradicting people, over those who walk in a way that is not good. They now ask judgment of me and dare to draw near to God." Again in other words he says through another prophet: "They pierced my hands and feet, and cast lots for my clothing." Now David, the king and prophet, who said this, suffered none of these things. But Jesus Christ stretched out his hands when he was crucified by the Jews, who contradicted him and denied that he was Christ. As the prophet said, "They placed him in mockery on the judgment seat and said, Judge us." "They pierced my hands and feet," was an announcement of the nails that were fastened in his hands and feet on the cross. After fastening him to the cross, those who crucified him cast lots for his clothing and divided it among themselves. That these things really happened, you can learn from the Acts of what was done under Pontius Pilate. And that it was distinctly prophesied that he would take his seat on the foal of an ass and so enter Jerusalem, we will quote the words of the prophecy of another prophet, Zephaniah, as follows: "Rejoice greatly, O daughter of Zion;

shout for joy, O daughter of Jerusalem; behold your King comes to you, meek, and riding upon an ass and a colt the foal of a donkey."

36. When you hear the words of the prophets spoken as in a particular character, do not think of them as spoken by the inspired men themselves, but by the divine Word that moved them. For sometimes he speaks as predicting the things that are to happen, sometimes he speaks as in the character of God the Master and Father of all, sometimes as in the character of Christ, sometimes in the character of the people answering the Lord or his Father. You can see the same thing in your own writers, where one man is the author of the whole work but introduces different characters in dialogue. Not understanding this, the Jews who are in possession of the books of the prophets did not recognize Christ even when he came, and they hate us who declare that he has come and show that he was crucified by them as had been predicted.

37. So that you may see this clearly, here is the kind of words spoken in the character of the Father through the above-mentioned prophet Isaiah: "The ox knows his owner, and the ass his master's crib, but Israel knows me not and my people does not understand. Woe, sinful nation, people full of sins, wicked seed, lawless children, you have forsaken the Lord."

Again in another place, where the same prophet speaks similarly for the Father: "What kind of house will you build for me? says the Lord. Heaven is my throne and the earth is my footstool." And again elsewhere: "My soul hates your new moons and sabbaths, I cannot endure the great day of the fast, and [your] idleness; nor when you come to appear before me will I hear you. Your hands are full of blood, and if you bring offerings of fine flour, [and] incense, it is an abomination to me; the fat of lambs and blood of bulls I do not wish. For who demanded this at your hands? But loose every bond of iniquity, tear apart the knots of the contracts of violence, cover the homeless and naked, deal out your bread to the hungry." You can now notice the kind of things that were taught by the prophets as from God.

38. When the prophetic Spirit speaks in the character of the Christ, he says, "I stretched out my hands over a disobedient and contradicting people, over those who walk in a way that is not good." And again: "I have offered my back to scourges and my cheeks to blows, and I did not turn away my face from the shame of spittings. And the Lord became my helper, therefore I was not confounded, but set my face as a hard rock, and I knew that I would not be put to shame, for he who justifies me is at hand." Again when he says: "They cast lots for my clothing, and pierced my feet and hands. I lay down and slept and rose up again, for the Lord supported me." Again when he says, "They spoke with their lips, they shook their heads, saying, Let him deliver himself." All these things were done by the Jews to Christ, as you can learn. For when he was crucified they stuck out their lips and shook their heads, saying, "He who raised the dead, let him now save himself."

39. When the prophetic Spirit speaks as prophesying things to come, he says: "For the law will go forth from Zion and the Word of the Lord from Jerusalem, and he shall judge in the midst of the nations and rebuke much people; and they shall beat

their swords into plowshares and their spears into pruning hooks, and nation will not lift up sword against nation, neither shall they learn to war any more." We can show you that this has really happened. For a band of twelve men went forth from Jerusalem, and they were common men, not trained in speaking, but by the power of God they testified to every race of mankind that they were sent by Christ to teach to all the Word of God; and [now] we who once killed each other not only do not make war on each other, but in order not to lie or deceive our inquisitors we gladly die for the confession of Christ. For it would be possible for us to follow the saying, "The tongue has sworn, the mind remains unsworn." But it would be ridiculous when the soldiers whom you have recruited and enrolled stick to their loyalty to you before their own life and parents and native land and all their families, though you have nothing incorruptible to offer them, for us, who desire incorruption, not to endure all things in order to receive what we long for from Him who is able to give it.

40. Hear now how predictions were made about those who were to proclaim his teaching and testify to his manifestation; for the above-mentioned prophet and king said this through the prophetic Spirit: "Day to day utters speech, and night to night shows forth knowledge. There is no language or speech where their words are not heard. Their sound went out into all the earth, and their words to the end of the inhabited world. He set his tabernacle in the sun, and he himself, as a bridegroom coming out of his chamber, will rejoice like a giant to run his course." In addition to these I have thought it good and appropriate to mention some other prophetic words spoken through the same David, from which you may learn how the prophetic Spirit exhorts men to live, and how he testifies of the conspiracy which was formed by Herod the king of the Jews and the Jews themselves and Pilate, who was your procurator among them, with his soldiers, against Christ. [He also testifies] that he would be believed in by men of every race, and that God calls him his Son and has declared that he will subject his enemies to him, and how the demons try as far as they can to escape the power of God the Father and Master of all and that of his Christ, and how God calls all men to repentance before the day of judgment comes. These words were as follows:

"Blessed is the man who has not walked in the council of the ungodly, nor stood in the way of sinners, nor taken his seat upon the seat of pestilence, but his will is in the law of the Lord, and in his law will he meditate day and night. And he shall be like the tree which is planted by the watercourses, which will give its fruit in its season, and his leaf will not wither, and whatever he does will be prospered. Not so are the ungodly, not so, but rather like the chaff which the wind blows away from the face of the earth. Therefore the ungodly will not arise in judgment, nor sinners in the council of the righteous, because the Lord knows the way of the righteous, and the way of the ungodly will be destroyed."

"Why have the nations raged and the peoples imagined new things? The kings of the earth stood up, and their rulers assembled together against the Lord and against his Christ, saying, Let us break their bonds and let us cast away from us their yoke. He that dwells in heaven will laugh them to scorn, and the Lord will mock at them.

Then will he speak to them in his wrath and vex them in his anger. I have been set up by him as king on Zion his holy mountain, proclaiming the Lord's decree. The Lord said to me, You are my Son, today have I begotten you; ask of me and I will give you nations for your inheritance, and the ends of the earth for your possession; you will shepherd them with a rod of iron, you will break them like potter's vessels. And now, O kings, understand; be instructed, all you who judge the earth. Serve the Lord with fear and rejoice before him with trembling. Accept discipline, lest the Lord should be angry, [and] wrathful, and you be destroyed from the right way when his anger is kindled in haste. Blessed are all those who have put their trust in him."

41.   And again in another prophecy the prophetic Spirit, testifying through the same David that after being crucified Christ would reign, said: "O sing to the Lord, all the earth, and proclaim his salvation from day to day; for great is the Lord and highly to be praised, terrible beyond all the gods. For all the gods of the nations are images of demons, but God made the heavens. Glory and praise are before him, and strength and pride in the place of his sanctification. Give glory to the Lord, the Father of the ages. Receive favor and go in before his face and worship in his holy courts. Let all the earth fear before him, and be set upright and not shaken. Let them exult among the nations; the Lord has reigned from the tree."

42.   Now when the prophetic Spirit speaks of things to come as already having happened, as is illustrated in the passages quoted – I will explain this too so that those who come on it will have no excuse [for not understanding]. Things he fully knows are to happen he speaks of in advance as if they had already occurred. Give careful attention to the passages quoted [and you will see] that this is the way they must be taken. David uttered the words quoted above fifteen hundred years before Christ, made man, was crucified, and none of those who were crucified before him gave joy to the nations, nor of those [crucified] after him either. But in our time Jesus Christ, who was crucified and died, rose again and, ascending into heaven, began to reign; and on account of what was proclaimed by the apostles in all nations as [coming] from him, there is joy for those who look forward to the incorruption which he has promised.

43.   So that none may infer from what we have said that the events we speak of, because they were foreknown and predicted, took place according to inevitable destiny – I can explain this too. We have learned from the prophets, and declare as the truth, that penalties and punishments and good rewards are given according to the quality of each man's actions. If this were not so, but all things happened in accordance with destiny, nothing at all would be left up to us. For if it is destined that one man should be good and another wicked, then neither is the one acceptable nor the other blameworthy. And if the human race does not have the power by free choice to avoid what is shameful and to choose what is right, then there is no responsibility for actions of any kind. But that [man] walks upright or falls by free choice we may thus demonstrate. We [often] observe the same man in pursuit of opposite things. If he were destined to be either wicked or virtuous, he would not be thus capable of opposites, and often change his mind. Nor would some be

virtuous and others wicked, for then we would have to declare fate to be the cause of evils and [at the same time] to act in opposition to itself – or to accept as true the opinion referred to above, that there is no real virtue or vice, but only by opinion are things considered good or bad; which, as the true Reason shows us, is the greatest impiety and wickedness. But we do say that deserved rewards are irrevocably destined for those who have chosen the good, and likewise their just deserts for those [who have chosen] the opposite. But God did not make man like other [beings], such as trees and animals, which have no power of choice. For he would not be worthy of rewards or praise if he did not choose the good of himself, but was so made, nor if he were evil would he justly deserve punishment, if he were not such of himself, but was unable to be anything different from that for which he was formed.

44. The holy prophetic Spirit taught us these things, saying through Moses that God said to the first-formed man, "Behold I have set before you good and evil, choose the good." And again through Isaiah, another prophet, this was said to the same purpose, as from God the Father and Master of all things: "Wash yourselves, be clean, take away wickednesses from your souls, learn to do good, give judgment for the orphan and defend the cause of the widow, and come and let us reason together, says the Lord. And though your sins be as scarlet, I will make them as white as wool, and though they be like crimson, I will make them as white as snow. And if you are willing and listen to me, you will eat the good of the land; but if you will not listen to me, the sword will devour you; for the mouth of the Lord has spoken these things." The phrase, "The sword will devour you," does not mean that the disobedient will be slain by swords, but the sword of God is the fire, of which those who choose to do what is evil are made the fuel. Because of this he says, "A sword will devour you, for the mouth of the Lord has spoken it." For if he were speaking of a sword that cuts and at once destroys, he would not have said, "Will devour."

So when Plato said, "The blame belongs to him who chooses, and God is free from blame," he took this from the prophet Moses. For Moses was earlier than Plato and all the Greek writers. And everything that philosophers and poets said about the immortality of the soul, punishments after death, contemplation of heavenly things, and teachings of that kind – they took hints from the prophets and so were able to understand these things and expounded them. So it seems that there were indeed seeds of truth in all men, but they are proved not to have understood them properly since they contradict each other.

So when we say that things yet to happen have been prophesied, we do not say that they take place by inevitable destiny, but since God foreknows what all men are to do, and it is his decree that each will be rewarded according to the quality of his actions, he foretells by the prophetic Spirit what he will do in accordance with the quality of what they do. So he is ever leading the human race to reflection and remembrance, showing that he cares for it and provides for men. But by the working of the wicked demons death has been decreed against those who read the books of Hystaspes or Sybil or the prophets, so that they might frighten people away from receiving the knowledge of good things by consulting them, and keep them in slavery to themselves. But they did not succeed in this forever, for we not only boldly consult these books, but also as you see offer them for your inspection, being sure that what they declare will be welcome to all. Even if we only persuade a few, this will be a great gain for us; for as good husbandmen we will receive our reward from our Master.

45.   Now hear how it was said through David the prophet, that God the Father of all would take up Christ into heaven after raising him from the dead, and then wait to smite the demons who are his enemies, until the number be completed of those whom he foreknows will be good and virtuous, for whose sake he has not yet brought about the destruction of the world by fire. The words are these: "The Lord said to my Lord, Sit on my right hand until I make your enemies your footstool. The Lord will send forth the rod of power from Jerusalem; and dominate in the midst of your enemies. The beginning is with you in the day of your power, in the splendors of your holy ones; I have begotten you from the womb before the morning star." The phrase, "He will send forth the rod of power for you from Jerusalem," is a prediction of the mighty word which his apostles, going forth from Jerusalem, preached everywhere, and which, although death is decreed against those who teach or even confess the name of Christ, we everywhere both receive and teach. If you respond to these words with hostility, you can do no more, as we said before, than to kill us, which will not do harm to us, but will leave to eternal punishment through fire for you and all who unjustly are enemies [to the gospel] and do not repent.

46.   Lest some should unreasonably object, in order to turn men away from what we teach, that we say that Christ was born a hundred and fifty years ago under Quirinius, and taught what we say he taught still later, under Pontius Pilate, and should accuse us [as supposing] that all men born before that time were irresponsible, I will solve this difficulty in advance. We have been taught that Christ is the First-begotten of God, and have previously testified that he is the Reason of which every race of man partakes. Those who lived in accordance with Reason are Christians, even though they were called godless, such as, among the Greeks, Socrates and Heraclitus and others like them; among the barbarians, Abraham, Ananiah, Azariah, and Mishael, and Elijah, and many others, whose deeds and names I forbear to list, knowing that this would be lengthy. So also those who lived without Reason were ungracious and enemies to Christ, and murderers of those who lived by Reason. But those who lived by Reason, and those who so live now, are Christians, fearless and unperturbed. For what cause a man was conceived of a virgin by the power of the Word according to the will of God, the Father and Master of all, and was named Jesus, and after being crucified and dying rose again and ascended into heaven, an intelligent man will be able to comprehend from the words that were spoken in various ways. But since the further demonstration of this does not seem necessary at the moment, I will pass on to more needed demonstrations.

47.   Hear how the prophetic Spirit said that the land of the Jews would be ravaged. The words are spoken as in the character of the people, wondering at what had

happened, as follows: "Zion has become a wilderness, Jerusalem has become like a wilderness, the house of our sanctuary [is made] a curse, and the glory which our fathers praised is burned with fire, and all its glorious things are fallen. And you abide these things, and have kept silence, and have humbled us greatly." You are well aware that Jerusalem was laid waste, as it was predicted would happen. That it would be laid waste, and no one permitted to dwell there, was said through Isaiah the prophet: "Their land is a desert, their enemies eat it up before them, and none of them will dwell in it." You certainly know that under your guard there is no one in it, and that death has been decreed against any Jew caught entering.

48. How it was prophesied that our Christ would heal all diseases and raise the dead, hear what was spoken, as follows: "At his coming the lame will leap like a hart, and the stammering tongue will be clear; blind will see and lepers be cleansed, and the dead will arise and walk." That he did these things, you can learn from the Acts of what took place under Pontius Pilate. How it was testified by the prophetic Spirit that he would be put to death, together with the men who hoped in him, hear what was said through Isaiah, as follows: "See how the Just One perishes and no one takes it to heart, and just men are slain and none consider it. The Just One is taken away from the presence of wickedness, and his burial will be in peace; he is taken away from the midst [of us]."

49. Here again is how it was said through the same Isaiah, that the peoples of the Gentiles who were not looking for him would worship him, and the Jews who were constantly looking for him would not recognize him when he came. These words are spoken as in the character of the Christ himself, as follows: "I became manifest to those who asked not after me, I was found by those who sought me not. I said, Here am I, to a nation who did not call upon my name. I stretched out my hands over a disobedient and contradicting people, over those who walked in a way that was not good, but after their sins, a people who rouse me to anger." For the Jews, having the prophecies, and constantly looking for the Christ, failed to recognize him when he came – more than that, they even mistreated him. But men of the Gentiles, who had never even heard about Christ until his apostles who came forth from Jerusalem testified to the things about him and gave them the prophecies, were filled with joy and faith, turned away from their idols, and dedicated themselves to the unbegotten God through Christ. That the slanders which would be spoken against those who confess Christ were foreknown, and how those would be afflicted who slander him and say that it is better to keep the ancient customs, hear what was briefly spoken through Isaiah as follows: "Woe to those who call sweet bitter and bitter sweet."

50. How, being made man for us, he endured suffering and dishonor, and will come again with glory – hear the prophecies which were spoken to this effect, as follows: "Because they delivered his soul to death, and he was counted with the wicked, he has borne the sins of many, and will make propitiation for the wicked. For behold, my servant will understand and be exalted and greatly glorified. As many will be astonished at you, so your form will be dishonored from [among] men and

your glory from men, so that many nations will wonder, and kings will shut their mouths; because those who were not told about him will see, and those who have not heard will understand. O Lord, who has believed our report, and to whom has the arm of the Lord been revealed? We have spoken before him as a child, as a root in thirsty ground. He has no form nor glory; and we saw him and he had no form nor beauty, but his form was dishonored and despised beyond [any of] mankind. He was a stricken man, knowing how to bear infirmity, because his face was turned away, and he was dishonored and not esteemed. It is he who bears our sins and undergoes travail for us, and we thought him to be in distress, smitten and afflicted. But he was wounded for our wickedness and suffered infirmity for our sins; the chastisement of [our] peace was upon him, and by his bruises we are healed. We have all as sheep gone astray, [every] man has gone astray in his own way. And he gave himself up for our sins, and did not open his mouth because of affliction. He was led as a sheep to slaughter, and as a lamb before its shearer is dumb, so he opened not his mouth. In his humiliation his judgment was taken away." For after he was crucified even all his acquaintances deserted him, denying him. But later, when he rose from the dead and appeared to them, and taught them to consult the prophecies, in which it was predicted that all these things would happen; and when they had seen him ascending into heaven, and believed on him, and received the power which he sent them from there, and went into every race of men, they taught these things and were known as apostles.

51.   In order to testify to us that he who suffered these things is of ineffable origin and reigns over his enemies, the prophetic Spirit spoke thus: "Who will declare his generation? For his life was taken away from the earth; on account of their wickedness he goes to death. And I will give the wicked for his burial and the rich for his death, for he did no wickedness nor was guilt found in his mouth. And the Lord wills to cleanse him from the blow. If you give an offering for sin, your soul will see a long-lived seed. And the Lord wills to remove his soul from sorrow, to show him light and to form him with understanding, to justify the Just One who is a good servant to many. And he shall bear away our sins. Because of this he will inherit many and divide the booty of the strong, for that his soul was delivered to death, and he was numbered among the wicked, and he himself bore the sins of many, and because of their wickednesses he was betrayed."

Hear how he was to go up to heaven, as it was prophesied. This was spoken: "Lift up the gates of heaven, be opened, that the King of glory may come in. Who is this King of glory? The Lord of might and the Lord of power." And that he is to come from heaven with glory, hear what was spoken to this effect through Jeremiah the prophet, as follows: "Behold how the Son of Man comes on the clouds of heaven, and his angels with him."

52.   Since we have shown that all these things that have already happened were proclaimed in advance through the prophets before they happened, it must similarly be believed that those things which were similarly prophesied and are yet to happen will certainly take place. Just as these things which have already happened came true, proclaimed in advance and [yet] unrecognized, so in the same way the remainder,

even if unacknowledged and disbelieved, will come to pass. For the prophets foretold two comings of Christ – one, which has already happened, as that of a dishonored and passible man, and the second, when as has been foretold he will come from heaven in glory with his angelic host, when he will raise the bodies of all the men who have ever lived, and will clothe the worthy with incorruption, but send those of the wicked, eternally conscious, into eternal fire with the evil demons. How it was predicted that these things will happen we will show. This was spoken through the prophet Ezekiel: "Joint will come together with joint and bone with bone, and flesh will grow again. And every knee will bow to the Lord and every tongue will confess him." That the wicked will be punished, still conscious, hear what was similarly spoken on this topic, as follows: "There worm shall not rest, and their fire shall not be extinguished." And then they will repent, when it will no longer do them any good. What the peoples of the Jews will say and do, when they see him coming in glory, was thus prophesied through the prophet Zechariah:

"I will command the four winds to bring together the scattered children; I will command the north wind to carry them, and the south wind not to keep them back. And then there will be great lamentation in Jerusalem, not a lamentation of mouths or lips, but a lamentation of the heart, and they shall rend not their garments but their minds. Tribe after tribe will lament, and then they will see him whom they pierced, and will say: Why, O Lord, did you make us wander astray from thy way? The glory which our fathers praised has become our disgrace."

53. I could cite many other prophecies too, but pause, thinking that these are sufficient to convince those who have ears to hear and understand, and considering that such people can understand that we do not, like those who tell the mythical stories about the so-called sons of Zeus, merely talk, without having proofs. For why should we believe a crucified man that he is First-begotten of the Unbegotten God, and that he will pass judgment on the whole human race, unless we found testimonies proclaimed about him before he came, and was made man, and see that things have thus happened? For we have seen the desolation of the land of the Jews, and the men of every nation who have been persuaded by the teaching that comes from his apostles, and have turned away from the old customs in which they lived, wandering astray – that is ourselves, since we know that the Gentile Christians are more numerous and truer than those from among the Jews and Samaritans. For all the other nations of mankind are called Gentiles by the prophetic Spirit, while the Jewish and Samaritan tribes are called Israel and House of Jacob. How it was prophesied that more of the Gentiles would be believers than of the Jews and Samaritans – I will cite what was prophesied. It was spoken thus: "Rejoice, O barren and bearing not, break forth and shout, you who did not travail, for the children of the desolate are more than those of her who had a husband." For all the Gentiles were desolate of the true God, serving the works of [men's] hands. But Jews and Samaritans, having the word from God given them through the prophets and constantly looking for the Christ, did not recognize him when he came, except only for a few, whose salvation the holy prophetic Spirit predicted through Isaiah. For he said, speaking as in their character, "Except the Lord had left us a seed, we should have been as

Sodom and Gomorrha." Moses tells the story of Sodom and Gomorrha, cities of godless men which God overthrew, burning them with fire and brimstone, none of the people in them being saved except a certain stranger of Chaldaean race, Lot by name, with whom his daughters were saved also. Those who want to can see their whole countryside, desolate and burned and still unproductive. That it was foreknown that those of the Gentiles would be truer and more faithful, we will cite what was said through Isaiah the prophet. He spoke thus, "Israel is uncircumcised in heart, and the Gentiles are the uncircumcision," seeing such things should reasonably bring conviction and faith to those who welcome the truth, and are not vainglorious or controlled by their passions.

Paganism an Imitation of Christianity

54.   But those who hand on the myths invented by the poets offer no demonstration to the youngsters who learn them – indeed I [am prepared to] show that they were told at the instigation of the wicked demons to deceive and lead astray the human race. For when they heard it predicted through the prophets that Christ was to come, and that impious men would be punished by fire, they put forward a number of so-called sons of Zeus, thinking that they could thus make men suppose that what was said about Christ was a mere tale of wonders like the stories told by the poets. These stories were spread among the Greeks and all the Gentiles, where, as they heard the prophets proclaiming, Christ would especially be believed in. But, as I will make clear, though they heard the words of the prophets they did not understand them accurately, but made mistakes in imitating what was told about our Christ. The prophet Moses was, as I said before, older than all [Greek] writers, and this prophecy was made through him, as previously cited: "The ruler shall not depart from Judah, nor the governor from his thighs, until he come for whom it is reserved; and he shall be the expectation of the nations, binding his colt to the vine, washing his robe in the blood of the grape." So when the demons heard these prophetic words they made out that Dionysus had been a son of Zeus, and handed down that he was the discoverer of the vine (hence they introduce wine in his mysteries), and taught that after being torn in pieces he ascended into heaven. Now the prophecy given through Moses did not precisely indicate whether he who was to come would be the Son of God, and whether, mounted on a colt, he would remain on earth or ascend into heaven; and the word "colt" can indicate the colt of an ass or a horse. So not knowing whether the predicted one would bring the colt of an ass or of a horse as the symbol of his coming, and, as said above, whether he was the Son of God or of a man, they said that Bellerophon, a man and born of men, had gone up to heaven on the horse Pegasus. Then when they heard it said through that other prophet Isaiah that he was to be born of a virgin and would ascend into heaven by his own [power], they put forward what is told about Perseus. When they learned that it was said, as has been quoted, in the ancient prophecies, "Strong as a giant to run his course," they said that Heracles was strong and had traveled over the whole earth.

Again when they learned that it was prophesied that he would heal every disease and raise the dead, they brought forward Asclepius.

55. But never was the crucifixion imitated in the case of any of the so-called sons of Zeus; for they did not understand it since, as has been explained, everything said about it was expressed symbolically. Yet, as the prophet predicted, it [the cross] is the greatest symbol of his power and authority, as [can be] shown from things you can see. Reflect on all things in the universe [and consider] whether they could be governed or held together in fellowship without this figure. For the sea cannot be traversed unless the sign of victory, which is called a sail, remain fast in the ship; the land is not plowed without it; similarly diggers and mechanics do not do their work except with tools of this form. The human figure differs from the irrational animals precisely in this, that man stands erect and can stretch out his hands, and has on his face, stretched down from the forehead, what is called the nose, through which goes breath for the living creature – and this exhibits precisely the figure of the cross. So it was said through the prophet, "The breath before our face is Christ the Lord." Even your own symbols display the power of this figure – on the standards and trophies, with which you make all your solemn processions, using these [cross-shaped objects] as signs of authority, even though without understanding what you're doing. Then you set up the images of your deceased emperors on this figure, and in the inscriptions call them gods. So now since I have done my best to persuade you, both by argument and by [appealing to] a visible figure, I am free from reproach even if you disbelieve; my part is done and finished.

56. The wicked demons were not satisfied with saying before the appearance of Christ that there had been the so-called sons of Zeus. After he had appeared and lived among men, when they learned how he had been predicted by the prophets, and saw how he was believed on and looked for in every race, they again, as we showed before, put forward others, Simon and Menander of Samaria, who by doing mighty works of magic deceived and are still deceiving many. For as I said before, Simon lived in your own imperial city of Rome under Claudius Caesar, and so impressed the Sacred Senate and the Roman people that he was thought to be a god and was honored with a statue like the other gods whom you honor. We ask you therefore to join the Sacred Senate and your people as joint judges of this petition of ours, so that if any are ensnared by his teachings they may be able to learn the truth and flee from this error. And, if you will, destroy the statue.

57. Nor can the wicked demons persuade men that there will be no burning for the punishment of the impious, just as they were not able to keep Christ hidden when he came. All they can do is to make men who live contrary to reason, having been brought up in bad habits of passion and prejudice, kill and hate us. Yet we do not hate them, but, as is evident, pity them and try to persuade them to reform. For we are not afraid of death, admitting that we are certainly going to die, and [since] there is nothing new [for unbelievers], but things continue the same in this dispensation – if boredom seizes those who share in such things even for a year, then in order to be free from suffering and want they should pay attention to our

teachings. If they do not believe that there is anything after death, but declare that those who die pass into unconsciousness, then they are our benefactors in delivering us from the sufferings and needs [of life] here. But they still show themselves to be wicked, misanthropic, and prejudiced. For they do not kill us in order to set us free, but rather murder us in order to deprive us of life and its pleasures.

58.   As I said before, the wicked demons have also put forward Marcion of Pontus, who is even now teaching men to deny that God is the Maker of all things in heaven and earth and that the Christ predicted by the prophets is his Son. He preaches another God besides the Fashioner of the universe, and likewise another Son. Many are persuaded by him, as if he alone knew the truth, and make fun of us, though they have no proof of the things they say, but are irrationally snatched away, like lambs by a wolf, and become the prey of godless teachings and of demons. For those who are called demons strive for nothing else than to draw men away from God who made [them] and from Christ his First-begotten. Those who cannot rise above the earth they have nailed down by [the worship of] earthly things and the works of men's hands. They even push back those who aim at the contemplation of things divine, unless their thinking is prudent and pure and their life free from passion, and drive them into ungodliness.

59.   So that you may learn that Plato borrowed from our teachers, I mean from the Word [speaking] through the prophets, when he said that God made the universe by changing formless matter, hear the precise words of Moses, who as declared above was the first of the prophets and older than the Greek writers. The prophetic Spirit testified through him how in the beginning God fashioned the universe, and out of what, saying: "In the beginning God made the heaven and the earth. And the earth was invisible and unfurnished, and darkness [was] over the abyss; and the Spirit of God was borne over the waters. And God said, Let there be light. And it was so." So by God's word the whole universe was made out of this substratum, as expounded by Moses, and Plato and those who agree with him, as well as we, have learned it [from him], and you can be sure of it too. We also know that Moses had already spoken of what the poets call Erebus.

60.   In the discussion of the nature of the Son of God in Plato's *Timaeus*, when he says, "He placed him like an X in the universe," this was similarly borrowed from Moses. For it is recorded in the writings of Moses that in his time, when the Israelites had gone out of Egypt and were in the wilderness, they encountered poisonous beasts, vipers and asps and every kind of snake which were killing the people. By an inspiration and influence that came from God, Moses took brass and made the form of a cross, and placed it over the holy tent, saying to the people, "If you look on this form and believe on it, you will be saved." And he records that when this was done, the snakes died, and so, he tells us, the people escaped death. Plato, reading this and not clearly understanding, nor realizing that it was the form of a cross, but thinking it was [the letter] *Chi*, said that the Power next to the first God was placed X-wise in the universe. And he spoke of a third, since he read what I have quoted from Moses, that the Spirit of God was borne over the waters. For he gives the second place to

the Word who is with God, who, he says, was placed X-wise in the universe, and the third to the Spirit which was said to be borne over the water, saying, "The third [order of] beings around the third." And hear how the prophetic Spirit has testified through Moses that there will be a destruction by fire. He said, "Everliving fire will descend and will devour even to the abyss below." So it is not that we hold the same opinions as others, but that what all others say is an imitation of ours. Among us you can hear and learn these things from those who do not even know the letters of the alphabet – uneducated and barbarous in speech, but wise and faithful in mind – even from cripples and the blind. So you can see that these things are not the product of human wisdom, but are spoken by the power of God.

Christian Worship

61.   How we dedicated ourselves to God when we were made new through Christ I will explain, since it might seem to be unfair if I left this out from my exposition. Those who are persuaded and believe that the things we teach and say are true, and promise that they can live accordingly, are instructed to pray and beseech God with fasting for the remission of their past sins, while we pray and fast along with them. Then they are brought by us where there is water, and are reborn by the same manner of rebirth by which we ourselves were reborn; for they are then washed in the water in the name of God the Father and Master of all, and of our Saviour Jesus Christ, and of the Holy Spirit. For Christ said, "Unless you are born again you will not enter into the Kingdom of heaven." Now it is clear to all that those who have once come into being cannot enter the wombs of those who bore them. But as I quoted before, it said through the prophet Isaiah how those who have sinned and repent shall escape from their sins. He said this: "Wash yourselves, be clean, take away wickedness from your souls, learn to do good, give judgment for the orphan and defend the cause of the widow, and come and let us reason together, says the Lord. And though your sins be as scarlet, I will make them as white as wool, and though they be as crimson, I will make them as white as snow. If you will not listen to me, the sword will devour you; for the mouth of the Lord has spoken these things." And we learned from the apostles this reason for this [rite]. At our first birth we were born of necessity without our knowledge, from moist seed, by the intercourse of our parents with each other, and grew up in bad habits and wicked behavior. So that we should not remain children of necessity and ignorance, but [become sons] of free choice and knowledge, and obtain remission of the sins we have already committed, there is named at the water, over him who has chosen to be born again and has repented of his sinful acts, the name of God the Father and Master of all. Those who lead to the washing the one who is to be washed call on [God by] this term only. For no one may give a proper name to the ineffable God, and if anyone should dare to say that there is one, he is hopelessly insane. This washing is called illumination, since those who learn these things are illumined within. The illuminand is also washed in the name of Jesus Christ, who was crucified

under Pontius Pilate, and in the name of the Holy Spirit, who through the prophets foretold everything about Jesus.

62.   When the demons heard this washing proclaimed through the prophets, they arranged that those who go into their temples and are about to approach them to offer libations and burnt offerings should sprinkle themselves – and further they have them wash themselves completely as they pass on into the sanctuaries where they are enshrined. The order given by the priests to devotees to remove their shoes as they enter the temples and approach them [the demons] is an imitation devised by the demons when they learned what happened to Moses, the above-mentioned prophet. For at the time when Moses was ordered to go down to Egypt and bring out the people of the Israelites who were there, as he was pasturing in the land of Arabia the sheep of his maternal uncle, our Christ addressed him in the form of fire out of a bush, and said, "Unloose your sandals and come near and hear." When he had taken them and approached, he heard [that he was] to go down into Egypt, and lead out the people of the Israelites there, and received great power from Christ, who spoke to him in the form of fire. He went down and led out the people after he had done great miracles – if you want to learn about them, you may learn in detail from his writings.

63.   Even now the Jews all teach that the unnamed God himself spoke to Moses. Wherefore the prophetic Spirit said in condemnation of them through Isaiah the above-mentioned prophet, as was quoted before: "The ox knows his owner and the ass his master's crib, but Israel does not know me and my people does not understand." Likewise Jesus the Christ, because the Jews did not know what the Father is and what the Son, himself said in condemnation of them: "No one knows the Father except the Son, nor the Son except the Father and those to whom the Son will reveal it." Now the Word of God is his Son, as I said before. He is also called "Angel" and "Apostle," for [as Angel] he announces what it is necessary to know, and [as Apostle] is sent forth to testify to what is announced, as our Lord himself said, "He that hears me hears him that sent me." This can be made clear from the writings of Moses, in which this is to be found: "And the Angel of God spoke to Moses in a flame of fire out of the bush and said, I am he who is, God of Abraham, God of Isaac, God of Jacob, the God of your fathers; go down to Egypt and bring out my people." Those who wish to can learn what followed from this; for it is not possible to put down everything in these [pages]. But these words were uttered to demonstrate that Jesus Christ is the Son of God and Apostle, who was first the Word, and appeared, now in the form of fire, now in the image of the bodiless creatures. Now, however, having become man by the will of God for the sake of the human race, he has endured whatever sufferings the demons managed to have brought upon him by the senseless Jews. For they have it clearly said in the writing of Moses, "And the Angel of God spoke to Moses in a flame of fire in the bush and said, I am he who is, the God of Abraham, the God of Isaac, and the God of Jacob," yet they say that he who said these things was the Father and Fashioner of the universe. Jesus again, as we cited, when he was with them said, "No one knows the Father except the Son, nor the Son except the Father and those to whom

the Son may reveal it." So the Jews, continuing to think that the Father of the universe had spoken to Moses, when it was the Son of God, who is called both Angel and Apostle, who spoke to him, were rightly censured both by the prophetic Spirit and by Christ himself, since they knew neither the Father nor the Son. For those who identify the Son and the Father are condemned, as neither knowing the Father nor recognizing that the Father of the universe has a Son, who being the Word and First-begotten of God is also divine. Formerly he appeared in the form of fire and the image of a bodiless being to Moses and the other prophets. But now in the time of your dominion he was, as I have said, made man of a virgin according to the will of the Father for the salvation of those who believe in him, and endured contempt and suffering so that by dying and rising again he might conquer death. What was said out of the bush to Moses, "I am he who is, the God of Abraham and the God of Isaac and the God of Jacob and the God of your fathers," was an indication that they though dead still existed and were Christ's own men. For they were the first of all men to devote themselves to seeking after God, Abraham being the father of Isaac, and Isaac of Jacob, as Moses also recorded.

64. From what has been said you can understand why the demons contrived to have the image of the so-called Kore erected at the springs of waters, saying that she was a daughter of Zeus, imitating what was said through Moses. For Moses said, as I have quoted: "In the beginning God made the heaven and the earth. And the earth was invisible and unfurnished, and the Spirit of God was borne over the waters." In imitation of the Spirit of God, spoken of as borne over the water, they spoke of Kore, daughter of Zeus. With similar malice they spoke of Athena as a daughter of Zeus, but not as a result of intercourse – since they knew that God designed the creation of the world by the Word, they spoke of Athena as the first Concept. This we consider very ridiculous, to offer the female form as the image of an intellectual concept. And similarly the other so-called sons of Zeus are condemned by their actions.

65. We, however, after thus washing the one who has been convinced and signified his assent, lead him to those who are called brethren, where they are assembled. They then earnestly offer common prayers for themselves and the one who has been illuminated and all others everywhere, that we may be made worthy, having learned the truth, to be found in deed good citizens and keepers of what is commanded, so that we may be saved with eternal salvation. On finishing the prayers we greet each other with a kiss. Then bread and a cup of water and mixed wine are brought to the president of the brethren and he, taking them, sends up praise and glory to the Father of the universe through the name of the Son and of the Holy Spirit, and offers thanksgiving at some length that we have been deemed worthy to receive these things from him. When he has finished the prayers and the thanksgiving, the whole congregation present assents, saying, "Amen." "Amen" in the Hebrew language means, "So be it." When the president has given thanks and the whole congregation has assented, those whom we call deacons give to each of those present a portion of the consecrated bread and wine and water, and they take it to the absent.

66.   This food we call Eucharist, of which no one is allowed to partake except one who believes that the things we teach are true, and has received the washing for forgiveness of sins and for rebirth, and who lives as Christ handed down to us. For we do not receive these things as common bread or common drink; but as Jesus Christ our Saviour being incarnate by God's word took flesh and blood for our salvation, so also we have been taught that the food consecrated by the word of prayer which comes from him, from which our flesh and blood are nourished by transformation, is the flesh and blood of that incarnate Jesus. For the apostles in the memoirs composed by them, which are called Gospels, thus handed down what was commanded them: that Jesus, taking bread and having given thanks, said, "Do this for my memorial, this is my body"; and likewise taking the cup and giving thanks he said, "This is my blood"; and gave it to them alone. This also the wicked demons in imitation handed down as something to be done in the mysteries of Mithra; for bread and a cup of water are brought out in their secret rites of initation, with certain invocations which you either know or can learn.

67.   After these [services] we constantly remind each other of these things. Those who have more come to the aid of those who lack, and we are constantly together. Over all that we receive we bless the Maker of all things through his Son Jesus Christ and through the Holy Spirit. And on the day called Sunday there is a meeting in one place of those who live in cities or the country, and the memoirs of the apostles or the writings of the prophets are read as long as time permits. When the reader has finished, the president in a discourse urges and invites [us] to the imitation of these noble things. Then we all stand up together and offer prayers. And, as said before, when we have finished the prayer, bread is brought, and wine and water, and the president similarly sends up prayers and thanksgivings to the best of his ability, and the congregation assents, saying the Amen; the distribution, and reception of the consecrated [elements] by each one, takes place and they are sent to the absent by the deacons. Those who prosper, and who so wish, contribute, each one as much as he chooses to. What is collected is deposited with the president, and he takes care of orphans and widows, and those who are in want on account of sickness or any other cause, and those who are in bonds, and the strangers who are sojorners among [us], and, briefly, he is the protector of all those in need. We all hold this common gathering on Sunday, since it is the first day, on which God transforming darkness and matter made the universe, and Jesus Christ our Saviour rose from the dead on the same day. For they crucified him on the day before Saturday, and on the day after Saturday, he appeared to his apostles and disciples and taught them these things which I have passed on to you also for your serious consideration.

Conclusion

68.   If what we say seems to you reasonable and true, treat it with respect – if it seems foolish to you, then despise us as foolish creatures and do not decree the death penalty, as against enemies, for those who do no wrong. I have said before

that you will not escape the future judgment of God if you continue unjust, while we will cry out, What God desires, let that be done. On the ground of a letter of your father, the great and illustrious Caesar Hadrian, we could demand that you order judgment to be given as we have asked. Yet we do not ask [for this] on the basis of Hadrian's judgment, but since we know that what we ask is just, we have made this petition and explanation. I have subjoined a copy of the letter of Hadrian, so that you may know that I speak the truth in this matter. Here is the copy:

Hadrian to Minucius Fundanus. I have received the letter addressed to me by your predecessor the Honorable Serenius Granianus, and it does not seem right to me to pass over this report in silence, lest innocent people should be molested and false accusers given the opportunity of doing harm. So if the people of your province can formally support their petition against the Christians by accusing them of something before [your] tribunal, I do not forbid their following this course; but I do not permit them to make use of mere requests and clamorous demands in this matter. It is much more proper, if anyone wishes to bring an accusation, for you to take cognizance of the matters brought forward. Therefore if anyone brings an accusation and proves that the men referred to have done anything contrary to the laws, you will assign penalties in accordance with the character of the offenses. But you must certainly take the greatest care, that if anyone accuses any of these people merely for the sake of calumny, you will punish him with severe penalties for his offense.

3

St Augustine, from *The City of God*

St Augustine was born to a pagan father and a Christian mother in the North African city of Tagaste in 354. He was a rebellious and somewhat aimless youth who received a classical education and who later became a teacher of rhetoric. Augustine's intellectual and personal restlessness prompted a search for answers to life's basic questions, especially with regard to the nature of evil. He was for a time a member of a religious group called the Manichees, which he eventually forsook for a philosophical school known as Neoplatonism. After much wrestling, he was dramatically converted to Christianity in his early thirties – an event he himself described in his autobiographical *Confessions*. Augustine subsequently became one of the greatest servants and theologians of the Christian Church, eventually becoming bishop of Hippo and authoring several classical theological treatises. He died in 430.

Central to Augustine's theological approach was his desire to understand his faith. He emphasized in his writings that one cannot come to God by reason alone; faith is necessary first. But reason is in no way to be rejected, for once one believes, reason serves to help one understand one's faith. This Augustinian conception of faith in search of understanding became a classical way of relating Christianity to philosophy, reason, and culture. The approach implies that without faith, one cannot understand. For this reason, the Greek philosophers, who loved wisdom (the literal meaning of the word *philosophia*), could not grasp it or truly understand. But because of the light of Christian revelation, believers can truly understand and, more important, be saved.

Based on his general theological approach, Augustine argued for the truth of Christianity over against other religious systems. In *The City of God*, he responded to the charge that Christianity was to blame for the sack of Rome. In his defense of Christianity, Augustine also marshals a critique of polytheism which includes an unfavorable evaluation of the views of the ancient historian of religion Varro. The bishop of Hippo argues that the gods should not be worshiped, for they cannot bring advantage to human beings in this life – to say nothing of eternal life, which they are incapable of providing. Augustine therefore concludes that there is one true God who has been revealed and who is deserving of worship.

In the selections from *The City of God* which follow, insertions of Latin terms are reprinted from the original source. All footnotes, however, have been deleted.

Book VI

· *Preface* ·

The argument of my first five books has, I believe, given a sufficient refutation of those who suppose that many false gods are to be venerated and worshiped for advantages in this mortal life and for benefits in temporal things. They would accord them the ceremonies and the humble devotion which the Greeks call *latreia*, a worship due only to the one true God. Christian truth proves those "gods" to be useless images or unclean spirits and malignant demons, creatures at any rate, and not the Creator.

To be sure, those five books are not enough to deal with all the extravagant folly and perversity of our opponents – nor would any number of additional books suffice. That is clear to all. Stupidity glories in never yielding to the force of truth; that is how it effects the ruin of anyone who is under the dominion of this monstrous moral fault. It is a disease proof against all efforts to treat it, not through any fault in the physician, but because the patient is himself incurable. But those who understand what they read, who reflect upon it and weigh the arguments without any obstinate adherence to their old errors, or at least without excessive and exaggerated attachment to them – such people will be ready to conclude that in the five books already completed our discussion has been more, not less, than the question demanded. The ignorant try to bring odium on the Christian religion in connection with the disasters to which human life is subject, and the calamities and catastrophes that beset human affairs; and the learned not merely connive at this but even support those slanders, in defiance of their own conscience, possessed by a raging madness of blasphemy. These judicious readers cannot doubt that such attempts are utterly devoid of any clear thinking or right reasoning and are composed of nothing but irresponsible frivolity and malignant spite.

1. *The assertion that the gods are worshipped not for blessings in this life, but with a view to life eternal*

The scheme I have prescribed for this work demands that I should now proceed to the task of refuting and instructing those who maintain that the pagan gods, which the Christian religion does away with, are to be worshipped, not with a view to this present life, but with a view to the life which is to come after death.

I should like to take as the opening of my discussion, the truthful oracle of a holy psalm, "Blessed is he whose hope is the Lord God, and who has not turned his attention to vain things and lying madnesses." However, on the subject of all those "vain things" and "lying madnesses", men are likely to give a far readier hearing to

Source: St Augustine, *The City of God*, trans. H. Bettenson.

the philosophers who reject the erroneous opinions of the peoples who have set up images to the divinities, and have either invented or accepted many false and unworthy stories about the "immortal gods", as they call them, and, having accepted them, have interwoven them into the worship and the sacred rites of those gods. Although they have not freely proclaimed their disapprobation of those practices, these philosophers have at least murmured it in their learned disputations; and so it is not inappropriate to discuss with them this question: Is it our duty to worship, with a view to the life after death, the one God, who made every spiritual and material creature; or those many gods who, according to some of the most eminent and famous of these same philosophers, were created by the one God and raised by him to their exalted state?

I have mentioned in my fourth book some of the gods who are distributed among particular functions, one god for each minute duty. Who could brook the suggestion, indeed the contention, that such divinities can assure eternal life to anyone? There were men of great learning and penetration, who gloried in having conferred a great benefit by giving written instructions to inform people why they should pray to each particular god, and what help should be asked for from each of them, so as to avoid the ludicrous kind of mistake which occurs in mime to raise a laugh, as when Bacchus is asked for water, and the Lymphae are asked for wine. Now, if a man who prays to the immortal gods, on asking the Lymphae for wine, receives the reply, "We only have water; apply to Liber", are those authorities likely to suggest that the correct rejoinder would be, "If you haven't wine, at least give me eternal life?" Could anything be more monstrously absurd? If those giggling goddesses (they are always so ready for a laugh!) are not aiming at leading their suppliant a dance (like the demons) they would surely reply, "My good man, why should you think we have life (*vitam*) at our disposal, when we have told you we haven't even the vine (*vitem*)?"

It is, then, a mark of the most unconscionable folly to ask or hope for eternal life from such divinities. Even supposing they are concerned with supporting and propping up this brief life of care, they watch over its particular departments, so it is asserted, in such a way that if anything belonging to one god's sphere of responsibility is sought from another god, a ridiculous anomaly arises, like some farcical situation in a mime. When those involved are actors, and know what they are doing, it gets a well-deserved laugh in the theatre; when they are fools, who do not know what they are about, it is treated with more justified scorn in the real world. That is why learned men were astute enough to determine, and put on record, which god or goddess should be entreated for what, as far as concerns the divinities established in their communities – for example, what one can obtain from Liber, or the Lymphae, or Vulcan, and the other gods, some of whom I mentioned in my fourth book, while I decided to pass over the rest. Doubtless it is an error to ask Ceres for wine, Liber for bread, Vulcan for water, the Lymphae for fire; we surely ought to realize how much more imbecile it would be to implore any of these deities for eternal life!

When we were discussing worldly dominion, and asking which gods or goddesses might be believed capable of granting it, we proved, after examining every possibility, that it would be utterly remote from the truth to imagine that even the kingdoms of this world are established by any of this host of false gods. If this is true, then surely it would show the craziest impiety to suppose that any of them could grant eternal life, which is, without any doubt, incomparably to be preferred to all earthly kingdoms. The reason why such gods are incapable, in our view, of giving earthly dominion is not that they are so great and exalted and earthly power a thing so lowly and contemptible that they would not deign, in their lofty state, to be concerned with it. However great the contempt which one may rightly feel for the precarious eminences of worldly power, when one considers the frailty of man, those gods are evidently of such a character as to be quite unworthy to be entrusted with the power to grant or to preserve even such transitory gifts. Therefore, if it be true (as the full discussion in my last two books has established) that not one of this host of gods, whether of the plebeian sort or, as one might say, the noble deities, is fit to grant mortal kingdoms to mortals, how much less could any of them turn mortals into immortals?

Furthermore, if we are now dealing with those who think that the gods are to be worshipped for the sake of the life after death and not with a view to this present life, we must conclude that it is utterly wrong to worship them even with the hope of obtaining those particular benefits which are severally assigned to the control of such gods, not on any rational grounds but by superstitious credulity. There are those who believe in the necessity of such worship, maintaining it essential for securing advantages in this mortal life; and I have refuted them, to the best of my ability, in the first five books. Accordingly, if the devotees of the goddess Juventas (Youth) enjoyed markedly greater prosperity in early life, while those who disclaimed her either deceased before maturity, or shrivelled into senile inertia while still young in years; if Bearded Fortune clothed the cheeks of her votaries with a growth of notable splendour and allurement, while we observed her detractors with hairless chins or with unconvincing beards, we should even so be perfectly right in saying that those goddesses only had power within the limits somehow assigned to their particular functions, and that one should not seek eternal life from Juventas, who does not produce beards, and that no benefit after this life is to be looked for from Bearded Fortune, for even in this life she could not even give us the youthful age in which the beard first grows. In reality, the worship of those goddesses is not essential to ensure the gifts supposedly under their control. Many worshippers of Juventas have been far from flourishing in their early years; while many non-worshippers enjoy robust health in youth; many suppliants of Bearded Fortune have no beard at all, or have achieved only an unprepossessing growth, and expose themselves to the ridicule of her bearded detractors for having venerated her in the hope of hirsute adornment. Are men such fools as to think in their hearts that the worship of these gods can be of advantage for eternal life, when they realize how futile and ridiculous it is even in respect of those temporal and evanescent gifts which the divinities are said to have in their particular charge? This would be too bold a claim even for those who parcelled out those temporal responsibilities to the gods to ensure that they should be worshipped by the unthinking; they thought there were too many of those deities, and they did not want to have any of them sitting about with time on their hands!

From *The City of God*

2. *What was Varro's opinion of the gods? His disclosures of their nature and their rites were such that he would have shown more reverence in keeping silent*

Has anyone pursued research in this subject further than Marcus Varro? Who has made more scholarly discoveries, or pondered the facts more assiduously? Who has made nicer distinctions, or written more carefully or more fully on those matters? His literary style is not particularly attractive; but he is so full of knowledge and ideas that in the kind of learning which we Christians call secular and the pagans call liberal he gives as much information to the student of history as Cicero gives pleasure to the connoisseur of style. In fact, Cicero himself gives Varro a fine testimonial in his *Academics* when he says that he had engaged in discussion on the subject of that work with Marcus Varro, "easily the most acute of intellects, and undoubtedly the most learned of men". He does not say "the most eloquent" or "the most fluent"; for in truth Varro is seriously inadequate in this department. What he says is "easily the most acute of intellects". And in that book, the *Academics*, where his thesis is that all things should be doubted, he added "undoubtedly the most learned of men". He was so convinced of this that he put aside the doubt which he normally applied to everything. It seems that although he was going to argue in defence of Academic doubt, he had forgotten when speaking of Varro, but only then, that he was an Academic. In the first book he acclaims the literary works of the same author in these terms,

> We were like strangers in our own city, visitors who had lost their way. It was your books that, as it were, brought us back home, so that at last we could recognize who we were, and where we were. It was you who revealed to us the age of our country, the sequence of events, the laws of religious ceremonies and of the priesthoods, the traditional customs of private and public life, the position of geographical areas and of particular places, and the terminology of all matters, human and divine, with their various kinds, and functions, and causes.

He was a man of pre-eminent, of unparalleled erudition, succinctly and neatly described in one line of Terentian,

Varro, that man of universal science;

a man who read so much that we marvel that he had any time for writing; who wrote so much that we find it hard to believe that anyone could have read it all. If this man, with all his talents and all his learning, had intended to attack and eradicate those "divine matters" of which he wrote, and to assert that they belonged to superstition not to religion, I do not know whether he would have recorded so many elements in "theology" which can arouse only derision, contempt, and abhorrence. In fact he worshipped those same gods and thought that they should be worshipped. So much so that in his written works he expresses the fear that the gods may perish, not through an attack of the enemy, but through the indifference of Roman citizens. It is, he says, from this disaster (as he thinks it) that he is rescuing the gods; by books of this kind he is securing and preserving for them a place in the memory of good men. This he regards as a more profitable service than the much-praised act of Metellus in saving the sacred emblems of Vesta from the fire, and that of Aeneas in rescuing the Penates from destruction: and yet he hands down, for the study of future generations, traditions which deserve to be rejected by the wise and the foolish alike as being, in their judgement, utterly inimical to the true religion. What ought we to think of this? Is it not that a man of acute intellect and vast erudition, but lacking the freedom given by the Holy Spirit, has succumbed to the pressure of the customs and laws of his country? At the same time he could not bring himself to keep silent about the things which troubled him, on the pretext of lending support to religion.

3. Varro's division of his "Antiquities" into "Human Matters" and "Divine Matters"

Varro wrote forty-one books of *Antiquities*; and he divided them by subjects into "human matters" and "divine matters", assigning twenty-five to "anthropology" and sixteen to "theology". In the anthropological section of his work he planned four parts, each of six books, concentrating in turn on the performers of the actions, the place, the time, and the nature of the action. Thus in the first six books he writes about men, in the next six about places, in the third group about times, while the fourth and last group deals with the performances. Four sixes make twenty-four; but he leads off with a separate book, which serves as a general introduction to the whole section.

In the section on "divine matters" the same scheme of division is kept, in regard to the rites to be performed in honour of the gods; for those rites are performed by men in certain places and at certain times. The four subjects mentioned are contained in groups of three books: the first group deals with the men involved, the second with the places, the third with the times, the fourth with the actual rites; as before, he employs the most subtle distinctions in describing the performers; the place and time of the performances, and the manner of the performances. But besides this he was bound to say – and this was what people especially looked for – to whom these ceremonies are offered. And so the three last books treat of the gods themselves; and that makes three fives, fifteen. As we have said, there are sixteen books in all, because here also he prefaces the section with a separate book to serve as an introduction.

After the end of this first book Varro goes on to subdivide the first group of three books, within his general five-part division. In this group, dealing with the men involved, the first book describes the priests, the second, the augurs, the third, the quindecimviri. In the second group, dealing with the places, Book One treats of shrines, Book Two, of temples, Book Three of sacred places. The next group, referring to feast days, contains one book about holy days; another about games in the circus, a third about stage plays. The fourth group, about the actual ceremonies, consists of a book devoted to consecrations, a book about private rites, while the last book handles public ceremonies. At the end of this kind of procession of observances the gods themselves, the recipients of the whole system of worship, bring up the rear; and they are dealt with in the remaining three books: in the first of these come the "certain gods", in the second, the "uncertain", in the third, the last of the whole work, the "principal and select" divinities.

4. *From Varro's account it emerges that "Human Matters" precede "Divine Matters" among the pagans*

In the whole of this impressive sequence, with all those subtle distinctions and this precise arrangement, it is in vain to seek eternal life; it would be the height of impudence to look for it or to hope for it in this context. So much is readily apparent, from what we have already said and from what we are to go on to say, to anyone who is not his own enemy because of the obstinacy of his heart. These institutions are either the work of men, or of demons, and not of "good demons", as the pagans call them, but, to speak frankly, of unclean spirits or undeniably malignant powers. Malignant, because with consummate spite they secretly instil into the thoughts of the impious, and at times openly suggest to their senses, pernicious notions which make the human soul more and more evanescent, and less and less able to adjust itself and attach itself to eternal truth; and they support those notions with fallacious evidence in every way they can.

Varro himself bears witness that the reason for writing about "human matters" before "divine matters" was that human communities first came into existence and divine institutions are afterwards established by them. Whereas it was not any terrestrial community that estabished true religion; it was true religion, without doubt, that established the Celestial City; and true religion is given to his true worshippers by the inspiration and teaching of the true God, the giver of eternal life.

Varro gives the following explanation of his treatment of "human matters" before "divine matters", on the ground that the "divine matters" were established by men: "The painter exists before the picture, the builder before the building: similarly, human communities precede their institutions." But he does say that he would have written about the gods before proceeding to men, if he were treating of every aspect of the gods. Are we really to suppose that in this work he is only treating of some part of the divine nature and not of the whole, or that the divine nature, even when considered only in a particular aspect ought not to take precedence over human nature? Further, in his last three books he carefully arranges the gods into the categories of "certain", "uncertain" and "select"; does it appear that he leaves any aspect unmentioned? What does he mean, then, when he says, "If I were treating of every aspect of the gods and of men, I would have dealt with the divine before starting on the human?" Either he is writing about every aspect, or some aspects, or no aspect at all. If about every aspect, then "divine matters" should precede "human"; but why should they not, even if he is writing only about some? Would it be improper to make even some aspects of the divine take precedence over the whole of human nature? If it would be too much that one part of the divine should have precedence over all the human matters, would it at least be right for it to do so over merely Roman affairs? For his books on "human affairs" treat only of Roman matters; they do not include the whole world. And yet he claims that he is justified in having given them precedence over his books on "divine affairs", as the painter precedes the picture, the builder comes before the building. Here he plainly admits that "divine matters" are of human institution, like pictures and buildings.

There remains the possibility that he is to be supposed to have written about no aspect of divinity at all; and that he was reluctant to admit this explicitly and left it to be inferred by the intelligent reader. For "I have not treated of all" means, in common usage, "I have treated of some"; but it *can* be understood as "I have treated of none"; since "none" is the negation of both "all" and "some". Varro himself declares that if he were writing about every aspect of the divine nature it would have to precede the treatment of human affairs; but truth cries out, without need of a word from Varro, that the divine nature, even if treated only in part, should have had precedence over Roman affairs, at least. Yet it properly takes second place; therefore it is not there at all. It was not that Varro decided to rank "human affairs" before "divine", but to give truth the precedence over falsehood. For in his books on "human affairs" he follows the course of history; but his account of what he calls "divine affairs" is a collection of frivolous fantasies. And this is doubtless what he intended to signify by a subtle hint, in writing of them after the other topics, and, not content with this, in giving an explanation for taking this course. If he had said nothing in explanation, others might have defended his procedure on different grounds. But the very explanation he has given leaves others no room for arbitrary speculation and is sufficient proof that he is giving men precedence over their institutions, not ranking human nature before the divine.

Thus Varro has admitted that his books on "divine affairs" do not deal with the truth relating to the divine nature but with the false notions which arise from error. As I have mentioned in the fourth book, he states this more clearly in another place, where he acknowledges that he would have written on the principles dictated by nature, if he had been founding a new community; but since he found himself in a community already ancient, the only course open to him was to conform to its traditional ways.

5.   *Varro's division of theology into "mythical", "natural", and "civil"*

Then again, what is the significance of Varro's division of "theology", that is the systematic theory of the gods, into the types: mythical, physical, and civil?" We should have called the first type "fabular", if Latin usage had permitted. Let us call it "fabulous", since the name "mythical" is derived from *mythos*, the Greek word for fable. Usage allows us to call the second type "natural" (*physis* being the Greek for "nature"). The third category, "civil", Varro himself designated by a Latin word.

He goes on to say, "The name 'mythical' applies to the theology used chiefly by the poets, 'physical' to that of the philosophers, 'civil' to that of the general public. The first type contains a great deal of fiction which is in conflict with the dignity and nature of the immortals. It is in this category that we find one god born from the head, another from the thigh, a third from drops of blood; we find stories about thefts and adulteries committed by gods, and gods enslaved to human beings. In fact we find attributed to gods not only the accidents that happen to humanity in general, but even those which can befall the most contemptible of mankind." In this passage he has the courage to take the chance, when he thinks he can do it with impunity, of casting off all obscurity and ambiguity, and making it quite clear what injustice is done to the nature of the gods by these lying fables. For he is talking, not about "natural", or "civil" theology but about "fabulous" theology, which he thinks he has the right to criticize quite candidly.

Let us see what he says about the second type:

> The second type which I have pointed out, is one on which the philosophers have left a number of works, in which they discuss who the gods are, where they are, of what kind and of what character they are: whether they came into being at a certain time, or have always existed: whether they derive their being from fire (the belief of Heraclitus) or from numbers (as Pythagoras thought) or from atoms (as Epicurus alleges). And there are other like questions all of which men's ears can more readily tolerate within the walls of a lecture-room than in the market-place outside.

He has no fault to find with this "physical" theology, which is the special preserve of philosophers, except for a mention of the philosophical controversies, which have given rise to a multitude of dissident sects. All the same, he removes the subject from the market-place, that is, from the general public, and shuts it up between the walls of a lecture-room. But he has not removed the first type – the mythical – with all its lies and filth. What sensitive ears ordinary people have, including the Roman people, in matters of religion! They cannot tolerate the discussions of philosophers about the immortal gods. Yet they not merely tolerate, they listen with pleasure to fictions, sung by poets and acted by players, which offend against the dignity and the nature of the gods, because such adventures are appropriate to human nature, or rather to human nature at its most contemptible. More than this, they have decided that such stories are pleasing to the gods, and must be employed to obtain their favour.

Now perhaps someone is going to say, "Let us make the same distinction as Varro himself makes between the 'mythical' and 'physical' ('fabulous' and 'natural') and the 'civil' variety of theology. We are now discussing 'civil' theology; let us see how Varro describes it." I do indeed see why Varro had to distinguish the fabulous type; because it is false, degraded, and unworthy. But to wish to separate natural theology from civil, is surely tantamount to an admission that civil theology itself is false. If "natural" theology is really natural, what is found wrong with it, to cause its exclusion from the city? While if so-called "civil" theology is not natural, what merit has it to cause its admission? This is, we may suppose, the reason why Varro treated "human affairs" before "divine affairs" – in "divine affairs" he was dealing not with something in nature but with purely human institutions.

Let us inspect this "civil theology". "The third variety", says Varro, "is that which the citizens in the towns, and especially the priests, ought to know and put into practice. It contains information about the gods which should be worshipped officially and the rites and sacrifices which should be offered to each of them." We should pay special attention to the statement which follows. Varro says, "The first type of theology is particularly suited to the theatre; the second is particularly concerned with the world; the special relevance of the third is to the city." It is easy to see to which he gives the first prize. Obviously it is the second type, the theology, as he said earlier, of the philosophers. He claims that this is concerned with the world, and, in the opinion of the philosophers, the world is the most important of all existing things. As for the other two theologies, the first (that of the theatre) and the second (that of the city), does he separate them or associate them? For what belongs to a city is not necessarily connected with the world, although a city is in the world. It may happen that cults are practised in a city, and beliefs held, which are based on mistaken ideas which correspond to no reality in the world or outside it. But a theatre must of necessity be in a city; for only a city community establishes a theatre. And the sole object of a theatre is the presentation of stage shows. And stage shows can only be classed among "divine affairs", which are treated with such subtlety in these books of Varro's.

6. *Criticism of Varro's treatment of "mythical" and "civil" theology*

Marcus Varro, you are the shrewdest of men, and, without a shadow of doubt, the most erudite. You are only a man, for all that; you are not God, and you have not been borne aloft by the Spirit of God into truth and liberty so that you could see things divine and bring news of them to men. You do indeed discern how important it is to separate divine matters from the follies and falsehoods of men. But you are afraid of falling foul of pernicious popular notions and traditional practices in state-established supersitions. You yourself feel, when you consider them in all their aspects, that they are utterly alien from the nature of the gods, even of those gods which the human mind, in its weakness, suspects to exist in the elements of this world; and the whole of your literature is loud in condemnation of them. And yet how does your native talent – which, for all its pre-eminence, is merely human – acquit itself at this point? What support do you derive, in this quandary, from your learning – which is also merely human, however manifold and immense? You desire to worship "natural" gods; you are compelled to worship the "gods of the city". You have found other gods, those of the fables, and you can be less reserved in loosing off your feelings about *them*. But, whether you like it or not, some of your shots land on the "civil" gods as well. You say, to be sure, that the "fabulous" gods are appropriate to the theatre, the "natural" gods are relevant to the world, the "civil" deities to the city. But, surely, the world is a divine work, while cities and theatres are works of men? And the gods who are laughed at in the theatres are the same as those adored in the temples, and the deities to whom you offer sacrifices are identical with those for whom you put on games. You would have shown much more candour and percipience in your division if you had distinguished between "natural gods" on one side and "gods of human institution" on the other, observing that the writings of poets on the latter display a different attitude from the teaching of the priests, but that poetry and priestcraft are allied in a fellowship of deception, and so are equally acceptable to the demons, whose enemy is the teaching of truth.

Leaving on one side, for later discussion, the so-called "natural theology", we may ask whether we are really prepared to ask or hope for eternal life from the gods of poetry and the theatre, the gods of the games and the plays? A thousand times, no! The God of truth forbids that we should entertain such monstrous, blasphemous insanity. What! Are we to seek eternal life from gods who are pleased and appeased by shows at which scandalous stories about them are enacted for all to see? No one, I conceive, has reached this degree of insanity, this bottomless pit of blasphemous delirium. It is agreed, then, that no one attains to everlasting life by means either of "fabulous" or "civil" theology. The former sows a crop of shame by inventing foul stories about the gods; the latter by supporting them, reaps the harvest. The one scatters lies: the other collects them. The one slanders "divine matters" with false reports: the other includes among "divine matters" the shows in which the slanders are presented. The one chants in verse the unspeakable fictions of human imagination about the gods; the other consecrates those fictions in the festivals of the gods. The one sings the crimes and shames of the deities; the other views them with complacence. The one reveals, or else invents them; the other either attests them as true, or enjoys them, even if false. Both "theologies" are disgusting, both deserve condemnation. The theology of the theatre proclaims the degradation of the people; the theology of the city makes that degradation into an amenity. Can eternal life be looked for from a source of corruption to this short life of time? Or are we to suppose that while association with evil men corrupts our life, if they insinuate themselves into our affections and secure our approval, the society of demons has no such effect, although those outrageous tales form part of their cult? If the tales are true, how degraded are the gods! If false, how degraded the worship!

In saying this we may give the impression to one who had but scant acquaintance with the subject, that it is only in the songs of the poets and in performances on the stage that these fables, so insulting to the divine majesty, so ludicrous and detestable, are presented to the public in honour of gods of this kind, while the sacred rites, which are conducted by priests, not by actors, are pure from any disgrace and unconnected with any such pollution. If this were true, no one would ever decide that obscenities should be presented on the stage in honour of the gods, and the gods themselves would never have ordered such exhibitions for themselves. In fact, it is just because this kind of thing goes on in the temples that there is no shame about putting on similar performances in the theatre.

It comes to this; that our authority, in attempting to distinguish "civil theology" as a third category separate from "fabulous" and "natural" theology, really meant it to be regarded as a mixture of the two others, rather than distinct from them. For he distinctly states that what the poets write is inadequate to serve as a model for the people to follow, while the writings of philosophers are too demanding for the common folk to find profit from their study. "These two theologies", says Varro, "are incompatible; and yet quite a number of ingredients have been taken from them to help to form the principles of 'civil' theology. For that reason, where elements in 'civil theology' coincide with elements in the other categories, we shall enter them under 'civil theology'. But we ought to cultivate the society of the philosophers more than that of the poets." This implies that we should not utterly shun the society of the poets. Besides, in another passage, dealing with the "generation of the gods", he says that people in general are more inclined to believe the poets than the "naturalists". In the former passage he is talking about what *ought* to happen, in the second about what actually does happen. He says that the "naturalists" have written with a view to edification; the poets to give pleasure. Thus the poets have written about the scandalous conduct of the gods, which gives pleasure to the general public – and to the gods; but they do not offer models for the people to imitate. As he says, poets write to give pleasure, not for edification. All the same, they write the kind of things the gods ask for and that the people present to them.

7. *The similarity and agreement of "mythical" and "civil" theology*

The truth is, then, that "fabulous" theology – the theology of theatre and stage, with all its abundant degradation and obscenity, is brought into "civil" theology. And all that theology which is rightly judged worthy of condemnation and rejection, is part of the theology which it is considered right to foster and put into practice. Clearly it is not a discrepant part, as I have undertaken to prove; not a part alien from the whole of the rest of the body, tacked on to it as an incongruous pendant; it is completely consonant with it, and is joined to it with perfect compatibility, like a component part of the same organism.

This is made plain by those images which show the shape, the age, the sex, and the clothing of the gods. The poets have their "bearded Jupiter" and "beardless Mercury"; so do the pontiffs. It is not only the mimes who give Priapus an enormous phallus; the priests do the same. He stands there in his sacred places to claim men's adoration in just the same guise as when he comes on the stage to provoke laughter. The old man Saturn and Apollo the stripling are not merely actors' parts; they are also statues in temples. Why is it that Forculus, who is in charge of doors (*fores*), and Limentinus, who looks after the threshold (*limen*), are masculine; while Cardea, who comes between them – she watches over the hinge (*cardo*) – is feminine? Do we not find details, in the books on "divine matters", which the serious poets judged unworthy of their verses? Is it true that only on the stage does Diana carry arms, while in the city she is shown simply as a maiden? Is it true that Apollo is a lute-player only in the theatre, while at Delphi he has no connection with that accomplishment?

But these details are quite respectable compared with the disgusting character of some of the others. What conception of Jupiter was in the minds of those who placed his nurse in the Capitol? Have they not given support to the theory of Euhemerus, who, writing as a careful researcher, not as a purveyor of legendary chatter, maintained that all those gods were originally men, mere mortals? And what of those banqueting gods, Jupiter's parasites? Surely those who set them round Jupiter's table intended to turn the ceremonies into scenes of farce! For if a mime had talked of Jupiter's parasites, admitted to his banquet, he would be taken to be asking for a laugh. It was, in fact, Varro who spoke of them. And he was not meaning to make fun of the gods, but to win them respect; this is witnessed by the fact that he wrote this in his books on "divine affairs" not in those on "human affairs"; not in the place where he describes the theatrical shows, but where he reveals the solemnities of the Capitol. In the end the evidence constrains him to admit that the Romans, having made gods in human form, believed them to take delight in human sensual pleasures.

The fact is that the malignant spirits did not fail in their proper task, which was to confirm these pernicious opinions by deluding men's minds. Hence such stories as the one about a guardian of the temple of Hercules, who had a day off with nothing to do and played dice by himself. He threw first with one hand for Hercules, then with the other for himself: the rule of the game being that if he won he would get himself a dinner at the temple's expense and pay for a mistress, while, if the game went to Hercules, he should supply the god with the same pleasures at his own expense. Then, being beaten by himself, representing Hercules, he provided for the god the dinner he owed him and the well-known courtesan Larentina. She went to sleep in the temple and had a dream in which Hercules lay with her, and told her that the first young man she met on leaving the temple would pay her a fee which she was to take as being her payment from Hercules. Now the first young man she met on her departure was the extremely wealthy Tarutius. He fell in love with her, and kept her as his mistress for many years; then he died, and left her as his heiress. Thus she came into a very handsome fortune and, not wishing to seem ungrateful for the divine payment, she did what she supposed would be most acceptable to the divine powers, in making the Roman people her heir. She disappeared, but her will was found; and for this benefit, so the story goes, she was accorded divine honours.

If the poets had invented this story, and if the mimes had acted it on the stage, it would, without any doubt, have been assigned to "fabulous" theology, and the decision would have been that it should be separated from the respectable category of "civil" theology. But such disgraceful stories are presented by so learned an authority as belonging not to the poets, but to the people; not to the mimes, but to the rites of religion; not to theatres, but to temples; in fact, not to "fabulous" but to "civil" theology. And that is why it is not idle for the actors to use their arts to represent the complete degradation of the gods; but it is utterly idle for the priests to try, by their supposed sacred rites, to invest the gods with an honour to which they have no claim whatsoever.

There are rites of Juno, celebrated in her favourite island of Samos, in which she is given in marriage to Jupiter. There are rites of Ceres, in which she searches for Proserpina, carried off by Pluto. Venus has her rites, in which she mourns the death of her beloved Adonis, a lovely youth, killed by the tusk of a boar. The Mother of the Gods has her rites, in which the beautiful youth Attis, whom she loved and castrated in feminine jealousy, is lamented by those called *Galli*, who themselves suffer the same misfortune. Such performances are more disgusting than any obscenity on the stage. What then is the point of ostensibly taking pains to separate the fabulous fictions of the poets about the gods, which belong to the theatre, from "civil" theology, which is, in theory, appropriate for the city, this being represented as a separation of what is honourable and decent from what is disgusting and dishonourable? In fact, we ought here to be grateful to the actors, who have had consideration for men's eyes, and have not unveiled in their shows everything that is concealed within the walls of sacred temples.

How can we think any good of the rites which are shrouded in darkness, when such abominations are produced in the light of day? Certainly, the practices performed in secret by those castrated perverts is their affair. But it has not been possible to keep out of sight those unfortunates, so foully unmanned and corrupted. The pagans should try to convince anyone that they perform any holy action through the ministry of such men, for they cannot deny that such men have an appointed role and activity among their ceremonies. We do not know the nature of the performances: we do know the nature of the ministers. In contrast, we do know what happens on the stage; we know that no eunuch or pervert finds a place there, even in a chorus of harlots. Yet the actors are regarded as degraded and outside the pale; and it would be wrong for respectable citizens to act such parts. Then what kind of sacred rites are these, seeing that holiness chooses as ministers the kind of men whom the stage, for all its obscenity, has refused to admit!

8. *The naturalistic explanations of the gods suggested by pagan scholars*

"But all these phenomena", we are told, "have what one may call 'physiological' explanations, explanations, that is, in terms of natural science." This is to assume that it is "physiology" we are looking for in this discussion and not theology, that is, the science of nature, not the science of God. Doubtless, the true God is God by nature, not in idea, but that does not mean that all nature is God; for there is a nature of man, of beast, of tree, of stone; and God is none of these. However, if the main point in this line of interpretation, when applied to the rites of the Mother of Gods, is that she is certainly the earth, do we need to look further and to examine other explanations? There could be no clearer support for the theory which alleges that all those gods were once mere men. They are "sons of earth", and so earth is their mother. But according to the true theology, the earth is the work of God, not his mother.

Besides, in whatever way the rites of the Mother of Gods may be interpreted in reference to the facts of nature, it remains true that for men to be treated as women is not in accordance with nature; it is contrary to nature. This disease, this scandal, this disgrace, is openly professed in these religious ceremonies; whereas it is reluctantly confessed, under torture, by men of corrupted morals. Then again, if those rites, which are proved to be more disgusting than the obscenities of the theatre, are excused and made pure by the interpretation which makes them symbolical of natural phenomena, why then does not the same excuse and purification affect the fictions of poets? Many interpreters have in fact explained them in the same way. Even the myth of Saturn devouring his children, regarded as the most brutal and shocking of all legends, is interpreted by a number of exegetes in this way;

the name Saturn signifies the long passage of time, which consumes all that it brings into existence; or, according to Varro's notion, Saturn refers to the seeds which issue from the ground and then fall back to the ground again. There are other similar interpretations of this legend, and of the other myths.

But still there is talk of "fabulous" theology; it is criticized, rejected, and scorned with all its interpretations of this kind; and it is distinguished, as rightly to be repudiated, not merely from the "natural" theology of the philosophers, but also from the "civil" theology, which we are now discussing; and it is rejected, on the ground that it has invented unworthy stories about the gods. The intention underlying this distinction is obvious. The men of acute intelligence and profound erudition who have written treatises on this subject realized that both "fabulous" and "civil" theology merit reprobation. Now they had the courage to find fault with the former, but not with the latter. They exposed the one for criticism; they put up the other, so like it, for comparison. It was not that they wanted "civil" theology to be chosen in preference to the other; they hoped that it would be realized that both ought equally to be cast aside. Thus, they thought, the contempt of both these theologies would give an opening for "natural" theology to establish itself in superior minds, and that without any risk to those who were afraid to criticize "civil" theology. For both "civil" and "fabulous" theologies are alike fabulous and civil. Anyone who intelligently examines the futile obscenities of both will conclude that both are fabulous; anyone who observes that stage shows closely related to "fabulous" theology are included in the festivals of the gods of the city and in the civic religious cult, will recognize that both theologies are, in fact, civil.

How is it, then, that the power of giving eternal life is ascribed to any of those gods, when their images and their ceremonies show quite unmistakably that they are precisely the same as those openly rejected "fabulous" divinities in respect of their physical form, their age, sex, clothing, their marriages, their children and their rites? All this makes it clear that they were originally human beings in whose honour rites and ceremonies were established in response to some special circumstance in their life or death and that this error has crept in with the encouragement of the demons who insinuated it, or at least through the activity of an unclean spirit, seizing any chance to delude the minds of men.

9. *The functions of individual gods*

Then what about functions assigned to the gods, portioned out in minute penny packets, with instructions that each of those divinities should be supplicated for this special responsibility? I have said a good deal about this already, though not all that could be said. But is it not all more appropriate to the buffoonery of farce than to the divine dignity? If anyone engaged two nurses for a child, one to give him solid food only, the other to give him nothing but drink, we should think him a clown, putting on a kind of farcical performance in his own home. But the Romans employ two divinities for these purposes, Educa and Potina! They want to derive the name Liber from *liberamentum* (deliverance), on the ground that through his assistance males

77

are "delivered" from semen in coition – and they will have it that Libera (whom they identify with Venus) renders the same service to women, because their story is that she ensures the emission. For this reason they prescribe the offering of the male part of the body to Liber, in his temple, and of the female to Libera. Besides this they have women, as well as wine, assigned to Liber, with a view to provoking sexual desire, and in this way the Bacchanalia were celebrated with all their limitless insanity; Varro himself admits that the Bacchants could not have performed their feats if their minds had not been deranged. However, these rites later incurred the displeasure of the senate when it came to its senses and ordered their abolition. It may be that here at any rate the Romans realized what power those unclean spirits, whom they took for gods, could exercise over men's minds. One thing is certain; such performances would never have taken place in the theatre; they had entertainment there, not raving madness. And yet to have gods who delight in such entertainments is a similar kind of lunacy.

Varro certainly lays down the distinction between a religious and a superstitious man. The superstitious, he says, is afraid of the gods. The religious man respects them as he respects his parents; he does not fear them as enemies, and when he calls them good, he means that they are more ready to spare the guilty than to harm one innocent person. And yet Varro records that three divinities are brought in as guards for a woman after childbirth to prevent Silvanus from entering and tormenting her; and, to symbolize the three guards, three men make the rounds of the doorways of the house at night. They strike the threshold first with an axe, then with a pestle, and afterwards they sweep it with besoms, these emblems of argiculture being used to prevent the entrance of Silvanus. They are agricultural emblems because axes are necessary for the polling or lopping of trees, pestles for the making of flour, besoms for the piling up of corn. The three gods get their names from those activities: Intercidona from the incision (*intercisio*) made by the axe, Pilumnus from *pilum* (pestle), Deverra from the besoms used in sweeping (*deverrere*). By these guardian deities the woman is protected after childbirth from the violence of the god Silvanus. Thus good gods could not offer strong enough protection against the savagery of a harmful deity unless they outnumbered him by three to one and opposed this rough, terrible, and uncouth god (he was, remember, the god of the forest) with the symbols of agriculture, as being contrary to him. Does this show the harmlessness of the gods? And their concord? Are those the protecting deities of cities – more laughable than the comic turns of the theatre?

The god Jugatinus is brought in when a man and a woman are united in the "yoke" (*iugum*) of marriage. So far, so good. But the bride has to be escorted home. The god Domiducus is employed to "lead her home" (*domum ducere*). To install her in the house, the god Domitius sees to her "going home" (*domum ire*). The goddess Manturna is called in as well, to see that she will "remain" (*manere*) with her husband. What else is needed? Should we not show consideration for human modesty, and let the sexual desire of flesh and blood achieve the rest, without violation of the secrets of modesty? Why fill the bridal chamber with a mob of divinities, when even the bridal escort retires? And what is the purpose of so crowding it? That the thought of the presence of the gods should make the couple more concerned to preserve decency? Not at all. It is to ensure that with their cooperation there shall be no difficulty in ravishing the virginity of a girl who feels the weakness of her sex and is terrified by the strangeness of her situation. For here are the goddess Virginensis, and Father Subigus (to subdue – *subigere*) and Mother Prema (to press – *premere*) and the goddess Pertunda (to pierce – *pertundere*) as well as Venus and Priapus. What does all this mean? If the husband finds the job altogether too much for him and needs divine assistance, would not one god, or one goddess be enough? Do you mean to tell me that Venus alone would not be adequate? She is, they say, so called (among other reasons) because "not without violence" (*vi non sine*) can a woman be robbed of her virginity! If there is any modesty in human beings (there seems to be none in the gods!), I feel sure that the belief in the presence of so many divinities of both sexes to urge on the business in hand would so embarrass the couple as to quench the enthusiasm of the one and stiffen the reluctance of the other! And then, if Virginensis is among those present, to see to the untying of the virgin girdle, and Subigus, to see that the bride is subdued to her husband, and Prema, to make sure that, when subdued, she is pressed tight, to prevent her moving – if they are there, what is the function of the goddess Pertunda? She should blush for shame and take herself off! Let the bridegroom have something to do for himself! It would be most improper for anyone but the husband to do what her name implies. But it may be that she is tolerated just because she is a goddess, not a god. If she were supposed to be masculine, with the name Pertundus, the husband would demand greater protection against him, in defence of his wife's honour, than the newly-delivered mother seeks, in order to ward off Silvanus. But what am I talking about? Priapus is there as well, that all-too-male divinity. And the newly wedded bride used to be told to sit on his phallus, that monstrous obscenity, following the most honourable and most religious custom of Roman matrons.

So let our friends go and try (and good luck to them!) to use all their subtlety to make a distinction between "civil" and "fabulous" theology, between the city and the theatre, the temple and the stage, priestly ceremonies and poets' verses – a supposed distinction between decency and obscenity, truth and falsehood, solemnity and frivolity, the serious and the farcical, between what is to be desired and what is to be rejected. We understand what they are up to. They know that the theology of the theatre and of fable depends on their "civil" theology, which is reflected in the verses of the poets as in a mirror. They have not the courage to condemn "civil" theology, but they give a detailed exposition of it, and then criticize its reflection in terms of reprobation. The purpose of this is that those who perceive their intention may repudiate the original also, of which this is the image. As for the gods, they look at themselves in the same mirror, and are so enamoured of what they see, that they can be more clearly recognized, in both image and original, for who they are and what they are.

This is why the gods have compelled their worshippers, by commandments backed by fearful threats, to dedicate to them the indecencies of "fabulous" theology, to include them in their festivals, to class them under "divine matters". In so doing they have made it all the more obvious that they themselves are unclean spirits; and at the same time, they have made this rejected and condemned theology, that of the theatre, a component part of "civil theology", which is regarded as chosen and approved. The whole of this "theology" is a mass of lies and delusions; yet we find part of it in the priestly books, the other part in the verses of poets.

Whether one could discover still more divisions is another question. For the present I have followed the distinctions made by Varro, and I believe that I have sufficiently shown that both the theology of the city and the theology of the theatre belong to one division, namely, "civil" theology. Hence, since they are both alike in their indecency, their absurdity, their unworthiness, their falsity, heaven forbid that any man of genuine religion should hope for life eternal from either of them.

Varro himself begins his enumeration of the gods with the moment of a man's conception and starts with Janus. Then he traces the sequence up to the moment of the death of a decrepit old man, and brings to an end the list of gods concerned with man himself with the goddess Nenia, who is invoked in song at the funerals of the aged. He then passes to a record of the gods who are concerned, not with man himself, but with the necessities of man's life, food, clothing, and the rest. And in every case he indicates the function of each god and the purpose for which prayer should be directed to each. Yet in the whole of this careful examination he never mentions or names any gods from whom eternal life is to be asked; and it is, strictly speaking, for the sake of eternal life alone that we are Christians.

Who is so slow-witted as to fail to realize that in expounding and exposing "civil" theology with such care, in showing its resemblance to the shameful and infamous "fabulous" theology, and in demonstrating quite clearly that it is part of the former – that, in this Varro is really making every effort to prepare a place in men's minds for "natural" theology, which, according to him, is the concern of the philosophers? He employs great subtlety in criticizing "fabulous" theology, without daring to criticize "civil", but demonstrating the reprehensible character of the latter by his manner of exposition. Thus, in his intention, both those theologies will be condemned by the judgement of intelligent readers, and only "natural" theology will remain for them to adopt. We shall treat of this theology more thoroughly in the appropriate place, with the help of God.

10. *Seneca's frankness in criticizing "civil" theology more vigorously than Varro denounced the "mythical"*

Varro lacked the frankness and courage to criticize the theology of the city with the same freedom he showed towards the theology of the theatre, which resembled it so closely. Annaeus Seneca had those qualities in some degree, if not in full measure. That is he had them in his writing; but he failed to display them in his life.

Seneca (who I suppose, on good evidence, to have been at the height of his fame in the time of our apostles) wrote a book *Against Superstitions*. In it he attacked this "civil" theology, the theology of the city, in much greater detail, and with much greater vehemence than Varro had used against the "fabulous" theology of the theatre. Thus, on the subject of images, he writes,

They dedicate images representing sacred, immortal, inviolable beings in base, inert matter; they give them the shapes of men, of wild beasts, or of fishes; some make bi-sexual gods, having bodies with incongruous characteristics. And they give the name of divinities to those images, though they would be classed as monsters if they suddenly came to life.

Somewhat later, he speaks in praise of "natural" theology, and sets out the opinions of some of the philosophers. He then confronts himself with a question. "At this point," he says, "someone asks, 'Am I to believe that the sky and the earth are gods? And that some gods live above the moon and some below? Am I to bear patiently with Plato, who proposed a god without a body; or Strato, the Peripatetic, who suggested a god without a soul?'" Seneca then replies, "Do you really suppose that the dreams of Titus Tatius, or Romulus, or Tullus Hostilius, were nearer to the truth? Tatius dedicated a statue to the goddess Cloacina; Romulus to Picus and Tiberinus. Hostilius made divinities of Panic and Pallor, the most unpleasant conditions of human beings; the one being the emotion of a terrified mind, the other not even a disease, but merely a change of complexion. Are you more inclined to believe in these deities, and to give them a place in heaven?"

Seneca was quite outspoken about the cruel obscenity of some of the ceremonies:

One man cuts off his male organs: another gashes his arms. If this is the way they earn the favour of the gods, what happens when they fear their anger? The gods do not deserve any kind of worship, if this is the worship they desire. So extreme is the frenzy of a mind disturbed and toppled from its throne, that the gods are appeased by rites which surpass the savagery of the foulest of mankind, whose cruelty has passed into legend. Tyrants have sometimes lacerated men's limbs: they have never ordered men to lacerate themselves. Men have been gelded to serve a monarch's lustful pleasure; but no one has ever unmanned himself with his own hands, at the bidding of his master. Men gash themselves in the temples, and offer their wounds and their blood as a supplication. If anyone had the time to notice what those people do and what they have done to them, he would discover things so unbecoming for men of honour, so unworthy of freemen, so incongruous for men of sane mind, that no one would hesitate to call them mad, if there were not so many sharing the same frenzy. As it is, their title to sanity rests on the multitude of the apparently insane.

He goes on to recount the ceremonies habitually observed in the Capitol itself, and he exposes them without the slightest reserve. No one would believe, he implies, that those were performed by any but lunatics – unless it were in a spirit of mockery. He himself speaks in derision of the mourning for Osiris in the Egyptian mysteries, followed soon by the joy at his finding, since both the loss and the discovery are fictitious, and yet the grief, and the joy, are expressed with every appearance of genuine emotion by people who have neither lost nor found anything. Seneca adds,

But at least this delirium has a limited period; it is allowable to go mad once a year. If you go to the Capitol, you will be ashamed at the demented performances presented to the public, which frivolous lunacy looks upon in the light of a duty. Jupiter has someone to announce the names of his callers; another to tell him the time; he has an attendant to wash him, another to oil him, and this one merely goes through the motions with his hands. There are women to do the hair of Juno and Minerva; these stand at a distance not only from the statues, but from the temple, and move their fingers like hairdressers, while others hold up a looking-glass. You find people praying the gods to stand bail for them; others handing them their writs and explaining their law cases. A leading pantomime actor of great experience, grown old and decrepit, used to put on his act every day on the Capitol, as if the gods still took pleasure in his performance now that human beings had abandoned him. Craftsmen of all kinds hang about the place waiting to do some work for the immortal gods.

Soon afterwards, Seneca adds,

At least the services they offer are not indecent or dishonourable, though they may be superfluous. But there are some women who haunt the Capitol in the belief that Jupiter is in love with them: and they are not deterred by the thought of Juno's jealous anger, which (if one is to believe the poets) can be formidable!

Here we have a freedom of speech such as Varro did not display. He could only bring himself to criticize poetic theology; he did not dare find fault with "civil", which Seneca cut to pieces. Yet, if we really want the truth, the temples where those rites go on are worse than the theatres where those fictions are enacted. Hence, in the rites of "civil" theology the role chosen by Seneca for the wise man is to simulate conformity in act while having no religious attachment. This is what he says: "The wise man will observe all these customs as being ordered by law, not as acceptable to the gods." And, a little later,

And what of the marriages we arrange among the gods, including the blasphemy of unions between brothers and sisters? We give Bellona to Mars, Venus to Vulcan, Salacia to Neptune. We leave some of the gods as bachelors, for lack, one assumes, of suitable matches. There are, to be sure, some unattached females available, such as Populonia, Fulgora, and Rumina; but it is not surprising that no suitors were forthcoming for them. All that undistingished mob of gods which long-standing superstition has amassed over the centuries, will receive our worship; but we shall bear in mind that their cult is a matter of custom, having little connection with truth.

Thus, what the laws and custom established in "civil" theology is not what was acceptable to the gods, nor anything related to reality. But Seneca, who had been, as it were, emancipated by the philosophers, but who was also an illustrious senator of the Roman people, worshipped what he criticized, performed acts which he reprehended, venerated what he condemned. Doubtless philosophy had taught him an important lesson, that he should not be superstitious in his conception of the physical universe; but, because of the laws of the country and the accepted customs, he also learnt that without playing an actor's part in theatrical fictions, he should imitate such a performance in the temple. This was to take a line the more reprehensible in that he acted this insincere part in such a way as to lead people to believe him sincere. The stage-player on the other hand, only aims at giving pleasure by his performance; he has no desire to mislead or deceive his audience.

11. *Seneca's opinion of the Jews*

Besides criticizing the superstitions of "civil" theology, Seneca attacks the rites of the Jews, and the Sabbath in particular. He maintains that the Sabbath is a harmful institution, since by the interposition of this one day in seven they practically lose a seventh part of their life in inactivity, and they suffer by having to put off urgent tasks. As for the Christians, who were at that time already bitterly opposed to the Jews, he did not dare to mention them for good or ill – not wishing to praise them in defiance of the ancient traditions of his country, nor to criticize them against (it may be) his personal feelings. It is in speaking of the Jews that he says: "The customs of this detestable race have become so prevalent that they have been adopted in almost all the world. The vanquished have imposed their laws on the conquerors." He expresses his surprise when he says this, and he shows his ignorance of the ways of God's working in adding a remark in which he reveals what he thought about the Jewish ritual system: "At least they know the origins of their ceremonies: the greater part of our people have no idea of the reason for the things they do."

The questions that arise about the Jewish religious practices, why, and to what extent, they have been established by divine authority, and afterwards taken over, with divine approval, by the people of God, to whom the mystery of eternal life has been revealed – these questions I have treated in other places, and in particular in my books against the Manicheans. And I shall have more to say on this topic at a more convenient moment in this present work.

12. *The falsity of the pagan gods has been exposed; they can give no help in respect of temporal life; they certainly cannot bestow life eternal*

Here then are three theologies: the Greeks call them "mythical", "physical" and "political", and in Latin they can be called "fabulous", "natural", and "civil". Men can look to neither the first nor the third of these for eternal life: not to "fabulous" theology, which the pagans themselves criticize with extreme candour, although they are worshippers of many false gods, nor to "civil" theology, for that has been proved to be a subdivision of the "fabulous", closely resembling it, or even morally inferior to it. If what I have said in this book is not enough to convince every reader, I would refer to the ample discussions in the previous volumes, and especially in the fourth, on God as the giver of felicity. For to whom should men consecrate themselves, with a view to eternal life, save to felicity alone, if felicity were a goddess? But felicity is not a goddess, but the gift of God. To what God then should we consecrate ourselves except to the giver of felicity, if we fix our devout affection on eternal life, where there is the true fulfilment of felicity?

After what has been already said, I do not imagine that anyone is likely to suppose that any of the pagan gods is the giver of felicity. Their worship has so much that is disgraceful in it, and even more disgraceful is their indignation if such worship is withheld; it is that which betrays them for the unclean spirits they are. Then how can one who does not give felicity be capable of giving eternal life? For what we mean by eternal life is the condition of unending felicity. If the soul lives in the eternal pains with which the unclean spirits themselves will be tormented, that is not eternal life, but eternal death. The greatest and worst of all deaths is where death does not die. Now since the soul, being created immortal, cannot be deprived of every kind of life, the supreme death of the soul is alienation from the life of God in an eternity of punishment. Therefore life eternal, that is, life of unending felicity, is the gift of him alone who gives true felicity. It has been proved that the gods worshipped by "civil" theology cannot give it. They are not to be worshipped, even with a view to temporal and earthly goods; we have demonstrated that in the five preceding books. Much less are they to be honoured with a view to eternal life, the life after death; that is the point we have made in this present book, with the support of the arguments in the previous discussions.

But inveterate custom has the strength derived from very deep roots: and some readers may think that my arguments have not adequately established the need to reject and to shun this "civil" theology. I would ask any such readers to give their attention to the next volume, which, with God's help, is to follow.

. . . .

Book VIII

1. *"Natural" theology is to be discussed with the most eminent philosophers*

Our present subject demands much more concentrated attention than was needed for the solution and explanation of the questions raised in the earlier books. We shall be treating of "natural" theology which is a different matter from "fabulous" or from "civil" theology, the theology of the theatre and that of the city; the former of those makes great play with the scandals of the gods, while the latter reveals their even more scandalous desires, showing them to be malignant demons rather than gods. But in discussing "natural" theology we shall have to cross swords not with the man in the street, but with philosophers; and that name means that they profess to be "lovers of wisdom".

Now if wisdom is identical with God, by whom all things were made, as we are assured by divine authority and divine truth, then the true philosopher is the lover of God. But the thing designated by the name is not found in all those who boast of the name. Because men call themselves philosophers it does not follow that they are lovers of true wisdom. In fact we have to choose some, from those whose opinions we have been able to discover from their writings, with whom we may discuss the subject on a reasonable level.

It is not my aim, in this present work, to refute all the baseless opinions of all the philosophers, but only those appertaining to theology – and I take this Greek word to signify reasoning or discussion about the Divinity. And I shall not deal with all the theological speculation of philosophers, but confine myself to those thinkers who, while admitting the existence of a Divinity and his concern for human affairs,

84

do not consider that the worship of one unchangeable God is sufficient for the attainment of a life of blessedness even after death, but suppose that for this end many gods are to be worshipped, gods who were created and established by him. Such philosophers certainly go far beyond Varro's ideas and come much nearer to the truth. For Varro could extend his "natural" theology as far as the visible world, or the World-Soul, but no further. But these thinkers acknowledge a God who transcends any kind of soul, being the maker not only of this visible world – heaven and earth, in the familiar phrase – but also of every soul whatsoever, a God who gives blessedness to the rational and intelligent soul – the class to which the human soul belongs – by giving it a share in his unchangeable and immaterial light. Those philosophers are called Platonists, a name derived from their master Plato, as is well known to those who have even a superficial acquaintance with these ideas. I shall touch briefly on Plato, saying as much as I think essential for the present discussion. But first I shall mention those who preceded him in this branch of study.

4

The Athanasian Creed

The Athanasian Creed was named for Athanasius, the champion of orthodoxy at the Council of Nicea in 325 and opponent of the heretic Arius. Beyond being named for Athanasius, the creed bearing his name was long mistakenly attributed to him as well. The true author of the creed remains unknown. Dating from approximately the sixth century and of Latin Christian origin, the Athanasian Creed is one of three ecumenical creeds (the others are the Apostles' Creed and the Nicene Creed) widely recognized by Western Christian churches. The Athanasian Creed, however, is not recognized by Eastern Orthodox Churches, for it expresses a peculiarly Western conception of the doctrine of the Trinity. It also contains the nucleus of the doctrine of the person and work of Christ. The first and last lines of the creed form a framework of inclusion, in which the believer is reminded of the requirement of orthodox belief for salvation. As such, the Athanasian Creed is one statement of the principle often articulated in the history of Christianity that outside the parameters of orthodoxy, of which the Church is guardian, there is no salvation.

The Text

Whoever desires to be saved should above all
hold to the catholic faith.
Anyone who does not keep it whole and unbroken
will doubtless perish eternally.

Now this is the catholic faith:

That we worship one God in trinity
and the trinity in unity,
neither blending their persons
nor dividing their essence.
  For the person of the Father is a distinct person,
  the person of the Son is another,
  and that of the Holy Spirit still another.
  But the divinity of the Father, Son, and Holy Spirit is one,
  their glory equal, their majesty coeternal.

What quality the Father has, the Son has, and the Holy Spirit has.
  The Father is uncreated,
  the Son is uncreated,
  the Holy Spirit is uncreated.

  The Father is immeasurable,
  the Son is immeasurable,
  the Holy Spirit is immeasurable.

  The Father is eternal,
  the Son is eternal,
  the Holy Spirit is eternal.

    And yet there are not three eternal beings;
    there is but one eternal being.
    So too there are not three uncreated or immeasurable beings;
    there is but one uncreated and immeasurable being.

  Similarly, the Father is almighty,
  the Son is almighty,
  the Holy Spirit is almighty.
    Yet there are not three almighty beings;
    there is but one almighty being.

  Thus the Father is God,
  the Son is God,
  the Holy Spirit is God.
    Yet there are not three gods;
    there is but one God.

Source: *Ecumenical Creeds and Reformed Confessions*.

The Athanasian Creed

Thus the Father is Lord,
the Son is Lord,
the Holy Spirit is Lord.
    Yet there are not three lords;
    there is but one Lord.

Just as Christian truth compels us
to confess each person individually
as both God and Lord,
so catholic religion forbids us
to say that there are three gods or lords.

The Father was neither made nor created nor begotten from anyone.
The Son was neither made nor created;
he was begotten from the Father alone.
The Holy Spirit was neither made nor created nor begotten;
he proceeds from the Father and the Son.

Accordingly there is one Father, not three fathers;
there is one Son, not three sons;
there is one Holy Spirit, not three holy spirits.

Nothing in this trinity is before or after,
nothing is greater or smaller;
in their entirety the three persons
are coeternal and coequal with each other.

So in everything, as was said earlier,
we must worship their trinity in their unity
and their unity in their trinity.

Anyone then who desires to be saved
should think thus about the trinity.

But it is necessary for eternal salvation
that one also believe in the incarnation
of our Lord Jesus Christ faithfully.

Now this is the true faith:
    That we believe and confess
    that our Lord Jesus Christ, God's Son,
    is both God and human, equally.

    He is God from the essence of the Father,
    begotten before time;
    and he is human from the essence of his mother,
    born in time;
    completely God, completely human,
    with a rational soul and human flesh;
    equal to the Father as regards divinity,
    less than the Father as regards humanity.

The Athanasian Creed

Although he is God and human,
yet Christ is not two, but one.
He is one, however,
not by his divinity being turned into flesh,
but by God's taking humanity to himself.

He is one,
certainly not by the blending of his essence,
but by the unity of his person.
For just as one human is both rational soul and flesh,
so too the one Christ is both God and human.

He suffered for our salvation;
he descended to hell;
he arose from the dead;
he ascended to heaven;
he is seated at the Father's right hand;
from there he will come to judge the living and the dead.
At his coming all people will arise bodily
and give an accounting of their own deeds.
Those who have done good will enter eternal life,
and those who have done evil will enter eternal fire.

This is the catholic faith:
one cannot be saved without believing it firmly and faithfully.

Part III

Medieval Texts
(*c*.500–*c*.1350)

5

Thomas Aquinas, from
Summa Theologiae

In the view of many theologians the greatest mind and system builder in the history of theology, Thomas Aquinas was born near Naples *c.*1225. He joined the Dominican Order, and eventually found his way to Paris, where he studied and taught at different periods of his life. Aquinas managed to compose a number of key philosophical and theological works, even though he died at a relatively young age in Naples in the year 1274.

Aquinas's master work, the *Summa Theologiae* ("Summation of Theology"), remained unfinished at his death. In it, he attempted to state all of Christian doctrine in a clear and orderly manner in the light of the recently rediscovered philosophy of Aristotle. The *Summa Theologiae* falls into three major divisions. The first part (*Prima Pars*, or I, or 1a) deals with "God." The first half of the second part (*Prima Secundae*, or I-II, or 1a2ae) and the second half of the second part (*Secunda Secundae*, or II-II, or 2a2ae) deal with "Journeying to God." The third part (*Tertia Pars*, or III, or 3a) deals with "The Road to God."

In the first two parts of the *Summa Theologiae*, Aquinas deals with topics such as the nature of theology, the relation of reason and revelation, kinds of truth, merit, grace, faith, unbelief, and religion. In the midst of these discussions, the reader can sense Aquinas's desire to contribute to an important task in his time – namely, the work of engaging non-Christians by presenting them with the truth of the Catholic faith. Aquinas understood the special challenges posed in confronting non-Christians with Christian doctrine, for non-Christians do not accept the authority of Christian Scripture. But because some non-Christians accept the authority of classical philosophy, truths known to reason are accessible and self-recommending to them, even though the other class of truths – revealed truths – remains beyond their grasp. With some non-Christians (at least Muslims – the principal group which Aquinas had in mind), thus, there exists some common ground on which discussion can take place.

Reflecting the disputational style of medieval philosophy and theology, each of the *Summa*'s parts is subdivided into questions; the questions are subdivided into articles. The standard way to refer to particular sections of the *Summa*, therefore, is to list part number, question number, and article number (e.g., 2a2ae.81.1 means second half of the second part, question 81, article 1). In each article Aquinas normally lists a title, notes some issues, provides a contrasting perspective (flagged by a phrase such as "On the contrary"), provides a reply (usually the nucleus of his own position and indicated by a phrase such as "I answer that"), and then replies to the issues with which the article began. In the following selections from the *Summa*, however, Aquinas's normal style has been replaced by a straightforward – and also more readable – prosaic style. This strategy has the advantages of efficiency (it gets to the heart of Aquinas's own view of a given matter without the customary dispute with the positions of others) and representation (it allows for a larger selection from the *Summa* than would otherwise be feasible). In order to get a sense of Aquinas's own style, however, the reader is strongly encouraged to consult an edition of the *Summa Theologiae* proper. To facilitate cross-reference, I have provided marginal numbers which indicate the precise place in Aquinas's masterwork where the article in question can be found. Omissions of articles in the otherwise continuous selections that follow are the work of the source editor, as are the brackets which appear in the text.

Introduction: The Learning of Men and the Teaching of God

My aim in this book is to introduce beginners to what God taught us [in the scriptures] as concisely and clearly as the subject-matter allows, and in scientific order.

Why we needed to be taught by God.   For our human well-being we needed teaching 1a.1.1 by God's revelation to supplement learning by our own natural powers of reasoning. God has destined us for a goal beyond the grasp of reason – *No eye has seen what you have prepared for those who love you* – and since we must set ourselves this goal and pursue it we needed teaching about it beforehand. We even needed revealed instruction in things reason can learn about God. If such truths had been left to us to discover they would have been learnt by few over long periods and mingled with much error; yet our whole well-being is centred on God and depends on knowing them. So, in order that more of us might more safely attain him, we needed teaching in which God revealed himself.

· ·

· *Grace* ·

God influences our behaviour from outside, [not only by instructing us with *law*, but also] by helping us to act rightly with *grace*.

Why we need God's grace.   All movement and activity presupposes in the agent a 1a2ae.109.1 quality [enabling it to act that way], and an initial activation. For physical movements this initial activation comes from some body in the heavens acting by necessity of its nature, but in the universe as a whole – bodily and spiritual – the absolute initiator of all activity is God, acting according to his own plan. However perfect the nature [disposing it to act], an agent cannot bring itself to act without God's initial activation. Our spiritual activity then (like any other activity) needs God in two ways: to give us a form disposing us to such activity, and to activate us.

The form God implants in a creature is sufficient to enable activity specific to that form, but activity beyond that will need a supplementing form: water as such cannot heat unless it is first made hot. Our human mind has a form, its own light of understanding, sufficiently enabling us to know and understand whatever we learn about through the senses; but to know anything beyond that the human mind needs completing by some stronger light (the light of faith, say, or prophecy): and that light must be grace-given, since it is beyond nature.

To sum up then: to know *any* truth we need God's help to activate our minds; but

Source: Thomas Aquinas, *Summa Theologiae: A Concise Translation*, ed. Timothy McDermott.

we need new light supplementing the light we have by nature only to know truths beyond our natural ability to know. *Every truth men utter comes from the Holy Spirit* bestowing on us the light of our nature and activating us to understand truth and utter it; but not every truth comes from the Holy Spirit dwelling in us himself by grace to make us holy and bestowing on us a disposition supplementary to our nature. We need this only when certain truths like the truths of faith are to be understood and uttered.

109.2 Before Adam sinned man's nature was integrated, but since that time it has been in disorder. Man's nature always need God's help to activate the doing or willing of any good whatever. But when his nature was integrated, it sufficiently enabled him to will and do what was by nature's standards good for him (the goodness of acquired virtue), though not any good beyond that (such as the goodness of instilled virtue). Now his nature is disordered, however, man falls short even of the goodness natural to him, and cannot wholly achieve it by his own natural abilities. Particular good actions he can still perform in virtue of his nature (building houses, planting vineyards and the like); but he falls short of the total goodness suited to his nature. He is like a sick man able to make certain movements by himself, but unable to move like a man in perfect health until he has had medicine to heal him.

In its integrated state, then, man's nature required strengthening by grace-given powers to do and will goodness surpassing nature. But in its disordered state it first needs even its natural strength healed, before it receives added strength to do what is supernaturally good and deserving. And in both states man needs God's help to activate him to act well.

Man is master of his own activity, willing or not willing it by making up his mind to turn this way or that. But if he is also to be master of making up his mind, this must come from some previous making up of mind, and so on endlessly, unless there is (as Aristotle argued) a point at which man's free decision is initiated from above and outside his mind by God. Even the mind of a man in health is not so much master of its activity as not to need God to activate it; but free decision by a man made sick by sin needs God even more, to overcome the obstacles to choosing good that are posed by disordered human nature. Man can run counter to his nature and commit faults on his own, but he is unable on his own to do and will good suited to his nature. For all created things exist by another's power and left on their own are nothing, needing another's help even to conserve in themselves their own natural good. Left on their own they can fail to be good, just as left on their own (without God to conserve them) they can fail to exist.

109.3 With an integrated nature man could achieve the goodness suited to his nature without additional gifts of grace, though not without God's help to activate him. Now to love God above everything else suits man's nature just as it does that of all other creatures – reasoning, non-reasoning or even non-living: interpreting love in a way appropriate to each creature. For things are naturally desired and loved for what they naturally are; so, since parts are good when serving the whole, each particular thing naturally desires and loves its own good as serving the general good of the whole universe, which is God. *God draws all things to love him.* When man's nature was integrated, he related his love of himself and all other creatures to love of God, loving God above himself and above everything else. But now that man's nature is disordered, his will fails to be reasonable in this respect and, unless God heals the disorder by his grace, pursues its own private good. To sum up then: in order naturally to love God above everything else man, when his nature was integrated, needed no gift of grace supplementing his natural gifts, though he needed God's help to activate the love. But now his nature is disordered, he also needs help from God's grace to heal his nature. Nature loves God above everything else as the source and goal of all natural good; charity loves him as the object of all happiness with whom we enjoy a kind of spiritual community. Charity moreover adds to our natural love the readiness and delight which virtuous dispositions add to all our good actions, for without such dispositions such actions are done merely from natural reason.

When his nature was integrated, man kept every commandment of the law in the sense that he did everything commanded; but now his nature is disordered he can't even do that unless grace heals him. Neither then nor now could he keep the commandments lovingly and charitably without grace; and both then and now he needed God's help to activate and initiate his keeping of them. *God doesn't command the impossible*; but what God can help us do is not altogether impossible: as Aristotle says, *what we can do through friends, we ourselves, in a sense, have the power to do.* 109.4

Eternal life is a goal out of all proportion to human nature; so man has no natural ability to earn it; for this he needs a greater grace-given ability. He is only able to achieve what is naturally good for him, by doing things like working the land, drinking, eating and making friends. Man does however will and do things which earn him eternal life, but only because his will has been prepared for it by God through his grace. *Eternal life is certainly a reward for good works; but those works themselves are done by God's grace*; for keeping the commandments of the law with charity in a deserving way needs grace. It is a mark of the dignity of human nature that it can, at least with the help of grace, achieve a higher goal than lower natures can in any way achieve. 109.5

There are two senses in which a man must prepare himself to will good. Firstly he must be willing to behave well and attain God, and for this he needs the gift of grace as a lasting disposition enabling him to earn [God] by his behaviour. So secondly, man must be willing to receive this gift of grace-as-disposition. Now for this it is not necessary to presuppose the gift of yet another disposition. For where would the process end? What we must presuppose is rather some gracious help from God activating our will from within, inspiring the good we propose. For when agents are acting in subordination to one another, their goals are correspondingly subordinated, the initial agent acting towards the ultimate goal and the secondary agents to the nearer goals. Thus God as absolute initiator of all activity is drawing all things to himself by initiating that general tendency to goodness through which everything tends to be as like God as in its own way it can. And he is also drawing good men to himself as to some special good they themselves aim to achieve and desire *to cling to as good for them*. So man can turn to God only if God draws him. And since willing grace is a sort of turning to God (like men turn to the sun for light), clearly we can't be willing to receive the light of grace unless God graciously helps by activating us 109.6

within. *Turn to me*, God says to man in Zechariah, *and I shall turn to you*: and man does turn to God by his free will; but since his free will cannot turn to God except God turn it, in Jeremiah man says go God: *turn me, and I shall be turned*. If a man does what he can, people say, God will not deny him grace. Yes, but a man can do whatever God moves him to do. We need our will to be prepared for grace-as-disposition in the way matter needs preparation to take on a new form; but to be acted on by God we don't need previous activation, since God is the initial activator. So the process of preparation is not endless. Man prepares himself by his own free will, but not without help from God activating him and drawing man to himself.

109.7   Man cannot rise from sin without the help of grace. When the actual sinning has stopped, certain damage has been sustained; so to rise from sin is not simply to stop sinning, but to have that damage repaired. The damage is threefold: a stain, by which we mean an eclipse of the brightness of grace by the tarnish of sin; a disorder of nature, in which man's will is no longer subject to God; and a liability to punishment, since fatal sin deserves to lose God for ever. Only God can repair such damage: he alone can shine his light on the soul again and restore the gift of grace-as-disposition; he alone can draw man's will to submit itself again to him; and he alone as plaintiff and judge can remit the liability to eternal punishment. So to rise from sin man needs the help of grace, both as disposition and as inner activation from God. Men cannot recuperate from sin on their own, because the light of grace has to be instilled in them afresh; just as a body cannot recover from death unless its soul is instilled afresh. Even an integrated nature couldn't have restored itself to a state beyond its natural capacity without external help. Human nature is now dissipated by an act of sin, no longer integrated but in disorder; so it cannot even restore itself to its own natural goodness, never mind to a state of rightness beyond its nature.

109.8   When his nature was integrated, man could refrain from sinning either fatally or non-fatally, even without any grace-as-disposition; for we sin when we deviate from the standards of nature, and men with integrated natures could avoid doing that as long as they had God's help conserving them in goodness (without that, of course, man's very nature would collapse into nothingness). But now that his nature is disordered, man also needs grace-as-disposition to heal the disorder, if he is wholly to refrain from sin. In the present life this healing already starts in the spirit, but the appetites of our flesh are not yet fully renewed: so we can refrain from fatal sins which need reasoned consent, but because of the disorder in our lower sensual appetites cannot avoid all non-fatal sins. Reason can indeed put down each individual movement of appetite (and that is enough to characterize such movements as voluntary and therefore sinful), but it cannot control all of them at once: while it is trying to resist one another arises, and reason can't always guard against that. In the same way, after fatally sinning and before being reconciled by grace, reason can avoid each individual fatal sin for a time – we don't have to sin continuously – but before long sins fatally again. For just as our lower appetites should submit to reason, so our reason should submit to God and make him the goal of our will; and just as our lower appetites, when not wholly subject to reason, are subject to disordered movements, so our reason, when stably fixed on God, is the seat of much disordered activity. Many things arise to obtain or avoid which a man will deviate from God, rejecting his commands and thus sinning fatally. Especially when things happen unexpectedly, we follow preconceived goals and pre-established dispositions, whereas if we had had time to think we would have acted otherwise. We cannot always be thinking ahead, and unless grace restores us quickly to proper orderedness, before long we will follow the lead of a will not submitted to God. It is our own fault if we are not prepared for grace, so the fact that without grace we cannot avoid sin doesn't excuse us from the sin.

A man established in grace has all the help he needs in the way of instilled 109.9 dispositions, but still needs the help of God activating him. For it is a general truth that no created thing can act at all except in virtue of God initiating the action; and in man's specific case, though his nature is healed in spirit by grace, it is still disordered in the flesh and darkened by ignorance (things never happen the same way twice, and we don't even fully know ourselves, so how can we always know what is the best thing to do?). We need God, who knows and can do all things, to direct and protect us. We are not given grace-as-disposition to preclude all further need of help from God; for all creatures need God to conserve them in the good they have already received. Even in the state of glory, when grace has reached its full perfection, man will need such help from God. The Holy Spirit moves and protects us not only through the disposition he gives us; but together with the Father and the Son in other ways as well.

What is grace?   In common speech we use the word *grace* in several ways: of love 110.1 and favour as when we say a certain soldier is *in the good graces of the king*, i.e. pleasing to him; of a free gift, as when we say *I confer this grace on you*; and of gratitude for such free gifts, as when we talk of *saying grace*. The third use derives from the second, and the second from the first. The second and third uses of the word *grace* name soemthing in the person favoured: the gift freely given or the acknowledgement of the gift. But whether grace in the first sense names something in the person favoured depends on whether we are thinking of God's grace or man's.

Creatures are good because God wills them so: their goodness derives from the love with which God wills their good; but man's will is moved by good already there in creatures, and man's love of things doesn't cause their good but presupposes it, in whole or in part. So if God loves a creature, some goodness will result at some time in that creature, though not co-eternally with the love itself. And because of differences in such goodness, we distinguish different loves of God for creatures. One is the general love with which he loves everything there is, and which gives natural existence to all created things. Another is the special love with which he draws reasoning creatures above their natural condition to share in his own good; and this is the way God loves creatures in an unqualified sense, willing them an etternal good which is nothing other than himself. To say then that a man is in God's grace implies some supernatural gift flowing out from God into that man. Although sometimes we refer to God's eternal love itself as his grace: the *grace of predestination*, for example, is God's free choosing of people without them earning it. As St Paul says: *He predestined us to be adopted sons, to the praise of the glory of his grace.*

So saying someone is in God's grace implies that God's gracious will is causing 110.2

something in him. Now God's gracious will helps men in two ways. Firstly, God activates our every act, stimulating us to know and will and do things, causing in us not a disposition but an actual movement: as Aristotle says, *the act of a mover is the movement of what it moves.* Secondly, God's gracious will helps us by instilling in us dispositions. For fittingly God's love is as thorough in caring for those to whom he wills good beyond their nature as he is for those to whom he wills natural good. He not only stimulates natural behaviour in creatures but bestows on them the natures and powers which make that behaviour natural and easy, disposing them to behave in that way of themselves; for *Wisdom orders all things sweetly.* All the more then does God instill into those he stimulates to achieve an eternal good beyond their nature, forms or qualities beyond nature whereby they move to that eternal good sweetly and readily. Grace given in this way is therefore a sort of quality or disposition. Grace is beyond human nature, so it cannot be man's substance or the form that makes him man, but some form supervening on that. For whenever man shares some divine good (like knowledge) what is God's substance in God becomes something supervening on substance in us. Grace is a sharing of God's good, and exists in the soul in a less perfect way than the soul itself, which exists substantially. As expressing and sharing God's goodness, grace is of a higher order of reality than the soul, but not in its mode of existing. Strictly speaking, a supervening quality is not so much in existence itself as a way in which something else exists; and so grace is not created, but men are created in it, established in a new existence out of nothing, without earning it: *Created in Christ Jesus in good works.*

110.3   The virtues we acquire by human activity dispose us in ways in keeping with our nature as men, but the virtues instilled in us by God dispose us in higher ways to the goal of sharing God's nature, into which we have been reborn as sons of God. So, just as our acquired virtues presuppose a natural light of reason, instilled virtues presuppose a light of grace, which is our sharing in God's nature. *Once you were darkness,* St Paul wrote, *but now you are light in the Lord; walk then like sons of light.* Acquired virtues strengthen us to walk according to the light of natural reason; instilled virtues strengthen us to walk according to the light of grace. St Augustine calls *faith acting through love* grace, because that is the activity which first manifests in us the grace that makes us pleasing to God. Grace then is a disposition presupposed

110.4   to instilled virtues as their origin and root. And since by grace we are reborn as sons of God, grace must modify our very nature in some way: it is presupposed to virtues, so affects what is presupposed to every ability of the soul, namely its nature. We share God's knowledge through the virtue of faith strengthening our mental ability, and God's love through the virtue of charity strengthening our power to will; we share some likeness to God's nature through a kind of rebirth or recreation taking place in the nature of our soul. The soul's abilities to act derive from its nature, and the virtues which strengthen those abilities derive from grace itself.

111.1   St Paul talks of grace both as making us pleasing – *He has taken us into his good grace through his beloved Son* – and as freely given – *If by grace then not by works, otherwise grace would no longer be grace.* So we should be able to distinguish graces that have both these elements from graces that have only one. And indeed God plans to draw men back to himself by grace through others. So there is not only grace-which-makes-pleasing, which unites its recipient to God; but also grace which allows its recipient to help draw another to God. This is a grace-freely-given since it surpasses natural abilities and personal deserts, but not grace-which-makes-pleasing since it is not given to set the recipient himself right with God but rather to enable the recipient to work for the setting right of someone else. This is the grace St Paul says *shows the Spirit is present in some way in that person for the good of all.* To say grace is freely given is to say it isn't owed either to personal desert or to nature (as man is owed a mind or whatever else is part of his nature). Not that God owes anything to creatures in either of these ways, but creation owes God submission to his plan, according to which this nature should possess these properties and dispositions, and doing this should earn that. Natural gifts are owed not as personal deserts but owed to nature; gifts beyond nature are owed in neither sense and so are specially entitled to the name of *graces.* Grace-that-makes-pleasing, then, adds another meaning of grace to this general notion of grace-freely-given. Only graces that don't do this retain the general name of grace-freely-given; so the distinction is really between graces that do or do not make pleasing.

Grace can mean God's help stimulating us to will and act well, or the gift of a 111.2 disposition implanted in us by God. In both cases we can fittingly distinguish grace working in us and with us. The working of an effect is never ascribed to what is acted on, but to the agent; so if our mind is stimulated to activity by God without activating itself – God being the only activator – we talk of what is done as the work of God alone, and of his grace as working in us; but if our mind, activated by God, activates itself, we talk of what is done as the work of both God and the soul, and of grace as working with us. Now we distinguish two levels of activity in man. We will interiorly, activated by God's activating (especially when the will is first starting to will good after previously having willed evil); so here grace is said to work in us. But we also engage in external behaviour under will's control, so that our will is at work and God is also helping, strengthing the inner will and providing the external means to act; and there grace is said to work with us. As Augustine says: *Working with us God completes what he started working in us; for at the beginning he works to make us will and at the end works with us when we will.* Grace then, thought of as the freely given activation of God moving us to act well and earn heaven, can fittingly be distinguished as working in us and working with us.

But also when grace is thought of as a disposition God gives us, we can distinguish two things it does: like every form it determines a way of existing and a way of doing things. Just as heat first makes something hot, then makes it able to heat other things, so grace-as-disposition first works in us to heal or set the soul to rights, making it pleasing to God, and then works with us as a source of those works of our free will which earn us heaven. (Grace-as-quality *does* things only in the sense that forms do things, not in the sense agents do: in the sense, that is to say, in which whiteness is said to make things white.) God does not set us to rights *despite* ourselves, for at the moment we are set right our free will consents to it. But that consent is not a cause of the grace but an effect of it, so the whole process is worked in us by grace. It is not only secondary agents involved in an action that are said to *work with,* but any agent that is helping towards an already presupposed goal. So God by grace works in us helping us to will good; and then, once that goal is presupposed, his grace works with us for its achievement. It is one and the same grace that works in us and works with us: the distinction lies solely in what the grace is doing.

111.3 Grace does five things: first it heals our soul, so that secondly we will to do good, thirdly actually do the good we will, fourthly persevere in doing good, and finally come to glory. Grace by causing one of these effects can be said to lead to the next effect; and in causing the next effect can be said to follow on from the first. And since these effects come before and after one another, grace can lead to and follow on from the same effect as related to different effects. As Augustine says: *It leads by healing and follows on when what is healed lives and grows; it leads by calling us and follows on by bringing us to glory.* God's love, being eternal, can never itself do anything but lead; but grace, its effect in time, can lead to one thing and follow on from another. It is the same grace that leads and follows; but doing different things, just as we said of grace working in us and with us. Even the grace which brings us to glory is the very same grace that now leads by setting us to rights. The love of charity we had on the way is not made void but comes to fulfilment when we come home to glory, and so it is with the light of grace; for neither charity nor grace is defined by its incompleteness [as faith and hope are].

111.4 St Paul distinguishes various graces-freely-given saying *The Spirit gives one person a message of wisdom, another knowledge. One and the same Spirit gives faith to one person, to another the gift of healing, to another power to work miracles, to another prophecy, to another reading the mind, to another speaking strange languages, to another explaining what is said.* Graces-freely-given are bestowed on men so they can help bring others back to God. Men can't work on others inwardly; only God can do that. But they can teach and persuade externally, and for this they need full knowledge of God (faith, wisdom and knowledge), the ability to confirm or prove what they say (the gifts of healing, miracles, prophecy and reading minds), and the ability to express their thoughts well

111.5 (speaking languages and explaining what is said). Graces-freely-given serve the general good within the church, but grace-that-makes-pleasing serves that universal good beyond the church which the church itself serves, namely God. So the grace-that-makes-pleasing is the more precious.

112.1 *Sources of grace.* Only God can give grace, since it surpasses the abilities of any created nature, and shares in the nature of God. Only God can make gods of us, sharing his nature and living like him in some way. Christ's human nature is *a sort of tool of his divine nature*, to quote Damascene, and tools don't do what we use them to do by their own power but by the power of the tool-user. So Christ gives grace not in virtue of his human nature but in virtue of the divine nature with which it is united, and which gives to Christ's human actions their power to save. And just as Christ's human nature gives grace only in virtue of being used by his divine power, so also the sacraments which Christ instituted in his New Law give grace only as tools used by the power of the Holy Spirit.

112.2 Sometimes grace means God's gift of a disposition, and sometimes God's active stimulation towards good. Grace in the first sense must be prepared for, since matter can only take on forms for which it is ready. But grace in the second sense, God's help, needs no preparing; rather whatever preparation occurs in man comes from

God helping him and stimulating him towards good. The very movement of free will by which someone readies himself to receive the gift of grace is such a good: an act of free will to which he is moved by God (and in that sense it is *up to man to prepare his spirit*), and an act of God moving our free will (and in that sense *man's will is prepared by God*). There is a preparation of man to receive grace which occurs at the same moment as grace is instilled: such activity cannot earn a man the grace he already possesses, but can earn the glory which is still to come. The incomplete preparation which God stimulates in us before the gift of grace-which-makes-pleasing, does not earn however, for only when grace has already set us to rights can we earn. Infinitely powerful agents don't need matter to work on, nor other agents predisposing matter for them. Though the circumstances of the thing being caused may require the infinite agent itself to create matter for the thing and dispose it in the way the form needs. So, when God instils grace in the soul he needs no other preparation than that which he himself provides.

We are prepared for grace by God activating us and by our free will thus activated. 112.3 Grace does not have to follow the preparation regarded as an act of free will, since the gift of grace is beyond anything human power can do. But grace has to follow the preparation regarded as an act of God. That doesn't mean God's grace is coerced, but that what God intends happens, and if God intends the man whose heart he moves to obtain grace he will. Every man's grace unites him to God, the 112.4 highest good, and in this respect one man's grace is equal to another's. Nevertheless one man may be more enlightened by grace than another; part of the reason being that one man is more prepared for grace than another. But this doesn't get to the root of the matter, since this preparation is man's doing only inasmuch as his free will has itself been prepared by God. So in the last analysis it is God who dispenses his gifts of grace unequally, to enhance the beauty and perfection of his church, just as he creates different levels of natural things to enhance the perfection of the universe. *Grace is given to every man in the measure Christ gives it, for perfecting the saints and building up Christ's body.*

God sometimes reveals to specially privileged people their graced state, but no 112.5 one can make certain for himself that he is graced. To be certain of something we must know the grounds for it, and the ground of grace is in God himself, whose sublimity is beyond all our knowing: *if he comes to me, I shall not see him.* We might guess from indications: seeing ourselves delight in God and despise worldly things, and being unconscious of any fatal sin. But such knowledge is incomplete: *I am not conscious of anything but I am not thereby justified.* For *who can discern his own sins?* Whatever is there in the soul can be experienced, for man experiences the inner springs of his action through acting; the will through willing, life through exercise of the activities of life. And since perfections of the mind involve certainty essentially, people possessing knowledge or faith can be sure they possess them. But the same doesn't hold for grace or love which are perfections of our faculty of desire.

Grace works in us to set sinners right. Justification is God setting man to rights. Now 113.1 being right can simply mean being personally just in our dealings with other people, and legally just and observant of the general good. But more broadly, it means being rightly disposed within ourselves with our lower powers subject to the higher power of reason, and that higher part subject to God. Such rightness is either a straight gift from God, as his original state of integrity was to Adam before he sinned; or it is a transformation from unrightness – *the justification of the unrighteous* – when a man who

113.2 has sinned has his sins forgiven. Now sin is forgiven when God is again at peace with us. This peace is God's love, which, though eternal and unalterable as an activity in God, imprints an effect in us which is interrupted from time to time as we fall away from God and then recover. That effect is the grace that fits man for eternal life, with which fatal sin is incompatible. So forgiveness of sin must be accompanied by instilling of grace. Men can be neutral towards one another, neither loving nor hating; but if one has offended the other then forgiveness of the offence will involve the other's special favour. So, although before man sinned he could have been in a neutral state, neither in God's graces nor guilty of sin, after sinning he can only escape guilt by possessing grace. Sin itself is a transient action, but a liability to punishment remains. Someone might stop one sin by passing on to another opposed to it, but then not only would the liability still be there, but the sinner would become liable for two opposed sins at once (for in that respect – as turning away from God

113.3 and attracting punishment – they are in fact not opposed). God moves things in keeping with their own way of moving: men, therefore, in a human way, by means of their own free choice. So in moving them towards rightness, he so instils his gift of reconciling grace, that he moves all those capable of receiving his movement to

113.4 accept his grace freely. Setting the unrighteous to rights, then, requires a free turning of man's spirit to God, the first step of which is an act of faith: for *whoever draws near to God must believe that he exists*. If the movement of faith is to be perfect it must be inspired by the love of charity, so in setting the unrighteous to rights two movements, of faith and love, occur together. One and the same act of free choice exercises two different virtues, one controlling the other, since actions can serve more than one goal. We cannot turn to God as object of our eternal happiness and cause of our reconciliation sheerly by natural knowledge: for reconciliation we need to make an

113.5 act of faith that God is reconciling us to himself through the mystery of Christ. And the movement of free will has another side: in desiring God's rightness it also renounces sin; for since charity is love of God, it is also renunciation of the sin which separates us from God.

113.6 So, since God in reconciling us, moves us from a state of sin to a state of rightness, we can describe that reconciliation in four ways: the one act of God instils grace, moves our free will away from sin by renunciation and towards God by faith, and ends up by achieving forgiveness of sin. In substance this is one action of God bestowing grace and forgiving sin. In the physical world, too, though coming is not going, the coming to be of one thing is identically the going away of another.

113.7 The start of the whole process is the instilling of grace, by which the free will is moved and sin forgiven. That instilling of grace is instantaneous and takes no time. The only disposing the soul needs to receive God's grace is the disposing he himself gives, and this need not be gradual: God has infinite power and can dispose any matter he himself creates to its form in an instant; especially man's free will which by nature acts instantaneously. Reconciliation as a whole, then, is instantaneous. A man may take time to consider his act of consent beforehand, but that is on the road leading up to reconciliation, which then happens instantaneously. There is nothing to stop us thinking two things at once when they form some kind of unity: for example, the subject and predicate of one affirmation are understood simultaneously. In the same way our free will can choose two things at once if they are related to one another; and that is how free will simultaneously renounces sin and turns to God, since the renunication of what sets us against God serves our willing unity with him. There is no timelag between acquiring a form, starting to act in keeping with it, and – if the act is instantaneous – finishing it. Now willing doesn't take time, so neither does reconciliation. In processes that do take time there is no instant immediately prior to any given instant, though there is a period of time ending at the given instant. When something is changing towards a given state, during the whole of the preceding period it is in some other state, and then at the last moment of that period (which is also the first moment of the next period) it is in the state it was moving towards. Only if the process is not in time will states succeed each other discretely rather than continuously; and then there will be a last instant in one state and a first instant in the next, without need of a time between, since no continuity will require it. Now the human spirit, though beyond time itself, is subject to time incidentally, since it understands the meanings of things as reflected in images involving space and time. So any changes in human minds must be thought of as subject to the same conditions as temporal processes; there is no last instant in which sin is present in the process of reconciliation, but only a last period of time, and then a first instant in which grace is present. So the four elements we 113.8 distinguished in the reconciliation of sinners are temporally simultaneous, even if they have a natural order of priority: first the instilling of grace, then the free willing of God, motivating the freely willed renunciation of sin, and finally the forgiveness of sin. For in any movement, the movement by the mover naturally precedes the change in what is being moved, and that precedes the achievement of the goal of the change. From the point of view of the thing being changed, leaving a previous state must naturally precede arriving at an opposite state; but from the agent's point of view the reverse is true. The agent expels the previous form because it already possesses the second. Thus the sun has to be luminous in order to expel darkness; but the atmosphere must lose its darkness before it can become light (though these processes are temporally simultaneous). Now the instilling of grace and the forgive-ness of sins are described from God's point of view, so the instilling of grace precedes forgiveness of sins by definition. But from the sinner's point of view the reverse is the case, and liberation from sin by definition precedes the obtaining of reconciling grace.

Judged by the way he does it – producing things out of nothing – creation is 113.9 God's greatest work. But judged by what he does, reconciliation is his greatest work: for what is achieved is the eternal good of sharing in God's nature, rather than the good of changeable nature, earth and sky. Absolutely speaking, the gift of glory is greater than the gift of reconciling grace, but proportionately speaking, the gift of grace is greater, exceeding the worth of the unrighteous man (who deserves punishment) by more than glory exceeds the worth of the righteous man (who as righteous deserves it). The good of one individual person's grace is greater than the natural good of the whole universe.

113.10 But the reconciliation of the unrighteous is not a miracle, outside the power of nature: for as Augustine says *to be able to have faith or the love of charity is natural to man, though actually having them is a grace reserved to believers.* If we characterize miracles – or marvels – as things that need a marvellous cause like the power of God, then the creation and all the other things only God can do are miracles. But if we limit miracles to cases of matter taking on some form beyond its natural capacity (e.g. dead bodies coming to life again), then the reconciliation of the unrighteous is not miraculous, since the soul has a *natural capacity for grace being made in God's image.* And if miracles are defined as events outside the usual customary order of cause and effect (e.g. instantaneous healing), then the reconciliation of the unjust is sometimes miraculous and sometimes not. The common and customary course of reconciliation starts with God moving the soul inwardly so that man turns to God firstly imperfectly and then more perfectly. But sometimes God moves the soul to perfection instantaneously (as in St Paul's case), and such a reconciliation is miraculous. Not every movement of natural things against their natural inclination is miraculous, otherwise water boiling and stones being thrown upwards would be miracles. But if such movements happen outside the established order of causes that normally cause them, then they are miraculous. Now only God can reconcile sinners, just as only fire can heat water. So in this sense God's reconciliation of sinners is not miraculous.

114.1 *Grace works with us to earn heaven.*   What we earn we call wages: a recompense made in return for work done, a sort of price paid for it. Justice demands we pay a proper price for goods bought, and pay proper wages for work done. But justice, strictly speaking, is the preservation of equality between equals; so earning wages is something that can only happen, strictly speaking, between equals; not between son and father, or slave and master. Between God and man there is no equality at all – the whole of what man has comes from God; so justice between God and man must be proportionate, each working to his own measure, a measure set up by God himself. Man can earn from God only what in God's plan God has allotted him power to earn. In the physical world too things achieve by their own power just what God has planned they can; but since reasoning creatures act freely, what they achieve is said to be earned. Man earns when he does freely even what he is obliged to do, otherwise acts of justice like repaying debts would not earn anything. God is not seeking profit for himself from our good works, but only the glorious revelation of his goodness. So we earn from him not by adding something to his store but by glorifying him. Our actions earn only because God has planned it so, so that God is not in our debt, strictly speaking, but rather in debt to himself, in the sense that he owes it to himself to fulfil his plan.

114.2 In the state of mankind before sin there was already one reason why man couldn't earn eternal life by his own purely natural abilities; for in God's plan things can't act beyond their abilities, and eternal life is a good quite out of proportion to created natures, unaided by grace. But when man sinned the obstacle of sin added a second reason, since we needed grace to forgive sin and reconcile us to God first; for *the wages of sin is death* not life. In God's plan, human nature attains the goal of eternal life not by its own power but aided by grace; and that is the way its actions earn eternal life. Men earn from God by God's gift; but we earn from men without any gift on their part, by means of gifts we have from God. Though we cannot earn from a man we have offended until we have first made recompense for that and been reconciled to him.

As acts of free will, our acts of earning from God are not commensurate with 114.3 what they earn because there is no equality between God and man; but a certain proportion exists, God recompensing to the excelling measure of *his* power what we do to the measure of ours. But as acts of the Holy Spirit, our acts earn eternal life commensurately. For the worth of these acts is now measured by the power of the Spirit moving us to eternal life, *becoming in us a fount of water springing up to eternal life.* Or we can measure the price of what we do by the worth of grace, through which we share in God's nature through adoption as sons, to whom inheritance is owed by the very law of adoption – *if sons, then heirs.* The grace of the Holy Spirit possessed in this life, though not the actual equal of glory is its virtual equal – as the seed is the equal of the tree. And through that grace the Holy Spirit dwells in man: cause enough of his eternal life, *the pledge of his inheritance.*

Our actions earn the good God has planned as man's reward. But what moves 114.4 man's spirit towards the enjoyment of God is love of charity, which directs all the acts of all other virtues to that goal. So earning eternal life primarily belongs to love of charity, and to other virtues as controlled by that love. Also, because earning must be voluntary it primarily belongs to charity, since clearly acts are most willed when done from love. Work is laborious and difficult either because there is a lot of it (and the greater the labour is in this sense the more it earns, and charity doesn't lessen our labours but urges us to attack even greater ones), or because the worker lacks skill and fitness or a ready will (and such labour lessens our earning capacity, but is removed by charity).

Earning is incompatible with the free gift character of grace (*if by works then no* 114.5 *longer by grace*). And in the nature of what we are given, someone without grace can't earn it; firstly, because it surpasses nature and secondly, because in the state of sin before grace, sin itself is an obstacle to earning grace. But once one has grace – to begin good works – one can earn further grace as a result of those works. Such further graces are not, however, the first grace; nobody earns that for themselves. Man is reconciled by faith, not because believing merits reconciliation, but because reconciliation involves belief, the movement of faith being a necessary element in the reconciliation.

What we do earns commensurately to God's movement within our actions, and 114.6 proportionately to our free willing of them. Clearly then only Christ can earn the first grace for others; only his soul is moved by God's grace to the glory of an eternal life for others, as well as for himself being constituted head of the church and author of salvation for all men. *For it is fitting that he who brought many sons to glory should perfect the author of their salvation.* Though we can earn someone else's first grace in a proportionate way. For if we do God's will in a state of grace, it is a fittingly friendly thing that God should do man's will in return and save the other person;

though sometimes of course that other person impedes his own reconciliation.

114.7   Prayers rely on mercy; only works of commensurate earning rely on justice. No one can earn a right to his own restoration from any future fall, neither commensurately nor proportionately. Commensurate earning depends on God moving one, and that sin has interrupted; whilst proportionate earning of a first grace can be impeded by the one it is earned for, and certainly will be in this case when the one earning and the one earned for are the same. Some have held that a man can unconditionally earn eternal life only with the last graced act he does; and that all earlier earning is conditional on perseverance. But this is absurd: indeed sickness sometimes makes our last graced acts less deserving than previous ones, not more. We hold that every act of charity earns eternal life unconditionally; but that later sin can impede the effect of such earning, just as obstacles can hinder the effect of natural causes.

114.8   The end that grace moves towards is eternal life, and the movement develops by growth in charity and grace. So growth in grace can also be earned commensurately. A tree is not beyond the seed's power just because it's bigger. Any deserving act earns man growth in grace just as it earns him that fulfilment of grace which is eternal life. And just as eternal life isn't given immediately but in its proper time, so grace will not grow immediately but in its proper time when a man is sufficiently disposed to receive it. What man can earn is the appointed end towards which God moves his free will. So perseverance in glory (which is the end in question) can be

114.9   earned. But perseverance in grace throughout life cannot be earned, since it depends only on God's movement, the source of all earning. God is free to bestow perseverance on whomsoever he wills to bestow it. But what can't be earned can always be prayed for.

. . . .

· *Faith* ·

We begin with the virtue of faith: what we believe, the act of believing and our disposition to believe.

2a2ae.1.1 *What we believe.* With regard to any disposition to know, we can distinguish what it disposes us to know from what makes that knowable; for example, in geometry what we know are proved conclusions, but what makes them knowable is the means by which geometry proves them. Now what makes things objects for faith is Truth himself, for faith believes only things God has revealed: his truth guarantees their truth. And what Truth makes believeable includes God but also much else related to Truth himself, namely, the works of God which help us attain him: e.g. the manhood of Christ, the sacraments of the church, creation itself.

1.2   Human minds know truths by making connections or disconnections. So by objects for faith we can mean either the realities believed in, or the mode in which they are presented to the believer: namely, through propositions stating certain connections. We formulate propositions only in order to know reality through them, so the act of believing moves through the propositions to rest in the reality – *I believe in God, in his only-begotten Son, in the church.*

Sometimes the mind's assent is determined by what it assents to, which is either 1.4
self-evident (like first premises) or provable (like conclusions from such premises).
Sometimes however what we assent to is insufficiently convincing, and our assent is
determined by a voluntary choice between alternative positions. If the choice is made
tentatively we call it *opinion*, but if with certainty and without doubt we call it *faith*.
But we talk of seeing things only when those things themselves determine the mind
or the senses to know them; so neither faith nor opinion concerns what we see.
Though a man sees what he believes under the general aspect of being believable,
since he wouldn't believe it unless he saw it as requiring his belief, evidenced by
miracles or in some other way. Indeed, any virtuous disposition enables us to see
what is in keeping with the disposition; so faith is an inclination to assent only to
what it is right to believe, and to nothing else. Unbelievers see neither the things that 1.5
believers believe nor their believability. Believers however do see that; they cannot
prove it but see it by the light of faith. Believers prove things from the premises of
faith (the authoritative sources of sacred scripture) in the way everybody proves
things from naturally known premises: as we said at the start of this book, theology
is a science. You can't *know* what you simultaneously hold as an opinion, because
knowledge (like faith) rules out the alternatives which opinion allows to be possible.
You can't *know* what you simultaneously put faith in, because knowledge sees and
faith doesn't.

Creeds articulate the faith of Christians into different *articles* so-called, into 1.6
connected parts. Where things we believe are unseen for different reasons they
constitute separate articles; where many truths are unknowable for the same reason
they join in one article. Thus we distinguish the article of Christ rising from the dead
from the article of his suffering, because it gives rise to different difficulties; but that
he suffered, died and was buried all raise the same difficulty and constitute one
article. The matters essential to faith are those directing us towards eternal life, so it
is these that are articulated in the creeds. Scripture asks us to believe other things,
like Abraham having two sons, but only in order that the essentials of faith should
get revealed, not as if such truths were themselves articles of faith. What makes all
the articles matters of faith is that though we cannot see them God's truth guarantees
them. God's guarantee unites them as objects of faith; our not being able to see
them differentiates them as articles. Articles of faith have the same role in the 1.7
teaching of the faith as self-evident premises in teaching what reason discovers
naturally. And just as such premises are subordinate to one another, some implicit in
others, so the articles of the faith are all implicit in a first belief *that God exists and
rewards those who seek him.* God's existence implicitly includes everything existing
eternally in him and constituting our eternal happiness; God's providence includes
everything God does in time to lead men to that happiness. The reality faith believes
in has never changed, but the number of explicit articles has grown as later believers
have become more explicitly aware of what earlier believers held implicitly. In the
sciences that human reason discovers the knowledge of teachers grow with time; but
when men grow in knowledge of the faith they are learners gradually absorbing over

time what their teacher always knew. God is the eternally knowing agent of revelation, and man is the material acted on, gradually knowing more and more. The last fulfilment of grace came through Jesus Christ: that was *the fullness of time*. So these nearest that time, whether just before like John the Baptist, or just after like the Apostles, knew most fully the mysteries of faith.

1.8   The creed proposes for our faith the hidden depths of the godhead, which we shall see when we enter bliss, and the mystery of Christ's manhood, through which *we enter the glory of the sons of God. This is eternal life: to know you, true God, and Jesus Christ whom you have sent.* Seven articles of faith concern the godhead: God's unity, the three persons in God, and the three works God alone does – creating nature, making us holy by his grace, and raising us to live for ever in his glory. Seven articles concern Christ's manhood: his taking flesh, his birth, his suffering through death to the tomb, his descent into the underworld, his being raised, his ascending into heaven, and his coming in judgment. Knowing the Father involves knowing his Son and their union in the Holy Spirit; and this favours those who talk of one article of faith in all three persons. But because separate errors arose about each person – Arius about the Son,

1.9 Macedonius about the Spirit – three articles became necessary. To extract the truths of faith from sacred scripture requires long study and practice, something not possible for everyone who needs to know such truths; many people are too occupied with other business to find the time for study. So there was a need to make a clear summary of scriptural theses that all could profess. The creed is not added to

1.10 scripture but extracted from it. Gratian's Decretals declare that making new versions of the creed is reserved to the Pope, along with everything else that affects the whole church, like the invoking of general councils, and so on.

2.1   *The act of believing.*   Believing, Augustine says, is giving assent to something one is still thinking about. Strictly speaking, we think about what we cannot yet fully see to be true. Mind sometimes firmly assents to things it is no longer thinking about in this way since it now knows or sees them to be true by self-evidence or proof. At other times it hasn't finished thinking about something so withholds firm assent: leaning towards neither alternative (doubting), or trying out one alternative (suspecting), perhaps accepting it but not firmly (holding an opinion). Believing, however, means putting faith in something, and this resembles knowing in giving firm assent, but resembles doubting, suspecting and holding opinions in having no finished vision of the truth. So we characterize it as assenting to something one is still thinking about. Not that faith is engaged in thinking about something hoping to prove what it believes by reasoned inquiry. Though it does inquire in a way into the credentials of what it believes: whether God said it and confirmed it by miracles. Faith's assent

2.2 is an act of mind not determined by reason but by will. In Augustine's words God is what, who and why we believe, the object of our faith in three different ways. He is what we assent to, the Truth guaranteeing what we assent to, and the goal our will is pursuing when it determines our mind to assent.

2.3   *Without faith we cannot please God.* When one thing is naturally subordinate to another, its perfection consists not only in what it can do on its own but also in what it derives from the higher nature: thus the sea not only moves downwards with

From *Summa Theologiae*

water's natural heaviness, but also moves in and out tidally under the influence of the moon. Now the only nature that relates immediately to God is that of reasoning creatures; they grasp the meaning of good and existence in general and so can relate immediately to the source of existence as such. The perfection of such creatures consists therefore not only in what they can do naturally on their own, but also in what they can do by supernaturally sharing God's own goodness. So man's ultimate happiness consists in a sort of supernatural sight of God, which he must learn from God as from a teacher, step by step as is man's natural way. But, as Aristotle says, *learners, if they are to attain full knowledge, must put faith in their teachers.* So to see God man must first believe him, as students believing a teacher. It is dangerous to assent to things one has no way of verifying; but just as men assent to first premises by a natural light of intelligence, and virtuous men are disposed by their virtue to judge rightly about what is in keeping with that virtue, so believers, by the light of faith divinely instilled into them, assent to what is worthy of faith, and to nothing else. Men must hold by faith many things discoverable by reason if they are to know God 2.4 quickly, generally and surely: for proving things about God presupposes long study in many different fields, many people can't follow such proofs anyway, and men make mistakes whereas God can't be doubted. The truths one person can prove, another must take on faith.

Whoever approaches God must believe that he exists and that he rewards those who seek him. 2.5 The essential matters of faith are those that contribute to men's eternal happiness; whatever else sacred scripture hands down from God (Abraham having two sons) is secondary. Man's obligation to believe obliges him to believe the primary matters of faith – the so-called *articles* – explicitly; but secondary matters only implicitly, by being ready in soul to believe whatever scripture contains. Only when it becomes clear to him that such matters are part of what faith teaches is he obliged to believe them explicitly. We might ask *How can anyone believe in someone he has never heard of? And how can he hear of him without preachers? And what if no preachers are sent?* But men are obliged to do many things that they can do only when healed by grace: they must love God and their fellowmen, and they must believe the articles of faith. They can do these things with the help of grace, which when given is mercifully given, and when withheld is justly withheld as penalty for earlier (if only inherited) sin.

Revelation is handed down from the more knowledgeable to the lesser. The faith 2.6 of the more knowledgeable teachers must be more explicit. The less knowledgeable learners are obliged to believe implicitly whatever their teachers are truly passing on from God, but only that. If some teachers teach falsehood this cannot harm the faith of the simple people who believe them to be teaching truth, unless they stick to the errors of some particular clique in the face of the universal teaching of the church. For that teaching can never fail, the Lord having said *I myself have prayed for you, Peter, that your faith will never fail.*

Man's road to happiness lies in the mystery of Christ's coming in the flesh and 2.7 dying for us: *there is no other name given to men to save us.* So in all periods everyone had to believe this mystery of Christ in some way or another. Adam, before he sinned, had explicit faith in Christ's coming in the flesh as the road to final glory (for Adam and Eve, as St Paul says, were *a great sacred symbol of Christ and his church,* and the first

111

man must surely have known his own sacred significance); but only after sinning could man believe explicitly in the sufferings and resurrection of Christ that were to liberate mankind from sin and death. Because of this faith, sacrifices before and under the Law could prefigure Christ's sufferings, though the reality prefigured was known explicitly only to the leaders, and to others under the veil of sacrificial actions that they believed divinely heralded a coming Messiah. Now that grace has been revealed, all, leaders and led, are obliged to believe explicitly the mysteries of Christ; particularly those articles of Christ's coming in the flesh that are commonly celebrated in the church and publicly preached. Christ was revealed to many pagans too: Job *knows that his redeemer liveth* and the Sibylline oracles (so Augustine says) predicted him. In any case, even people saved without such revelation were saved by faith in God's go-between; for they had implicit faith in God's providence, believing God would deliver men in ways of his own choosing that his Spirit would reveal to some

2.8 knowers of truth. Explicit belief in Christ's coming in the flesh presupposes faith in the three persons: in a son of God taking flesh and renewing the world by the grace of the Holy Spirit through whom he was conceived. We can know God's goodness in his effects without understanding that he is three persons, but not in himself as the blessed in heaven know him. To that blessed happiness we are led by the sending of those three persons.

2.9 *Through faith the blessed did what was right and received what God promised.* All human behaviour freely willed and directed towards God earns a reward, and believing is such behaviour, mentally assenting to God's truth in obedience to a will activated by God's grace. Our natures are like matter that the love of charity (the source of all earning) gives life to; and faith is the final disposition which prepares nature for charity. So neither nature nor faith can earn without charity, but given charity, acts of faith and nature and natural free will all earn. Our assent to what we prove scientifically is forced, not freely willed, and cannot earn; but reflecting about such things is under our control, and when it serves the goal of charity – the honour of God and the well-being of our fellowmen – it can earn a reward. In believing, however, both assent and reflection are freely willed and can earn. Opinions though are assented to only weakly with an undecided will, and that cannot earn much, though actually thinking about them can earn. Believers do not believe frivolously; they have inducement enough to believe: the authority of God's teaching confirmed by miracles and (more importantly) by the inner inspiration of God attracting them. But because the inducement is not enough to prove what is believed, the believers'

2.10 assent can still earn a reward. Human reasons for believing may lead to our act of will or follow from it. They lead to willing when we wouldn't so easily will without them, and then they detract from faith's merit; for just as acts of virtue should be done from judgment rather than passion, so we should believe on the authority of God rather than human reason. On the other hand, the readier our will to believe the more we love what we believe, meditating on its truth and cherishing any reasons for it we discover. So human reasons that follow on faith are an indication of additional merit; just as passion following on virtue indicates greater readiness of will. Reasons supporting faith's authority cannot prove what we believe and remove its unseenness or its meritorious character as faith, but they can remove obstacles to believing. When reason proves certain preliminaries to the articles of faith, those preliminaries are no longer matters of belief but are *seen* to be true. That however doesn't detract from the love of charity which made our will ready to believe them even when they were unseen; so there is no loss of meritoriousness.

We speak externally in order to express our inner thoughts; so since inner belief is 3.1 an act of faith so too is its external profession, just as professing thanks and praise is an act of worship, and confessing sins an act of repentance. All external virtuous behaviour is the work of our inner faith working through love, commanding other virtues to evoke that behaviour rather than evoking it itself; professing the faith is faith's own external act, unmediated by any other virtue. [What precepts prohibit we 3.2 must never do;] what they positively command we need not always do, but only when circumstances make the act a virtuous one. So professing the faith always and everywhere is not necessary for salvation, but only when omitting to do so would jeopardize God's honour or our fellowmen's well-being.

The disposition to believe — faith. *Faith is the substance of what we hope for, the evidence of* 4.1 *what we cannot see*, says the letter to the Hebrews. Faith is a disposition we characterize by the activity of believing it disposes us to, and that activity we characterize by the object believed in. Now believing is an assent of mind commanded by will, so faith's activity relates to its object both as to a good willingly pursued and as to a truth mentally assented to. Moreover, being a theological virtue in which goal and object are identical, the way the object is faith's goal will correspond to the way it is its object. Now faith's object is unseen Truth itself and whatever else we assent to because of that Truth. So faith's goal is also Truth itself as unseen, that is to say, as still unachieved yet hoped for. So Hebrews express the way faith relates to Truth as goal, the object willed, by saying *Faith is the substance*, or seed, *of what we hope for*, since what we hope for is to see openly the Truth we already assent to by faith. And the epistle expresses the way faith relates to Truth as object of the mind by calling faith *the evidence*, or conviction, *of what we cannot see*. Throwing this into the form of a definition, we could say that faith is the mental disposition through which eternal life starts up in us, causing our mind to assent to what it does not see. Calling faith *conviction* distinguishes it from opinion, suspicion and doubt; saying it is *of things unseen* distinguishes it from both proven and self-evident knowledge; and calling it *the substance of things hoped for* distinguishes it from all faith unrelated to our hoped-for happiness.

Believing is an act of mental assent commanded by will, perfected by dispositions 4.2 both of will and of mind; but since its object is truth (the object of mind) believing is more immediately an activity of mind and the disposition proper to it — faith — disposes our mind. For the will to be disposed to obey would not be enough unless the mind was ready to follow the will's command; so we need a strengthening disposition not only in the will commanding, but in the mind assenting. Every 4.3 voluntary act is given life, so to speak, by the goal it serves; that goal determines its species and mode of activity. Now the goal of faith is the good God himself, the object defining the love we call charity. So charity gives life to faith, perfecting and enlivening faith's activity. Faith as such is a perfection of mind and what defines 4.4

113

faith is its relation to mind; its relation to will does not define it and cannot be used to differentiate types of faith. Now the distinction of faith as living or lifeless relates to the will and the love of charity; so this distinction doesn't differentiate two

4.5 dispositions. Only dispositions that dispose us always to act well are human virtues, and living faith is such a disposition. Believing is an act of mental assent commanded by will, and to believe perfectly our mind must tend unfailingly towards the perfection of truth, in unfailing service of that ultimate goal for the sake of which our will is commanding our mind's assent. Both elements are present in living faith: as faith it sets the mind always on course to truth, and as living by the love of charity it sets the will always on course to a good goal. But lifeless faith is no virtue: it has the perfection needed on the part of the mind but not the perfection needed on the part of the will. And faith that does not rely on divine truth can fail and believe falsehood, so such faith is also no virtue.

4.7 The goal is the first thing in behaviour, so theological virtues, which have our ultimate goal as their object, precede other virtues. And since we must have our ultimate goal in mind before we can will it (for we can only will what we perceive), faith must precede hope and love, making it the first of all virtues. Natural knowledge can't substitute, since it can't embrace God as source of our ultimate happiness, which is the way we hope for him and love him. We cannot, for example, hope for eternal happiness unless we believe it possible; what is impossible can't be hoped for. A building's foundation, however, is not only its beginning but that to which all its parts are made fast. Now what ties the whole spiritual building together is charity: *above all things have love, which is the bond of perfection.* So without charity faith can't be a foundation, though that doesn't mean charity precedes faith. Faith presupposes an act of will but not necessarily an act of charity; but acts of charity presuppose faith, since will cannot tend to God in perfect love unless the mind has a right faith about

4.8 him. Two virtues of mind are concerned with variable and uncertain events, namely prudence and technical skill. Faith has greater certainty than these since its matter is eternal and invariant. Three other mental virtues are also concerned with the invariant: wisdom, scientific knowledge, and understanding. Now if we judge certainty by its cause, faith which relies on divine truth is more certain than these three which rely on human reason. If however we judge certainty by the degree to which the mind takes hold of what it knows, then faith is less certain since it deals with things beyond the mind's grasp. But it is the cause which matters, simply speaking, so faith has the greater certainty simply speaking though not in regard to our grasp of it. Other things being equal sight is more certain than hearing; but if the person one is listening to can see more, then hearing gives the better certainty. So what we hear from God, who cannot be mistaken, is much more certain than what we see by reason, which makes mistakes.

5.1 Believers assent to what they believe not because their minds see it to be true, either directly or by reduction to self-evident premises, but because their wills command their minds to assent. And this is either because believing is willed as a good (the way Christians believe) or because the mind, though not seeing what it believes, is somehow convinced of its truth: and this is the way the devil assents, seeing clearly that the teaching of the church comes from God, though not seeing the realities taught: the three persons, for example. The devil's faith is forced from him by the evidence of signs. Faith given by grace inclines men to believe from love (even if not always the love of charity); but the devil is not inclined by grace but forced to believe by his natural intelligence of mind. Heretics who disbelieve one 5.3 article of faith lose all faith, living and lifeless. For what makes something a matter of faith is God's truth revealed in sacred scripture and the church's teaching. So whoever does not adopt the church's teaching, derived from the truth revealed in scripture, as an infallible and divine rule, doesn't have the disposition of faith, but is holding matters of faith in some other way than by faith. Because he picks and chooses from the church's teaching what he takes as his infallible rule is his own will. When such a person is not stubborn he is not a heretic but only mistaken; but a heretic who stubbornly disbelieves one article clearly doesn't have faith in the others, but is only following his own wilful opinion.

Truth itself, one and simple, defines what are matters of faith, and from that point 5.4 of view we all have one faith. But since matters of faith can be held more or less explicitly, one man's faith can be more explicit than another's. And also deeper: either because his mind assents more firmly and certainly, or because his will has a more ready devotion and trust.

If it is to be explicit, faith needs matters of belief to be proposed to it, which it 6.1 can then assent to. Clearly the proposing must come from God: to apostles and prophets immediately, and to others by *preachers sent* from God. But as to the assent, all external inducements and persuasions of men and witness of miracles are insufficient, for faced with such things some believe and some don't. So there has to be some other inner cause moving us to assent, which Pelagians held to be our own free will. We begin our faith, they said, by being ready to assent, and God completes it by proposing to us what we should believe. But that is a mistake. To assent to matters of faith is something surpassing our natures, and requires supernatural interior stimulus from God. So our assent, the chief act of faith, is an interior movement of God's grace. Even lifeless faith is essentially faith, so God is its only cause too.

Knowing and understanding the faith. Understanding implies depth of knowledge, 8.1 penetrating under the surface. Thus, though our senses perceive the outer qualities of things, we need understanding to penetrate what those things are. However, there are many ways of being *under*: the essences of things underlie their outer supervening qualities, meanings underlie words used to express them, truth lies behind images and figures, spiritual realities behind the things we sense, effects lie hidden in their causes; and in all these cases penetrating beyond the surface is called *understanding.* Our natural light of understanding has limited powers of penetration, however, so we require a supernatural light to penetrate further; and this is appropriately called the *the gift of understanding.* Reasoning is a process that starts from something we already understand and leads to the understanding of something new; but grace doesn't issue from natural understanding but adds to it perfecting it. So such an addition is better called understanding than reason, its relation to what we know supernaturally being the same as that of our natural understanding to the

8.3 fundamentals of our knowledge. It shows the worth of the gift of understanding that it penetrates eternal realities not only in themselves, but as setting the standard for human behaviour. Human reason and eternal law both set us such standards, but eternal law so surpasses human reason that its understanding requires the supernatu-

8.4 ral light of a gift of the Holy Spirit. The Holy Spirit by the gift of charity disposes our wills directly to intend supernatural good, and by his gift of understanding enlightens our minds to know the supernatural truth on which our good will must be intent. Not all believers fully understand what is proposed for their belief, but

8.5 they must at least understand that it is to be believed and never abandoned. Such enlightenment of the mind is called a gift of the Holy Spirit because it makes our mind responsive to the Spirit's stimulus, rightly appreciative of our ultimate goal, making no mistakes about it, and cleaving firmly to it as our greatest good. This needs grace-that-makes-pleasing, just as dispositions of virtue are needed to jduge our moral goals rightly. Faith implies only assent to what is believed, but understanding adds a certain perception of truth, which we cannot have about our ultimate goal

8.6 unless we have grace-that-makes-pleasing. We need to respond to what we believe in two ways: to grasp or penetrate it soundly with our mind we need the gift of understanding; to judge rightly what to accept and what to shun we need the gifts of wisdom (in divine matters), knowledge (in creaturely), and counsel (when applying judgment to particular actions).

9.1   We need *the gift of knowledge* to enable us to discern rightly and surely what and what not to believe. Man's knowledge comes by reasoning and proof, but God's by simple insight, and the Holy Spirit's gift is a shared likeness in God's knowledge. All people with grace-that-makes-pleasing share this gift of knowing what is and what is not to be believed. But not all have the grace-freely-given (also called knowledge) which would enable them not only to know what to believe, but also how to witness

9.2 and preach and argue it. When a class of objects includes one more perfect than the rest that object is often given a special name while the rest are known by the common name of the class. Thus in logic one of the characterizing attributes proper to a thing actually states what it is and is specially called its definition; whilst the rest are collectively known as its characteristic properties. Similarly, all knowledge implies certainty, but, when the certainty is based on the deepest possible grounds and causes, we give the knowledge the special name of wisdom: so knowledge of divine things is called wisdom, and all knowledge of human things shares the more general term of knowledge. Wisdom knows – by a kind of unity with them – the actual things in which we believe, and so corresponds to the virtue which unites us to God – charity. But knowing how and what to believe is knowing something temporal about the human mind, [so corresponds to faith]. Every cognitive disposition is a disposition to know certain things by way of something that makes them knowable, and this latter is what decides the type of that disposition. Thus sciences which prove truths about natural things by mathematical arguments are more akin to mathematics than to natural philosophy. In the same way, knowing God through creatures is more knowledge than wisdom, whilst judging creatures in God's light is

9.3 more wisdom than knowledge. Faith is first and foremost a fidelity to truth, indeed to Truth himself; but since Truth himself is the ultimate goal of our activities faith also directs our behaviour. In the same way the gift of knowledge first and foremost tells us what we should believe but secondarily directs our behaviour. Only when our judgments about what should be believed and done come from instilled grace are we said to have the gift of knowledge.

Disbelief. Disbelief in the strict sense is an opposition to faith, resisting it and even 10.1 despising listening to it; so it is a sin. But disbelief as sheer absence of belief because we haven't heard about it is not so much a sin as a penalty consequent on Adam's sin. And if men who lack faith in this sense are lost, that is because of other sins that cannot be forgiven without faith, rather than because their disbelief is sinful. Strict disbelief, like faith, is a disposition of mind under the influence of will. It 10.2 distances us from God by depriving us of true knowledge of him, and as such is a 10.3 greater sin than any moral wrongdoing, though not than wrong against the other theological virtues. There are several types of disbelief: pagans resist a faith they have 10.5 never accepted, Jews a faith they accept in figure, and heretics a faith that was clearly revealed to them. But there are numberless mistaken positions contrary to the faith. What makes a sin the type of sin it is is what the sinner intends; but what makes it evil and a sin at all is the good it rejects, which does not so much decide the sin's type as deprive it of all type. So, though faith is a single virtue unified by adherence to the one Truth himself, there are as many types of disbelief as there are false opinions to follow. Disbelief of heretics, who resist and distort a gospel they once 10.6 professed, is a worse sin than the disbelief of Jews who never accepted it; but because Jews accept the gospel faith in figure in the Old Testament, but distort it by bad interpretation, their disbelief is worse than that of pagans who have never accepted the gospel at all. Nevertheless pagans are more mistaken than Jews, and they than heretics: except perhaps for the Manichean heresy which is more mistaken about the faith than even pagans are.

When arguing about the faith we should remember two things: our intention in 10.7 arguing and the danger to those listening. If genuine doubt leads us to test out the faith with argument, this is clearly a sin of disbelief; but arguing to repel error, or even as an exercise, can be praised. As to those listening, there is no danger if they are firmly educated in the faith, but uneducated listeners with an unstable faith should not be disturbed by argument unless they live where they are already bothered and attacked by disbelievers distorting the faith, in which case people suitably trained for the job should publicly argue for the faith before them.

In Luke we are told: *Go out into the country roads and lanes and compel people to come in,* 10.8 *that my house may be full.* So some people are to be compelled to believe and enter the church. But only people who had once accepted the faith: pagans and Jews can't be forced to believe, since believing is a matter of will. The faithful, if they have the power, may use it to stop such disbelievers hindering the faith by blasphemy or propaganda or openly persecuting it. This is the reason Christians frequently wage war on disbelievers: not to force them to believe (because even if conquered and held captive they must be left their freedom to believe or not as they will), but to stop them hindering the faith. However, disbelievers who once accepted and professed the faith – heretics and apostates – can be compelled, even physically, to fulfil their promises and hold to what they once professed. For even though making a vow is a voluntary matter, keeping it is an obligation. So adopting the faith is voluntary, but sticking to it once adopted is obligatory. As Augustine says, *none of us would want a heretic to die. But the house of David could not have had peace if Absalom had not died in the war he waged against his father. And in the same way, if the catholic church loses some in gathering others, freeing the many heals the wound in her maternal heart.*

10.9   The faithful are forbidden communication with certain persons partly to punish those persons and partly to safeguard the faithful. The church therefore visits the penalty of excommunication on heretics and apostates, but not on disbelievers who have never accepted the Christian faith – Jews and pagans – since over them she has no spiritual jurisdiction, and temporal jurisdiction only if they live in a Christian community and when in fault are punishable by Christians. But as regards the safety of the faithful: if their faith is strong enough one can hope more for conversion of the disbelievers than subversion of believers, and in this case the faithful should not be forbidden communication with Jews or pagans. But if the faithful are weak and uneducated they should be forbidden such communication, especially in intimate or unnecessary ways.

10.10   Authority is instituted by human law, but believers and disbelievers are distinguished by God's law. Since the law of grace does not abrogate human law based on reason, being believers does not as such exempt us from the already established authority of disbelievers. The church, however, does have God's authority to take authority away from disbelievers, since their disbelief makes them unworthy to exercise power over believers, who have become sons of God. And sometimes the church exercises this right, sometimes not. As regards disbelievers subject to the temporal authority of the church or its members, church law states that slaves of Jews must be freed immediately on becoming Christians, with no ransom paid if they were born slaves or sold into slavery. But if in the market they must be offered for ransom within three months. The church has the right to dispose of the Jew's goods since he is subject to the church. And secular princes have enacted similar laws for their own subjects, favouring freedom. But as regards disbelievers not subject to the church's temporal authority the church – in order to avoid scandal – has made no such law, though it has the right to. The church permits Christians to work Jewish lands, because that doesn't involve living together; but if such contact did hold dangers for the faith of Christians it would be altogether forbidden.

10.11   God, despite his omnipotence and supreme goodness, allows evils he could prevent to exist in the world, if removing them would cause greater goods to be lost or greater evils to ensue. So human rulers may also tolerate some evils for the same reasons; *forbid prostitution*, says Augustine, *and lust will turn everything upside down.* The religious rites of disbelievers, though sinful, can be tolerated if doing so brings good and avoids evil.

10.12   The greatest authority of all is church tradition, which should always be jealously observed. Even the teaching of the great Catholic theologians gets its authority from the church, the authority of which is greater than that of Augustine or Jerome or any other thinker. Now it has never been the church's custom to baptize Jewish children without their parents' permission; though in past ages many powerful Catholic princes with holy bishops as their friends – Constantius with Sylvester, Theodosius with Ambrose – would surely have claimed authority to do it if they had thought they reasonably could. But it is a practice dangerous to the faith, for when the children grow up their parents will easily persuade them to abandon what they unknowingly received. And it is also repugnant to natural justice, since children belong by nature to their parents, and to remove them from their parents' care or arrange things against their parents' wishes while the children are still without use of their own reasons is an offence against natural justice. When children start to use their own free will they begin to belong to themselves, and then they can be brought to believe – but by persuasion, not by coercion – and be baptized without their parents' permission. People married to each other have free will, so can assent to the faith without each other's permission.

Heresy.   People deviate from the straight path of the Christian faith in two ways: 11.1
pagans and Jews, by being unwilling to assent to Christ, get the goal wrong; heretics, however, intend to assent to Christ but make a wrong choice of what to assent to, choosing what their own mind proposes rather than what Christ handed down. Canon law quotes Augustine: *However false and perverse people's opinions are, we mustn't* 11.2
accuse them of heresy when they aren't stubborn in those opinions, but seek truth with anxious care and when they find it are ready to change their minds. Such people are not choosing to contradict the teaching of the church. Even doctors of the church have disagreed about matters of no consequence to the faith or not yet decided by the church; but when such matters are decided by the authority of the universal church (vested principally in the Pope) anyone who stubbornly resists the decision must be adjudged a heretic. About heretics there are two things to say. Their sin deserves 11.3
banishment not only from the church by excommunication but also from the world by death. But the church seeks with mercy to turn back those who go astray, and condemns them not immediately but only *after a first or second warning.* If, however, a heretic remains stubborn, the church, despairing of his conversion, takes care of the salvation of others, separates the heretic from the church with a sentence of excommunication, and delivers him to the secular courts to be removed from the world by death. The church, as the Lord commands, extends her charity to all, 11.4
willing good to her enemies and persecutors as well as her friends. But there is spiritual good and temporal good. Spiritual good is the soul's salvation, the main objective of charity; so heretics who return, no matter how often they have fallen away, are readmitted to repentance, the way to salvation. But temporal goods are things like bodily life, worldly possessions, reputation, and ecclesiastical or civil position. Charity does not oblige us to will such things for others unless that serves their, and others', eternal salvation. Now were heretics so received on their return that they kept life and temporal possessions, this might prejudice the salvation of others; and so the church admits them to repentance and to life the first time, and sometimes by dispensation to their ecclesiastical positions, should their conversion appear sincere. Often this is done for the sake of peace. But if they lapse again, on their second return they are admitted to repentance but not delivered from sentence

of death. God can read the heart and knows those genuinely returning and always receives them. But the church is not able to imitate this, and presumes that those who lapse a second time did not genuinely return. So though it does not deny them the way to salvation, it does not save them from death. Our Lord told Peter we should forgive *seventy times seven times* – meaning always – offences committed against ourselves; but that does not mean we are free to forgive offences against God and our fellowmen: there the law sets the standard, taking into account God's honour and our fellowmen's well-being.

12.1 *Apostasy.* Men can turn their backs on God by forsaking religious or clerical vows, or by rebelling against his commandments, while remaining united to him by faith. But if they forsake faith then they turn from God altogether. So apostasy in an unqualified sense means forsaking the faith. It is not a special type of disbelief but
12.2 an aggravating circumstance of it. Being disbelievers does not of itself deprive men of authority to rule, for that is a right recognized by human law, whereas believing or not believing is a distinction made by God's law which does not abrogate human law. But disbelievers can be deposed for disbelief just as for other crimes. It is not the church's job to punish the disbelief of those who have never believed, but she can pass sentence on those who once believed and as a suitable punishment depose them from ruling over believers. Excommunication for apostasy from the faith automatically releases a ruler's subjects from his authority and from their oaths of allegiance to him. In her early days the church wasn't yet able to suppress earthly rulers, so, to avoid greater dangers to the faith, allowed believers to obey Julian the Apostate in matters not contrary to faith.

13.1 *Blasphemy.* Blasphemy is vilification of God's excellence and goodness. Whoever denies truth or affirms untruth of God vilifies his goodness; sometimes accompanying his false opinion with hatred (as contrariwise love perfects faith), and sometimes
13.2 adding blasphemy by mouth to blasphemy in the heart. Of its nature vilification of God's goodness is a fatal sin irreconcible with God's love it cuts us off from that love, the first source of spiritual life. But blasphemy can burst out thoughtlessly. Sometimes we don't even realize what we are saying, because passion breaks out in words we haven't yet weighed in our minds: and this is non-fatal sin and not really blasphemy. But sometimes we know what we're saying, and then thoughtlessness no more excuses a blasphemer from fatal sin than it does a man who in a fit of anger
13.3 kills the man sitting next to him. The gravity of a fault depends more on wicked intention than on the deed's actual outcome, so that blasphemy which intends to harm God's honour is graver, simply speaking, than murder, the gravest sin against
13.4 our fellowmen. The hatred of the damned for God's justice is an innner blasphemy of the heart, but after the resurrection it will probably break out in words just as the blessed in heaven will praise God with their voices.

. . . .

2a2ae.81.1 *Religion.* Religion consists in performing services and rites in honour of a superior
81.2 nature called divine. *Virtues make men and their actions good.* Since paying our debts is

good, religion, which pays our debt of honour to God, is a virtue. Where there is a 81.4 special kind of good we need a special virtue. Now honour is owed to people of excellence and God's excellence is unparalleled, so religion must pay him special honour and be a special virtue. Everything we do, if done to the glory of God, is an action subject to the command of religion, even if not primarily an exercise of religion. For only those deeds are primary exercises of religion which are defined as acts of reverence for God. Love loves the good; reverence honours the excellent. God's goodness he shares with his creatures, but the excellence of that goodness is his alone. So the charity with which we love God is the charity with which we love our fellowmen; but religion, which honours God, is distinct from the virtues which honour our fellowmen.

Religion offers to God honour owed to him. But acts done in God's honour 81.5 don't embrace God in the way acts of faith do. God is the object of our faith: not only what we believe but also the person in whom we believe, the person we put our faith in. But God is only the goal of religion, and its matter or object is the acts of service, sacrifices and offerings we make to show him reverence. Religion is not a theological virtue like faith, hope and charity taking our ultimate goal as its object, but a moral virtue concerned with actions that serve that goal. The acts of theological virtues have God as their proper object, and employ religion as an instrument, directing its acts to God. That is what Augustine means by saying *we honour God through faith, hope and charity*. Religion in itself is a moral virtue, allied to justice, seeking out not a balance of emotions but an equality of actions directed to God. The equality is not absolute since we cannot give God as much honour as we ought, but only as much as is possible to us and acceptable to him. We can't offer God more honour than he warrants, but the honour we offer can be excessive and unbalanced in other ways: shown to false gods or at the wrong time. Moral 81.6 virtues are concerned with everything done to serve our ultimate goal, which is God. Religion approaches God more closely than other moral virtues, since what it does directly and immediately honours God. So religion is the greatest of the moral virtues.

We show God reverence not for his benefit, since creatures can add nothing to 81.7 the fullness of glory he already has in himself; we do it for our benefit, so as to subject our spirit to him and perfect it. Every creature gains perfection by subjecting itself to higher ones: the body gets life from the soul, and the air light from the sun. The minds needs leading to unity with God by way of the world we sense, and in the service of God this means using bodily things as symbols and signs, to arouse our mind to the spiritual acts that unite it to God. So there are interior acts of religion (and in these religion primarily consists), and secondary external acts subordinate to the interior ones. Not only men but also things like churches and 81.8 sacred vessels are said to be made holy by being devoted to God's honour. Man's holiness consists in devoting himself and his actions to God, and doesn't differ essentially from religion. We call it religion when it offers God the service owed him in ways specially adapted to honouring him: things like sacrifices, offerings and suchlike; we call the same virtue holiness when it offers to God not only such works but every work of virtue, or when man disposes himself to honour God by doing virtuous works. In essence holiness is a special virtue, that of religion, but it can embrace virtue in general in so far as it directs the actions of all other virtues to the divine good in the way legal or general justice directs them all to the general good.

6

Boniface VIII, "Unam Sanctam"

In 1302, Pope Boniface VIII issued a famous official edict or decree, known as a "bull" in the Roman Catholic Church, the first Latin words and title of which are "Unam Sanctam" ("One Holy"). Embroiled in a political struggle with King Philip IV of France, the Pope in this bull declares the supreme ultimate authority of his office in both earthly and spiritual matters. Submitting to the authority of the Pope is furthermore declared to be a requirement for salvation, for there is no salvation outside the "one holy Catholic and apostolic Church," of which the Pope is the one head. "Unam Sanctam" thus stands out to this day as a famous declaration of the principle that there is no salvation outside the Church – understood in this context as the Roman Catholic Church.

The Text

We are compelled, our faith urging us, to believe and to hold – and we do firmly
believe and simply confess – that there is only holy Catholic and apostolic Church,
outside of which there is neither salvation nor remission of sins; her Spouse
proclaiming it in the canticles: "My dove, my undefiled, is but one, she is the choice
one of her that bare her"; which represents one mystic body, of which body the
head is Christ; but of Christ, God. In this church there is one Lord, one faith and
one baptism. There was one ark of Noah, indeed, at the time of the flood,
symbolizing one church; and this being finished in one cubit had, namely, one Noah
as helmsman and commander. And, with the exception of this ark, all things existing
upon the earth were, as we read, destroyed. This church, moreover, we venerate as
the only one, the Lord saying through His prophet: "Deliver my soul from the
sword, my darling from the power of the dog." He prayed at the same time for His
soul – that is, for Himself the Head – and for His body, – which body, namely, he
called the one and only church on account of the unity of the faith promised, of the
sacraments, and of the love of the church. She is that seamless garment of the Lord
which was not cut but which fell by lot. Therefore of this one and only church there
is one body and one head – not two heads as if it were a monster: – Christ, namely,
and the vicar of Christ, St Peter, and the successor of Peter. For the Lord Himself
said to Peter, Feed my sheep. My sheep, He said, using a general term, and not
designating these or those particular sheep; from which it is plain that He committed
to Him *all* His sheep. If, then, the Greeks or others say that they were not committed
to the care of Peter and his successors, they necessarily confess that they are not of
the sheep of Christ; for the Lord says, in John, that there is one fold, one shepherd
and one only. We are told by the word of the gospel that in this His fold there are
two swords, – a spiritual, namely, and a temporal. For when the apostles said
"Behold here are two swords" – when, namely, the apostles were speaking in the
church – the Lord did not reply that this was too much, but enough. Surely he who
denies that the temporal sword is in the power of Peter wrongly interprets the word
of the Lord when He says: "Put up thy sword in its scabbard." Both swords, the
spiritual and the material, therefore, are in the power of the church; the one, indeed,
to be wielded for the church, the other by the church; the one by the hand of the
priest, the other by the hand of kings and knights, but at the will and sufferance of
the priest. One sword, moreover, ought to be under the other, and the temporal
authority to be subjected to the spiritual. For when the apostle says "there is no
power but of God," and the powers that are of God are ordained, they would not
be ordained unless sword were under sword and the lesser one, as it were, were led
by the other to great deeds. For according to St Dionysius the law of the divinity is
to lead the lowest through the intermediate to the highest things. Not therefore
according to the law of the universe, are all things reduced to order equally and

Source: *The Papal Encyclicals In Their Historical Context*, ed. Anne Freemantle.

immediately; but the lowest through the intermediate, the intermediate through the higher. But that the spiritual exceeds any earthly power in dignity and nobility we ought the more openly to confess the more spiritual things excel temporal ones. This also is made plain to our eyes from the giving of tithes, and the benediction and the sanctification; from the acceptation of this same power, from the control over those same things. For, the truth bearing witness, the spiritual power has to establish the earthly power, and to judge it if it be not good. Thus concerning the church and the ecclesiastical power is verified the prophecy of Jeremiah: "See, I have this day set thee over the nations and over the kingdoms," and the other things which follow. Therefore if the earthly power err it shall be judged by the spiritual power; but if the lesser spiritual power err, by the greater. But if the greatest, it can be judged by God alone, not by man, the apostle bearing witness. A spiritual man judges all things, but he himself is judged by no one. This authority, moreover, even though it is given to man and exercised through man, is not human but rather divine, being given by divine lips to Peter, and founded on a rock for him and his successors through Christ himself whom he has confessed, the Lord himself, saying to Peter "Whatsoever thou shalt bind," etc. Whoever, therefore, resists this power thus ordained by God, resists the ordination of God, unless he makes believe, like the Manichaean, that there are two beginnings. This we consider false and heretical, since by the testimony of Moses not "in the beginnings" but "in the beginning" God created the Heaven and the earth. Indeed we declare, announce and define, that it is altogether necessary to salvation for every human creature to be subject to the Roman pontiff. *The Lateran, November 14, in our 8th year.* As a perpetual memorial of this matter.

Part IV

Renaissance and Reformation Texts

(*c*.1350–*c*.1600)

7

Martin Luther, "Preface to the Complete Edition of Luther's Latin Writings"

Born in 1483, Martin Luther studied at the University of Erfurt in preparation for a legal career. As a result of a dramatic series of events in his life, he chose instead to join the Augustinian monastery at Erfurt and pursue the study of theology. There he wrestled with the question of justification, vexed by how he could claim divine mercy and grace rather than fall subject to divine justice and wrath. Unsure of the sacramental solution to his dilemma provided by the Roman Church of the day, Luther continued to struggle with the question of justification. He went on to teach Bible and theology at the universities of Erfurt and Wittenberg. In his early thirties, in Wittenberg, he had a conversion experience in which he came to understand that divine righteousness is based on grace alone – an idea which would become central to the imminent Protestant Reformation. Armed with this new understanding of the gospel, Luther could not but protest Johann Tetzel's preaching about indulgences, in which the papal emissary promised forgiveness of sins in addition to release from temporal punishment for wrongdoing. Luther's Ninety-Five Theses of 1517, written for the purpose of starting a debate about the theology of indulgences, were published and launched the protest against Rome which dominated sixteenth-century Western Christianity. Luther subsequently entered the arena of conflict and debate with Rome. His understanding of how the gospel and grace free believers from the law and incorrect views of works came to expression in his 1520 open letter to Pope Leo X entitled "The Freedom of a Christian." His words at the Diet of Worms in 1521, in which he argued that ultimate authority is found in Scripture and not in popes or councils, represent one of the foundational teachings of

Protestantism. Luther was excommunicated from the Roman Catholic Church. He died in 1546.

In the "Preface to the Complete Edition of Luther's Latin Writings," written very near the end of his life, the greatest figure in the sixteenth-century Reformation ruminates about his life, his struggles, his conversion experience, and his new understanding of St Paul's teaching concerning divine righteousness: humanity cannot justify or save itself, but is instead justified and saved by grace, by the gift of faith.

In the text which follows, footnotes in the source edition have been eliminated.

The Text

Martin Luther wishes the sincere reader salvation!

For a long time I strenuously resisted those who wanted my books, or more correctly my confused lucubrations, published. I did not want the labors of the ancients to be buried by my new works and the reader kept from reading them. Then, too, by God's grace a great many systematic books now exist, among which the *Loci communes* of Philip excel, with which a theologian and a bishop can be beautifully and abundantly prepared to be mighty in preaching the doctrine of piety, especially since the Holy Bible itself can now be had in nearly every lanaguage. But my books, as it happened, yes, as the lack of order in which the events transpired made it necessary, are accordingly crude and disordered chaos, which is now not easy to arrange even for me.

Persuaded by these reasons, I wished that all my books were buried in perpetual oblivion, so that there might be room for better ones. But the boldness and bothersome perseverance of others daily filled my ears with complaints that it would come to pass, that if I did not permit their publication in my lifetime, men wholly ignorant of the causes and the time of the events would nevertheless most certainly publish them, and so out of one confusion many would arise. Their boldness, I say, prevailed and so I permitted them to be published. At the same time the wish and command of our most illustrious Prince, Elector, etc., John Frederick was added. He commanded, yes, compelled the printers not only to print, but to speed up the publication.

But above all else, I beg the sincere reader, and I beg for the sake of our Lord Jesus Christ himself, to read those things judiciously, yes, with great commiseration. May he be mindful of the fact that I was once a monk and a most enthusiastic papist when I began that cause. I was so drunk, yes, submerged in the pope's dogmas, that I would have been ready to murder all, if I could have, or to co-operate willingly with the murderers of all who would take but a syllable from obedience to the pope. So great a Saul was I, as are many to this day. I was not such a lump of frigid ice in defending the papacy as Eck and his like were, who appeared to me actually to defend the pope more for their own belly's sake than to pursue the matter seriously. To me, indeed, they seem to laugh at the pope to this day, like Epicureans! I pursued the matter with all seriousness, as one, who in dread of the last day, nevertheless from the depth of my heart wanted to be saved.

So you will find how much and what important matters I humbly conceded to the pope in my earlier writings, which I later and now hold and execrate as the worst blasphemies and abomination. You will, therefore, sincere reader, ascribe this error, or, as they slander, contradiction, to the time and my inexperience. At first I was all alone and certainly very inept and unskilled at conducting such great affairs. For I

Source: *Martin Luther: Selections from His Writings*, ed. John Dillenberger.

got into these turmoils by accident and not by will or intention. I call upon God himself as witness.

Hence, when in the year 1517 indulgences were sold (I wanted to say promoted) in these regions for most shameful gain – I was then a preacher, a young doctor of theology, so to speak – and I began to dissuade the people and to urge them not to listen to the clamors of the indulgence hawkers; they had better things to do. I certainly thought that in this case I should have a protector in the pope, on whose trustworthiness I then leaned strongly, for in his decrees he most clearly damned the immoderation of the quaestors, as he called the indulgence preachers.

Soon afterward I wrote two letters, one to Albrecht, the archbishop of Mainz, who got half of the money from the indulgences, the pope the other half – something I did not know at the time – the other to the ordinary (as they call them) Jerome, the bishop of Brandenburg. I begged them to stop the shameless blasphemy of the quaestors. But the poor little brother was despised. Despised, I published the *Theses* and at the same time a German *Sermon on Indulgences*, shortly therafter also the *Explanations*, in which, to the pope's honor, I developed the idea that indulgences should indeed not be condemned, but that good works of love should be preferred to them.

This was demolishing heaven and consuming the earth with fire. I am accused by the pope, am cited to Rome, and the whole papacy rises up against me alone. All this happened in the year 1518, when Maximilian held the diet at Augsburg. In it, Cardinal Cajetan served as the pope's Lateran legate. The most illustrious Duke Frederick of Saxony, Elector Prince, approached him on my behalf and brought it about that I was not compelled to go to Rome, but that he himself should summon me to examine and compose the matter. Soon the diet adjourned.

The Germans in the meantime, all tired of suffering the pillagings, traffickings, and endless impostures of Roman rascals, awaited with bated breath the outcome of so great a matter, which no one before, neither bishop nor theologian, had dared to touch. In any case that popular breeze favored me, because those practices and "Romanations," with which they had filled and tired the whole earth, were already hateful to all.

So I came to Augsburg, afoot and poor, supplied with food and letters of commendation from Prince Frederick to the senate and to certain good men. I was there three days before I went to the cardinal, though he cited me day by day through a certain orator, for those excellent men forbade and dissuaded me most strenuously, not to go to the cardinal without a safe conduct from the emperor. The orator was rather troublesome to me, urging that if I should only revoke, everything would be all right! But as great as the wrong, so long is the detour to its correction.

Finally, on the third day he came demanding to know why I did not come to the cardinal, who expected me most benignly. I replied that I had to respect the advice of those very fine men to whom I had been commended by Prince Frederick, but it was their advice by no means to go to the cardinal without the emperor's protection or safe conduct. Having obtained this (but they took action on the part of the imperial senate to obtain it), I would come at once. At this point he blew up. "What?" he said, "Do you suppose Prince Frederick will take up arms for your sake?" I said, "This I do not at all desire." "And where will you stay?" I replied, "Under heaven." Then he, "If you had the pope and the cardinals in your power, what would you do?" "I would," said I, "show them all respect and honor." Thereupon he, wagging his finger with an Italian gesture, said, "Hem!" And so he left, nor did he return.

On that day the imperial senate informed the cardinal that the emperor's protection or a safe conduct had been granted me and admonished him that he should not design anything too severe against me. He is said to have replied, "It is well. I shall nevertheless do whatever my duty demands." These things were the start of that tumult. The rest can be learned from the accounts included later.

Master Philip Melanchthon had already been called here that same year by Prince Frederick to teach Greek literature, doubtless so that I should have an associate in the work of theology. His works attest sufficiently what the Lord has performed through this instrument, not only in literature but also in theology, though Satan is mad and all his adherents.

Maximilian died, in the following year, '19, in February, and according to the law of the empire Duke Frederick was made deputy. Thereupon the storm ceased to rage a bit, and gradually contempt of excommunication or papal thunderbolts arose. For when Eck and Caraccioli brought a bull from Rome condemning Luther and revealed it, the former here, the latter there to Duke Frederick, who was at Cologne at the time together with other princes in order to meet Charles who had been recently elected, Frederick was most indignant. He reproved that papal rascal with great courage and constancy, because in his absence he and Eck had disturbed his and his brother John's dominion. He jarred them so magnificently that they left him in shame and disgrace. The prince, endowed with incredible insight, caught on to the devices of the Roman Curia and knew how to deal with them in a becoming manner, for he had a keen nose and smelled more and farther than the Romanists could hope or fear.

Hence they refrained from putting him to a test. For he did not dignify with the least respect the Rose, which they call "golden," sent him that same year by Leo X, indeed ridiculed it. So the Romanists were forced to despair of their attempts to deceive so great a prince. The gospel advanced happily under the shadow of that prince and was widely propagated. His authority influenced very many, for since he was a very wise and most keen-sighted prince, he could incur the suspicion only among the hateful that he wanted to nourish and protect heresy and heretics. This did the papacy great harm.

That same year the Leipzig debate was held, to which Eck had challenged us two, Karlstadt and me. But I could not, in spite of all my letters, get a safe conduct from Duke George. Accordingly, I came to Leipzig not as a prospective debater, but as a spectator under the safe conduct granted to Karlstadt. Who stood in my way I do not know, for till then Duke George was not against me. This I knew for certain.

Here Eck came to me in my lodging and said he had heard that I refused to debate. I replied, "How can I debate, since I cannot get a safe conduct from Duke George?" "If I cannot debate with you," he said, "neither do I want to with Karlstadt, for I have come here on your account. What if I obtain a safe conduct for you? Would you then debate with me?" "Obtain," said I, "and it shall be." He left and soon a safe conduct was given me too and the opportunity to debate.

Eck did this because he discerned the certain glory that was set before him on account of my proposition in which I denied that the pope is the head of the church by divine right. Here a wide field was open to him and a supreme occasion to flatter in praiseworthy manner the pope and to merit his favor, also to ruin me with hate and envy. He did this vigorously throughout the entire debate. But he neither proved his own position nor refuted mine, so that even Duke George said to Eck and me at the morning meal, "Whether he be pope by human or divine right, yet he is pope." He would in no case have said this had he not been influenced by the arguments, but would have approved of Eck only.

Here, in my case, you may also see how hard it is to struggle out of and emerge from errors which have been confirmed by the example of the whole world and have by long habit become a part of nature, as it were. How true is the proverb, "It is hard to give up the accustomed," and, "Custom is second nature." How truly Augustine says, "If one does not resist custom, it becomes a necessity." I had then already read and taught the sacred Scriptures most diligently privately and publicly for seven years, so that I knew them nearly all by memory. I had also acquired the beginning of the knowledge of Christ and faith in him, i.e., not by works but by faith in Christ are we made righteous and saved. Finally, regarding that of which I speak, I had already defended the proposition publicly that the pope is not the head of the church by divine right. Nevertheless, I did not draw the conclusion, namely, that the pope must be of the devil. For what is not of God must of necessity be of the devil.

So absorbed was I, as I have said, by the example and the title of the holy church as well as my own habit, that I conceded human right to the pope, which nevertheless, unless it is founded on divine authority, is a diabolical lie. For we obey parents and magistrates not because they themselves command it, but because it is God's will, 1 Peter 3 [2:13]. For that reason I can bear with a less hateful spirit those who cling too pertinaciously to the papacy, particularly those who have not read the sacred Scriptures, or also the profane, since I, who read the sacred Scriptures most diligently so many years, still clung to it so tenaciously.

In the year 1519, Leo X, as I have said, sent the Rose with Karl von Miltitz, who urged me profusely to be reconciled with the pope. He had seventy apostolic briefs that if Prince Frederick would turn me over to him, as the pope requested by means of the Rose, he should tack one up in each city and so transfer me safely to Rome. But he betrayed the counsel of his heart toward me when he said, "O Martin, I believed you were some aged theologian who, sitting behind the stove, disputed thus with himself; now I see you are still young and strong. If I had twenty-five thousand armed men, I do not believe I could take you to Rome, for I have sounded out the people's mind all along the way to learn what they thought of you. Behold, where I found one standing for the pope, three stood for you against the pope." But that was ridiculous! He had also asked simple little women and girls in the hostelries, what they thought of the Roman chair. Ignorant of this term and thinking of a domestic chair, they replied, "How can we know what kind of chairs you have in Rome, wood or stone?"

Therefore he begged me to seek the things which made for peace. He would put forth every effort to have the pope do the same. I also promised everything abundantly. Whatever I could do with a good conscience with respect to the truth, I would do most promptly. I, too, desired and was eager for peace. Having been drawn into these disturbances by force and driven by necessity, I had done all I did: the guilt was not mine.

But he had summoned Johann Tetzel of the preaching order, the primary author of this tragedy, and had with verbose threats from the pope so broken the man, till then so terrible to all, a fearless crier, that from that time on he wasted away and was finally consumed by illness of mind. When I found this out before his death, I comforted him with a letter, written benignly, asking him to be of good cheer and not to fear my memory. But perhaps he succumbed a victim of his conscience and of the pope's indignation.

Karl von Miltitz was regarded as vain and his advice as vain. But, in my opinion, if the man at Mainz had from the start, when I admonished him, and, finally, if the pope, before he condemned me unheard and raged with his bulls, had taken this advice, which Karl took although too late, and had at once quenched Tetzel's fury, the matter would not have come to so great a tumult. The entire guilt belongs to the one at Mainz, whose smartness and cleverness fooled him, with which he wanted to suppress my doctrine and have his money, acquired by the indulgences, saved. Now counsels are sought in vain; in vain efforts are made. The Lord has awakened and stands to judge the people. Though they could kill us, they still do not have what they want, yes, have less than they have, while we live in safety. This some of them who are not entirely of a dull nose smell quite enough.

Meanwhile, I had already during that year returned to interpret the Psalter anew. I had confidence in the fact that I was more skilful, after I had lectured in the university on St Paul's epistles to the Romans, to the Galatians, and the one to the Hebrews. I had indeed been captivated with an extraordinary ardor for understanding Paul in the Epistle to the Romans. But up till then it was not the cold blood about the heart, but a single word in Chapter 1 [:17], "In it the righteousness of God is revealed," that had stood in my way. For I hated that word "righteousness of God," which, according to the use and custom of all the teachers, I had been taught to understand philosophically regarding the formal or active righteousness, as they called it, with which God is righteous and punishes the unrighteous sinner.

Though I lived as a monk without reproach, I felt that I was a sinner before God with an extremely disturbed conscience. I could not believe that he was placated by my satisfaction. I did not love, yes, I hated the righteous God who punishes sinners, and secretly, if not blasphemously, certainly murmuring greatly, I was angry with God, and said, "As if, indeed, it is not enough, that miserable sinners, eternally lost through original sin, are crushed by every kind of calamity by the law of the decalogue, without having God add pain to pain by the gospel and also by the gospel threatening us with his righteousness and wrath!" Thus I raged with a fierce and troubled conscience. Nevertheless, I beat importunately upon Paul at that place, most ardently desiring to know what St Paul wanted.

At last, by the mercy of God, meditating day and night, I gave heed to the context of the words, namely, "In it the righteousness of God is revealed, as it is written, 'He who through faith is righteous shall live.'" There I began to understand that the righteousness of God is that by which the righteous lives by a gift of God, namely by faith. And this is the meaning: the righteousness of God is revealed by the gospel, namely, the passive righteousness with which merciful God justifies us by faith, as it is written, "He who through faith is righteous shall live." Here I felt that I was altogether born again and had entered paradise itself through open gates. There a totally other face of the entire Scripture showed itself to me. Thereupon I ran through the Scriptures from memory. I also found in other terms an analogy, as, the work of God, that is, what God does in us, the power of God, with which he makes us strong, the wisdom of God, with which he makes us wise, the strength of God, the salvation of God, the glory of God.

And I extolled my sweetest word with a love as great as the hatred with which I had before hated the word "righteousness of God." Thus that place in Paul was for me truly the gate to paradise. Later I read Augustine's *The Spirit and the Letter*, where contrary to hope I found that he, too, interpreted God's righteousness in a similar way, as the righteousness with which God clothes us when he justifies us. Although this was heretofore said imperfectly and he did not explain all things concerning imputation clearly, it nevertheless was pleasing that God's righteousness with which we are justified was taught. Armed more fully with these thoughts, I began a second time to interpret the Psalter. And the work would have grown into a large commentary, if I had not again been compelled to leave the work begun, because Emperor Charles V in the following year convened the diet at Worms.

I relate these things, good reader, so that, if you are a reader of my puny works, you may keep in mind, that, as I said above, I was all alone and one of those who, as Augustine says of himself, have become proficient by writing and teaching. I was not one of those who from nothing suddenly become the topmost, though they are nothing, neither have labored, nor been tempted, nor become experienced, but have with one look at the Scriptures exhausted their entire spirit.

To this point, to the year 1520 and 21, the indulgence matter proceeded. Upon that followed the sacramentarian and the Anabaptist affairs. Regarding these a preface shall be written to other tomes, if I live.

Farewell in the Lord, reader, and pray for the growth of the Word against Satan. Strong and evil, now also very furious and savage, he knows his time is short and the kingdom of his pope is in danger. But may God confirm in us what he has accomplished and perfect his work which he began in us, to his glory, Amen. March 5, in the year 1545.

8

John Calvin, from *Institutes of the Christian Religion*

The French scholar, theologian, churchman, and father of the Reformed tradition, John Calvin, was born in 1509. A Renaissance humanist by training, originally intent on a career in law, Calvin underwent a conversion in his early twenties, and became an active supporter of the fledgling Protestant cause. After Martin Luther, who was born a quarter of a century earlier, Calvin is widely regarded as the most important figure of the sixteenth century in the Protestant struggle to reform the Roman Catholic Church. He spent most of his adult, post-conversion life working in the city of Geneva, where he advanced the Reformation cause, and where he died in 1564.

The work for which Calvin is best known is his *Institutes of the Christian Religion*. The first edition of the *Institutes* was published in 1536. Calvin's purpose in writing the *Institutes* was twofold. First, he sought to provide a guide for the reading of Scripture, as well as a clear statement of doctrine. Second, he wished to make an appeal to King Francis I of France for tolerant and fair treatment of Protestants in his domain. The definitive edition of the *Institutes* was published in 1559, and is divided into four books. The theological structure of the definitive edition, however, is broadly trinitarian. Book One deals with the knowledge of God the Father; Book Two discusses the knowledge of God the Redeemer; and Books Three and Four treat the means of grace and the mediating work of God the Holy Spirit.

In Book One of the *Institutes*, Calvin deals, among other things, with universal human religiosity or divine awareness, natural or general revelation, and scriptural or special revelation. In a fashion typical of the Protestant Reformation, he argues that Scripture is necessary for all who would come to know God in a saving way. Having established the necessity and authority of Scripture for knowledge of God, Calvin

John Calvin

goes on in Book One to discuss doctrines of God, creation, humanity, and providence.

In the selections from the *Institutes* which follow, insertions in the text in brackets are the work of the source editor (p. indicates paraphrase(d)). Footnotes in the source edition, however, have been eliminated.

BOOK ONE: The Knowledge of God the Creator

CHAPTER I: The knowledge of God and that of ourselves are connected. How they are interrelated

1. *Without knowledge of self there is no knowledge of God*

Nearly all the wisdom we possess, that is to say, true and sound wisdom, consists of two parts: the knowledge of God and of ourselves. But, while joined by many bonds, which one precedes and brings forth the other is not easy to discern. In the first place, no one can look upon himself without immediately turning his thoughts to the contemplation of God, in whom he "lives and moves" [Acts 17:28]. For, quite clearly, the mighty gifts with which we are endowed are hardly from ourselves; indeed, our very being is nothing but subsistence in the one God. Then, by these benefits shed like dew from heaven upon us, we are led as by rivulets to the spring itself. Indeed, our very poverty better discloses the infinitude of benefits reposing in God. The miserable ruin, into which the rebellion of the first man cast us, especially compels us to look upward. Thus, not only will we, in fasting and hungering, seek thence what we lack; but, in being aroused by fear, we shall learn humility. For, as a veritable world of miseries is to be found in mankind, and we are thereby despoiled of divine raiment, our shameful nakedness exposes a teeming horde of infamies. Each of us must, then, be so stung by the consciousness of his own unhappiness as to attain at least some knowledge of God. Thus, from the feeling of our own ignorance, vanity, poverty, infirmity, and – what is more – depravity and corruption, we recognize that the true light of wisdom, sound virtue, full abundance of every good, and purity of righteousness rest in the Lord alone. To this extent we are prompted by our own ills to contemplate the goods things of God; and we cannot seriously aspire to him before we begin to become displeased with ourselves. For what man in all the world would not gladly remain as he is – what man does not remain as he is – so long as he does not know himself, that is, while content with his own gifts, and either ignorant or unmindful of his own misery? Accordingly, the knowledge of ourselves not only arouses us to seek God, but also, as it were, leads us by the hand to find him.

2. *Without knowledge of God there is no knowledge of self*

Again, it is certain that man never achieves a clear knowledge of himself unless he has first looked upon God's face, and then descends from contemplating him to scrutinize himself. For we always seem to ourselves righteous and upright and wise and holy – this pride is innate in all of us – unless by clear proofs we stand convinced of our own unrighteousness, foulness, folly, and impurity. Moreover, we are not thus convinced if we look merely to ourselves and not also to the Lord, who

Source: John Calvin, *Institutes of the Christian Religion*, Library of Christian Classics, 20, trans. F. L. Battles, ed. J. T. McNeill.

is the sole standard by which this judgment must be measured. For, because all of us are inclined by nature to hypocrisy, a kind of empty image of righteousness in place of righteousness itself abundantly satisfies us. And because nothing appears within or around us that has not been contaminated by great immorality, what is a little less vile pleases us as a thing most pure – so long as we confine our minds within the limits of human corruption. Just so, an eye to which nothing is shown but black objects judges something dirty white or even rather darkly mottled to be whiteness itself. Indeed, we can discern still more clearly from the bodily senses how much we are deluded in estimating the powers of the soul. For if in broad daylight we either look down upon the ground or survey whatever meets our view round about, we seem to ourselves endowed with the strongest and keenest sight; yet when we look up to the sun and gaze straight at it, that power of sight which was particularly strong on earth is at once blunted and confused by a great brilliance, and thus we are compelled to admit that our keenness in looking upon things earthly is sheer dullness when it comes to the sun. So it happens in estimating our spiritual goods. As long as we do not look beyond the earth, being quite content with our own righteousness, wisdom, and virtue, we flatter ourselves most sweetly, and fancy ourselves all but demigods. Suppose we but once begin to raise our thoughts to God, and to ponder his nature, and how completely perfect are his righteousness, wisdom, and power – the straightedge to which we must be shaped. Then, what masquerading earlier as righteousness was pleasing in us will soon grow filthy in its consummate wickedness. What wonderfully impressed us under the name of wisdom will stink in its very foolishness. What wore the face of power will prove itself the most miserable weakness. That is, what in us seems perfection itself corresponds ill to the purity of God.

3. Man before God's majesty

Hence that dread and wonder with which Scripture commonly represents the saints as stricken and overcome whenever they felt the presence of God. Thus it comes about that we see men who in his absence normally remained firm and constant, but who, when he manifests his glory, are so shaken and struck dumb as to be laid low by the dread of death – are in fact overwhelmed by it and almost annihilated. As a consequence, we must infer that man is never sufficiently touched and affected by the awareness of his lowly state until he has compared himself with God's majesty. Moreover, we have numerous examples of this consternation both in The Book of Judges and in the Prophets. So frequent was it that this expression was common among God's people: "We shall die, for the Lord has appeared to us" [Judg. 13:22; Isa. 6:5; Ezek. 2:1; 1:28; Judg. 6:22–23; and elsewhere]. The story of Job, in its description of God's wisdom, power, and purity, always expresses a powerful argument that overwhelms men with the realization of their own stupidity, impotence, and corruption [cf. Job 38:1 ff]. And not without cause: for we see how Abraham recognizes more clearly that he is earth and dust [Gen. 18:27] when once he had come nearer to beholding God's glory; and how Elijah, with uncovered face, cannot bear to await his approach, such is the awesomeness of his appearance [I Kings 19:13]. And what can man do, who is rottenness itself [Job 13:28] and a worm

[Job 7:5; Ps.22:6], when even the very cherubim must veil their faces out of fear [Isa. 6:2]? It is this indeed of which the prophet Isaiah speaks: "The sun will blush and the moon be confounded when the Lord of Hosts shall reign" [Isa. 24:23]; that is, when he shall bring forth his splendor and cause it to draw nearer, the brightest thing will become darkness before it [Isa. 2:10, 19 p.].

Yet, however the knowledge of God and of ourselves may be mutually connected, the order of right teaching requires that we discuss the former first, then proceed afterward to treat the latter.

· *CHAPTER II: What it is to know God, and to what purpose the knowledge of Him tends* ·

1. *Piety is requisite for the knowledge of God*

Now, the knowledge of God, as I understand it, is that by which we not only conceive that there is a God but also grasp what befits us and is proper to his glory, in fine, what is to our advantage to know of him. Indeed, we shall not say that, properly speaking, God is known where there is no religion or piety. Here I do not yet touch upon the sort of knowledge with which men, in themselves lost and accursed, apprehend God the Redeemer in Christ the Mediator; but I speak only of the primal and simple knowledge to which the very order of nature would have led us if Adam had remained upright. In this ruin of mankind no one now experiences God either as Father or as Author of salvation, or favorable in any way, until Christ the Mediator comes forward to reconcile him to us. Nevertheless, it is one thing to feel that God as our Maker supports us by his power, governs us by his providence, nourishes us by his goodness, and attends us with all sorts of blessings – and another thing to embrace the grace of reconciliation offered to us in Christ. First, as much in the fashioning of the universe as in the general teaching of Scripture the Lord shows himself to be simply the Creator. Then in the face of Christ [cf. II Cor. 4:6] he shows himself the Redeemer. Of the resulting twofold knowledge of God we shall now discuss the first aspect; the second will be dealt with in its proper place.

Moreover, although our mind cannot apprehend God without rendering some honor to him, it will not suffice simply to hold that there is One whom all ought to honor and adore, unless we are also persuaded that he is the fountain of every good, and that we must seek nothing elsewhere than in him. This I take to mean mean that not only does he sustain this universe (as he once founded it) by his boundless might, regulate it by his wisdom, preserve it by his goodness, and especially rule mankind by his righteousness and judgment, bear with it in his mercy, watch over it by his protection; but also that no drop will be found either of wisdom and light, or of righteousness or power or rectitude, or of genuine truth, which does not flow from him, and of which he is not the cause. Thus we may learn to await and seek all these things from him, and thankfully to ascribe them, once received, to him. For this sense of the powers of God is for us a fit teacher of piety, from which religion is born. I call "piety" that reverence joined with love of God which the knowledge of his benefits induces. For until men recognize that they owe everything to God,

141

that they are nourished by his fatherly care, that he is the Author of their every good, that they should seek nothing beyond him – they will never yield him willing service. Nay, unless they establish their complete happiness in him, they will never give themselves truly and sincerely to him.

2. *Knowledge of God involves trust and reverence*

What is God? Men who pose this question are merely toying with idle speculations. It is more important for us to know of what sort he is and what is consistent with his nature. What good is it to profess with Epicurus some sort of God who has cast aside care of the world only to amuse himself in idleness? What help is it, in short, to know a God with whom we have nothing to do? Rather, our knowledge should serve first to teach us fear and reverence; secondly, with it as our guide and teacher, we should learn to seek every good from him, and, having received it, to credit it to his account. For how can the thought of God penetrate your mind without your realizing immediately that, since you are his handiwork, you have been made over and bound to his command by right of creation, that you owe your life to him? – that whatever you undertake, whatever you do, ought to be ascribed to him? If this be so, it now assuredly follows that your life is wickedly corrupt unless it be disposed to his service, seeing that his will ought for us to be the law by which we live. Again, you cannot behold him clearly unless you acknowledge him to be the fountainhead and source of every good. From this too would arise the desire to cleave to him and trust in him, but for the fact that man's depravity seduces his mind from rightly seeking him.

For, to begin with, the pious mind does not dream up for itself any god it pleases, but contemplates the one and only true God. And it does not attach to him whatever it pleases, but is content to hold him to be as he manifests himself; furthermore, the mind always exercises the utmost diligence and care not to wander astray, or rashly and boldly to go beyond his will. It thus recognizes God because it knows that he governs all things; and trusts that he is its guide and protector, therefore giving itself over completely to trust in him. Because it understands him to be the Author of every good, if anything oppresses, if anything is lacking, immediately it betakes itself to his protection, waiting for help from him. Because it is persuaded that he is good and merciful, it reposes in him with perfect trust, and doubts not that in his loving-kindness a remedy will be provided for all its ills. Because it acknowledges him as Lord and Father, the pious mind also deems it meet and right to observe his authority in all things, reverence his majesty, take care to advance his glory, and obey his commandments. Because it sees him to be a righteous judge, armed with severity to punish wickedness, it ever holds his judgment seat before its gaze, and through fear of him restrains itself from provoking his anger. And yet it is not so terrified by the awareness of his judgment as to wish to withdraw, even if some way of escape were open. But it embraces him no less as punisher of the wicked than as benefactor of the pious. For the pious mind realizes that the punishment of the impious and wicked and the reward of life eternal for the righteous equally pertain to God's glory. Besides, this mind restrains itself from sinning, not out of dread of punishment alone; but, because it loves and reveres God as Father, it worships and adores him as Lord. Even if there were no hell, it would still shudder at offending him alone.

Here indeed is pure and real religion: faith so joined with an earnest fear of God that this fear also embraces willing reverence, and carries with it such legitimate worship as is prescribed in the law. And we ought to note this fact even more diligently: all men have a vague general veneration for God, but very few really reverence him; and wherever there is great ostentation in ceremonies, sincerity of heart is rare indeed.

· *CHAPTER III: The knowledge of God has been naturally implanted in the minds of men* ·

1. The character of this natural endowment

There is within the human mind, and indeed by natural instinct, an awareness of divinity. This we take to be beyond controversy. To prevent anyone from taking refuge in the pretense of ignorance, God himself has implanted in all men a certain understanding of his divine majesty. Ever renewing its memory, he repeatedly sheds fresh drops. Since, therefore, men one and all perceive that there is a God and that he is their Maker, they are condemned by their own testimony because they have failed to honor him and to consecrate their lives to his will. If ignorance of God is to be looked for anywhere, surely one is most likely to find an example of it among the more backward folk and those more remote from civilization. Yet there is, as the eminent pagan says, no nation so barbarous, no people so savage, that they have not a deep-seated conviction that there is a God. And they who in other aspects of life seem least to differ from brutes still continue to retain some seed of religion. So deeply does the common conception occupy the minds of all, so tenaciously does it inhere in the hearts of all! Therefore, since from the beginning of the world there has been no region, no city, in short, no household, that could do without religion, there lies in this a tacit confession of a sense of deity inscribed in the hearts of all.

Indeed, even idolatry is ample proof of this conception. We know how man does not willingly humble himself so as to place other creatures over himself. Since, then, he prefers to worship wood and stone rather than to be thought of as having no God, clearly this is a most vivid impression of a divine being. So impossible is it to blot this from man's mind that natural disposition would be more easily altered, as altered indeed it is when man voluntarily sinks from his natural haughtiness to the very depths in order to honor God!

2. Religion is no arbitrary invention

Therefore it is utterly vain for some men to say that religion was invented by the subtlety and craft of a few to hold the simple folk in thrall by this device and that those very persons who originated the worship of God for others did not in the least believe that any God existed. I confess, indeed, that in order to hold men's minds in greater subjection, clever men have devised very many things in religion by which to inspire the common folk with reverence and to strike them with terror. But they would never have achieved this if men's minds had not already been imbued with a firm conviction about God, from which the inclination toward religion springs as from a seed. And indeed it is not credible that those who craftily imposed upon the ruder folk under pretense of religion were entirely devoid of the knowledge of God. If, indeed, there were some in the past, and today not a few appear, who deny that God exists, yet willy-nilly they from time to time feel an inkling of what they desire not to believe. One reads of no one who burst forth into bolder or more unbridled contempt of deity than Gaius Caligula; yet no one trembled more miserably when any sign of God's wrath manifested itself; thus – albeit unwillingly – he shuddered at the God whom he professedly sought to despise. You may see now and again how this also happens to those like him; how he who is the boldest despiser of God is of all men the most startled at the rustle of a falling leaf [cf. Lev. 26:36]. Whence does this arise but from the vengeance of divine majesty, which strikes their consciences all the more violently the more they try to flee from it? Indeed, they seek out every subterfuge to hide themselves from the Lord's presence, and to efface it again from their minds. But in spite of themselves they are always entrapped. Although it may sometimes seem to vanish for a moment, it returns at once and rushes in with new force. If for these there is any respite from anxiety of conscience, it is not much different from the sleep of drunken or frenzied persons, who do not rest peacefully even while sleeping because they are continually troubled with dire and dreadful dreams. The impious themselves therefore exemplify the fact that some conception of God is ever alive in all men's minds.

3. *Actual godlessness is impossible*

Men of sound judgment will always be sure that a sense of divinity which can never be effaced is engraved upon men's minds. Indeed, the perversity of the impious, who though they struggle furiously are unable to extricate themselves from the fear of God, is abundant testimony that this conviction, namely, that there is some God, is naturally inborn in all, and is fixed deep within, as it were in the very marrow. Although Diagoras and his like may jest at whatever has been believed in every age concerning religion, and Dionysius may mock the heavenly judgment, this is sardonic laughter, for the worm of conscience, sharper than any cauterizing iron, gnaws away within. I do not say, as Cicero did, that errors disappear with the lapse of time, and that religion grows and becomes better each day. For the world (something will have to be said of this a little later) tries as far as it is able to cast away all knowledge of God, and by every means to corrupt the worship of him. I only say that though the stupid hardness in their minds, which the impious eagerly conjure up to reject God, wastes away, yet the sense of divinity, which they greatly wished to have extinguished, thrives and presently burgeons. From this we conclude that it is not a doctrine that must first be learned in school, but one of which each of us is master from his mother's womb and which nature itself permits no one to forget, although many strive with every nerve to this end.

Besides, if all men are born and live to the end that they may know God, and yet if knowledge of God is unstable and fleeting unless it progresses to this degree, it is clear that all those who do not direct every thought and action in their lives to this goal degenerate from the law of their creation. This was not unknown to the philosophers. Plato meant nothing but this when he often taught that the highest good of the soul is likeness to God, where, when the soul has grasped the knowledge of God, it is wholly transformed into his likeness. In the same manner also Gryllus, in the writings of Plutarch, reasons very skilfully, affirming that, if once religion is absent from their life, men are in no wise superior to brute beasts, but are in many respects far more miserable. Subject, then, to so many forms of wickedness, they drag out their lives in ceaseless tumult and disquiet. Therefore, it is worship of God alone that renders men higher than the brutes, and through it alone they aspire to immortality.

CHAPTER IV: This knowledge is either smothered or corrupted, partly by ignorance, partly by malice

1. Supersititon

As experience shows, God has sown a seed of religion in all men. But scarely one man in a hundred is met with who fosters it, once received, in his heart, and none in whom it ripens – much less shows fruit in season [cf. Ps. 1:3]. Besides while some may evaporate in their own superstitions and others deliberately and wickedly desert God, yet all degenerate from the true knowledge of him. And so it happens that no real piety remains in the world. But as to my statement that some erroneously slip into superstition, I do not mean by this that their ingenuousness should free them from blame. For the blindness under which they labor is almost always mixed with proud vanity and obstinacy. Indeed, vanity joined with pride can be detected in the fact that, seeking God, miserable men do not rise above themselves as they should, but measure him by the yardstick of their own carnal stupidity, and neglect sound investigation; thus out of curiosity they fly off into empty speculations. They do not therefore apprehend God as he offers himself, but imagine him as they have fashioned him in their own presumption. When this gulf opens, in whatever direction they move their feet, they cannot but plunge headlong into ruin. Indeed, whatever they afterward attempt by way of worship or service of God, they cannot bring as tribute to him, for they are worshipping not God but a figment and a dream of their own heart. Paul eloquently notes this wickedness: "Striving to be wise, they make fools of themselves" [Rom. 1:22 p.]. He had said before that "they became futile in their thinking" [Rom. 1:21]. In order, however, that no one might excuse their guilt, he adds that they are justly blinded. For not content with sobriety but claiming for themselves more than is right, they wantonly bring darkness upon themselves – in fact, they become fools in their empty and perverse haughtiness. From this it follows that their stupidity is not excusable, since it is caused not only by vain curiosity but by an inordinate desire to know more than is fitting, joined with a false confidence.

2. Conscious turning away from God

David's statement that ungodly men and fools feel in their hearts that there is no God [Ps. 14:1; 53:1] must first, as we shall see again a little later, be limited to those who, by extinguishing the light of nature, deliberately befuddle themselves. Accordingly, we see that many, after they have become hardened in insolent and habitual sinning, furiously repel all remembrance of God, although this is freely suggested to them inwardly from the feeling of nature. But to render their madness more detestable, David represents them as flatly denying God's existence; not that they deprive him of his being, but because, in despoiling him of his judgment and providence, they shut him up idle in heaven. Now there is nothing less in accord with God's nature than for him to cast off the government of the universe and abandon it to fortune, and to be blind to the wicked deeds of men, so that they may lust unpunished. Accordingly, whoever heedlessly indulges himself, his fear of heavenly judgment extinguished, denies that there is a God. And it is God's just punishment of the wicked that fatness envelops their hearts, so that after they have closed their eyes, in seeing they see not [Matt. 13:14–15; cf. Isa. 6:9–10 and Ps. 17:10]. And David is the best interpreter of his thought when in another place he says that "the fear of God is not before the eyes of the ungodly" [Ps. 36:1 p.]. Likewise, because they persuade themselves that God does not see, they proudly applaud their own wrongdoings [Ps. 10:11].

Even though they are compelled to recognize some god, they strip him of glory by taking away his power. For, as Paul affirms, just as "God cannot deny himself," because "he remains forever like himself" [II Tim. 2:13], so they, by fashioning a dead and empty idol, are truly said to deny God. At this point we ought to note that, however much they struggle against their own senses, and wish not only to drive God thence but also to destroy him in heaven, their stupidity never increases to the point where God does not at times bring them back to his judgment seat. But because no fear restrains them from rushing violently against God, it is certain that so long as this blind urge grips them, their own oafish forgetfulness of God will hold sway over them.

3. We are not to fashion God according to our own whim

Thus is overthrown that vain defense with which many are wont to gloss over their superstition. For they think that any zeal for religion, however preposterous, is sufficient. But they do not realize that true religion ought to be conformed to God's will as to a universal rule; that God ever remains like himself, and is not a specter or phantasm to be transformed according to anyone's whim. One can clearly see, too, how superstition mocks God with pretenses while it tries to please him. For, seizing almost solely upon what God has testified to be of no concern to himself, superstition either holds in contempt or else openly rejects that which he prescribes and enjoins as pleasing to himself. Thus all who set up their own false rites to God worship and adore their own ravings. Unless they had first fashioned a God to match the absurdity of their trifling, they would by no means have dared trifle with God in this way. The apostle accordingly characterizes that vague and erroneous opinion of the divine as ignorance of God. "When you did not know God," he says, "you were in bondage to beings that by nature were no gods" [Gal. 4:8 p.]. And elsewhere he teaches that the Ephesians were "without God" at the time they were straying away from the right knowledge of the one God [Eph. 2:12]. Nor is it of much concern, at least in this circumstance, whether you conceive of one God or several; for you continually depart from the true God and forsake him, and, having left him, you have nothing left except an accursed idol. Therefore it remains for us to assert with Lactantius that no religion is genuine unless it be joined with truth.

4. *Hypocrisy*

A second sin arises, that they never consider God at all unless compelled to; and they do not come nigh until they are dragged there despite their resistance. And not even then are they impressed with the voluntary fear that arises out of reverence for the divine majesty, but merely with a slavish, forced fear, which God's judgment extorts from them. This, since they cannot escape it, they dread even to the point of loathing. That saying of Statius' that fear first made gods in the world corresponds well to this kind of irreligion, and to this alone. Those who are of a mind alien to God's righteousness know that his judgment seat stands ready to punish transgressions against him, yet they greatly desire its overthrow. Feeling so, they wage war against the Lord, who cannot be without judgment. But while they know that his inescapable power hangs over them because they can neither do away with it nor flee from it, they recoil from it in dread. And so, lest they should everywhere seem to despise him whose majesty weighs upon them, they perform some semblance of religion. Meanwhile they do not desist from polluting themselves with every sort of vice, and from joining wickedness to wickedness, until in every respect they violate the holy law of the Lord and dissipate all his righteousness. Or at least they are not so restrained by that pretended fear of God from wallowing blithely in their own sins and flattering themselves, and preferring to indulge their fleshly intemperance rather than restrain it by the bridle of the Holy Spirit.

This, however, is but a vain and false shadow of religion, scarcely even worth being called a shadow. From it one may easily grasp anew how much this confused knowledge of God differs from the piety from which religion takes its source, which is instilled in the breasts of believers only. And yet hypocrites would tread these twisting paths so as to seem to approach the God from whom they flee. For where they ought to have remained consistently obedient throughout life, they boldly rebel against him in almost all their deeds, and are zealous to placate him merely with a few paltry sacrifices. Where they ought to serve him in sanctity of life and integrity of heart, they trump up frivolous trifles and worthless little observances with which to win his favor. Nay, more, with greater license they sluggishly lie in their own filth, because they are confident that they can perform their duty toward him by ridiculous acts of expiation. Then while their trust ought to have been placed in him, they neglect him and rely upon themselves, his creatures though they be. Finally, they entangle themselves in such a huge mass of errors that blind wickedness stifles and finally extinguishes those sparks which once flashed forth to show them God's glory. Yet that seed remains which can in no wise be uprooted: that there is some sort of divinity; but this seed is so corrupted that by itself it produces only the worst fruits.

From this, my present contention is brought out with greater certainty, that a sense of divinity is by nature engraven on human hearts. For necessity forces from the reprobate themselves a confession of it. In tranquil times they wittily joke about God, indeed are facetious and garrulous in belittling his power. If any occasion for despair presses upon them, it goads them to seek him and impels their perfunctory prayers. From this it is clear that they have not been utterly ignorant of God, but that what should have come forth sooner was held back by stubbornness.

CHAPTER V: The knowledge of God shines forth in the fashioning of the universe and the continuing government of it ·

(God manifested in his created works, 1–10)

1. The clarity of God's self-disclosure strips us of every excuse

The final goal of the blessed life, moreover, rests in the knowledge of God [cf. John 17:3]. Lest anyone, then, be excluded from access to happiness, he not only sowed in men's minds that seed of religion of which we have spoken but revealed himself and daily discloses himself in the whole workmanship of the universe. As a consequence, men cannot open their eyes without being compelled to see him. Indeed, his essence is incomprehensible; hence, his divineness far escapes all human perception. But upon his individual works he has engraved unmistakable marks of his glory, so clear and so prominent that even unlettered and stupid folk cannot plead the excuse of ignorance. Therefore the prophet very aptly exclaims that he is "clad with light as with a garment" [Ps. 104:2 p.]. It is as if he said: Thereafter the Lord began to show himself in the visible splendor of his apparel, ever since in the creation of the universe he brought forth those insignia whereby his shows his glory to us, whenever and wherever we cast our gaze. Likewise, the same prophet skillfully compares the heavens, as they are stretched out, to his royal tent and says that he has laid the beams of his chambers on the waters, has made the clouds his chariot, rides on the wings of the wind, and that the winds and lightning bolts are his swift messengers [Ps. 104:2–4]. And since the glory of his power and wisdom shine more brightly above, heaven is often called his palace [Ps. 11:4]. Yet, in the first place, wherever you cast your eyes, there is no spot in the universe wherein you cannot discern at least some sparks of his glory. You cannot in one glance survey this most vast and beautiful system of the universe, in its wide expanse, without being completely overwhelmed by the boundless force of its brightness. The reason why the author of The Letter to the Hebrews elegantly calls the universe the appearance of things invisible [Heb. 11:3] is that this skillful ordering of the universe is for us a sort of mirror in which we can contemplate God, who is otherwise invisible. The reason why the prophet attributes to the heavenly creatures a language known to every nation [Ps. 19:2 ff.] is that therein lies an attestation of divinity so apparent that it ought not to escape the gaze of even the most stupid tribe. The apostle declares this more clearly: "What men need to know concerning God has been disclosed to them, ... for one and all gaze upon his invisible nature, known from the creation of the world, even until his eternal power and divinity" [Rom. 1:19–20 p.].

2. *The divine wisdom displayed for all to see*

There are innumerable evidences both in heaven and on earth that declare his wonderful wisdom; not only those more recondite matters for the closer observation of which astronomy, medicine, and all natural science are intended, but also those which thrust themselves upon the sight of even the most untutored and ignorant persons, so that they cannot open their eyes without being compelled to witness them. Indeed, men who have either quaffed or even tasted the liberal arts penetrate with their aid far more deeply into the secrets of the divine wisdom. Yet ignorance of them prevents no one from seeing more than enough of God's workmanship in his creation to lead him to break forth in admiration of the Artificer. To be sure, there is need of art and of more exacting toil in order to investigate the motion of the stars, to determine their assigned stations, to measure their intervals, to note their properties. As God's providence shows itself more explicitly when one observes these, so the mind must rise to a somewhat higher level to look upon his glory. Even the common folk and the most untutored, who have been taught only by the aid of the eyes, cannot be unaware of the excellence of divine art, for it reveals itself in this innumerable and yet distinct and well-ordered variety of the heavenly host. It is, accordingly, clear that there is no one to whom the Lord does not abundantly show his wisdom. Likewise, in regard to the structure of the human body one must have the greatest keenness in order to weigh, with Galen's skill, its articulation, symmetry, beauty, and use. But yet, as all acknowledge, the human body shows itself to be a composition so ingenious that its Artificer is rightly judged a wonder-worker.

3. *Man as the loftiest proof of divine wisdom*

Certain philosophers, accordingly, long ago not ineptly called man a microcosm because he is a rare example of God's power, goodness, and wisdom, and contains within himself enough miracles to occupy our minds, if only we are not irked at paying attention to them. Paul, having stated that the blind can find God by feeling after him, immediately adds that he ought not to be sought afar off [Acts 17:27]. For each one undoubtedly feels within the heavenly grace that quickens him. Indeed, if there is no need to go outside ourselves to comprehend God, what pardon will the indolence of that man deserve who is loath to descend within himself to find God? For the same reason, David, when he has briefly praised the admirable name and glory of God, which shine everywhere, immediately exclaims: "What is man that thou art mindful of him?" [Ps. 8:4]. Likewise, "Out of the mouths of babes and sucklings thou hast established strength" [Ps. 8:2]. Indeed, he not only declares that a clear mirror of God's works is in humankind, but that infants, while they nurse at their mothers' breasts, have tongues so eloquent to preach his glory that there is no need at all of other orators. Consequently, also, he does not hesitate to bring their infant speech into the debate, as if they were thoroughly instructed, to refute the madness of those who might desire to extinguish God's name in favor of their own devilish pride. Consequently, too, there comes in that which Paul quotes from Aratus, that we are God's offspring [Acts 17:28], because by adorning us with such great excellence he testifies that he is our Father. In the same way the secular poets, out of a common feeling and, as it were, at the dictation of experience, called him "the

Father of men." Indeed, no one gives himself freely and willingly to God's service unless, having tasted his fatherly love, he is drawn to love and worship him in return.

4. But man turns ungratefully against God

Here, however, the foul ungratefulness of men is disclosed. They have within themselves a workshop graced with God's unnumbered works and, at the same time, a storehouse overflowing with inestimable riches. They ought, then, to break forth into praises of him but are actually puffed up and swollen with all the more pride. They feel in many wonderful ways that God works in them; they are also taught, by the very use of these things, what a great variety of gifts they possess from his liberality. They are compelled to know – whether they will or not – that these are the signs of divinity; yet they conceal them within. Indeed, there is no need to go outside themselves, provided they do not, by claiming for themselves what has been given them from heaven, bury in the earth that which enlightens their minds to see God clearly.

Even today the earth sustains many monstrous spirits who, to destroy God's name, do not hesitate to misdirect all the seed of divinity spread abroad in human nature. How destestable, I ask you, is this madness: that man, finding God in his body and soul a hundred times, on this very pretense of excellence denies that there is a God? They will not say it is by chance that they are distinct from brute creatures. Yet they set God aside, the while using "nature," which for them is the artificer of all things, as a cloak. They see such exquisite workmanship in their individual members, from mouth and eyes even to their very toenails. Here also they substitute nature for God. But such agile motions of the soul, such excellent faculties, such rare gifts, especially bear upon the face of them a divinity that does not allow itself readily to be hidden – unless the Epicureans, like the Cyclopes, should from this height all the more shamelessly wage war against God. Do all the treasures of heavenly wisdom concur in ruling a five-foot worm while the whole universe lacks this privilege? First, to establish that there is something organic in the soul that should correspond to its several parts in no way obscures God's glory, but rather illumines it. Let Epicurus answer what concourse of atoms cooks food and drink, turns part of it into excrement, part into blood, and begets such industry in the several members to carry out their tasks, as if so many souls ruled one body by common counsel!

5. The confusion of creature with Creator

But now I have no concern with that pigsty; rather, I take to task those given to fanciful subtleties who willingly drag forth in oblique fashion that frigid statement of Aristotle both to destroy the immortality of the soul and to deprive God of his right. For, since the soul has organic faculties, they by this pretext bind the soul to the body so that it may not subsist without it, and by praising nature they suppress God's name as far as they can. Yet the powers of the soul are far from being confined to functions that serve the body. Of what concern is it to the body that you measure the heavens, gather the number of the stars, determine the magnitude of each, know what space lies between them, with what swiftness or slowness they complete their courses, how many degrees this way or that they decline? I confess, indeed, that astronomy has some use; but I am only showing that in this deepest investigation of heavenly things there is no organic symmetry, but here is an activity of the soul distinct from the body. I have put forth one example, from which it will be easy for my readers to derive the rest. Manifold indeed is the nimbleness of the soul with which it surveys heaven and earth, joins past to future, retains in memory something heard long before, nay, pictures to itself whatever it pleases. Manifold also is the skill with which it devises things incredible, and which is the mother of so many marvelous devices. These are unfailing signs of divinity in man. Why is it that the soul not only vaguely roves about but conceives many useful things, ponders concerning many, even divines the future – all while man sleeps? What ought we to say here except that the signs of immortality which have been implanted in man cannot be effaced? Now what reason would there be to believe that man is divine and not to recognize his Creator? Shall we, indeed, distinguish between right and wrong by that judgment which has been imparted to us, yet will there be no judge in heaven? Will there remain for us even in sleep some remnant of intelligence, yet will no God keep watch in governing the world? Shall we think ourselves the inventors of so many arts and useful things that God may be defrauded of his praise even though experience sufficiently teaches that what we have has been unequally distributed among us from another source?

Some persons, moreover, babble about a secret inspiration that gives life to the whole universe, but what they say is not only weak but completely profane. Vergil's famous saying pleases them:

> "First of all, an inner spirit feeds
> Sky, earth, and watery fields, the shining orb
> Of Moon, and Titan's star; and mind pervades
> Its members, sways all the mass, unites
> With its great frame. Thence come the race of man
> And beast, the life of winged things, strange shapes
> That ocean bears beneath his glassy floor.
> Of fire the vigor, and divine the source
> Of those life-seeds."

As if the universe, which was founded as a spectacle of God's glory, were its own creator! For thus the same author has elsewhere followed the view common to Greeks and Latins alike:

> "The bees, some teach, received a share of mind,
> Divine, ethereal draught. For God, men say,
> Pervades all things, the earth, expanse of seas
> And heaven's depth. From him the flocks and herds,
> Men and beasts of every sort, at birth
> Draw slender life; yea, unto him all things
> Do then return; unmade, are then restored;

> Death has no place; but still alive they fly
> Unto the starry ranks, to heaven's height."

See, of what value to beget and nourish godliness in men's hearts is that jejune speculation about the universal mind which animates and quickens the world! This shows itself even more clearly in the sacrilegious words of the filthy dog Lucretius which have been deduced from that principle. This is indeed making a shadow deity to drive away the true God, whom we should fear and adore. I confess, of course, that it can be said reverently, provided that it proceeds from a reverent mind, that nature is God; but because it is a harsh and improper saying, since nature is rather the order prescribed by God, it is harmful in such weighty matters, in which special devotion is due, to involve God confusedly in the inferior course of his works.

6. The Creator reveals his lordship over the creation

Let us therefore remember, whenever each of us contemplates his own nature, that there is one God who so governs all natures that he would have us look unto him, direct our faith to him, and worship and call upon him. For nothing is more preposterous than to enjoy the very remarkable gifts that attest the divine nature within us, yet to overlook the Author who gives them to us at our asking. With what clear manifestations his might draws us to contemplate him! Unless perchance it be unknown to us in whose power it lies to sustain this infinite mass of heaven and earth by his Word: by his nod alone sometimes to shake heaven with thunderbolts, to burn everything with lightnings, to kindle the air with flashes; sometimes to disturb it with various sorts of storms, and then at his pleasure to clear them away in a moment; to compel the sea, which by its height seems to threaten the earth with continual destruction, to hang as if in mid-air; sometimes to arouse it in a dreadful way with the tumultuous force of winds; sometimes, with waves quieted, to make it calm again! Belonging to this theme are the praises of God's power from the testimonies of nature which one meets here and there especially indeed in The Book of Job and in Isaiah. These I now intentionally pass over, for they will find a more appropriate place where I shall discuss from the Scriptures the creation of the universe. Now I have only wanted to touch upon the fact that this way of seeking God is common both to strangers and to those of his household, if they trace the outlines that above and below sketch a living likeness of him. This very might leads us to ponder his eternity; for he from whom all things draw their origin must be eternal and have beginning from himself. Furthermore, if the cause is sought by which he was led once to create all these things, and is now moved to preserve them, we shall find that it is his goodness alone. But this being the sole cause, it ought still to be more than sufficient to draw us to his love, inasmuch as there is no creature, as the prophet declares, upon whom God's mercy has not been poured out [Ps. 145:9; cf. Ecclus. 18:11; 18:9, Vg.].

7. God's government and judgment

In the second kind of works, which are outside the ordinary course of nature also, proofs of his powers just as clear are set forth. For in administering human society he so tempers his providence that, although kindly and beneficent toward all in numberless ways, he still by open and daily indications declares his clemency to the godly and his severity to the wicked and criminal. For there are no doubts about what sort of vengeance he takes on wicked deeds. Thus he clearly shows himself the protector and vindicator of innocence, while he prospers the life of good men with his blessing, relieves their need, soothes and mitigates their pain, and alleviates their calamities; and in all these things he provides for their salvation. And indeed the unfailing rule of his righteousness ought not to be obscured by the fact that he frequently allows the wicked and malefactors to exult unpunished for some time, while he permits the upright and deserving to be tossed about by many adversities, and even to be oppressed by the malice and iniquity of the impious. But a far different consideration ought, rather, to enter our minds: that, when with a manifest show of his anger he punishes one sin, he hates all sins; that, when he leaves many sins unpunished, there will be another judgment to which have been deferred the sins yet to be punished. Similarly, what great occasion he gives us to contemplate his mercy when he often pursues miserable sinners with unwearied kindness, until he shatters their wickedness by imparting benefits and by recalling them to him with more than fatherly kindness!

8. *God's sovereign sway over the life of men*

To this end, the prophet is mindful that in their desperate straits God suddenly and wonderfully and beyond all hope succors the poor and almost lost; those wandering through the desert he protects from wild beasts and at last guides them back to the way [Ps. 107:4–7]; to the needy and hungry he supplies food [v. 9]; the prisoners he frees from loathsome dungeons and iron bands [vs. 10–16]; the shipwrecked he leads back to port unharmed [vs. 23–30]; the half dead he cures of disease [vs. 17–20]; he burns the earth with heat and dryness, or makes it fertile with the secret watering of grace [vs. 33–38]; he raises up the humblest from the crowd, or casts down the lofty from the high level of their dignity [vs. 39–41]. By setting forth examples of this sort, the prophet shows that what are thought to be chance occurrences are just so many proofs of heavenly providence, especially of fatherly kindness. And hence ground for rejoicing is given to the godly, while as for the wicked and the reprobate, their mouths are stopped [v. 42]. But because most people, immersed in their own errors, are struck blind in such a dazzling theater, he exclaims that to weigh these works of God wisely is a matter of rare and singular wisdom [v. 43], in viewing which they who otherwise seem to be extremely acute profit nothing. And certainly however much the glory of God shines forth, scarcely one man in a hundred is a true spectator of it!

In no greater degree is his power or his wisdom hidden in darkness. His power shows itself clearly when the ferocity of the impious, in everyone's opinion unconquerable, is overcome in a moment, their arrogance vanquished, their strongest defenses destroyed, their javelins and armor shattered, their strength broken, their machinations overturned, and themselves fallen of their own weight; and when their audacity, which exalted them above heaven, lays them low even to the center of the earth; when, conversely the humble are raised up from the dust, and the needy are lifted up from the dung heap [Ps. 113:7]; the oppressed and afflicted are rescued from their extreme tribulation; the despairing are restored to good hope; the unarmed, few and weak, snatch victory from the armed, many and strong. Indeed, his wisdom manifests his excellence when he dispenses everything at the best opportunity; when he confounds all wisdom of the world [cf. I Cor. 1:20]; when "he catches the crafty in their own craftiness" [I Cor. 3:19 p.; cf. Job 5:13]. In short, there is nothing that he does not temper in the best way.

9. *We ought not to rack our brains about God; but rather, we should contemplate him in his works*

We see that no long or toilsome proof is needed to elicit evidences that serve to illuminate and affirm the divine majesty; since from the few we have sampled at random, whithersoever you turn, it is clear that they are so very manifest and obvious that they can easily be observed with the eyes and pointed out with the finger. And here again we ought to observe that we are called to a knowledge of God: not that knowledge which, content with empty speculation, merely flits in the brain, but that which will be sound and fruitful if we duly perceive it, and if it takes root in the heart. For the Lord manifests himself by his powers, the force of which we feel within ourselves and the benefits of which we enjoy. We must therefore be much more profoundly affected by this knowledge than if we were to imagine a God of whom no perception came through to us. Consequently, we know the most perfect way of seeking God, and the most suitable order, is not for us to attempt with bold curiosity to penetrate to the investigation of his essence, which we ought more to adore than meticulously to search out, but for us to contemplate him in his works whereby he renders himself near and familiar to us, and in some manner communicates himself. The apostle was referring to this when he said that we need not seek him far away, seeing that he dwells by his very present power in each of us [Acts 17:27–28]. For this reason, David, having first confessed his unspeakable greatness [Ps. 145:3], afterward proceeds to mention his works and professes that he will declare his greatness [Ps. 145:5–6; cf. Ps. 40:5]. It is also fitting, therefore, for us to pursue this particular search for God, which may so hold our mental powers suspended in wonderment as at the same time to stir us deeply. And as Augustine teaches elsewhere, because, disheartened by his greatness, we cannot grasp him, we ought to gaze upon his works, that we may be restored by his goodness.

10. *The purpose of this knowledge of God*

Knowledge of this sort, then, ought not only to arouse us to the worship of God but also to awaken and encourage us to the hope of the future life. For since we notice that the examples that the Lord shows us both of his clemency and of his serverity are inchoate and incomplete, doubtless we must consider this to presage even greater things, the manifestation and full exhibition of which are deferred to another life. On the other hand – since we see the pious laden with afflictions by the impious, stricken with unjust acts, overwhelmed with slanders, wounded with abuses and reproaches; while the wicked on the contrary flourish, are prosperous, obtain repose with dignity and that without punishment – we must straightaway conclude that there will be another life in which iniquity is to have its punishment, and righteousness is to be given its reward. Furthermore since we observe that believers are often chastised by the Lord's rods, we may with full assurance believe that one day the wicked must no less suffer his lash. Indeed, Augustine's remark is well known: "If now every sin were to suffer open punishment, it would seem that nothing is reserved for the final judgment. Again, if God were now to punish no sin openly, one would believe that there is no providence."

We must therefore admit in God's individual works – but especially in them as a whole – that God's powers are actually represented as in a painting. Thereby the whole of mankind is invited and attracted to recognition of him, and from this to true and complete happiness. Now those powers appear most clearly in his works. Yet we comprehend their chief purpose, their value, and the reason why we should ponder them, only when we descend into ourselves and contemplate by what means the Lord shows in us his life, wisdom, and power; and exercises in our behalf his righteousness, goodness, and mercy. For even though David justly complains that unbelievers are foolish because they do not ponder the deep designs of God in the governance of mankind [Ps. 92:5–6], yet what he says elsewhere is very true: that God's wonderful wisdom here abounds more than the hairs of our head [cf. Ps. 40:12]. But because this argument is to be treated more amply below, I now pass over it.

(Man nevertheless, failing to know and worship him, falls into superstition and confusion, 11–12)

11. *The evidence of God in creation does not profit us*

But although the Lord represents both himself and his everlasting Kingdom in the mirror of his works with very great clarity, such is our stupidity that we grow increasingly dull toward so manifest testimonies, and they flow away without profiting us. For with regard to the most beautiful structure and order of the universe, how many of us are there who, when we lift up our eyes to heaven or cast them about through the various regions of earth, recall our minds to a remembrance of the Creator, and do not rather, disregarding their Author, sit idly in comtemplation of his works? In fact, with regard to those events which daily take place outside the ordinary course of nature, how many of us do not reckon that men are whirled and twisted about by blindly indiscriminate fortune, rather than governed by God's providence? Sometimes we are driven by the leading and direction of these things to contemplate God; this of necessity happens to all men. Yet after we rashly grasp a conception of some sort of divinity, straightaway we fall back into the ravings or evil imaginings of our flesh, and corrupt by our vanity the pure truth of God. In one respect we are indeed unalike, because each one of us privately forges his own particular error; yet we are very much alike in that, one and all, we forsake the one true God for prodigious trifles. Not only the common folk and dull-witted men, but also the most excellent and those otherwise endowed with keen discernment, are infected with this disease.

In this regard how volubly has the whole tribe of philosophers shown their stupidity and silliness! For even though we may excuse the others (who act like utter fools), Plato, the most religious of all and the most circumspect, also vanishes in his round globe. And what might not happen to others when the leading minds, whose task it is to light the pathway for the rest, wander and stumble! It is the same where the governance of human affairs shows providence so manifestly that we cannot deny it; yet we profit no more by it than if we believed that all things were turned topsy-turvy by the heedless will of fortune – so great is our inclination toward vanity and error! I always speak of the most excellent, not of those vulgar folk whose madness in profaning God's truth is beyond measure.

12. *The manifestation of God is choked by human superstition and the error of the philosophers*
Hence arises that boundless filthy mire of error wherewith the whole earth was filled and covered. For each man's mind is like a labyrinth, so that it is no wonder that individual nations were drawn aside into various falsehoods; and not only this – but individual men, almost, had their own gods. For as rashness and superficiality are joined to ignorance and darkness, scarcely a single person has ever been found who did not fashion for himself an idol or specter in place of God. Surely, just as waters boil up from a vast, full spring, so does an immense crowd of gods flow forth from the human mind, while each one, in wandering about with too much license, wrongly invents this or that about God himself. However, it is not necessary here to draw up a list of the superstitions with which the world has been entangled, because there would be no end to it, and so without a word of them it is sufficiently clear from so many corruptions how horrible is the blindness of the human mind. I pass over the rude and untutored crowd. But among the philosophers who have tried with reason and learning to penetrate into heaven, how shameful is the diversity! As each was furnished with higher wit, graced with art and knowledge, so did he seem to camouflage his utterances; yet if you look more closely upon all these, you will find them all to be fleeting unrealities. The Stoics thought themselves very clear when they said that one could elicit from all parts of nature various names for God, yet without on this account destroying the unity of God – as if, indeed, we were not already more than prone to vanity, without being drawn farther and more violently into error by the multiplicity of gods foisted upon us! Even the mystic theology of the Egyptians shows all have sedulously brooded upon this so as not to appear to rave without reason. And perchance even at first glance something that seemed probable would deceive the simple and careless; but no mortal ever contrived anything that did not basely corrupt religion.

And this very confused diversity emboldened the Epicureans and other crass despisers of piety to cast out all awareness of God. For when they saw the wisest persons contending with contrary opinions, from the disagreements of these – and even from their frivolous or absurd teaching – they did not hesitate to gather that men vainly and foolishly bring torments upon themselves when they seek for a god that is not. And this they thought to do with impunity because it would be preferable to deny outright God's existence than to fashion uncertain gods, and then stir up endless quarrels. But these folk pass a purely foolish judgment, or, rather, they conjure up a cloud out of men's ignorance to conceal their own impiety; in such ignorance there is not the least justification for departing from God. But since all confess that there is nothing concerning which the learned and the unlearned at the same time disagree so much, hence one may conclude that the minds of men which thus wander in their search after God are more than stupid and blind in the heavenly mysteries. Some praise the reply of Simonides, who, asked by the tyrant Hiero what God was, begged to be given a day to ponder. When on the following day the tyrant asked the same question, he asked for two days more, and after having frequently doubled the number of days, finally answered, "The longer I consider this, the more obscure it seems to me." He wisely indeed suspended judgment on a subject so obscure to himself. Yet hence it appears that if men were taught only by nature, they would hold to nothing certain or solid or clear-cut, but would be so tied to confused principles as to worship an unknown god [cf. Acts 17:23].

(Persistent in error, we are without excuse, 13–15)
13. The Holy Spirit rejects all cults contrived by men
Now we must also hold that all who corrupt pure religion – and this is sure to happen when each is given to his own opinion – separate themselves from the one and only God. Indeed, they will boast that they have something else in mind; but what they intend, or what they have persuaded themselves of, has not much bearing on the matter, seeing that the Holy Spirit pronounces them all to be apostates who in the blindness of their own minds substitute demons in place of God [cf. I Cor. 10:20]. For this reason, Paul declares the Ephesians were without God until they learned from the gospel what it was to worship the true God [Eph. 2:12–13]. And this must not be restricted to one people, since elsewhere he states generally that all mortals "became vain in their reasonings" [Rom. 1:21] after the majesty of the Creator had been disclosed to them in the fashioning of the universe. For this reason, Scripture, to make place for the true and only God, condemned as falsehood and lying whatever of divinity had formerly been celebrated among the heathen; nor did any divine presence remain except on Mt Zion, where the proper knowledge of God continued to flourish [Hab. 2:18, 20]. Certainly among the pagans in Christ's lifetime the Samaritans seemed to come closest to the true piety; yet we hear from Christ's mouth that they knew not what they worshiped [John 4:22]. From this it follows that they were deluded by vain error.

In short, even if not all suffered under crass vices, or fell into open idolatries, yet there was no pure and approved religion, founded upon common understanding alone. For even though few persons did not share in the madness of the common herd, there remains the firm teaching of Paul that the wisdom of God is not understood by the princes of this world [I Cor. 2:8]. But if even the most illustrious wander in darkness, what can we say of the dregs? It is therefore no wonder that the Holy Spirit rejects as base all cults contrived through the will of men; for in the heavenly mysteries, opinion humanly conceived, even if it does not always give birth to a great heap of errors, is nevertheless the mother of error. And though nothing more harmful may result, yet to worship an unknown god [cf. Acts 17:23] by chance is no light fault. Nevertheless, by Christ's own statement all who have not been taught from the law what god they ought to worship are guilty in this matter [John 4:22]. And surely they who were the best legislators did not progress farther than to hold that religion was founded upon public agreement. Nay, according to Xenophon, Socrates praises the oracle of Apollo, which commanded that every man worship the gods after the manner of his forefathers and according to the custom of his own city. But whence comes this law to mortals that they may by their own authority define what far surpasses the world? Or who could so acquiesce in decrees of his ancestors, or enactments of the people, as to receive without hesitation a god humanly taught him? Each man will stand upon his own judgment rather than subject himself to another's decision. Therefore, since either the custom of the city or the agreement of tradition is too weak and frail a bond of piety to follow in worshiping God, it remains for God himself to give witness of himself from heaven.

14. *The manifestation of God in nature speaks to us in vain*

It is therefore in vain that so many burning lamps shine for us in the workmanship of the universe to show forth the glory of its Author. Although they bathe us wholly in their radiance, yet they can of themselves in no way lead us into the right path. Surely they strike some sparks, but before their fuller light shines forth these are smothered. For this reason, the apostle, in that very passage where he calls the worlds the images of things invisible, adds that through faith we understand that they have been fashioned by God's word [Heb. 11:3]. He means by this that the invisible divinity is made manifest in such spectacles, but that we have not the eyes to see this unless they be illumined by the inner revelation of God through faith. And where Paul teaches that what is to be known of God is made plain from the creation of the universe [Rom. 1:19], he does not signify such a manifestation as men's discernment can comprehend; but, rather, shows it not to go farther than to render them inexcusable. The same apostle also, even if he somewhere denies that God is to be sought far off, inasmuch as he dwells within us [Acts 17:27], in another place teaches of what avail that sort of nearness is, saying: "In past generations the Lord let the nations follow their own ways. Yet God did not leave himself without witness, sending benefits from heaven, giving rain and fruitful seasons, filling men's hearts with food and gladness" [Acts 14:16–17; vs. 15–16, Vg.]. Therefore, although the Lord does not want for testimony while he sweetly attracts men to the knowledge of himself with many and varied kindnesses, they do not cease on this account to follow their own ways, that is, their fatal errors.

15. *We have no excuse*

But although we lack the natural ability to mount up unto the pure and clear knowledge of God, all excuse is cut off because the fault of dullness is within us. And, indeed, we are not allowed thus to pretend ignorance without our conscience itself always convicting us of both baseness and ingratitude. As if this defense may properly be admitted: for a man to pretend that he lacks ears to hear the truth when there are mute creatures with more than melodious voices to declare it; or for a man to claim that he cannot see with his eyes what eyeless creatures point out to him; or for him to plead feebleness of mind when even irrational creatures give instruction! Therefore we are justly denied every excuse when we stray off as wanderers and vagrants even though everything points out the right way. But, however that may be, yet the fact that men soon corrupt the seed of the knowledge of God, sown in their minds out of the wonderful workmanship of nature (thus preventing it from coming to a good and perfect fruit), must be imputed to their own failing; nevertheless, it is very true that we are not at all sufficiently instructed by this bare and simple testimony which the creatures render splendidly to the glory of God. For at the same time as we have enjoyed a slight taste of the divine from contemplation of the universe, having neglected the true God, we raise up in his stead dreams and specters of our own brains, and attribute to anything else than the true source the praise of righteousness, wisdom, goodness, and power. Moreover, we so obscure or overturn his daily acts by wickedly judging them that we snatch away from them their glory and from their Author his due praise.

· *CHAPTER VI: Scripture is needed as guide and teacher for anyone who would come to God the Creator* ·

1. *God bestows the actual knowledge of himself upon us only in the Scriptures*

That brightness which is borne in upon the eyes of all men both in heaven and on earth is more than enough to withdraw all support from men's ingratitude – just as God, to involve the human race in the same guilt, sets forth to all without exception his presence portrayed in his creatures. Despite this, it is needful that another and better help be added to direct us aright to the very Creator of the universe. It was not in vain, then, that he added the light of his Word by which to become known unto salvation; and he regarded as worthy of this privilege those whom he pleased to gather more closely and intimately to himself. For because he saw the minds of all men tossed and agitated, after he chose the Jews as his very own flock, he fenced them about that they might not sink into oblivion as others had. With good reason he holds us by the same means in the pure knowledge of himself, since otherwise even those who seem to stand firm before all others would soon melt away. Just as old or bleary-eyed men and those with weak vision, if you thrust before them a most beautiful volume, even if they recognize it to be some sort of writing, yet can scarcely construe two words, but with the aid of spectacles will begin to read distinctly; so Scripture, gathering up the otherwise confused knowledge of God in our minds, having dispersed our dullness, clearly shows us the true God. This, therefore, is a special gift, where God, to instruct the church, not merely uses mute teachers but also opens his own most hallowed lips. Not only does he teach the elect to look upon a god, but also shows himself as the God upon whom they are to look. He has from the beginning maintained this plan for his church, so that besides these common proofs he also put forth his Word, which is a more direct and more certain mark whereby he is to be recognized.

(Two sorts of knowledge of God in Scripture)

There is no doubt that Adam, Noah, Abraham, and the rest of the patriarchs with this assistance penetrated to the intimate knowledge of him that in a way distinguished them from unbelievers. I am not yet speaking of the proper doctrine of faith whereby they had been illumined unto the hope of eternal life. For, that they might pass from death to life, it was necessary to recognize God not only as Creator but also as Redeemer, for undoubtedly they arrived at both from the Word. First in order came that kind of knowledge by which one is permitted to grasp who that God is who founded and governs the universe. Then that other inner knowledge was added, which alone quickens dead souls, whereby God is known not only as the Founder of the universe and the sole Author and Ruler of all that is made, but also in the person of the Mediator as the Redeemer. But because we have not yet come to the fall of the world and the corruption of nature, I shall now forego discussion of the remedy. My readers therefore should remember that I am not yet going to discuss that covenant by which God adopted to himself the sons of Abraham, or that part of doctrine which has always separated believers from unbelieving folk, for it was founded in Christ. But here I shall discuss only how we should learn from Scripture that God, the Creator of the universe, can by sure marks be distinguished from all the throng of feigned gods. Then, in due order, that series will lead us to the redemption. We shall derive many testimonies from the New Testament, and other testimonies also from the Law and the Prophets, where express mention is made of Christ. Nevertheless, all things will tend to this end, that God, the Artificer of the universe, is made manifest to us in Scripture, and that what we ought to think of him is set forth there, lest we seek some uncertain deity by devious paths.

2. *The Word of God as Holy Scripture*

But whether God became known to the patriarchs through oracles and visions or by the work and ministry of men, he put into their minds what they should then hand down to their posterity. At any rate, there is no doubt that firm certainty of doctrine was engraved in their hearts, so that they were convinced and understood that what they had learned proceeded from God. For by his Word, God rendered faith unambiguous forever, a faith that should be superior to all opinion. Finally, in order that truth might abide forever in the world with a continuing succession of teaching and survive through all ages, the same oracles he had given to the patriarchs it was his pleasure to have recorded, as it were, on public tablets. With this intent the law was published, and the prophets afterward added as its interpreters. For even though the use of the law was manifold, as will be seen more clearly in its place, it was especially committed to Moses and all the prophets to teach the way of reconciliation between God and men, whence also Paul calls "Christ the end of the law" [Rom. 10:4]. Yet I repeat once more: besides the specific doctrine of faith and repentance that sets forth Christ as Mediator, Scripture adorns with unmistakable marks and tokens the one true God, in that he has created and governs the universe, in order that he may not be mixed up with the throng of false gods. Therefore, however fitting it may be for man seriously to turn his eyes to contemplate God's works, since he has been placed in this most glorious theater to be a spectator of them, it is fitting that he prick up his ears to the Word, the better to profit. And it is therefore no wonder that those who were born in darkness become more and more hardened in their insensibility; for there are very few who, to contain themselves within bounds, apply themselves teachably to God's Word, but they rather exult in their own vanity. Now, in order that true religion may shine upon us, we ought to hold that it must take its beginning from heavenly doctrine and that no one can get even the slightest taste of right and sound doctrine unless he be a pupil of Scripture. Hence, there also emerges the beginning of true understanding when we reverently embrace what it pleases God there to witness of himself. But not only faith, perfect and in every way complete, but all right knowledge of God is born of obedience. And surely in this respect God has, by his singular providence, taken thought for mortals through all ages.

3. *Without Scripture we fall into error*

Suppose we ponder how slippery is the fall of the human mind into forgetfulness of God, how great the tendency to every kind of error, how great the lust to fashion constantly new and artificial religions. Then we may perceive how necessary was such written proof of the heavenly doctrine, that it should neither perish through forgetfulness nor vanish through error nor be corrupted by the audacity of men. It is therefore clear that God has provided the assistance of the Word for the sake of all those to whom he has been pleased to give useful instruction because he foresaw that his likeness imprinted upon the most beautiful form of the universe would be insufficiently effective. Hence, we must strive onward by this straight path if we seriously aspire to the pure contemplation of God. We must come, I say, to the Word, where God is truly and vividly described to us from his works, while these very works are appraised not by our depraved judgment but by the rule of eternal truth. If we turn aside from the Word, as I have just now said, though we may strive with strenuous haste, yet, since we have got off the track, we shall never reach the goal. For we should so reason that the splendor of the divine countenance, which even the apostle calls "unapproachable" [I Tim. 6:16], is for us like an inexplicable labyrinth unless we are conducted into it by the thread of the Word; so that it is better to limp along this path than to dash with all speed outside it. David very often, therefore, teaching that we ought to banish superstitions from the earth so that pure religion may flourish, represented God as regnant [Ps. 93:1; 96:10; 97:1; 99:1; and the like]. Now he means by the word "regnant" not the power with which he is endowed, and which he exercises in governing the whole of nature, but the doctrine by which he asserts his lawful sovereignty. For errors can never be uprooted from human hearts until true knowledge of God is planted therein.

4. *Scripture can communicate to us what the revelation in the creation cannot*

Accordingly, the same prophet, after he states, "The heavens declare the glory of God, the firmament shows forth the works of his hands, the ordered succession of days and nights proclaims his majesty" [Ps. 19:1–2 p.], then proceeds to mention his Word: "The law of the Lord is spotless, converting souls; the testimony of the Lord is faithful, giving wisdom to little ones; the righteous acts of the Lord are right, rejoicing hearts; the precept of the Lord is clear, enlightening eyes" [Ps. 18:8–9, Vg.; 19:7–8]. For although he also includes other uses of the law, he means in general that, since God in vain calls all peoples to himself by the contemplation of heaven and earth, this is the very school of God's children. Psalm 29 looks to this same end, where the prophet – speaking forth concerning God's awesome voice, which strikes the earth in thunder [v. 3], winds, rains, whirlwinds and tempests, causes mountains to tremble [v. 6], shatters the cedars [v. 5] – finally adds at the end that his praises are sung in the sanctuary because the unbelievers are deaf to all the voices of God that resound in the air [vs. 9–11]. Similarly, he thus ends another psalm where he has described the awesome waves of the sea: "Thy testimonies have been verified, the beauty and holiness of thy temple shall endure forevermore" [Ps. 93:5 p.]. Hence, also, arises that which Christ said to the Samaritan woman, that her people and all other peoples worshiped they knew not what; that the Jews alone offered worship to the true God [John 4:22]. For, since the human mind because of its feebleness can in no way attain to God unless it be aided and assisted by his Sacred Word, all mortals at that time – except for the Jews – because they were seeking God without the Word, had of necessity to stagger about in vanity and error.

. . . .

CHAPTER X: Scripture, to correct all superstition, has set the True God alone over against all the gods of the heathen

3. Because the unity of God was also not unknown to the heathen, the worshipers of idols are the more inexcusable

But here I propose to summarize the general doctrine. And first, indeed, let readers observe that Scripture, to direct us to the true God, distinctly excludes and rejects all the gods of the heathen, for religion was commonly adulterated throughout almost all ages. Indeed, it is true that the name of one God was everywhere known and renowned. For men who worshipped a swarm of gods, whenever speaking from a real feeling of nature, as if content with a single God, simply used the name "God"; and Justin Martyr, wisely noting this, composed a book, *God's Monarchy*, in which he showed by very many testimonies that the unity of God has been engraved upon the hearts of all. Tertullian likewise proves the same point by phrases in common use. But all the heathen, to a man, by their own vanity either were dragged or slipped back into false inventions, and thus their perceptions so vanished that whatever they had naturally sensed concerning the sole God had no value beyond making them inexcusable. For even the wisest of them openly display the vague wanderings of their minds when they long for some god or other to be present among them, and so invoke dubious gods in their prayers. Besides this, in imagining a god of many natures – although they held a view less absurd than the ignorant multitude with its Jupiter, Mercury, Venus, Minerva, and the rest – they, too, were not free of Satan's deceptions. As we have already said elsewhere, all the evasions the philosophers have skillfully contrived do not refute the charge of defection; rather, the truth of God has been corrupted by them all. For this reason, Habakkuk, when he condemned all idols, bade men seek God "in his temple" [Hab. 2:20] lest believers admit someone other than him who revealed himself by his Word.

9

The Creed of the Council of Trent

The Protestant Reformation posed a challenge to the theology and practice of the Roman Catholic Church in the sixteenth century. In response, the Roman Church launched some initiatives of its own, among them a church council which met on and off over eighteen years (1545–63). What came to be called the "Council of Trent" rectified some problems in the Catholic Church of the day, and officially defined certain positions for the Church in the face of the Protestant challenge to its authority – including statements on authority (Scripture and tradition), justification, and the sacraments. Issued as a bull by Pope Pius IV in 1564, the following "Creed of the Council of Trent" reiterates, and so underscores, the necessity of the Catholic faith for salvation. The first paragraph contains a version of the Nicene Creed. Statements in parentheses in the last paragraph were added in 1877 by order of Pope Pius IX and reflect a key dogma proclaimed at the First Vatican Council in 1870: namely, papal infallibility.

The Text

I, N., with firm faith believe and profess each and every article contained in the Symbol of faith which the holy Roman Church uses; namely: I believe in one God, the Father almighty, maker of heaven and earth, and of all things visible and invisible; and in one Lord Jesus Christ, the only-begotten Son of God, born of the Father before all ages; God from God, light from light, true God from true God; begotten not made, of one substance with the Father, through whom all things were made; who for us men and for our salvation came down from heaven, and was made incarnate by the Holy Spirit of the Virgin Mary, and was made man. He was crucified also for us under Pontius Pilate, died, and was buried; and he rose again the third day according to the Scriptures, and ascended into heaven; he sits at the right hand of the Father, and he shall come again in glory to judge the living and the dead, and of his kingdom there will be no end. And I believe in the Holy Spirit the Lord, and giver of life, who proceeds from the Father and the Son; who equally with the Father and the Son is adored and glorified; who spoke through the prophets. And I believe that there is one, holy, Catholic, and apostolic Church. I confess one baptism for the remission of sins; and I hope for the resurrection of the dead, and the life of the world to come. Amen.

I resolutely accept and embrace the apostolic and ecclesiastical traditions and the other practices and regulations of that same Church. In like manner I accept Sacred Scripture according to the meaning which has been held by holy Mother Church and which she now holds. It is her prerogative to pass judgment on the true meaning and interpretation of Sacred Scripture. And I will never accept or interpret it in a manner different from the unanimous agreement of the Fathers.

I also acknowledge that there are truly and properly seven sacraments of the New Law, instituted by Jesus Christ our Lord, and that they are necessary for the salvation of the human race, although it is not necessary for each individual to receive them all. I acknowledge that the seven sacraments are: baptism, confirmation, Eucharist, penance, extreme unction, holy orders, and matrimony; and that they confer grace; and that of the seven, baptism, confirmation, and holy orders cannot be repeated without committing a sacrilege. I also accept and acknowledge the customary and approved rites of the Catholic Church in the solemn administration of these sacraments. I embrace and accept each and every article on original sin and justification declared and defined in the most holy Council of Trent.

I likewise profess that in the Mass a true, proper, and propitiatory sacrifice is offered to God on behalf of the living and the dead, and that the body and blood together with the soul and divinity of our Lord Jesus Christ is truly, really, and substantially present in the most holy sacrament of the Eucharist, and that there is a change of

Source: *The Church Teaches: Documents of the Church in English Translation*, eds J. F. Clarkson et al.

the whole substance of the bread into the body, and of the whole substance of the wine into blood; and this change the Catholic Church calls transubstantiation. I also profess that the whole and entire Christ and a true sacrament is received under each separate species.

I firmly hold that there is a purgatory, and that the souls detained there are helped by the prayers of the faithful. I likewise hold that the saints reigning together with Christ should be honored and invoked, that they offer prayers to God on our behalf, and that their relics should be venerated. I firmly assert that images of Christ, of the Mother of God ever Virgin, and of the other saints should be owned and kept, and that due honor and veneration should be given to them. I affirm that the power of indulgences was left in the keeping of the Church by Christ, and that the use of indulgences is very beneficial to Christians.

I acknowledge the holy, Catholic, and apostolic Roman Church as the mother and teacher of all churches; and I promise and swear true obedience to the Roman Pontiff, vicar of Christ and successor of Blessed Peter, Prince of the Apostles.

I unhesitatingly accept and profess all the doctrines (especially those concerning the primacy of the Roman Pontiff and his infallible teaching authority) handed down, defined, and explained by the sacred canons and ecumenical councils and especially those of this most holy Council of Trent (and by the ecumenical Vatican Council). And at the same time I condemn, reject, and anathematize everything that is contrary to those propositions, and all heresies without exception that have been condemned, rejected, and anathematized by the Church. I, N., promise, vow, and swear that, with God's help, I shall most constantly hold and profess this true Catholic faith, outside which no one can be saved and which I now freely profess and truly hold. With the help of God, I shall profess it whole and unblemished to my dying breath; and, to the best of my ability, I shall see to it that my subjects or those entrusted to me by virtue of my office hold it, teach it, and preach it. So help me God and his holy Gospel.

Part V

Modern and Postmodern Texts

(*c.*1600 to the present)

10

Herbert of Cherbury, "Common Notions Concerning Religion"

The post-Reformation wars of religion in Europe tended to provoke one of two reactions in many people: either they took sides (which often amounted to a kind of sectarianism) or they pronounced a plague on the houses of both sides in a conflict (which often amounted to secularism). Some critics of religious wars, however, recognized the importance of religion insofar as they discerned that religion functions in a number of important ways in human life, including keeping affairs from becoming amoral or chaotic. Instead of choosing to identify with a particular sect or to embrace secular nonbelief, some thinkers sought a middle way which took into account both some form of religious belief and the emerging and increasingly credible scientific advances of the early modern period.

The thinking went as follows. Modern science seems to provide evidence that nature is regular, like a machine; a machine-maker seems a good explanation for such regularity. This machine-maker is none other than God, who established order and law in nature which reason can decipher. In such natural religion, religion is accordingly purged of superstition and shown to be rational. There is still therefore a God, but this God is the engineer of the universe, a watchmaker, a machine-maker – and not necessarily the God revealed in the Bible. This view came to be called "deism," from the Latin word for God (*deus*). It came to be associated with heterodoxy, and was therefore distingushed from theism, from the Greek word for God (*theos*), which came to be associated with orthodoxy. Deism became a key ingredient in many influential eighteenth-century Enlightenment views of religions and their relations.

The chief architect of this way of thinking was Edward Herbert (1583–1648), also known as Lord Herbert of Cherbury and the founder of English deism. He articulated this view a century or so before it became influential. In the face of religious conflict and scientific skepticism, Herbert sought in his work *De Veritate* ("On Truth"), from which the following reading is taken, to establish a new theory of knowledge and new criteria for determining truth. He concluded that natural instinct indicates that there are intellectual truths, the content of which he called the "Common Notions." The Common Notions are a priori, independent of other principles, universal, certain, necessary for life, and immediately apprehensible – as well as the final court of appeal for our beliefs and the essence of the deistic viewpoint. Concerning religion, Herbert argued, God has inscribed five Common Notions in the human mind; they deal with the existence of God, worship, piety, virtue, morality, eternal life, and the like. Religions are therefore all *essentially* similar, according to Herbert, differing only regarding what they add to the original endowment. In the end, Herbert judged Christianity to be superior for its faithfulness to – or least corruption of – the Common Notions.

The Text

Before I proceed to discuss revelation, I think that certain assumptions which underlie our notions of revelation ought to be examined. Every religion which proclaims a revelation is not good, nor is every doctrine which is taught under its authority always essential or even valuable. Some doctrines due to revelation may be, some of them ought to be, abandoned. In this connection the teaching of Common Notions is important; indeed, without them it is impossible to establish any standard of discrimination in revelation or even in religion. Theories based upon implicit faith, though widely held not only in our own part of the world but also in the most distant regions, are here irrelevant. Instances of such beliefs are: that human reason must be discarded, to make room for Faith; that the Church, which is infallible, has the right to prescribe the method of divine worship, and in consequence must be obeyed in every detail; that no one ought to place such confidence in his private judgment as to dare to question the sacred authority of priests and preachers of God's word; that their utterances, though they may elude human grasp, contain so much truth that we should rather lay them to heart than debate them; that to God all the things of which they speak and much more are possible. Now these arguments and many other similar ones, according to differences of age and country, may be equally used to establish a false religion as to support a true one. Anything that springs from the productive, not to say seductive, seed of Faith will yield a plentiful crop. What pompous charlatan can fail to impress his ragged flock with such ideas: Is there any fantastic cult which may not be proclaimed under such auspices? How can any age escape deception, especially when the cunning authorities declare their inventions to be heaven-born, though in reality they habitually confuse and mix the truth with falsehood? If we do not advance toward truth upon a foundation of Common Notions, assigning every element its true value, how can we hope to reach any but futile conclusions? Indeed, however those who endeavor to base their beliefs upon the disordered and licentious codes of superstition may protest, their behavior is precisely similar to people who with the purpose of blinding the eyes of the wayfarer with least trouble to themselves offer with singular courtesy to act as guides on the journey. But the actual facts are otherwise. The supreme Judge requires every individual to render an account of his actions in the light, not of another's belief, but of his own. So we must establish the fundamental principles of religion by means of universal wisdom, so that whatever has been added to it by the genuine dictates of Faith may rest on that foundation as a roof is supported on a house. Accordingly, we ought not to accept any kind of religion lightly, without first enquiring into the sources of its prestige. And the Reader will find all these considerations depend upon Common Notions. Can anyone, I beg to ask, read the huge mass of books composed with such immense display of learning, without feeling scorn for these age-long impostures and fables, save in so far as they point the way to holiness? What man

Source: *Attitudes Toward Other Religions: Some Christian Interpretations*, ed. Owen C. Thomas.

could yield unquestioning faith to a body which, disguised under the name of the Church, wastes its time over a multitude of rites, ceremonies, and vanities, which fights in so many parts of the world under different banners, if he were not led to perceive, by the aid of conscience, some marks of worship, piety, penance, reward, and punishment? Who, finally, would attend to the living voice of the preacher if he did not refer all his deeds and words to the Sovereign Deity? It would take too long to deal with every instance. It is sufficient to make clear that we cannot establish any of them without the Common Notions. I value these so highly that I would say that the book, religion, and prophet which adheres most closely to them is the best. The system of Notions, so far at least as it concerns theology, has been clearly accepted at all times by every normal person, and does not require any further justification. And, first of all, the teaching of Common Notions, or true Catholic Church, which has never erred, nor ever will err, and in which alone the glory of Divine Universal Providence is displayed, asserts that

There is a Supreme God

No general agreement exists concerning the Gods, but there is universal recognition of God. Every religion in the past has acknowledged, every religion in the future will acknowledge, some sovereign deity among the Gods, Thus to the Romans this supreme Power is Optimus Maximus; to the Greeks He is "Ὁ ἐπὶ πᾶσι Θεός αὐτοφυής, παντοκράτωρ, ἀρχὴ πάντων τε τελευτῇ"; to the Jews He is יהוה, Jehovah; to the Mohammedans, Allah; to the Indians of the West, Pachama Viracocha, etc. The Eastern Indians have similar names for Him. Accordingly that which is everywhere accepted as the supreme manifestation of deity, by whatever name it may be called, I term God. I pass on to consider His attributes, using the same method. And in the first place I find that He is Blessed. Secondly, He is the end to which all things move. Thirdly, He is the cause of all things, at least in so far as they are good. From which follows, according to His providence that, in the fourth place, He is the means by which all things are produced; for how could we pass from the beginning to the end but by the means provided? We need not be deterred by the type of philosophers who have refused to grant the medium any share of providence. Since circumstances seldom fall out in accordance with their wishes, they make a desperate attempt to abolish particular Providence as though the course of events were ordained by themselves and not by the Divine will. We must realize that writers of this kind are only wrangling about the means by which Divine Providence acts; they are not, I think, disputing Providence itself. Meanwhile the utmost agreement exists concerning Universal Providence, or Nature. But every religion believes that the Deity can hear and answer prayers; and we are bound to assume a special Providence – to omit other sources of proof – from the universal testimony of the sense of divine assistance in times of distress. In the fifth place, He is eternal. For we are taught by a Common Notion that what is first is eternal. In the sixth place a common Notion tells us that the Deity is good, since the cause of all good is supremely good. In the seventh place, He is just; a Common Notion, experience and history bear witness at every point that the world is ruled under His

Providence with absolute justice. For as I have often observed, Common Notions, which solve the most difficult questions of philosophy and theology, teach us that all things are governed with righteousness and justice, though their causes may be hidden from us. In the eighth place, He is wise; for marks of His wisdom do not only appear in the attributes of which I have spoken but are manifest daily in His works.

In addition to these qualities there are certain attributes, such as Infinity, Omnipotence, and Liberty, concerning which I find there is much difference of opinion. But His infinity is proved by the infinity of position or space. For the supreme God penetrates all things, according to the teaching of Common Notions. His Omnipotence follows from His infinity, for it is certain that there is nothing which is beyond the power of the infinite. His omnipotence proves His liberty, since no man in his senses has ever doubted that He who can do everything is absolutely free. I think, however, that those who feel otherwise must be approached from a different angle. And here there is a Common Notion that what exists in us in a limited degree is found absolutely in God. If He is so far beyond our capacity as to be illimitable He will be infinite. If He has created all things without using any existing matter He will be omnipotent. And finally if He is the Author of our liberty He will be supremely free. The ancient Schools were wrong in holding that men were free while God was fettered to the first Sphere. The Divine Attributes prove these points as effectively when taken separately as when taken together. On the attributes and their synonyms the Schools may usefully be consulted, and I find that in general they discuss them very fairly. It is true that I have found that the names which they have given these attributes are conflicting and often inappropriate. Thus the Pagans confuse the attribute of infinity with that of unity, and invent a number of Gods. Even if you suppose with some that under the names of Apollo, Mars, and Ceres, various aspects of Divine Providence were recognized, you cannot deny that the fables which the ancients invented under these names have always been thought foolish, since no one has ever doubted (so far as I am aware) the evils of their creed. As for the attributes which are rejected in our discussion, they are those which make the Deity strange, physical, composite, particular, or capable of condemning men for His own pleasure. Such a God is nothing but an idol of the imagination, and exists nowhere else. I pass now to the second Common Notion of theology.

This Sovereign Deity Ought to be Worshipped

While there is no general agreement concerning the worship of Gods, sacred beings, saints, and angels, yet the Common Notion or Universal Consent tells us that adoration ought to be reserved for the one God. Hence divine religion – and no race, however savage, has existed without some expression of it – is found established among all nations, not only on account of the benefits which they received from general providence but also in recognition of their dependence upon Grace, or particular providence. Hence, too, men have been convinced, as I have observed above, that they can not only supplicate that heavenly Power but prevail upon Him, by means of the faculties implanted in every normal man. Hence, finally, what is a more important indication, this Power was consulted by the seers in order to

173

interpret the future, and they undertook no important action without referring to it. So far the peoples were surely guided by the teaching of Natural Instinct. The All Wise Cause of the universe does not suffer itself to be enclosed within its own sphere, but it bestows general Grace on all and special Grace on those whom it has chosen. Since everyone can experience this in himself, would it not be unjust to refuse the same power to God? God does not suffer us to beseech Him in vain, as the universal experience of divine assistance proves, to pass over all other arguments. Although I find that the doctrine of special providence, or Grace, was only grudgingly acknowledged by the ancients, as may be gathered from their surviving works, yet since the worship of the Divine Power was recognized in every age, and carried with it this doctrine of Grace or Special Providence, I assert that this doctrine is a Common Notion. From this source spring supplications, prayers, sacrifices, acts of thanksgiving; to this end were built shrines, sanctuaries, and finally for this purpose appeared priests, prophets, seers, pontiffs, the whole order of ministers. And even if their activity has been equally evident in human affairs as in the affairs of God, since they have often been a crafty and deceitful tribe, prone to avarice, and often ineffective, this is because they have introduced much under the pretext of Religion which has no bearing upon Religion. In this way with extraordinary skill they have confused sacred matters with profane, truth with falsehood, possibility with probability, lawful worship with licentious ceremonies and senseless superstitions; with the result, I make bold to say, that they have corrupted, defiled, and prostituted the pure name of Religion. However necessary the priests were, whenever they brought contempt upon themselves, the fear of God and the respect due to sacred things diminished in proportion. Accordingly, we must give them the honor which is due to them. I obtain, then, proof of this external aspect of divine worship in any type of religion from every age, country, and race. It is therefore a Common Notion. It is no objection that temples or regions sacred to the Gods are not found among savages. For in their own fashion they consulted oracles and undertook no serious task without propitiating their Deity. I am aware that an author of reputation has said that in one remote region no religious practice can be observed. But this statement has been rejected by a later writer who pointed out that the author was ignorant of the language of that country. However, if anyone denies the assertion we must reply that the same religious faculties which anyone can experience in himself exist in every normal human being, though they appear in different forms and may be expressed without any external ceremony or ritual. And in postulating this principle I draw the conclusion that religion is the ultimate difference of man. I am not deterred by the fact that irreligious men exist, and even some who appear to be atheists. In reality they are not atheists; but because they have noticed that some people apply false and shocking attributes to God, they have preferred not to believe in God than to believe in a God of such a character. When He is endowed with true attributes, so far from not believing in Him they would pray that such a God might exist, if there were no such Being. If, however, you still maintain that irreligious persons and even atheists can be found (which I do not believe), reflect that there may be not a few madmen and fools included among those who maintain that rationality is the final difference of man. Otherwise there would hardly have been such endless disputes about Religion, nor such a multitude of martyrs; for there is no Church which does not boast of its legendary heroes, men who for the sake of religion have not only adopted lives of the utmost austerity but have endured death itself. Such conflicts would not have occurred if there had not been men so stubborn and unreasonable that they were incapable of distinguishing truth from probability, possibility, and falsity.

I pass now to aspects of worship which are universally recognized. Those which can be referred to the analogy between man and God, between man and things, and between things themselves, I include under the right conformation of the faculties. I say then that

> The connection of Virtue with Piety, defined in this work as the right conformation of the faculties, is and always has been held to be, the most important part of religious practice

There is no general agreement concerning rites, ceremonies, traditions, whether written or unwritten, or concerning Revelation; but there is the greatest possible consensus of opinion concerning the right conformation of the faculties. The way in which this right conformation of the faculties may be established I have discussed at length above, and the reader is invited to refer to that passage. There he will learn how Conscience guided by Common Notions produces virtue combined with piety, how from this there springs true hope, from such true hope, faith, from true faith, love, from true love, joy, and from true joy, Blessedness. Thus we now see that no faculty which leads to piety, purity of life, holiness, and virtue is not included under this heading. If I am to make some survey of these faculties, in respect of a person's years and the degree of wisdom which it has pleased God to give him, I would say that children recognize and seek God in their own way in the form of happiness, and acknowledge Him in the spontaneous gratitude which they accord their benefactors. No trait, therefore, is so excellent as gratitude, nothing so base as ingratitude. And when gratitude is expressed by more mature persons and the Common Notions gradually reveal their objects more clearly, Religion becomes enriched and appears in a greater variety of ways, though no practice emerges which is more admirable than this gratitude. With the advantage of age, piety and holiness of life take deeper roots within the conscience, and give birth to a profound love and faith in God. Very often, too, vanities and superstitions and even vices and crimes spring up and multiply together with these virtues, like tares and weeds which grow from the decaying seed of wheat. Though they blossom more slowly, they mature quickly, unless they are uprooted in good time. I assign this growth to those factors which compose the body. Accordingly, while our animal nature actually comes into being later, it reaches its completion in us before the reasoning element. This will not surprise those who notice that the animals attain their maturity in three years. Whether this fact is to be traced to their fallen state or to some other cause I will not stay to discuss. It may seem paradoxical that moral virtue which is so strict and severe is, and always has been, esteemed by men in every age and place and respected in every land, in spite of the fact that it conflicts with our physical and, I may say, agreeable feelings. But the reason for this is as follows. Since Nature unceasingly labors to deliver the soul from its physical burden, so Nature itself instils men with its secret conviction that virtue constitutes the most effective means by which our mind may be gradually separated and released from the body, and enter into its lawful realm. And though many arguments could be cited to the same purpose, I know no more convincing proof than the fact that it is only virtue that has the power to draw our soul from the delights which engulf it, and even to restore it to its native region, so that freed from the foul embrace of vice, and finally from the fear of death itself, it can apply itself to its proper function and attain inward everlasting joy.

> The minds of men have always been filled with horror for their wickedness. Their
> vices and crimes have been obvious to them. They must be expiated by repentance.

There is no general agreement concerning the various rites or mysteries which the priests have devised for the expiation of sin. Among the Romans, ceremonies of purification, cleansing, atonement, among the Greeks, rites of expiation and purging, and in nearly all races, sacrifices, even of human victims, a cruel and abominable device of the priests, were instituted for this purpose. Among the Egyptians and all the heathen races observances of a similar kind prevailed. I have referred to many of them in my book *On the Religion of the Gentiles* and also in my work, not yet published, *On the Causes of Errors*. Among the Mohammedans, Ramadan is held twice each year after the manner of our Forty Days. But above all other races the Eastern Indians display the most energy in exercises of this kind. At a certain sacred period of the year they gather in the forests, and taking a piece of sharp rock or stone, let forth a quantity of blood, until their spirits are on the point of leaving them, protesting at the same time that the root-causes of their sins had lain hidden in their blood and that by allowing it to gush forth they atone for their sins. But we may pass over such rites, some of which may well appear ridiculous. General agreement among religions, the nature of divine goodness, and above all conscience, tell us that our crimes may be washed away by true penitence, and that we can be restored to new union with God. For this inner witness condemns wickedness while at the same time it can wipe out the stain of it by genuine repentance, as the inner form of apprehension under proper conditions proves. I do not wish to consider here whether any other more appropriate means exists by which the divine justice may be appeased, since I have undertaken in this work only to rely on truths which are not open to dispute but are derived from the evidence of immediate perception and admitted by the whole world. This alone I assert, whatever may be said to the contrary, that unless wickedness can be abolished by penitence and faith in God, and unless the Divine goodness can satisfy the Divine justice (and no further appeal can be invoked), then there does not exist, nor ever has existed any universal source to which the wretched mass of men, crushed beneath the burden of sin, can turn to obtain grace and inward peace. If this were the case, God has created and condemned certain men; in fact, the larger part of the human race, not only without their desire, but without their knowledge. This idea is so dreadful and consorts so ill with the providence and goodness, and even the justice of God, that it is more charitable to suppose that the whole human race has always possessed in repentance the opportunity of becoming reconciled with God. And as long as men did not cut themselves off from it their damnation would not have been due to the benevolent will of God but to their own sins, nor could God have been charged with blame if they failed to find salvation. All the teaching of the greatest preachers concerning eternal salvation coincides on this issue, since every means of redress is useless except penitence and becomes, as they tell us, empty and futile. Accordingly, they hold it to be of such importance in relation to the divine goodness that they consider that when no readier way presents itself the entire secret of salvation may be revealed in this process. Some critics of Nature or Divine Universal Providence object that it is not always within our power to experience remorse. I have myself pointed out that wisdom is always within our grasp. But these critics fail to notice the distinction which I have made above, between voluntary and involuntary actions, nor do they recognize that some movements cannot be prevented, and others cannot be provoked into action. Man does not remember, or keep awake, or sleep, just as he desires. Some of these activities, like many other inner movements, admit of degrees and exceptions. But to declare that God has cut us off from the means by which we can return to Him, provided that we play our part to the utmost of our ability, is a blasphemy so great that those who indulge in it seek to destroy not merely human goodness but also the goodness of God. They must abandon these ideas, and their ideas and utterances, at least concerning the secret judgments of God, must be more guarded. For they cannot deny that if not from general providence, yet from particular providence or Grace, may flow the means by which God's favor may be won. We realize what we owe to Grace when we reflect that by it our works are accomplished, by it they are made acceptable to God. I think that it is chiefly by this means that God's mercy meets the demands of His goodness. For in the mutual relationship which exists between us, when our goods are seized by plunder or theft, the common laws of nations or universal consent requires that in addition to repentance there should be restoration. Now, if anyone with perverted curiosity asks me why we possess the liberty to commit sin and crime I can only answer that it is due to the secret judgments of God. If he persists in asking what can be known within the moderate limits of the human faculties I must reply that man is a finite animal, and therefore cannot do anything which is absolutely good or even absolutely bad. Yet the nature of each is modified in every action, so that the action shares to some extent in both, though it is named according to the element which has the larger share. Anyone who desires further discussion on this problem may refer to what I have said on an earlier page. I have now briefly examined the principal Common Notions about the way of God which refer to the journey of life. I pass on to treat of the state of the future life. And this I shall comprise in a single proposition.

There is Reward or Punishment after this Life

The rewards that are eternal have been variously placed in heaven, in the stars, in the Elysian fields, or in contemplation. Punishment has been thought to lie in metempsychosis, in hell (which some describe as filled with fire, but the Chinese imagine pervaded with smoke), or in some infernal regions, or regions of the middle air, or in temporary or everlasting death. But all religion, law, philosophy, and, what is more, conscience teach openly or implicitly that punishment or reward awaits us after this life. Religion teaches us this explicitly when it used the terms which I have mentioned. It teaches the same doctrine indirectly by establishing the immortality of the soul or by proving that God avenges crimes which are committed with impunity in this life. In this sense there is no nation, however barbarous, which has not and will not recognize the existence of punishments and rewards. That reward and punishment exist is, then, a Common Notion, though there is the greatest difference of opinion as to their nature, quality, extent, and mode. It is no objection that the soul perishes with the body, as some people assert. For they refer this very fact to punishment for sin, or else they mean only that part of the soul with which they have been familiar, namely, the physical senses; or finally, they must be ignored, since they talk sheer nonsense; for there is nothing in the faculties of the mind to suggest such ideas. That the soul could be immortal if God willed it is clearly a Common Notion, in that among the most distant races, seething with every type of superstition, there exists a general conviction that purity of life and courage of mind promote happiness. It is on this account that they are said to honor the bones of those who have died bravely in battle. But I do not trouble myself about such matters, since I am not concerned with superstitions and sacred rites; it is not what a large number of men assert, but what all men of normal mind believe, that I find important. Scanning the vast array of absurd fictions, I am content to discover a tiny Common Notion. And this is of the utmost importance, since when the general mass of men have rejected a whole range of beliefs which it has found valueless, it proceeeds to acquire new beliefs by this method, until the point is reached where faith can be applied.

It follows from these considerations that the Dogmas which recognize a sovereign Deity enjoin us to worship Him, command us to live a holy life, lead us to repent our sins, and warn us of future recompense or punishment, proceed from God and are inscribed within us in the form of Common Notions. But those dogmas which postulate a plurality of Gods, which do not forbid crimes and sins, which rail against penitence, and which express doubts about the eternal state of the soul cannot be considered either Common Notions or truths. Accordingly, every religion, if we consider it comprehensively, is not good; nor can we admit that salvation is open to men in every religion. For how could anyone who believes more than is necessary, but who does less than he ought, be saved? But I am convinced that in every religion, and indeed in every individual conscience, either through Grace or Nature, sufficient means are granted to men to win God's goodwill; while all additional and peculiar features which are found at any period must be referred to their inventors. It is not sufficient that they should be old if they have once been new. Ideas which are superfluous or even false may be not only novel but ancient, and truths which are only seized by a few cannot be essential to all. The truth which belongs to revelation occupies a special place here; and no faith in it is in any way disparaged by the principles which I have described. On the contrary, whatever it adds to them

I hold to be valuable. The fundamental principles of Revelation itself are here established, so that it is possible to reduce all disputes to the question, On what faculty does the argument depend? Accordingly, so far from these views conflicting with ordinary beliefs or depending on new principles, I have asserted nothing but the symbol of Common Notions and what has been universally accepted by every religion, age, and country. I do not deny that sacred ceremonies can form part of religion; on the contrary, I find that some ceremonies are included in every religion and serve to embellish it; sofar they are valuable. But when they are made by the priests the essential elements of divine worship, then religion, and we who practise it, are the victims of imposture. Rites must be kept within bounds. We can only accept them on the understanding that religion is chaste and only requires such ornaments as render a matron more venerable and respected. When she paints and dyes herself her appearance is too suggestive of the harlot.

Such, then, are the Common Notions of which the true Catholic or universal Church is built. For the church which is built of clay or stone or living rock or even of marble cannot be claimed to be the infallible Church. The true Catholic Church is not supported on the inextricable confusion of oral and written tradition to which men have given their allegiance. Still less is it that which fights beneath any one particular standard, or is comprised in one organization so as to embrace only a restricted portion of the earth, or a single period of history. The only Catholic and uniform Church is the doctrine of Common Notions which comprehends all places and all men. This Church alone reveals Divine Universal Providence, or the wisdom of Nature. This Church alone explains why God is appealed to as the common Father. And it is only through this Church that salvation is possible. The adoration which has been bestowed on every particular Church belongs to it.· Every Church, as I have pointed out above, is the more exposed to error the further it is separated from it. Anyone who courts uncertain doctrines in place of the sure truths of divine providence, and forges new articles of Faith, forsakes this Church. If, however, anyone receives some truth by revelation, which I think can occur both in the waking state and in sleep, he must use it as occasion warrants, remembering that unless he is entrusted with a message of interest to all, he should reserve it to himself. For it is not likely that what is not evident to the faculties of all can have any bearing on the whole human race. I have often observed that we can take much on faith with true piety, and we need not abandon any belief as long as it does not conflict with the divine attributes. It is not the case therefore, as some critic may point out, that after examining the means by which Divine Universal Providence acts and admitting that it is universal in its operation, I then restrict it to its own kingdom. I desire that every feature which redounds to the glory of God may be added to the characteristics which have been mentioned. For my part I accept with earnest faith and gratitude all that preceding ages have uttered in praise of God's goodness and mercy. I agree with the majority of mankind that all that they tell us not merely could have come to pass but that it actually did so. But I maintain that the principles of faith are to be found in the truths of Divine Universal Providence, since I cannot see that in any other way the harmony of Nature or general Providence, with Grace or particular

Providence, can be preserved. This does not exclude the right of the Church to decide all matters which concern external worship, or ecclesiastical organization, or the publication for future generations of the records of earlier times, and especially those events which confirm the true attributes of God. For when these Catholic truths are received into the recesses of the soul they rest on a foundation of indubitable faith, and anything which remains can and ought to be believed with piety upon the authority of the Church; provided, that is, that all contradictions are avoided or recognized, and only those doctrines are impressed on men's minds which promote universal peace and concord, and make for purity of life. Whether these means are sufficient to prepare us for eternal salvation I leave in the hands of God. I, at least, do not seek to pry into the secret judgments of God. I am content to have shown that the human mind informed by the Common Notions has been able in every age and place to apprehend these principles. If we set aside superstitions and legends the mind takes its stand on my five articles, and upon nothing else. To deny this would be to allow less sense to men than to sheep; for they at least when they are let into the pastures avoid those herbs which are harmful and only eat those which are good for them. Whether indeed human wisdom has undertaken this examination in any age or place, or whether, even if it has done so, all who have rejected the inferior and trifling portions of religion, or possibly have accepted a mystical interpretation of them on the authority of their priests, equally enjoy the supreme happiness, I have not attempted to discuss. I firmly maintain, however, that it is, and always has been, possible for all men to reach the truths I have described. But whether they have been manifest, or whether, even when they are manifest, they are immediately accepted, I am so far from wishing to discuss that all matters of this nature which depend upon the secret counsels of God, I leave to be inferred from the Divine wisdom and goodness. But if anyone calls them in dispute I am prepared stoutly to defend them. For by no other method could the existence of Divine Universal Providence, the highest attribute of God, be proved by the principles of common reason. If we abandon these principles – and as I have often pointed out Nature or the Common Providence of the world does not operate beyond the means at its disposal – and if we give way to wicked blasphemies, terrible crimes, and finally to impenitence, to which we are sacramentally bound; if we defile the purity of Religion with foolish superstitions and degrading legends; it would be wholly unjust to blame the Supreme Goodness for our sins. It would be like accusing a host who provides a feast set out with a splendid profusion of dishes, of encouraging drunkenness, gluttony, and license. For what is sufficient is due to God, excess is due to us. Why, then, as I have said elsewhere, following the law of common reason, can we not apply the same rule to the perfect sphere of the religion of God that we apply to any circle? If anything is added to it or taken from it its shape is destroyed, and its perfection ruined. I do not, however, wish to decide too hastily on this question. I would, indeed, firmly maintain that it is impossible to remove any feature from religion. But whether anything can suitably be added to the orb of religion, as is possible with a circle, I am not so certain; though the shape of a visible circle is continuous so that no part of it is hidden. The fair form of Divine Universal Providence ought to stand forth in all its beauty and not lurk behind a mask.

Whatever feature is added to this circular shape should fitly and exactly correspond in a form which is harmonious and congruent both with its centre and its circumference. The chief reason for this is that no other genuine and Almighty God can be accepted but He who directs universal providence to those ends which essentially concern the salvation of the soul. But since no other clear pattern of that Providence can be found than that which lies open to the whole human race in these Articles, and in these alone, we ought to consider whether it is possible to conceive of any stricter or purer religion, or of any means by which it is possible for a man to become more virtuous or more just, than is contained in these Catholic Articles. Accordingly, if the priests have agreed to emphasize for the sake of Universal Peace not merely these principles (since Dogmas are permissible in matters of faith) but have further resolved to add those parts of beliefs in historical events which display great mercy toward the human race, a procedure with which I am in full accord, yet they should not suffer elements to be introduced which disparage the work of Universal Providence or confine it within strict or narrow limits. But neither must they allow features to be introduced which, through too hasty a desire for forgiveness, soften or destroy the austere outline of religion; otherwise men may relapse more quickly and with less foresight into sin. I humbly recommend these considerations to the judgment of the priests, with the hope that they may abandon their mysteries, and direct themselves to accomplishing their function toward God and His interests in accordance with the most sacred maxims given us to that end, and so exert themselves on behalf of the people. Anyone may add for himself, their substance, quality, quantity, mode, etc., to these articles. I shall now discuss what may be derived from Revelation.

11

G. E. Lessing, from *Nathan the Wise*

G. E. Lessing (1729–81) was a German Enlightenment scholar and critic. He believed that religion was not primarily a matter of creeds and doctrines; rather, religion concerns humanitarianism and tolerance. Lessing was accused of heterodoxy and pressured by certain authorities of the day not to commit his views to print. Cleverly, he took to writing literary works in which he could disguise his views and claim innocence.

In Act III, Scene 7 of his play *Nathan the Wise* Lessing relates a parable about a man in Eastern lands who had a ring of priceless worth with a stone of magic power. Whoever wore the ring and trusted in its strength was said to be loved of God and humanity. The ring was bequeathed by the man to his son and passed down through the generations until it came into the possession of a man with three sons whom he loved equally. Nearing death and having promised the ring to each of them, the father had two identical rings made. As all three rings were indistinguishable, the father called in each son, blessed him, and gave him the/a ring. After the father's death, the sons discovered each other's rings and began to squabble about who possessed the true ring. But they argue in vain, says Lessing in a highly instructive and suggestive line, for "the genuine ring was not Demonstrable . . . almost as little as Today the genuine faith." The sons went to a judge to make a complaint and have him decide the case. His refusal or inability to deliver a decisive verdict, coupled with a consequent plea for tolerance, comes close, the reader suspects, to the heart of Lessing's own view of the relations among Judaism, Christianity, and Islam.

The Text

SALADIN (*returning, aside*). There, now the coast is clear! – (*Aloud.*) I hope I come
   Not prematurely? – You are at an end
   With your deliberations. – Well, then, speak!
   No soul will hear us.
NATHAN.   Let the whole world listen.
SALADIN. So sure is Nathan of his case? Now there
   Is wisdom! Not to hide the truth! To stake
   One's all upon it! Life and limb! One's goods
   And blood!
NATHAN.   Yes, when it's needful and of use.
SALADIN. Henceforth I may expect to hold by rights
   One of my names, Reformer of the world   10
   And of the law.
NATHAN.   Indeed, a handsome title!
   But, Sultan, ere I draw the final veil,
   Allow me, please, to tell an ancient story.
SALADIN. Why not? I always was a friend of tales
   Well told.
NATHAN.   To tell them *well* is not, I fear,
   My forte.
SALADIN.   Proud modesty again? – Tell on!
NATHAN. In days of yore, there dwelt in eastern lands
   A man who had a ring of priceless worth
   Received from hands beloved. The stone it held,
   An opal, shed a hundred colors fair,   20
   And had the magic power that he who wore it,
   Trusting its strength, was loved of God and men.
   No wonder therefore that this eastern man
   Would never cease to wear it; and took pains
   To keep it in his household for all time.
   He left the ring to that one of his sons
   He loved the best; providing that in turn
   That son bequeath to his most favorite son
   The ring; and thus, regardless of his birth,
   The dearest son, by virtue of the ring,   30
   Should be the head, the prince of all his house. –
   You follow, Sultan.
SALADIN.   Perfectly. continue!
NATHAN. At last this ring, passed on from son to son,
   Descended to a father of three sons;
   All three of whom were duly dutiful,
   All three of whom in consequence he needs

Source: G. E. Lessing, *Nathan the Wise*, trans. B. Q. Morgan.

Must love alike. But yet from time to time,
Now this, now that one, now the third – as each
Might be with him alone, the other two
Not sharing then his overflowing heart – 40
Seemed worthiest of the ring; and so to each
He promised it, in pious frailty.
This lasted while it might. – Then came the time
For dying, and the loving father finds
Himself embarrassed. It's a grief to him
To wound two of his sons, who have relied
Upon his word. – What's to be done? – He sends
In secret to a jeweler, of whom
He orders two more rings, in pattern like
His own, and bids him spare nor cost nor toil 50
To make them in all points identical.
The jeweler succeds. And when he brings
The rings to him, the sire himself cannot
Distinguish them from the original.
In glee and joy he calls his sons to him,
Each by himself, confers on him his blessing –
His ring as well – and dies – You hear me, Sultan?

SALADIN. (*who, taken aback, has turned away*). I hear,
I hear you! – Finish now your fable
Without delay. – I'm waiting!

NATHAN.   I am done.
For what ensues is wholly obvious – 60
Scarce is the father dead when all three sons
Appear, each with his ring, and each would be
The reigning prince. They seek the facts, they quarrel,
Accuse. In vain; the genuine ring was not
Demonstrable; – (*he pauses for a reply*)
almost as little as
Today the genuine faith.

SALADIN.   You mean this as
The answer to my question? . . .

NATHAN.   What I mean
Is merely an excuse, if I decline
Precisely to distinguish those three rings
Which with intent the father ordered made 70
That sharpest eyes might not distinguish them.

SALADIN. The rings! – Don't trifle with me! – I should think
That those religions which I named to you
Might be distinguished readily enough.
Down to their clothing; down to food and drink!

NATHAN. In all respects except their basic grounds. –
Are they not grounded all in history,
Or writ or handed down? – But history
Must be accepted wholly upon faith –

Not so? – Well then, whose faith are we least like 80
To doubt? Our people's surely? Those whose blood
We share? the one's who from our childhood gave
Us proofs of love? who never duped us, but
When it was for our good to be deceived? –
How can I trust my fathers less than you
Trust yours? Or turn about. – Can I demand
That to your forebears you should give the lie
That mine be not gainsaid? Or turn about.
The same holds true of Christians. Am I right? –
SALADIN. (*aside*). By Allah, yes! The man is right. I must 90
  Be still.
NATHAN. Let's come back to our rings once more.
  As we have said: the sons preferred complaint;
  And each swore to the judge, he had received
  The ring directly from his father's hand. –
  As was the truth! – And long before had had
  His father's promise, one day to enjoy
  The privilege of the ring. – No less than truth! –
  His father, each asserted, could not have
  Been false to him; and sooner than suspect
  This thing of him, of such a loving father: 100
  He must accuse his brothers – howsoever
  Inclined in other things to think the best
  Of them – of some false play; and he the traitors
  Would promptly ferret out; would take revenge.
SALADIN. And then, the judge? – I am all ears to hear
  What you will have the judge decide. Speak on!
NATHAN. Thus said the judge: unless you swiftly bring
  Your father here to me, I'll bid you leave
  My judgment seat. Think you that I am here
  For solving riddles? Would you wait, perhaps, 110
  Until the genuine ring should rise and speak? –
  But stop! I hear the genuine ring enjoys
  The magic power to make its wearer loved,
  Beloved of God and men. That must decide!
  For spurious rings can surely not do that! –
  Whom then do two of you love most? Quick, speak!
  You're mute? The rings' effect is only backward,
  Not outward? Each one loves himself the most? –
  O then you are, all three, deceived deceivers!
  Your rings are false, all three. The genuine ring 120
  No doubt got lost. To hide the grievous loss,
  To make it good, the father caused three rings
  To serve for one.
SALADIN.   O splendid, splendid!
NATHAN.   So,
  The judge went on, if you'll not have my counsel,

185

Instead of verdict, go! My counsel is:
==Accept the matter wholly as it stands.==
If each one from his father has his ring,
Then let each one believe his ring to be
The true one. – Possibly the father wished
To tolerate no longer in his house   130
The tyranny of just one ring! – And know:
That you, ==all three, he loved;== and loved alike;
Since two of you he'd not humiliate
To favor one. – Well then! Let each aspire
To emulate his father's unbeguiled,
Unprejudiced affection! Let each strive
To match the rest in bringing to the fore
The magic of the opal in his ring!
Assist that power with all humility,
With benefaction, hearty peacefulness,   140
And with profound submission to God's will!
And when the magic powers of the stones
Reveal themselves in children's children's children:
I bid you, in a thousand thousand years,
To stand again before this seat. For then
A wiser man than I will sit as judge
Upon this bench, and speak. Depart! – So said
The modest judge.
SALADIN.   God! God!
NATHAN.   Now, Saladin,
    If you would claim to be that wiser man,
    The promised one . . .   150
SALADIN. (*rushing to him and seizing his hand, which he retains*)
                              I, dust? I, nothing? God!
NATHAN. What is the matter, Saladin?
SALADIN.   Dear Nathan! –
    The thousand thousand years your judge assigned
    Are not yet up. – His judgment seat is not
    For me. – Go! – Go! – But be my friend.
NATHAN.   Nought else
    Had Saladin to tell me?
SALADIN.   Nought.
NATHAN.   Nought?
SALADIN.   Nothing. –
    Why ask?
NATHAN. May I seek opportunity
    To ask a favor?
SALADIN.   And for that you need
    An opportunity? – Speak out!
NATHAN.   I have returned
    From distant parts, where I collected debts. –
    I've almost too much cash on hand. – The times   160

Are once more looking doubtful; – and I know
Not rightly where to find security. –
I wondered, then, if you perhaps – because
Prospective war needs money more and more –
Could use some.

SALADIN. (*Looking him fixedly in the eye*). Nathan! – I'll not ask you if
Al-Hafi has been with you; – nor explore
If some suspicion urges you to make
This voluntary offer . . .

NATHAN.   A suspicion?

SALADIN. I'd be to blame. – Forgive me! – What's the use?
I must confess to you – I was indeed   170
Intending –

NATHAN.   Surely not, the selfsame thing
To ask of me?

SALADIN.   Quite so.

NATHAN.   Then both of us
Are helped at once! – But that I cannot send
All of my cash to you, ascribe that to
The youthful Templar. – One well known to you. –
To him I first must pay a goodly sum.

SALADIN. A Templar? Surely you would not support
My fiercest foes with means of yours?

NATHAN.   I speak
But of the one whose life you spared . . .

SALADIN.   Ah! that
Reminds me! – I had quite forgot the youth! –   180
Where is he? Do you know him?

NATHAN.   What? Then you
Are not aware, how much of what you gave
To him in mercy flowed through him to me?
For, risking all his newly granted life,
He saved my daughter from the fire.

SALADIN.   He did? –
Ha! So he looked, I thought. My brother would
Have done the same, whom he so much resembles. –
Is he still here? Then bring him to me! – For
I've told my sister of her brother, whom
She never knew, so many things that I   190
Must have her see his living image too! –
Go, fetch him! – Strange, how out of *one* good deed,
Though but a child of passion, such a wealth
Of other goodly deeds is born. Go, fetch him!

NATHAN. (*dropping Saladin's hand*). At once! And, our agreement stays in force? (*Exit.*)

SALADIN. Too bad I did not let my sister listen! –
To her! – How shall I tell her all of this?
(*Exit at the other side.*)

12

Friedrich Schleiermacher, from
The Christian Faith

Athough Friedrich Schleiermacher (1768—1834) was reared in a Pietist community which hardly encouraged intellectual or worldly engagement, he became the first great modern theologian to step into the arena of cultural conflict in order to face the challenge of modernity squarely. While he never broke with his Pietist beginnings, his inquiring spirit led him beyond the confines of the simple life of piety and devotion. He read the Enlightenment thinkers carefully and took seriously the challenge that they posed for Christianity. His pioneering response to the provocation of modernity has earned Schleiermacher the honor of being widely recognized as the father of modern Protestant theology.

Schleiermacher found himself in Berlin near the end of the eighteenth century, breathing the intuitively and imaginatively charged air of the Romantics and their protest against the Enlightenment. He was dismayed, however, to learn that the Romantics with whom he felt a certain kinship had jettisoned religion in the name of culture, in the name of higher expressions of the human spirit. He wished to restore the place of religion in human life, convinced that the Romantics had misunderstood something fundamental. In his famous *On Religion: Speeches to Its Cultured Despisers*, he tried to convince the Romantics that they had mistaken religion for something else, that they had confused its husk with its kernel. Schleiermacher believed that religion is neither knowledge or doctrine (as many eighteenth-century orthodox Protestants taught) nor action or morality (as the philosopher Immanuel Kant taught), but something else: a sense and taste for the infinite, the universe, the whole, or God.

Schleiermacher eventually became a professor at the University of Berlin. In his work *The Christian Faith*, he defines religion as the feeling (*Gefühl*) of absolute dependence or consciousness of relation

188

to God. The seat of religion is therefore not reason or conscience, but feeling or affectivity. Religion is furthermore irreducible to anything more basic; it is a genus unto itself (*sui generis*). Schleiermacher believed that the feeling of dependence was articulated in various ways in a number of different religions. In each case, the religion in question emphasizes one kind of consciousness of being related to God. Gradations of the feeling of dependence, from relative to absolute, can therefore be said to exist; Christianity is the religion in which this feeling comes to purest and exemplary expression as seen in the Redeemer, Jesus Christ – the most God-conscious of all human beings.

In the following selections from *The Christian Faith*, insertions of German phrases found in the source edition have been retained, while footnotes have been eliminated.

The Text

§4.   *The common element in all howsoever diverse expressions of piety, by which these are conjointly distinguished from all other feelings, or, in other words, the self-identical essence of piety, is this: the consciousness of being absolutely dependent, or, which is the same thing, of being in relation with God.*

1.   In any actual state of consciousness, no matter whether it merely accompanies a thought or action or occupies a moment for itself, we are never simply conscious of our Selves in their unchanging identity, but are always at the same time conscious of a changing determination of them. The Ego in itself can be represented objectively; but every consciousness of self is at the same time the consciousness of a variable state of being. But in this distinction of the latter from the former, it is implied that the variable does not proceed purely from the self-identical, for in that case it could not be distinguished from it. Thus in every self-consciousness there are two elements, which we might call respectively a self-caused element (*ein Sichselbstsetzen*) and a non-self-caused element (*ein Sichselbstnichtsogesetzthaben*); or a Being and a Having-by-some-means-come-to-be (*ein Sein und ein Irgendwiegewordensein*). The latter of these presupposes for every self-consciousness another factor besides the Ego, a factor which is the source of the particular determination, and without which the self-consciousness would not be precisely what it is. But this other is not objectively presented in the immediate self-consciousness with which alone we are here concerned. For though, of course, the double constitution of self-consciousness causes us always to look objectively for an other to which we can trace the origin of our particular state, yet this search is a separate act with which we are not at present concerned. In self-consciousness there are only two elements: the one expresses the existence of the subject for itself, the other its co-existence with an other.

Now to these two elements, as they exist together in the temporal self-consciousness, correspond in the subject its *Receptivity* and its (spontaneous) *Activity*. If we could think away the co-existence with an other, but otherwise think ourselves as we are, then a self-consciousness which predominantly expressed an affective condition of receptivity would be impossible, and any self-consciousness could then express only activity – an activity, however, which, not being directed to any object, would be merely an urge outwards, an indefinite "agility" without form or colour. But as we never do exist except along with an other, so even in every outward-tending self-consciousness the element of receptivity, in some way or other affected, is the primary one; and even the self-consciousness which accompanies an action (acts of knowing included), while it predominantly expresses spontaneous movement and activity, is always related (though the relation is often a quite indefinite one) to a

Source: Friedrich Schleiermacher, *The Christian Faith*, trans. H. R. Mackintosh et al., eds H. R. Mackintosh and J. S. Stewart.

prior moment of affective receptivity, through which the original "agility" received its direction. To these propositions assent can be unconditionally demanded; and no one will deny them who is capable of a little introspection and can find interest in the real subject of our present inquiries.

2.   The common element in all those determinations of self-consciousness which predominantly express a receptivity affected from some outside quarter is the *feeling of Dependence*. On the other hand, the common element in all those determinations which predominantly express spontaneous movement and activity is the *feeling of Freedom*. The former is the case not only because it is by an influence from some other quarter that we have come to such a state, but particularly because we *could* not so become except by means of an other. The latter is the case because in these instances an other is determined by us, and without our spontaneous activity could not be so determined. These two definitions may, indeed, seem to be still incomplete, inasmuch as there is also a mobility of the subject which is not connected with an other at all, but which seems to be subject to the same antithesis as that just explained. But when we become such-and-such from within outwards, for ourselves, without any other being involved, that is the simple situation of the temporal development of a being which remains essentially self-identical, and it is only very improperly that this can be referred to the concept "Freedom." And when we cannot ourselves, from within outwards, become such-and-such, this only indicates the limits which belong to the nature of the subject itself as regards spontaneous activity, and this could only very improperly be called "Dependence."

Further, this antithesis must on no account be confused with the antithesis between gloomy or depressing and elevating or joyful feelings, of which we shall speak later. For a feeling of dependence may be elevating, if the "having-become-such-and-such" which it expresses is complete; and similarly a feeling of freedom may be dejecting, if the moment of predominating receptivity to which the action can be traced was of a dejecting nature, or again if the manner and method of the activity prove to be a disadvantageous combination.

Let us now think of the feeling of dependence and the feeling of freedom as *one*, in the sense that not only the subject but the corresponding other is the same for both. Then the total self-consciousness made up of both together is one of *Reciprocity* between the subject and the corresponding other. Now let us suppose the totality of all moments of feeling, of both kinds, as one whole: then the corresponding other is also to be supposed as a totality or as one, and then that term "reciprocity" is the right one for our self-consciousness in general, inasmuch as it expresses our connexion with everything which either appeals to our receptivity or is subjected to our activity. And this is true not only when we particularize this other and ascribe to each of its elements a different degree of relation to the twofold consciousness within us, but also when we think of the total "outside" as one, and moreover (since it contains other receptivities and activities to which we have a relation) as one together with ourselves, that is, as a *World*. Accordingly our self-consciousness, as a consciousness of our existence in the world or of our co-existence with the world, is a series in which the feeling of freedom and the feeling of dependence are divided.

But neither an absolute feeling of dependence, *i.e.* without any feeling of freedom in relation to the co-determinant, nor an absolute feeling of freedom, *i.e.* without any feeling of dependence in relation to the co-determinant, is to be found in this whole realm. If we consider our relations to Nature, or those which exist in human society, there we shall find a large number of objects in regard to which freedom and dependence maintain very much of an equipoise: these constitute the field of equal reciprocity. There are other objects which exercise a far greater influence upon our receptivity than our activity exercises upon them, and also *vice versa*, so that one of the two may diminish until it is imperceptible. But neither of the two members will ever completely disappear. The feeling of dependence predominates in the relation of children to their parents, or of citizens to their fatherland; and yet individuals can, without losing their relationship, exercise upon their fatherland not only a directive influence, but even a counter-influence. And the dependence of children on their parents, which very soon comes to be felt as a gradually diminishing and fading quantity, is never from the start free from the admixture of an element of spontaneous activity towards the parents: just as even in the most absolute autocracy the ruler is not without some slight feeling of dependence. It is the same in the case of Nature: towards all the forces of Nature – even, we may say, towards the heavenly bodies – we ourselves do, in the same sense in which they influence us, exercise a counter-influence, however minute. So that our whole self-consciousness in relation to the World or its individual parts remains enclosed within these limits.

3.   There can, accordingly, be for us no such thing as a feeling of absolute freedom. He who asserts that he has such a feeling is either deceiving himself or separating things which essentially belong together. For if the feeling of freedom expresses a forthgoing activity, this activity must have an object which has been somehow given to us, and this could not have taken place without an influence of the object upon our receptivity. Therefore in every such case there is involved a feeling of dependence which goes along with the feeling of freedom, and thus limits it. The contrary could only be possible if the object altogether came into existence through our activity, which is never the case absolutely, but only relatively. But if, on the other hand, the feeling of freedom expresses only an inward movement of activity, not only is every such individual movement bound up with the state of our stimulated receptivity at the moment, but, further, the totality of our free inward movements, considered as a unity, cannot be represented as a feeling of absolute freedom, because our whole existence does not present itself to our consciousness as having proceeded from our own spontaneous activity. Therefore in any temporal existence a feeling of absolute freedom can have no place. As regards the feeling of absolute dependence which, on the other hand, our proposition does postulate: for just the same reason, this feeling cannot in any wise arise from the influence of an object which has in some way to be *given* to us; for upon such an object there would always be a counter-influence, and even a voluntary renunciation of this would always involve a feeling of freedom. Hence a feeling of absolute dependence, strictly speaking, cannot exist in a single moment as such, because such a moment is always determined, as regards its total content, by what is *given*, and thus by objects towards which we have a feeling of

freedom. But the self-consciousness which accompanies all our activity, and therefore, since that is never zero, accompanies our whole existence, and negatives absolute freedom, is itself precisely a consciousness of absolute dependence; for it is the consciousness that the whole of our spontaneous activity comes from a source outside of us in just the same sense in which anything towards which we should have a feeling of absolute freedom must have proceeded entirely from ourselves. But without any feeling of freedom a feeling of absolute dependence would not be possible.

4. As regards the identification of absolute dependence with "relation to God" in our proposition: this is to be understood in the sense that the *Whence* of our receptive and active existence, as implied in this self-consciousness, is to be designated by the word "God," and that this is for us the really original signification of that word. In this connexion we have first of all to remind ourselves that, as we have seen in the foregoing discussion, this "Whence" is not the world, in the sense of the totality of temporal existence, and still less is it any single part of the world. For we have a feeling of freedom (though, indeed, a limited one) in relation to the world, since we are complementary parts of it, and also since we are continually exercising an influence on its individual parts; and, moreover, there is the possibility of our exercising influence on all its parts; and while this does permit a limited feeling of dependence, it excludes the absolute feeling. In the next place, we have to note that our proposition is intended to oppose the view that this feeling of dependence is itself conditioned by some previous knowledge about God. And this may indeed be the more necessary since many people claim to be in the sure possession of a concept of God, altogether a matter of conception and original, *i.e.* independent of any feeling; and in the strength of this higher self-consciousness, which indeed may come pretty near to being a feeling of absolute freedom, they put far from them, as something almost infra-human, that very feeling which for us is the basic type of all piety. Now our proposition is in no wise intended to dispute the existence of such an original knowledge, but simply to set it aside as something with which, in a system of Christian doctrine, we could never have any concern, because plainly enough it has itself nothing to do directly with piety. If, however, word and idea are always originally one, and the term "God" therefore presupposes an idea, then we shall simply say that this idea, which is nothing more than the expression of the feeling of absolute dependence, is the most direct reflection upon it and the most original idea with which we are here concerned, and is quite independent of that original knowledge (properly so called), and conditioned only by our feeling of absolute dependence. So that in the first instance God signifies for us simply that which is the co-determinant in this feeling and to which we trace our being in such a state; and any further content of the idea must be evolved out of this fundamental import assigned to it. Now this is just what is principally meant by the formula which says that to feel oneself absolutely dependent and to be conscious of being in relation with God are one and the same thing; and the reason is that absolute dependence is the fundamental relation which must include all others in itself. This last expression includes the God-consciousness in the self-consciousness in such a way that, quite in

accordance with the above analysis, the two cannot be separated from each other. The feeling of absolute dependence becomes a clear self-consciousness only as this idea comes simultaneously into being. In this sense it can indeed be said that God is given to us in feeling in an original way; and if we speak of an original revelation of God to man or in man, the meaning will always be just this, that, along with the absolute dependence which characterizes not only man but all temporal existence, there is given to man also the immediate self-consciousness of it, which becomes a consciousness of God. In whatever measure this actually takes place during the course of a personality through time, in just that measure do we ascribe piety to the individual. On the other hand, any possibility of God being in any way *given* is entirely excluded, because anything that is outwardly given must be given as an object exposed to our counter-influence, however slight this may be. The transference of the idea of God to any perceptible object, unless one is all the time conscious that it is a piece of purely arbitrary symbolism, is always a corruption, whether it be a temporary transference, *i.e.* a theophany, or a constitutive transference, in which God is represented as permanently a particular perceptible existence.

. . . .

§7. *The various religious communions which have appeared in history with clearly defined limits are related to each other in two ways: as different stages of development, and as different kinds.*

1.   The religious communion which takes the form of household worship within a single family cannot fitly be regarded as an appearance in the realm of history, because it remains in the obscurity of an inner circle. Moreover, the transition from this to a really historical appearance is often very gradual. The beginning of it is seen in the large style of the patriarchal household, and the persisting association between families of sons and grandsons that live near each other; and it is out of these alone that the two fundamental forms previously mentioned (§6, 4) can be developed. In these transitions, if several of them are placed beside each other, both kinds of difference can be found at least in germ.

Now in the first place, as regards the different stages of development: the historical appearance is in itself a higher stage, and stands above the mere isolated household worship, just as the civic condition, even in its most incomplete forms, stands above the formless association of the pre-civic condition. But this difference by no means relates only to the form or the compass of the fellowship itself, but also to the constitution of the underlying religious affections, according as they attain to clearness in conscious antithesis to the movements of the sensible self-consciousness. Now this development depends partly on the whole development of the mental powers, so that for that reason alone many a communion cannot continue longer in its own peculiar mode of existence; as, *e.g.*, many forms of idol-worship, even though they might claim a high degree of mechanical skill, are incompatible with even a moderate scientific and artistic education, and perish when confronted by it. Yet it is also partly true that the development takes its own course; and there is no contradiction in saying that, in one and the same whole, the piety may develop to its highest consummation, while other mental functions remain far behind.

But all differences are not to be thus regarded as distinct stages or levels. There are communal religions (Greek and Indian polytheism are good cases in point), of which one might well seem to be at the same point in the scale as the other, but which are yet very definitely different from each other. If, then, several such exist which belong to the same stage or level, the most natural course will be to call them different kinds or species. And indisputably it can be shown, even at the lowest stage, that most religious communions which are geographically separated from each other are also divided by inner differences.

2.   But of course these two distinctions, into stages of development and into kinds (genera) or species, cannot in this realm, or indeed generally in the realm of history or of so-called moral "persons," be maintained so definitely or carried through so surely as in the realm of Nature. For we are not here dealing with invariable forms which always reproduce themselves in the same way. Each individual communion is capable of a greater or lesser development within the character of its kind or genus. Let us, now, consider that in this way, just as the individual may pass from a more imperfect religious communion to a higher one, so a particular communion might, without prejudice to its generic character, develop beyond its original level, and that this may happen equally to all. Then the idea of stages would naturally disappear, for the last phase of the lower and the first of the higher might be continuously connected, and it would then be more correct to say that each genus works itself up by a series of developments from the imperfect to the more perfect. But, on the other hand, we may take the fact that, just as we say an individual becomes in a certain sense a new man by passing to a higher form of religion, so the generic character of a communion must be lost when it rises to a higher level. Then even on any one level, if the inner development is to go on, the generic character would become uncertain and altogether unstable, while the levels or stages would be all the more sharply and definitely distinguished.

This variability, however, does not discredit the reality of our twofold distinction. For every religious communion which appears in history will be related to the others in this twofold way. It will be co-ordinate with some, and subordinate or superior to others; and thus it is distinguished from the former in the one manner and from the latter in the other. And if those who busy themselves most with the history and criticism of religions have given less attention to the task of fitting the different forms into this framework, this may be partly because they confine themselves almost exclusively to the individual, and partly also because it may be difficult in particular cases to lay bare these relationships and properly to distinguish and separate co-ordinates and subordinates. It may here suffice us to have established the twofold distinction in a general way, since our sole concern is to investigate how Christianity is related, in both respects, to other religious communions and forms of faith.

3.   Our proposition does not assert, but it does tacitly presuppose the possibility, that there are other forms of piety which are related to Christianity as different forms

on the same level of development, and thus so far similar. But this does not contradict the conviction, which we assume every Christian to possess, of the exclusive superiority of Christianity. In the realm of Nature also we distinguish perfect and imperfect animals as different stages of the development of animal life, and again on each of these stages different genera, which thus resemble each other as expressions of the same state; but this does not mean that one genus of the lower stage may not be nearer to the higher, and thus more perfect, than the others. Similarly, though several kinds of piety belong to the same stage as Christianity, it may yet be more perfect than any of them.

Our proposition excludes only the idea, which indeed is often met with, that the Christian religion (piety) should adopt towards at least most other forms of piety the attitude of the true towards the false. For if the religions belonging to the same stage as Christianity were entirely false, how could they have so much similarity to Christianity as to make that classification requisite? And if the religions which belong to the lower stages contained nothing but error, how would it be possible for a man to pass from them to Christianity? Only the true, and not the false, can be a basis of receptivity for the higher truth of Christianity. The whole delineation which we are here introducing is based rather on the maxim that error never exists in and for itself, but always along with some truth, and that we have never fully understood it until we have discovered its connexion with truth, and the true thing to which it is attached. With this agrees what the apostle says when he represents even Polytheism as a perversion of the original consciousness of God which underlies it, and when, in this evidence of the longing which all these fancies have failed to satisfy, he finds an obscure presentiment of the true God.

§8. *Those forms of piety in which all religious affections express the dependence of everything finite upon one Supreme and Infinite Being, i.e. The monotheistic forms, occupy the highest level; and all others are related to them as subordinate forms, from which men are destined to pass to those higher ones.*

1. As such subordinate stages we set down, generally speaking, Idol-worship proper (also called Fetishism) and Polytheism; of which, again the first stands far lower than the second. The idol-worshipper may quite well have only one idol, but this does not give such Monolatry any resemblance to Monotheism, for it ascribes to the idol an influence only over a limited field of objects or processes, beyond which its own interest and symapthy do not extend. The addition of several idols is merely an accident, usually caused by the experience of some incapacity in the original one, but not aiming at any kind of completeness. Indeed, the main reason why people remain on this level is that the sense of totality has not yet developed. The old ξόανα of the original Greek tribes were probably idols in the proper sense, each being something in itself alone. The unification of these different worships, by which one Being was substituted for several such idols, and the rise of several cycles of myths by which these creations were brought into connexion with each other – this was the development through which the transition from Idol-worship to Polytheism proper

took place. But the more the idea of a multiplicity of local habitations clung to the Beings thus constituted, the more did Polytheism continue to savour of Idol-worship. Polytheism proper is present only when the local references quite disappear, and the gods, spiritually defined, from an organized and coherent plurality, which, if not exhibited as a totality, is nevertheless presupposed and striven after as such. The more, then, any single one of these Beings is related to the whole system of them, and this system, in turn, to the whole of existence as it appears in consciousness, the more definitely is the dependence of everything finite, not indeed on a Highest One, but on this highest totality, expressed in the religious self-consciousness. But in this state of religious faith there cannot fail to be here and there at least a presentiment of One Supreme Being behind the plurality of higher Beings; and then Polytheism is already beginning to disappear, and the way to Monotheism is open.

2.   As for this difference, of believing in one God on whom the religious man regards himself as being (along with the world of which he is a part) absolutely dependent, or in a group of gods to whom he stands in different relations according as they divide the government of the world among them, or finally in particular idols which belong to the family or the locality or the particular occupation in which he lives: it seems at first, indeed, to be only a difference in the mode of representation, and therefore, from our point of view, only a derivative difference. And only a difference in the immediate self-consciousness can for us be a fit measure of the development of religion. But it is also very easy to show that these different representations depend on different states of self-consciousness. Idol-worship proper is based upon a confused state of the self-consciousness which marks the lowest condition of man, since in it the higher and the lower are so little distinguished that even the feeling of absolute dependence is reflected as arising from a particular object to be apprehended by the senses. So, too, with Polytheism: in its combination of the religious susceptibility with diverse affections of the sensible self-consciousness, it exhibits this diversity in such a very preponderant degree that the feeling of absolute dependence cannot appear in its complete unity and indifference to all that the sensible self-consciousness may contain; but, instead, a plurality is posited as its source. But when the higher self-consciousness, in distinction from the sensible, has been fully developed, then, in so far as we are open in general to sensible stimulation, *i.e.* in so far as we are constituent parts of the world, and therefore in so far as we take up the world into our self-consciousness and expand the latter into a general consciousness of finitude, we are conscious of ourselves as absolutely dependent. Now this self-consciousness can only be described in terms of Monotheism, and indeed only as we have expressed it in our proposition. For if we are conscious of ourselves, as such and in our finitude, as absolutely dependent, the same holds true of all finite existence, and in this connexion we take up the whole world along with ourselves into the unity of our self-consciousness. Thus the different ways of representing that existence outside of us to which the consciousness of absolute dependence refers, depend partly on the different degrees of extensiveness of the self-consciousness (for as long as a man identifies himself only with a small part of finite existence, his god will remain a fetich); and partly on the degree of clearness

with which the higher self-consciousness is distinguished from the lower. Polytheism naturally represents in both respects an indeterminate middle stage, which sometimes is very little different from Idol-worship, but sometimes, when in the handling of the plurality there appears a secret striving after unity, may border very closely on Monotheism; whether it be that the gods rather represent the forces of Nature, or that they symbolize the human qualities which are operative in social relationships, or that both these tendencies are united in the same cult. Otherwise it could not in itself be explained how the correlative term in the feeling of absolute dependence could be reflected as a plurality of beings. But if the higher consciousness has not become quite distinct from the lower, then the correlative can only be conceived in a sensible way, and then for that very reason it contains the germs of plurality. Thus it is only when the religious consciousness expresses itself as capable of being combined with all the states of the sensible self-consciousness without discrimination, but also as clearly distinct from the latter, in such a way that in the religious emotions themselves no sharper distinction appears than that between the joyful and the depressing tone – it is only then that man has successfully passed beyond those two stages, and can refer his feeling of absolute dependence solely to one Supreme Being.

3.   It can therefore justly be said that as soon as piety has anywhere developed to the point of belief in one God over all, it may be predicted that man will not in any region of the earth remain stationary on one of the lower planes. For this belief is always and everywhere very particularly engaged, if not always in the best way, in the endeavour to propagate itself and disclose itself to the receptive faculties of mankind; and this succeeds eventually, as we can see, even among the rudest human races, and by a direct transition from Fetichism without any intermediate passage through a stage of Polytheism. On the other hand, there is nowhere any trace, so far as history reaches, of a relapse from Monotheism, in the strict sense. In the case of most of those Christians who under persecution went back to heathenism, it was only an apparent return. Where it was a matter of real earnest, these people must, previously, at their conversion to Christianity, have been simply carried on by a general movement, without having appropriated the essence of this belief into their own personal consciousness. However, we must not, from all this, draw the conclusion that the existence of Fetichism requires for its explanation the assumption of a still lower stage, in which religious emotion would be altogether lacking. Many have, indeed, described the original state of mankind as such a brute-existence; but, even if we cannot deny all trace of such a state, it can be neither proved historically nor imagined in a general way how of itself this state should have given rise to the development of something higher. No more can it be shown that Polytheism has anywhere transformed itself, by a sheer process from within, into genuine Monotheism; although this can at least be conceived as possible, as has been indicated above. In any case, we must secure ourselves against the demand that, since we have definitely exhibited such a gradation, we are bound also to give a definite account of such an original state of religion; for in other connexions also it is the case that we never get back to origins. If, then, we keep simply to our presuppositions, without resorting to any historical statements about a period which is althogether prehistoric,

we are left with a choice between two ways of conceiving it. Either that quite obscure and confused form of religion was everywhere the original form, and advanced to Polytheism through the concentration of several small tribes into one larger community; or a childish Monotheism (which for that very reason was subject to a confused mingling of the higher and the lower) was the original stage, and among some people darkened completely into Idol-worship, while among others it clarified into a pure belief in God.

4.   On this highest plane, of Monotheism, history exhibits only three great communions – the Jewish, the Christian, and the Mohammedan; the first being almost in process of extinction, the other two still contending for the mastery of the human race. Judaism, by its limitation of the love of Jehovah to the race of Abraham, betrays a lingering affinity with Fetichism; and the numerous vacillations towards Idol-worship prove that during the political heyday of the nation the monotheistic faith had not yet taken fast root, and was not fully and purely developed until after the Babylonian Exile. Islam, on the other hand, with its passionate character, and the strongly sensuous content of its ideas, betrays, in spite of its strict Monotheism, a large measure of that influence of the sensible upon the character of the religious emotions which elsewhere keeps men on the level of Polytheism. Thus Christianity, because it remains free from both these weaknesses, stands higher than either of those other two forms, and takes its place as the purest form of Monotheism which has appeared in history. Hence there is strictly no such thing as a wholesale relapse from Christianity to either Judaism or Mohammedanism, any more than there is from any monotheistic religion to Polytheism or Idol-worship. Individual exceptions will always be connected with pathological states of mind; or, instead of religion, it will prove to be simply one form of irreligion that is exchanged for another, which indeed is what always happens in the case of renegades. And so this comparison of Christianity with other similar religions is in itself a sufficient warrant for saying that Christianity is, in fact, the most perfect of the most highly developed forms of religion.

Postscript 1 – The above account is at variance with the view which sees no real piety at all, but only superstition, in the religions of the lower levels, mainly because they are supposed to have had their source simply in fear. But the honour of Christianity does not at all demand such an assertion. For since Christianity itself affirms that only perfect love casts out all fear, it must admit that imperfect love is never entirely free from fear. And likewise it is always the case, even in Idol-worship, if the idol is worshipped as a protector at all, and not as an evil being, that the fear is by no means quite without any impulses of love, but is rather an adaptation, corresponding to the imperfect love, of the feeling of absolute dependence. Moreover (quite apart from the fact that many of these religions are too cheerful to be explicable by fear), if we should set out to discover for them a quite different origin from that of true religion, it would be difficult to show what sort of tendency this is in the human soul, and what its inner aim is, which engenders Idol-worship, and which must again be lost when the latter gives place to Religion. The truth is, rather, that we must never deny the homogeneity of all these products of the human spirit, but must acknowledge the same root even for the lower powers.

Postscript 2 – But for the assonance of the names there would scarcely be any occasion for us expressly to remark that it is not at all our present business to say anything about that way of thinking which is called Pantheism. For it has never been the confession of a religious communion which actually appeared in history, and it is only with these that we are concerned. Moreover, this name was not originally used even by individuals to designate their own views, but crept in as a taunt and nickname; and in such cases it always remains difficult to hold consistently to any one meaning. The one thing concerning the subject which can be discussed in this place (and indeed *only* in such a place as this) is the question of the relation of this way of thinking to piety. It is admitted that it does not, like the three above-described theories, spring from the religious emotions, by direct reflection upon them. But it may be asked whether, having once arisen in some other way – by the way of speculation or simply of reasoning – it is yet compatible with piety. To this question an affirmative answer may be given without hesitation, provided that Pantheism is taken as expressing some variety or form of Theism, and that the word is not simply and solely a disguise for a materialistic negation of Theism. If we look at Idol-worship, and consider how it is always conjoined with a very limited knowledge of the world, and is also full of magic and sorcery of every sort, it is very easy to see that in very few cases can one speak of a clear distinction on this level between what is assigned to God and what is assigned to the world. And why could not a Hellenic polytheist, embarrassed by the entirely human shapes of the gods, have identified his great gods with the evolved gods of Plato, leaving out the God whom Plato represents as addressing them, and positing only the enthroned Necessity? This would not imply any change in his piety, yet his representation of it would have become pantheistic. But let us think of the highest stage of religion, and let us accordingly hold Pantheism fast to the usual formula of One and all: then God and world will remain distinct at least as regards function, and thus such a man, since he reckons himself as belonging to the world, can feel himself along with this All, to be dependent on that which is the corresponding One. Such states of mind can scarcely be distinguished from the religious emotions of many a Monotheist. At any rate, the distinction (always rather a curious one, and, if I may say so, roughly drawn) between a God who is outside of and above the world, and a God who is in the world, does not particularly meet the point, for nothing can strictly be said about God in terms of the antithesis between internal and external without imperilling in some way the divine omnipotence and omnipresence.

. . . .

§11. *Christianity is a monotheistic faith, belonging to the teleological type of religion, and is essentially distinguished from other such faiths by the fact that in it everything is related to the redemption accomplished by Jesus of Nazareth.*

1. The only pertinent way of discovering the peculiar essence of any particular faith and reducing it as far as possible to a formula is by showing the element which remains constant throughout the most diverse religious affections within this same

communion, while it is absent from analogous affections within other communions. Now since we have little reason to expect that this peculiarity is equally strongly marked in all the different varieties of emotions, there is all the greater possibility of our missing the mark in this attempt, and so coming in the end to the opinion that there is no hard-and-fast inward difference at all, but only the outward difference as determined by time and place. However, we may with some certainty conclude from what has been said above, that we shall be least likely to miss the peculiarity if we keep principally to what is most closely connected with the basal fact, and this is the procedure which underlies the formula of our proposition. But Christianity presents special difficulties, even in this fact alone, that it takes a greater variety of forms than other faiths and is split up into a multiplicity of smaller communions or churches; and thus there arises a twofold task, first, to find the peculiar essence, common to all these communions, of Christianity as such, and secondly, to find the peculiar essence of the particular communion whose right is to be authenticated or whose system of doctrine is to be established. But still further difficulty lies in the fact that even in each particular ecclesiastical communion almost every doctrine appears with the most multifarious variations at different times and places; and this implies as its basis, not indeed, perhaps, an equally great diversity in the religious affections themselves, but always at least a great diversity in the manner of understanding and appraising them. Indeed, the worst of all is that, owing to this variation, the bounds of the Christian realm become a matter of dispute even among Christians themselves, one asserting of this form of teaching, and another of that form, that though it was indeed engendered within Christianity it is nevertheless really un-Christian in content. Now, if he who wishes to solve our problem belongs himself to one of these parties, and assumes at the outset that only what is found within the realm of that one view ought to be taken into account in ascertaining what is distinctive of Christianity, he is at the outset taking controversies as settled, for the settlement of which he professes to be only discovering the conditions. For only when the peculiar essence of Christianity has been ascertained can it be decided how far this or that is compatible or incompatible with it. But if the investigator succeeds in freeing himself from all partiality, and therefore takes into account everything, however opposed, so long as it professes to be Christian, then on the other hand he is in danger of reaching a result far scantier and more colourless in its content, and consequently less suitable to the aims of our present task. That is the present state of affairs, and it cannot be concealed. Now since each man, the more religious he is, usually brings his individual religion the more into this investigation, there is a large majority of the people who form their idea of the peculiar essence of Christianity according to the interests of their party. But for the interests of Apologetics as well as of Dogmatics it seems advisable rather to be content with a scanty result at the beginning and to hope for its completion in the course of further procedure, than to begin with a narrow and exclusive formula, which is of necessity confronted by one or more opposing formulæ, with which there must be a conflict sooner or later. And it is in this sense that the formula of our proposition is set up.

2. It is indisputable that all Christians trace back to Christ the communion to

which they belong. But here we are also presupposing that the term *Redemption* is one to which they all confess: not only that they all *use* the word, with perhaps different meanings, but that there is some common element of meaning which they all have in mind, even if they differ when they come to a more exact description of it. The term itself is in this realm merely figurative, and signifies in general a passage from an evil condition, which is represented as a state of captivity or constraint, into a better condition – this is the passive side of it. But it also signifies the help given in that process by some other person, and this is the active side of it. Further, the usage of the word does not essentially imply that the worse condition must have been preceded by a better condition, so that the better one which followed would really be only a restoration: that point may at the outset be left quite open. But now apply the word to the realm of religion, and suppose we are dealing with the teleological type of religion. Then the evil condition can only consist in an obstruction or arrest of the vitality of the higher self-consciousness, so that there comes to be little or no union of it with the various determinations of the sensible self-consciousness, and thus little or no religious life. We may give to this condition, in its most extreme form, the name of *Godlessness*, or, better, *God-forgetfulness*. But we must not think this means a state in which it is quite impossible for the God-consciousness to be kindled. For if that were so, then, in the first place, the lack of a thing which lay outside of one's nature could not be felt to be an evil condition; and in the second place, a re-creating in the strict sense would then be needed in order to make good this lack, and that is not included in the idea of redemption. The possibility, then, of kindling the God-consciousness remains in reserve even where the evil condition of that consciousness is painted in the darkest colours. Hence we can only designate it as an absence of facility for introducing the God-consciousness into the course of our actual lives and retaining it there. This certainly makes it seem as if these two conditions, that which exists before redemption and that which is to be brought about by redemption, could only be distinguished in an indefinite way, as a more and a less; and so, if the idea of redemption is to be clearly established, there arises the problem of reducing this indefinite distinction to a relative opposition. Such an opposition lies in the following formulae. Given an activity of the sensible self-consciousness, to occupy a moment of time and to connect it with another: its "exponent" or "index" will be greater than that of the higher self-consciousness for uniting itself therewith; and given an activity of the higher self-consciousness, to occupy a moment of time through union with a determination of the sensible, its "exponent" or "index" will be less than that of the activity of the sensible for completing the moment for itself alone. Under these conditions no satisfaction of the impulse towards the God-consciousness will be possible; and so, if such a satisfaction is to be attained, a redemption is necessary, since this condition is nothing but a kind of imprisonment or constraint of the feeling of absolute dependence. These formulae, however, do not imply that in all moments which are so determined the God-consciousness or the feeling of absolute dependence is at zero, but only that in some respect it does not dominate the moment; and in proportion as that is the case the above designations of Godlessness and God-forgetfulness may fitly be applied to it.

3.   The recognition of such a condition undeniably finds a place in all religious communions. For the aim of all penances and purifications is to put an end to the consciousness of this condition or to the condition itself. But our proposition establishes two points which in this connexion distinguish Christianity from all other religious communions. In the first place, in Christianity the incapacity and the redemption, and their connexion with each other, do not constitute simply one particular religious element among others, but all other religious emotions are related to this, and this accompanies all others, as the principal thing which makes them distinctively Christian. And secondly, redemption is posited as a thing which has been universally and completely accomplished by Jesus of Nazareth. And these two points, again, must not be separated from each other, but are essentially interconnected. Thus it could not by any means be said that Christian piety is attributable to every man who in all his religious moments is conscious of being in process of redemption, even if he stood in no relation to the person of Jesus or even knew nothing of Him – a case which, of course, will never arise. And no more could it be said that a man's religion is Christian if he traces it to Jesus, even supposing that therein he is not at all conscious of being in process of redemption – a case which also, of course, will never arise. The reference to redemption is in every Christian consciousness simply because the originator of the Christian communion is the Redeemer; and Jesus is Founder of a religious communion simply in the sense that its members become conscious of redemption through Him. Our previous exposition ensures that this will not be understood to mean that the whole religious consciousness of a Christian can have no other content than simply Jesus and redemption, but only that all religious moments, so far as they are free expressions of the feeling of absolute dependence, are set down as having come into existence through that redemption, and, so far as the feeling appears still unliberated, are set down as being in need of that redemption. It likewise goes without saying that, while this element is always present, different religious moments may and will possess it in varying degrees of strength or weakness, without thereby losing their Christian character. But it *would*, of course, follow from what has been said, that if we conceive of religious moments in which all reference to redemption is absent, and the image of the Redeemer is not introduced at all, these moments must be judged to belong no more intimately to Christianity than to any other monotheistic faith.

4.   The more detailed elaboration of our proposition, as to how the redemption is effected by Christ and comes to consciousness within the Christian communion, falls to the share of the dogmatic system itself. Here, however, we have still to discuss, with reference to the general remarks we made above, the relation of Christianity to the other principal monotheistic communions. These also are traced back each to an individual founder. Now if the difference of founder were the only difference, this would be a merely external difference, and the same thing would be true if these others likewise set up their founder as a redeemer and thus related everything to redemption. For that would mean that in all these religions the religious moments were of like content, only that the personality of the founder was different. But such is not the case: rather must we say that only through Jesus, and thus only in

Christianity, has redemption become the central point of religion. For inasmuch as these other religions have instituted particular penances and purifications for particular things, and these are only particular parts of their doctrine and organization, the effecting of redemption does not appear as their main business. It appears rather as a derivative element. Their main business is the founding of the communion upon definite doctrine and in definite form. If, however, there are within the communion considerable differences in the free development of the God-consciousness, then some people, in whom it is most cramped, are more in need of redemption, and others, in whom it works more freely, are more capable of redemption; and thus through the influence of the latter there arises in the former an approximation to redemption; but only up to the point at which the difference between the two is more or less balanced, simply owing to the fact that there exists a communion or fellowship. In Christianity, on the other hand, the redeeming influence of the Founder is the primary element, and the communion exists only on this presupposition, and as a communication and propagation of that redeeming activity. Hence within Christianity these two tendencies always rise and fall together: the tendency to give pre-eminence to the redeeming work of Christ, and the tendency to ascribe great value to the distinctive and peculiar element in Christian piety. And the same is true of the two opposite tendencies: the tendency to regard Christianity simply as a means of advancing and propagating religion in general (its own distinctive nature being merely accidental and secondary), and the tendency to regard Christ principally as a teacher and the organizer of a communion, while putting the redeeming activity in the background.

Accordingly, in Christianity the relation of the Founder to the members of the communion is quite different from what it is in the other religions. For those other founders are represented as having been, as it were, arbitrarily elevated from the mass of similar or not very different men, and as receiving just as much for themselves as for other people whatever they do receive in the way of divine doctrine and precept. Thus even an adherent of those faiths will hardly deny that God could just as well have given the law through another as through Moses, and the revelation could just as well have been given through another as through Mohammed. But Christ is distinguished from all others as Redeemer alone and for all, and is in no wise regarded as having been at any time in need of redemption Himself; and is therefore separated from the beginning from all other men, and endowed with redeeming power from His birth.

Not that we mean here to exclude at the outset from the Christian communion all those who differ from this presentation of the matter (which is itself capable of manifold shades of variation) in holding that Christ was only later endowed with redeeming power, provided only that this power is recognized as something different from the mere communication of doctrine and rule of life. But if Christ is regarded entirely on the analogy of the founders of other religions, then the distinctive peculiarity of Christianity can only be asserted for the content of the doctrine and rule of life, and the three monotheistic faiths remain separate only in so far as each holds unflinchingly to what it has received. But now suppose them all together capable of advancing still to perfection, and suppose they were able to find for themselves, sooner or later, the better doctrines and precepts of Christianity: then the inward difference would entirely disappear. Suppose that finally the Christian Church is likewise to move on beyond what has been received from Christ: then nothing else remains for Christ but to be regarded as an outstanding point in the development, and this in such a sense that there is a redemption *from* Him as well as a redemption through Him. And since the perfecting principle can only be Reason, and this is everywhere the same, all distinction between the progress of Christianity and that of other monotheistic faiths would gradually disappear, and all alike would only have a validity limited to a definite period, so far as their distinctive character was concerned.

In this way the difference becomes clear between two widely divergent conceptions of Christianity. But at the same time the lines leading from the one to the other become visible. If the latter of the two conceptions were ever to present itself as a complete doctrine, such a communion would perhaps of its own accord sever its connexion with the other Christian communions. But otherwise it could still be recognized as a Christian communion, unless it actually declared itself to be now freed from the necessity of adherence to Christ. Still less should participation in the Christian communion be denied to *individuals* who approximate to that view, so long as they desire to maintain in themselves a living consciousness of God along with, and by means of, that communion.

5.   This development of the argument will, it is hoped, serve to confirm what we have established for the purpose of determining the distinctive element of Christianity. For we have tried, as it were by way of experiment, to single out from among the common elements of Christian piety that element by which Christianity is most definitely distinguished externally; and in this attempt we were guided by the necessity of regarding the inner peculiarity and the outward delimitation in their interconnexion. Perhaps in a universal Philosophy of Religion, to which, if it were properly recognized, Apologetics could then appeal, the inner character of Christianity in itself could be exhibited in such a way that its particular place in the religious world would thereby be definitely fixed. This would also mean that all the principal moments of the religious consciousness would be systematized, and from their interconnexion it would be seen which of them were fitted to have all the others related to them and to be themselves a constant concomitant of all the others. If, then, it should be seen that the element which we call "redemption" becomes such a moment as soon as a liberating fact enters a region where the God-consciousness was in a state of constraint, Christianity would in that case be vindicated as a distinct form of faith and its nature in a sense construed. But even this could not properly be called a proof of Christianity, since even the Philosophy of Religion could not establish any necessity, either to recognize a particular Fact as redemptive, or to give the central place actually in one's own consciousness to any particular moment, even though that moment should be capable of occupying such a place. Still less can this present account claim to be such a proof; for here, in accordance with the line we have taken, and since we can only start from a historical consideration, we cannot even pretend to do as much as might be done in a complete Philosophy of Religion.

Moreover, it is obvious that an adherent of some other faith might perhaps be completely convinced by the above account that what we have set forth is really the peculiar essence of Christianity, without being thereby so convinced that Christianity is actually the truth, as to feel compelled to accept it. Everything we say in this place is relative to Dogmatics, and Dogmatics is only for Christians; and so this account is only for those who live within the pale of Christianity, and is intended only to give guidance, in the interests of Dogmatics, for determining whether the expressions of any religious consciousness are Christian or not, and whether the Christian quality is strongly and clearly expressed in them, or rather doubtfully. We entirely renounce all attempt to prove the truth or necessity of Christianity; and we presuppose, on the contrary, that every Christian, before he enters at all upon inquires of this kind, has already the inward certainty that his religion cannot take any other form than this.

§12. *Christianity does indeed stand in a special historical connexion with Judaism; but as far as concerns its historical existence and its aim, its relations to Judaism and Heathenism are the same.*

1. We here take Judaism to mean primarily the Mosaic institutions, but also, as preparing the way for these, every earlier usage which helped to separate the people from other peoples. With this Judaism, then, Christianity has an historical connexion through the fact that Jesus was born among the Jewish people, as indeed a universal Redeemer could scarcely spring from any other than a monotheistic people, once such a people was in existence. But we must not represent the historical connexion in a too exclusive manner. At the time of the appearance of Christ the religious thought of the people was no longer based exclusively on Moses and the prophets, but had been in many ways remoulded through the influence of non-Jewish elements which it had absorbed during and after the Babylonian Dispersion. And, on the other hand, Greek and Roman Heathendom had been in many ways prepared for Monotheism, and in these quarters the expectation of a new phase was most intense; while contrariwise among the Jews the Messianic promises had been partly given up and partly misunderstood. So that when one puts together all the historical circumstances, the difference becomes much smaller than it appears at the first glance. And Christ's descent from Judaism is largely counterbalanced by the facts that so many more heathen than Jews went over to Christianity, and that Christianity would not have been received by the Jews even as much as it was, had they not been permeated by those foreign elements.

2. The truth rather is that the relations of Christianity to Judaism and Heathenism are the same, inasmuch as the transition from either of these to Christianity is a transition to another religion. The leap certainly seems greater in the case of Heathenism, since it had first to become monotheistic in order to become Christian. At the same time, the two processes were not separated, but Monotheism was given to the heathen directly in the form of Christianity, as it had been previously in the form of Judaism. And the demand made upon the Jews, to give up their reliance

upon the law, and to put a different interpretation upon the Abrahamitic promises, was just as large a demand. Accordingly we must assume that Christian piety, in its original form, cannot be explained by means of the Jewish piety of that or of an earlier time, and so Christianity cannot in any wise be regarded as a remodelling or a renewal and continuation of Judaism. Paul does indeed regard the faith of Abraham as the prototype of Christian faith, and represents the Mosaic Law simply as something slipped in between; and from this it might, of course, be inferred that he meant to represent Christianity as a renewal of that original and pure Abrahamitic Judaism. But his meaning was only that Abraham's faith was related to the promise as ours is to the fulfilment, and not by any means that the promise was the same to Abraham as the fulfilment is to us. Where he expressly speaks of the relation of the Jews and the Heathen to Christ, he represents it as being exactly the same: he represents Christ as being the same for both, and both as being alike very far from God and so in need of Christ. Now if Christianity has the same relation to Judaism as to Heathenism, it can no more be regarded as a continuation of the former than of the latter: if a man comes from either of them to Christianity, he becomes, as regards his religion, a new man. But the promise to Abraham, so far as it has been fulfilled in Christ, is represented as having had its reference to Christ only in the divine decree, not in the religious consciousness of Abraham and his people. And since we can only recognize the self-identity of a religious communion when there is a uniformity of the religious consciousness, we can no more recognize an identity between Christianity and Abrahamitic Judaism than between it and the later Judaism or Heathenism. And neither can it be said that that purer original Judaism carried within itself the germ of Christianity, so that it would have developed of itself by natural progress from Judaism without the intervention of any new factor; nor that Christ Himself lay in the line of this progress in such a way that a new communal life and existence could not begin with Him.

3.　The widely prevalent notion of one single Church of God, existing from the beginning of the human race to the end of it, is opposed to our proposition more in appearance than in reality. If the Mosaic Law belongs to the one chain of this divine economy of salvation, then we must, according to approved Christian teachers, include also the Greek philosophy, especially that which tended towards Monotheism; and yet we cannot, without quite destroying the peculiarity of Christianity, assert that its teaching forms a single whole with the heathen philosophy. If, on the other hand, this doctrine of the one Church is chiefly intended to express the fact that Christ's active relation to all that is human knows no limits, even with regard to the time that was past, this is an intention upon which we cannot yet pass judgment, but which is quite compatible with our proposition. And even in Old Testament prophecy there is ascribed to the New Covenant a different character from the Old, and this direct antithesis expresses the inward separation in the most definite way. Hence the rule may be set up that almost everything else in the Old Testament is, for our Christian usage, but the husk or wrapping of its prophecy, and that whatever is most definitely Jewish has least value. So that we can find rendered with some exactness in Old Testament passages only those of our religious emotions which are of a somewhat general nature without anything very distinctively Christian. For those which are distinctively Christian, Old Testament sayings will not provide a suitable expression, unless we think certain elements away from them and read other things into them. And that being the case, we shall certainly find quite as near and accordant echoes in the utterances of the nobler and purer Heathenism; as indeed the older Apologists were no less glad to appeal to what they held to be heathen Messianic prophecies, and thus recognized there a striving of human nature towards Christianity.

13

Ernst Troeltsch, "The Place
of Christianity among the
World Religions"

In the wake of the theology of Schleiermacher, nineteenth-century liberal Protestantism came to believe that God is revealed not in a book or in the church but in the process of history. In particular, there was a group of German Protestant theologians centered at the University of Göttingen who applied the method of the fledgling field of history of religion to the study of Christianity. They held that the Bible and Christianity could be understood only if studied as individual historical phenomena seen in the context of other religio-historical phenomena in the ancient world. It was assumed that resemblances between cultures indicated borrowing and that, therefore, claims to Christian uniqueness or absoluteness were historically dubious. This group of scholars came to be known as "the History of Religions School" (*die Religionsgeschichtliche Schule*). One of their key theorists was Ernst Troeltsch (1865–1923).

Much in the fashion of Schleiermacher, Troeltsch conceived of religion as nonrational experience not reducible to anything else. Troeltsch was interested in the place of religion in human intellectual development, as well as the historical process by which religion, including Christianity, came into being. In his essay "The Place of Christianity among the World Religions," written near the end of his life, Troeltsch notes the conflict between historical reflection on the one hand and the determination of standards of truth and value on the other hand. In response to the transitoriness, contingency, and relativity which the study of history indicates, theology has attempted to provide a defense of its own uniqueness or absoluteness by seeking to establish the ultimate validity of the Christian revelation. In Troeltsch's judgment, such defensive strategies are bound to end in failure because such ultimate validity is not historically demonstrable; and because the tendency of history is not toward unity and universality, Christianity cannot be said to be the goal of history. Troeltsch therefore counseled Christianity to renounce claims of absolute validity and to content itself with the declaration that – at least for its adherents – it has the highest degree of validity possible to date. Presumably, other religions have a similar degree of validity for their adherents. Recognizing that objective and final pronouncements on validity are thus not possible, the task is to understand each religion as an individuality in the context of the civilization in which it was located and work for mutual understanding. So doing allows one "to apprehend the One in the Many."

The Text

It has long been my great desire to visit the famous University of Oxford, which shines across to us in my country with the splendor of its medieval days, and is most closely associated for us with the problem of the development of Nominalism and Empiricism out of the Scholastic philosophy. But that it would be my privilege to survey it from the height of an Oxford lecture-platform was a thing which exceeded my boldest aspirations. I am indebted for this high honor to Professor Clement C. J. Webb, and to the kind interest which you have shown in my literary work. I am deeply conscious how great an honor it is, and I should like to offer you and Mr Webb my very sincere thanks. I can only hope that you will not miss today the wisdom and learning of your ordinary teacher.

In view of these unusual circumstances, I could not select any other subject than the one which contains the center and starting-point of my academic work. This central theme is most clearly, I think, set forth in my little book on *The Absolute Validity of Christianity*, which forms the conclusion of a series of earlier studies and the beginning of new investigations of a more comprehensive kind in the philosophy of history. Moreover, this subject is for me the point at which my own original interests and the problems presented by the modern religious situation have met together. It was recognized as such by a countryman of your own, Mr A. C. Bouquet, in his book *Is Christianity the Final Religion?* and I am indebted to him for a very able statement and criticism of the position. I should like, therefore, to occupy this hour in explaining the position I adopted in my little book, and in elucidating the further development of my thought by means of this small work.

To put it briefly, the central meaning of this book consists in a deep and vivid realization of the clash between historical reflection and the determination of standards of truth and value. The problem thus arising presented itself to me at a very early age. I had had a predominantly humanistic and historical education, from which I had been led to extend my studies and interests over a wide field of historical investigation, using the terms "history" and "humanity" in the sense we in Germany have been wont to attribute to them in our best periods – namely, in the objective sense of a contemplation of objects which covers as far as possible the whole extent of human existence, and which finds its delight in all the abundant diversity and ceaseless movement characteristic of human existence, and this without seeking any precise practical ends. It seems to us that it is the wealth of moral life and development that manifests itself in this endlessly diversified world of history, and imparts some of its own loftiness and solemnity to the soul of the observer.

I was, however, inspired by a smaller interest, which was quite as strong and quite as much a part of my natural endowment as the first, I mean the interest in reaching a vital and effective religious position, which could alone furnish my life with a center of reference for all practical questions, and could alone give meaning and

Source: *Attitudes Toward Other Religions: Some Christian Interpretations*, ed. Owen C. Thomas.

purpose to reflection upon the things of this world. This need of mine led me to theology and philosophy, which I devoured with an equally passionate interest. I soon discovered, however, that the historical studies which had so largely formed me, and the theology and philosophy in which I was now immersed, stood in sharp opposition, indeed even in conflict, with one another. I was confronted, upon the one hand, with the perpetual flux of the historian's data and the distrustful attitude of the historical critic toward conventional traditions, the real events of the past being, in his view, discoverable only as a reward of ceaseless toil, and then only with approximate accuracy. And, upon the other hand, I perceived the impulse in men toward a definite practical standpoint – the eagerness of the trusting soul to receive the divine revelation and to obey the divine commands. It was largely out of this conflict, which was no hypothetical one, but a fact of my own practical experience, that my entire theoretical standpoint took its rise.

Though this conflict was a personal one, however, it was no mere accident of my personal experience. It was rather the personal form in which a vital problem characteristic of the present stage of human development presented itself to me. I am, of course, aware that the sting of this problem is not equally felt in all parts of the civilized world of Europe and America. As Bouquet has explained in the work I have already mentioned, we must not apply without reservation to England, still less to America with its very undeveloped historical sense, what is true, in this respect, of other countries.

Nevertheless, there exists at bottom, everywhere, an impression that historical criticism and the breadth of historical interest are fraught with danger to the recognition of simple standards of value, be they of rational or traditional origin. In the Anglo-Saxon countries it is especially ethnography and the comparative study of religion, together with careful philosophical criticism, that produce this attitude. In my own country it is primarily an examination of European civilization itself that has impressed us with the relativity and transitoriness of all things, even of the loftiest values of civilization. The effect, however, is very similar in the two cases. Whether we approach it from the standpoint of Herbert Spencer and the theory of evolution, or from that of Hegel and Ranke and German Romanticism, history presents a spectacle of bewildering diversity, and of historical institutions as all in a perpetual state of movement from within.

Indeed, the comparative study of religion, which gives an additional impulse to the tendency to relativity produced by historical reflection, has been pre-eminently the work of the great colonizing nations, especially of the English and the Dutch. And the criticism of the Bible and of dogma is not without representatives in England; and thus a growing feeling of uncertainty has been created here in this department also. The difference between this English line of reflection and the historical thought of Germany really consists simply in the fact that the latter is less wont to consider the practical needs and interests of society, while in theory it is determined more by the concept of individuality than by sociological or evolutionary principles which tend to regard all processes as leading to a single goal presented by nature.

Important as these differences are, however, they are all but different aspects of the one fundamental conflict between the spirit of critical scepticism generated by the ceaseless flux and manifold contradictions within the sphere of history and the demand of the religious consciousness for certainty, for unity, and for peace. Whether this conflict becomes more apparent in the critical analysis of details or in the challenging of fundamental principles, the cause and the general effect remain very much the same.

In my book on *The Absolute Validity of Christianity* I examined the means whereby theology is able to defend itself against these difficulties. This, of course, involved an examination of the fundamental concepts of theology as such. I believed that I could here determine two such concepts, both of which claimed to establish the ultimate validity of the Christian revelation in opposition to the relativities revealed by the study of history.

The first of these concepts was the theory that the truth of Christianity is guaranteed by miracles. In our times we are no longer primarily concerned here with miracles in the external world, i.e. with the so-called "nature-miracles", involving an infringement of natural law, but with the miracles of interior conversion and the attainment of a higher quality of life through communion with Jesus and His community. In this connection, it is claimed, an entirely different type of causation comes into operation from that which is operative anywhere else in the world. The Christian life may indeed be compared to an island in the midst of the stream of history, exposed to all the storms of secular life, and lured by all its wiles, yet constituting, in reality, a stronghold of experience of quite another order. The absolute validity of Christianity rests upon the absoluteness of God Himself, who is made manifest here directly in miracles but who manifested Himself beyond this island only as a *causa remota* – as the ground of the interconnection of all relative things. In this way both a natural and a supernatural theology are possible, the latter resting upon the new birth and experience of the inner man, while natural theology is based upon the facts and forces of the external world. This theory is simply a restatement of the old miracle apologetic in the more intimate and spiritual form which it acquired under the influence of Methodism and Pietism.

The second fundamental concept of theology, which I have called the concept of evolution, presents a considerable contrast to the first. Its most important exponent is Hegel. According to this view, Christianity is simply the perfected expression of religion as such. In the universal process of the unfolding of Spirit, the fundamental impulse toward salvation and communion with God overcomes all the limitations of sense experience, of the natural order, of mythological form, until it attains perfect expression in Christianity, and enters into combination with the loftiest and most spiritual of all philosophies, namely, that of Platonism. Christianity, it is maintained, is not *a particular* religion, it is *religion*. It is no isolated manifestation of Spirit, but the flower of spiritual life itself. All religion implies salvation and rebirth, but outside Christianity these are subject to the limitations of physical nature and are baulked by human selfishness. In the prophets and in Christ the Divine Life breaks through these limits and flows unrestrained into the thirsty world, which finds therein the solution of all its conflicts and the goal of all its striving. The whole history of religion and its obvious trend are thus a completely adequate proof of Christianity.

The historical process does not stand in opposition to it. When regarded as a whole, and as one process, it rather affords a demonstration of its supreme greatness and all-embracing power. The miracles which attend its development are partly explicable, as in other religions, as mythical elements, accumulated during the growth of tradition, but they are partly effects of the shock produced by the spiritual revolution traceable here. They are thus not so much its credentials as its attendant phenomena, and as such they may be left without anxiety in the hands of the historical critic.

I found myself obliged to dismiss both these views as untenable. The former I rejected on the ground that an inward miracle, though it is indeed a powerful physical upheaval, is not a miracle in the strict sense of the term. Are we justified in tracing the Platonic *Eros* to a natural cause, while we attribute a supernatural origin to the Christian *Agape*? And how can we prove such origin, even if we care to assume it? This would only be possible by having recourse once more to the visible signs which accompany these inward miracles, which would be again to treat the accompaniment as if it were itself the melody. Moreover, we should then be faced with the competition furnished by similar miracles in non-Christian religions, not to mention the negative results of historical criticism and the trouble attendant upon every theory of miracles.

If, however, we turn for this reason to the second view we find the difficulties to be different, indeed, but not less formidable. The actual history of religion knows nothing of the common character of all religions, or of their natural upward trend toward Christianity. It perceives a sharp distinction between the great world religions and the national religions of heathen tribes, and further discovers certain irresolvable contradictions between these world religions themselves which render their ultimate fusion and reconciliation in Christianity highly improbable, either in theory or in practice. Moreover, Christianity is itself a theoretical abstraction. It presents no historical uniformity, but displays a different character in every age, and is, besides, split up into many different denominations, hence it can in no wise be represented as the finally attained unity and explanation of all that has gone before, such as religious speculation seeks. It is rather a particular, independent, historical principle, containing, similarly to the other principles, very diverse possibilities and tendencies.

This leads us finally to a conception which has, I think, obtained less recognition in other countries than in Germany – I mean the conception which dominates the whole sphere of history, viz. Individuality. History cannot be regarded as a process in which a universal and everywhere similar principle is confined and obscured. Nor is it a continual mixing and remixing of elemental psychical powers, which indicate a general trend of things toward a rational end or goal of evolution. It is rather an immeasurable, incomparable profusion of always-new, unique, and hence individual tendencies, welling up from undiscovered depths, and coming to light in each case in unsuspected places and under different circumstances. Each process works itself out in its own way, bringing ever-new series of unique transformations in its train, until its powers are exhausted, or until it enters as component material into some new combination. Thus the universal law of history consists precisely in this, that the Divine Reason, or the Divine Life, within history, constantly manifests itself in always-new and always-peculiar individualizations – and hence that its tendency is not toward unity or universality at all, but rather toward the fulfillment of the highest potentialities of each separate department of life. It is this law which, beyond all else, makes it quite impossible to characterize Christianity as the reconciliation and goal of all the forces of history, or indeed to regard it as anything else than a historical individuality.

These are the historical ideas which have been handed down to us from German Romanticism, the great opposition movement to Rationalism and to all the clumsy miracle apologetic. They illustrate the special character and significance of German Romanticism, considered as a part of the great Romantic Movement of Europe. They form the starting-point of all the German history and most of the German theology of the nineteenth century. They present our problem in its most crucial form, and explain why it became a more burning problem in Germany than elsewhere, except where it was envisaged in the same way, either as a result of independent reflection or under German influence.

What, then, is the solution? This is the question which I attempted to answer in my book. I first endeavored to show that it was in any case impossible to return to the old miracle apologetic. This has been rendered untenable, not by theories but by documents, by discoveries, by the results of exploration. The force of such evidence cannot be resisted by anyone whose sense of truth has been educated by philology, or even by anyone possessing an average amount of ordinary "common sense". I then submitted that the mere fact of the universality of Christianity – of its presence in all the other religions – would, even if true – be irrelevant. The point at issue was not whether Christianity was as a matter of fact universal or at least implicit in all religion, but whether it possessed ultimate truth, a truth which might easily depend upon a single instance of itself.

This formed a position for further reflection. It is quite possible, I maintained, that there is an element of truth in every religion, but that this is combined with innumerable transitory, individual features. This element of truth can only be disentangled through strife and disruption, and it should be our constant endeavor to assist in this process of disentanglement. The recognition of this truth is, however, an intuition which is born of deep personal experience and a pure conscientiousness. No strict proof of it is possible, for to demonstrate the actual presence of this truth in all the other cases would not be to establish its validity, even if this demonstration were easier than it is. Such an intuition can only be confirmed retrospectively and indirectly by its practical fruits, and by the light that it sheds upon all the problems of life. Thus in relation to Christianity such an intuition can only arise from immediate impression and personal conviction. Its claim to universal validity can only be felt and believed, in the first instance, and must be confirmed retrospectively through its genuine ability to furnish a solution of the various problems of life.

Now, validity of this kind seems always to rest upon the fine point of personal conviction. We still require a broader foundation upon actual, objective facts. I believed that I had discovered such a foundation for Christianity in the terms in which its claim to ultimate validity finds instinctive and immediate expression; in other words, in its faith in revelation and in the kind of claim it makes to truth. I thought it necessary to compare it from this point of view with other religions, whose belief in revelation and claim to validity were in every case of quite a different kind. If we examine any of the great world religions we shall find that all of them, Judaism, Islam, Zoroastrianism, Buddhism, Christianity, even Confucianism, indeed claim absolute validity, but quite naïvely, and that in a very different manner in each case, the differences being illustrative of differences in their inner structure. These claims are always naïve – simple and direct. They are not the outcome of an apologetic reasoning, and the differences they exhibit in their naïve claims to absolute validity indicate the varying degree of such absolute validity as they really mean and intend within their own minds. This seemed to me to be nearly the most important point in every comparison between the religions, and the one which furnished the most searching test of the character of the dogmatic contents to be compared – contents which, in themselves, reveal so little as to the manner of their foundation in immediate religious experience.

A similar line of thought is to be found in the excellent book on *National and Universal Religions*, by the Dutch writer, Abraham Kuenen. If we make his distinction the basis of our investigation and comparison we at once perceive that Judaism and Zoroastrianism were explicitly national religions, associated with a particular country and concerned with tasks presented by a particular type of civilization – in the case of the Jews primarily with questions of national loyalty and national aspiration. Islam, too, is at bottom the national religion of the Arab peoples, compelling by the sword recognition of the prophetic claims of Mohammed in all the countries to which the Arab races have penetrated. Where, on the other hand, it has spread beyond the boundaries of Arabian territory, it has not as a rule attempted to convert unbelievers, but has simply maintained them as a source of revenue. And where Islam has developed great missionary activity, as, for example, in Africa and in the islands of the Malay Archipelago, it shows itself to be bound to certain conditions of civilization which render it more readily acceptable to primitive races than Christianity, but which prove it, at the same time, to be indissolubly connected with a particular type of civilization. Finally, where it has adopted Persian or Indian mysticism, or Greek or modern philosophy, it loses its essential character, and becomes no more than a sign and a proof of national autonomy. Confucianism and Buddhism again are rather philosophies than religions, and owe their claim to absolute validity more to the common character of thought than to belief in a specific religious revelation, while Confucianism is essentially a national movement and Buddhism is, as a matter of fact, bound to the conditions of life in tropical countries.

Now, the naïve claim to absolute validity made by Christianity is of quite a different kind. All limitation to a particular race or nation is excluded on principle, and this exclusion illustrates the purely human character of its religious ideal, which appeals only to the simplest, the most general, the most personal and spiritual needs of mankind. Moreover, it does not depend in any way upon human reflection or a laborious process of reasoning, but upon an overwhelming manifestation of God in the persons and lives of the great prophets. Thus it was not a theory but a life – not a social order but a power. It owes its claim to universal validity not to the correctness of its reasoning nor to the conclusiveness of its proofs, but to God's revelation of Himself in human hearts and lives. Thus the naïve claim to absolute validity of Christianity is as unique as its conception of God. It is indeed a corollary of its belief in a revelation within the depths of the soul, awakening men to a new and higher quality of life, breaking down the barriers which the sense of guilt would otherwise set up, and making a final breach with the egoism obstinately centered in the individual self. It is from this point of view that its claim to absolute validity, following as it does from the content of its religious ideal, appears to be vindicated. It possesses the highest claim to universality of all the religions, for this its claim is based upon the deepest foundations, the nature of God and of man.

Hence we may simply leave aside the question of the measure of validity possessed by the other religions. Nor need we trouble ourselves with the question of the possible further development of religion itself. It suffices that Christianity is itself a developing religion, constantly striving toward a fresh and fuller expression. We may content ourselves with acknowedging that it possesses the highest degree of validity attained among all the historical religions which we are able to examine. We shall not wish to become Jews, nor Zoroastrians, nor Mohammedans, nor again Confucianists, nor Buddhists. We shall rather strive continually to bring our Christianity into harmony with the changing conditions of life, and to bring its human and divine potentialities to the fullest possible fruition. It is the loftiest and most spritiual revelation we know at all. It has the highest validity. Let that suffice.

Such was the conclusion I reached in the book which I wrote some twenty years ago, and, from the practical standpoint at least, it contains nothing that I wish to withdraw. From the point of view of theory, on the other hand, there are a number of points which I should wish to modify today, and these modifications are, of course, not without some practical effects.

My scruples arise from the fact that, while the significance for history of the concept of Individuality impresses me more forcibly every day, I no longer believe this to be so easily reconcilable with that of supreme validity. The further investigations, especially into the history of Christianity, of which I have given the results in my *Social Teachings (Die Soziallehren der christlichen Kirchen und Gruppen, 1912)*, have shown me how thoroughly individual is historical Christianity after all, and how invariably its various phases and denominations have been due to varying circumstances and conditions of life. Whether you regard it as a whole or in its several forms, it is a purely historical, individual, relative phenomenon, which could, as we actually find it, only have arisen in the territory of the classical culture, and among the Latin and Germanic races. The Christianity of the Oriental peoples – the Jacobites, Nestorians, Armenians, Abyssinians – is of quite a different type, indeed even that of the Russians is a world of its own. The inference from all that is, however, that a religion, in the several forms assumed by it, always depends upon the intellectual, social, and national conditions among which it exists. On the other hand, a study of the non-Christian religions convinced me more and more that their naïve claims to absolute validity are also genuinely such. I found Buddhism and Brahminism especially to be really humane and spiritual religions, capable of appealing in precisely the same way to the inner certitude and devotion of their followers as Christianity, though the particular character of each has been determined by the historical, geographical, and social conditions of the countries in which it has taken shape.

The subject to which I devoted most attention, however, was that of the relation of individual historical facts to standards of value within the entire domain of history in connection with the development of political, social, ethical, aesthetic, and scientific ideas. I have only lately published the results of these investigations in my new book on *The Historical Standpoint and Its Problems* (*Der Historismus und seine Probleme*, 1922). I encountered the same difficulties in each of these provinces – they were not confined to religion. Indeed, even the validity of science and logic seemed to exhibit, under different skies and upon different soil, strong individual differences present even in their deepest and innermost rudiments. What was really common to mankind, and universally valid for it, seemed, in spite of a general kinship and capacity for mutual understanding, to be at bottom exceedingly little, and to belong more to the province of material goods than to the ideal values of civilization.

The effect of these discoveries upon the conclusions reached in my earlier book was as follows:

The individual character of European civilization, and of the Christian religion which is intimately connected with it, receives now much greater emphasis, while the somewhat rationalistic concept of validity, and specifically of *supreme validity*, falls considerably into the background. It is impossible to deny facts or to resist the decrees of fate. And it is historical facts that have welded Christianity into the closest connection with the civilizations of Greece, Rome, and Northern Europe. All our thoughts and feelings are impregnated with Christian motives and Christian presuppositions; and, conversely, our whole Christianity is indissolubly bound up with elements of the ancient and modern civilizations of Europe. From being a Jewish sect Christianity has become the religion of all Europe. It stands or falls with European civilization; while, on its own part, it has entirely lost its Oriental character and has become hellenized and westernized. Our European conceptions of personality and its eternal, divine right, and of progress toward a kingdom of the spirit and of God, our enormous capacity for expansion and for the interconnection of spiritual and temporal, our whole social order, our science, our art – all these rest, whether we know it or not, whether we like it or not, upon the basis of this deorientalized Christianity.

Its primary claim to validity is thus the fact that only through it have we become what we are, and that only in it can we preserve the religious forces that we need. Apart from it we lapse either into a self-destructive titanic attitude, or into effeminate trifling, or into crude brutality. And at the same time our life is a consistent compromise, as little unsatisfactory as we can manage, between its lofty spirituality and our practical everyday needs – a compromise that has to be renewed at every fresh ascent and every bend in the road. This tension is characteristic of our form of human life and rouses us to many a heroic endeavor, though it may also lead us into the most terrible mendacity and crime. Thus we are, and thus we shall remain, as long as we survive. We cannot live without a religion, yet the only religion that we can endure is Christianity, for Christianity has grown up with us and has become a part of our very being.

Now, obviously we cannot remain in these matters at the level of brute fact. Christianity could not be the religion of such a highly developed racial group if it did not possess a mighty spiritual power and truth; in short, if it were not, in some degree, a manifestation of the Divine Life itself. The evidence we have for this remains essentially the same, whatever may be our theory concerning absolute validity – it is the evidence of a profound inner experience. This experience is undoubtedly the criterion of its validity, but, be it noted, only of its validity *for us.* It is God's countenance as revealed to us; it is the way in which, being what we are, we receive, and react to, the revelation of God. It is binding upon us, and it brings us deliverance. It is final and unconditional for us, because we have nothing else, and because in what we have we can recognize the accents of the divine voice.

But this does not preclude the possibility that other racial groups, living under entirely different cultural conditions, may experience their contact with the Divine Life in quite a different way, and may themselves also possess a religion which has grown up with them, and from which they cannot sever themselves so long as they remain what they are. And they may quite sincerely regard this as absolutely valid for them, and give expression to this absolute validity according to the demands of their own religious feeling. We shall, of course, assume something of this kind only among nations which have reached a relatively high stage of civilization, and whose whole mental life has been intimately connected with their religion through a long period of discipline. We shall not assume it among the less developed races, where many religious cults are followed side by side, nor in the simple animism of heathen tribes, which is so monotonous in spite of its many variations. These territories are gradually conquered by the great world religions which possess a real sense of their own absolute validity. But among the great spiritual religions themselves the fundamental spiritual positions which destiny has assigned to them persist in their distinctness. If we wish to determine their relative value it is not the religions alone that we must compare but always only the civilizations of which the religion in each case constitutes a part incapable of severance from the rest. But who will presume to make a really final pronouncement here? Only God Himself, who has determined these differences, can do that. The various racial groups can only seek to purify and enrich their experience, each within its own province and according to its own standards, and to win the weaker and less-developed races for their own faith, always remembering that the religion thus adopted by another people will individualize itself anew.

The practical bearing of this new manner of thinking differs but little from that of my earlier view, or indeed from that of any theology which seeks to retain the essential basis of Christianity, and intends merely to substantiate and to interpret it. Its detailed application, however, brings to light one or two important consequences.

In the first place, it has a considerable influence upon the question of foreign missions. Missionary enterprise has always been in part simply a concomitant of the political, military, and commercial expansion of a state or nation, but in part also an outcome of the religious enthusiast's zeal for conversion. The former aspect is exceedingly important as a factor in human history, but is irrelevant in the present connection. The latter aspect, on the other hand, is intimately connected with the claim to absolute validity. But here we have to maintain, in accordance with all our conclusions hitherto, that directly religious missionary enterprise must stand in quite a different relation to the great philosophical world religions from that in which it stands to the crude heathenism of smaller tribes. There can be always only a spiritual wrestling of missionary Christianity with the other world religions, possibly a certain contact with them. The heathen races, on the other hand, are being morally and spiritually disintegrated by the contact with European civilization; hence they demand a substitute from the higher religion and culture. We have a missionary duty towards these races, and our enterprise is likely to meet with success among them, although Christianity, be it remembered, is by no means the only religion which is taking part in this missionary campaign. Islam and Buddhism are also missionary religions. But in relation to the great world religions we need to recognize that they are expressions of the religious consciousness corresponding to certain definite types of culture, and that it is their duty to increase in depth and purity by means of their own interior impulses, a task in which the contact with Christianity may prove helpful, to them as to us, in such processes of development from within. The great religions might indeed be described as crystallizations of the thought of great races, as these races are themselves crystallizations of the various biological and anthropological forms. There can be no conversion or transformation of one into the other, but only a measure of agreement and of mutual understanding.

The second practical consequence of my new trend of thought concerns the inner development of Christianity itself. If my theory is correct this development is closely related to the whole spiritual and cultural development of European civilization. True, the religious consciousness, whose object is God and eternal peace, is less exposed to restlessness and change than are the purely temporal constituents of the movement; hence it has become institutionalized in the various large denominations which, because of these internal reasons, constitute the most conservative element in the life of Europe. Nevertheless, Christianity is drawn into the stream of spiritual development even within the Churches, and still more outside and beyond them, in the free speculation of literature and philosophy. Moreover, it contains, like all the world religions, and perhaps more than any other world religion, an impulse and the power to a continual self-purification and self-deepening, for it has been assigned to that Spirit which shall lead men into all truth, and which seeks its fulfillment in the coming Kingdom of God; and again, because it has been bound up from the first with all the intellectual forces of Hellenism.

Under these circumstances the course of its development is unpredictable, for it is capable of assuming always new individualizations. A new era in the world's history is beginning for it at this moment. It has to ally itself anew to a new conception of nature, a new social order, and a profound interior transformation of the spiritual outlook, and has to bring to the suffering world a new peace and a new brotherhood. How this can be accomplished it is not for me to say here; indeed, the answer is as yet very far from clear. All that is certain is that Christianity is at a critical moment of its further development, and that very bold and far-reaching changes are necessary, transcending anything that has yet been achieved by any denomination. I have, in this respect, become more and more radical and super-denominational while, at the same time, I have come more and more to regard the specific kernel of religion as a unique and independent source of life and power.

Can we, then, discover no common goal of religion, nothing at all that is absolute, in the objective sense of constituting a common standard for mankind? Instinctive conviction makes us reluctant to admit such a skeptical conclusion, and it will especially be combated on the ground of the reality of the subjective validities which we have discovered. These are not simply illusions or the products of human vanity. They are the products of the impulse toward absolute objective truth, and take effect in the practical sphere under constant critical self-purification and effort at self-improvement. I have already drawn attention to this fact in my earlier work. I only wish to emphasize now more strongly than I did then that this synthesis cannot as yet be already attained in any one of the historical religions, but that they all are tending in the same direction, and that all seem impelled by an inner force to strive upward toward some unknown final height, where alone the ultimate unity and the final objective validity can lie. And, as all religion has thus a common goal in the Unknown, the Future, perchance in the Beyond, so, too, it has a common ground in the Divine Spirit ever pressing the finite mind onward toward further light and fuller consciousness, a Spirit Which indwells the finite spirit, and Whose ultimate union with it is the purpose of the whole many-sided process.

Between these two poles, however – the divine Source and the divine Goal – lie all the individual differentiations of race and civilization, and, with them also, the individual differences of the great, comprehensive religions. There may be mutual understanding between them if they are willing to renounce those sorry things, self-will and the spirit of violent domination. If each strives to fulfil its own highest potentialities, and allows itself to be influenced therein by the similar striving of the rest, they may approach and find contact with each other. Some striking examples of such contact are recorded in Canon Streeter's *The Sadhu,* and in a book called *On the Verge of the Primitive Forest,* by the Alsatian physician and writer on the philosophy of religion, Albert Schweitzer. But, so far as human eye can penetrate into the future, it would seem probable that the great revelations to the various civilizations will remain distinct, in spite of a little shifting of their several territories at the fringes, and that the question of their several relative values will never be capable of objective determination, since every proof thereof will presuppose the special characteristics of the civilization in which it arises. The conception of personality itself is, for instance, different in the east and in the west, hence arguments starting from it will lead to different conclusions in the two cases. Yet there is no other concept which could furnish a basis for argument concerning practical values and truths save this concept of personality, which is always itself already one of the fundamental positions of the several religions, and is determined by them according to these respective general attitudes of theirs.

This is what I wish to say in modification of my former theories. I hope you feel that I am not speaking in any spirit of skepticism or uncertainty. A truth which, in the first instance, is *a truth for us* does not cease, because of this, to be very Truth

Ernst Troeltsch

and Life. What we learn daily through our love for our fellow-men, viz. that they are independent beings with standards of their own, we ought also to be able to learn through our love for mankind as a whole – that here too there exist autonomous civilizations with standards of their own. This does not exclude rivalry, but it must be a rivalry for the attainment of interior purity and clearness of vision. If each racial group strives to develop its own highest potentialities we may hope to come nearer to one another. This applies to the great world religions, but it also applies to the various religious denominations, and to individuals in their intercourse with one another. In our earthly experience the Divine Life is not One, but Many. But to apprehend the One in the Many constitutes the special character of love.

222

14

Karl Barth, "The Revelation of God as the Abolition of Religion"

Born in 1886, the Swiss Reformed theologian Karl Barth is widely considered to be the greatest Protestant theologian of the twentieth century. Trained in Germany in the liberal tradition inaugurated by Schleiermacher, Barth's experiences as a pastor in the small Swiss village of Safenwil in the second decade of the twentieth century simmered within him until they came to expression in theological writings that in many ways redirected the course of subsequent Protestant thought. Barth came to believe that the liberal theology in which he had been schooled ill-prepared him to preach the gospel. Furthermore, when many of his German theological mentors lent their support to the German war effort at the outbreak of the First World War in 1914, Barth came to question the liberal tradition in which he had been trained. He began a careful study of Paul's Letter to the Romans and eventually produced a study entitled *The Letter to the Romans* (*Der Römerbrief*) – a work which shook the Protestant theological world.

In part as a result of the fame which this work brought him, Barth was offered a professorship in Germany. As a full-time theological scholar, he began work on his magisterial *Church Dogmatics*, on which he worked for the rest of life and which remained unfinished at his death. In the early 1930s, with a Fascist cloud gathering over Germany, Barth voiced his opposition to Hitler's regime and spoke against the "German Christians" who supported the Nazis and saw no conflict between Nazism and Christianity. He simultaneously became a leader of the "Confessing Church," which declared that allegiance to Jesus Christ entails rejection of Nazism. For his protest against the Nazis' claim to complete allegiance and obedience, Barth was forced from his university post in the mid-1930s. He returned to his native Switzerland and spent the remainder of his career as a professor at the University of Basel. He died in 1968.

As Barth's theological identity was negatively forged in the crucible of the theology of Schleiermacher and his heirs, the Swiss theologian's thought has about it a certain spirit of opposition. Against the nineteenth-century tradition, Barth asserted that theology is not talk about pious human feelings (religion), but talk about God (revelation). Talk about God can only become a reality by first listening reverently to revelation, the word of the wholly other God. The task of the theologian, according to Barth, is proclamation of the Divine Word in the Church, not arguing with the cultured despisers of religion. Barth's theology is accordingly sometimes characterized as being a new statement of orthodoxy, by comparison with liberalism, and is therefore sometimes called "neo-orthodoxy." It is also known as "dialectical theology" or the "theology of crisis."

In section 17 of *Church Dogmatics*, entitled "The Revelation of God as the Abolition of Religion," Barth renders his view of revelation's verdict on religion. By revelation, Barth has the revelation of God in Jesus Christ in mind; he was an opponent of natural theology and the notion of general revelation. By religion, he has liberal theology in mind at least as much as the religions of the world; he therefore conceives religion as humanity's futile attempt to reach God on its own. He first addresses what he considers to be the problem of religion in theology: namely, the failure of liberal theology to reckon centrally with divine revelation, by making human religion the central theological category. Next, Barth argues that in the light of revelation, religion is shown to be unbelief, the human attempt to reach God independent of, and in resistance to, divine revealing and willing. The German term for "Abolition" in the title is *Aufhebung*, a complex philosophical term which can mean "abolition" but can also mean "elevation." In the last section, accordingly, Barth calls Christianity the true religion, for God has graciously elevated it in a fashion analogous to the way in which undeserving sinners are sought out by God and justified.

In the text which follows, Barth's digressional notes, which appear in smaller type in the actual text of the source edition, have been omitted. An ellipsis notes each such omission. Omissions of portions of the text proper are marked by a line of ellipsis dots.

The Text

The revelation of God in the outpouring of the Holy Spirit is the judging but also reconciling presence of God in the world of human religion, that is, in the realm of man's attempts to justify and to sanctify himself before a capricious and arbitrary picture of God. The Church is the locus of true religion, so far as through grace it lives by grace.

1. The Problem of Religion in Theology

The event of God's revelation has to be understood and expounded as it is attested to the Church of Jesus Christ by Holy Scripture. It is within this concrete relationship that theology has to work. That is why when we asked how God does and can come to man in His revelation, we were compelled to give the clear answer that both the reality and the possibility of this event are the being and action only of God, and especially of God the Holy Spirit. Both the reality and the possibility! It was only for the sake of a better understanding that we could distinguish between the two. And what we had to understand was ultimately just this, that we must seek both of them in God, and only in God. Therefore we could not take the distinction seriously. We could not fix the reality of revelation in God, and yet find in man a possibility for it. We could not ascribe the event to God, and yet attribute to man the instrument and point of contact for it. We could not regard divine grace as the particular feature and man's suitability and capacity as the universal. We could not interpret God as the substance and man as the form. We could not, therefore, regard the event of revelation as in interplay between God and man, between grace and nature. On the contrary, as we tried to be faithful to Holy Scripture as the only valid testimony to revelation, we saw that we were committed to the statement that as an event which encounters man, this event represents a self-enclosed circle. Not only the objective but also the subjective element in revelation, not only its actuality but also its potentiality, is the being and action of the self-revealing God alone.

But this revelation is in fact an event which encounters man. It is an event which has at least the form of human competence, experience and activity. And it is at this point that we come up against the problem of man's religion. The revelation of God by the Holy Spirit is real and possible as a determination of man's existence. If we deny this, how can we think of it as revelation? But if we do not deny it, we have to recognise that it has at least the aspect and character of a human phenomenon. It is something which may be grasped historically and psychologically. We can inquire into its nature and structure and value as we can in the case of all others. We can compare it with other phenomena of a more or less similar type. We can understand

Source: Karl Barth, *Church Dogmatics: The Doctrine of the Word of God*, trans. G. T. Thomson and H. Knight, ed. G. W. Bromiley and T. F. Torrance.

it and judge it according to that comparison. But the sphere to which this problem introduces us is the sphere of religion. On their subjective side, too, we have tried as strictly and logically as possible to expound the reality and possibility of revelation as the divine reality and possibility. But how could we do that without having to speak no less definitely and concretely about an encounter and fellowship between God and man, about the Church and the sacrament, about a definite existence and attitude of man in the presence of God? And in speaking about these things we have spoken about things which are human. They are singular, perhaps, but not unique. They are astounding, but not inconceivable. And they are not unparalleled elsewhere. From this aspect what we call revelation seems necessarily to be only a particular instance of the universal which is called religion. "Christianity" or the "Christian religion" is one predicate for a subject which may have other predicates. It is a species within a genus in which there may be other species. Apart from and alongside Christianity there is Judaism, Islam, Buddhism, Shintoism and every kind of animistic, totemistic, ascetic, mystical and prophetic religion. And again, we would have to deny revelation as such if we tried to deny that it is also Christianity, that it has this human aspect, that from this standpoint it can be compared with other human things, that from this standpoint it is singular but certainly not unique. We have to recognise the fact calmly, and calmly think it through. If we are going to know and acknowledge the revelation of God as revelation, then there is this general human element which we cannot avoid or call by any other name. It is always there even apart from Christianity as one specific area of human competence, experience and activity, as one of the worlds within the world of men. . . .

Always and even necessarily men seem to feel that they are confronted by definite forces which stand over their own life and that of the world and influence it. Even at the most primitive cultural levels they seem to be aware not only of nature but also of the spirit and of spirits and their operation. Human culture in general and human existence in detail seem always and everywhere to be related by men to something ultimate and decisive, which is at least a powerful rival to their own will and power. Both culture and existence seem to have been determined or partly determined by a reverence for something ostensibly more than man, for some Other of wholly Other, for a supreme Relative or even the Absolute. There seems always and everywhere to be an awareness of the reality and possibility of a dedication, or even a sanctification of the life of man, on the basis of an individual or social striving, which is almost always and everywhere referred to an event which comes from beyond. As a result, the representation of the object and aim of the striving, or of the origin of the event, has always and everywhere been compressed into pictures of deities, with almost always and everywhere the picture of a supreme and only deity more or less clearly visible in the background. It is difficult to find any time or place when man was not aware of his duty to offer worship to God or gods in the form of concrete cults: by occupying himself with pictures and symbols of deity, by sacrifice, acts of atonement, and prayers, by customs, games and mysteries, by the formation of communions and churches. It is difficult to find any time or place when it was not thought that the voice of the deity had been heard and that it ought to be asserted and its meaning investigated. The Veda to the Indians, the Avesta to the Persians, the Tripitaka to the Buddhists, the Koran to its believers: are they not all "bibles" in exactly the same way as the Old and New Testaments? Are not at any rate the elements and problems in the basic outlook of all religions the same as those of Christian doctrine: the world's beginning and end, the origin and nature of man, moral and religious law, sin and redemption? And even in its supreme and finest forms, although it may be at the highest level, is not Christian "piety" on the same scale as all other forms of piety? And what are the criteria by which the highest place is necessarily accorded to it?

To allow that there is this whole world apart from and alongside "Christianity" is to recognise that in His revelation God has actually entered a sphere in which His own reality and possibility are encompassed by a sea of more or less adequate, but at any rate fundamentally unmistakable, parallels and analogies in human realities and possibilities. The revelation of God is actually the presence of God and therefore the hiddenness of God in the world of human religion. By God's revealing of Himself the divine particular is hidden in a human universal, the divine content in a human form, and therefore that which is divinely unique in something which is humanly only singular. Because and in so far as it is God's revelation to man, God Himself and the outpouring of the Holy Spirit, and therefore the incarnation of the Word, can be seen from this side too, in the hiddenness which is obviously given to it along with its true humanity as a religious phenomenon, as a member of that series, as a particular concept within general observation and experience, as one content of a human form, which can have other contents and in which the divine uniqueness of that content cannot be perceived directly. . . .

If we do not wish to deny God's revelation as revelation, we cannot avoid the fact that it can also be regarded from a standpoint from which it may in certain circumstances be denied as God's revelation. In fact, it can and must also be regarded as "Christianity," and therefore as religion, and therefore as man's reality and possibility. In this section we will have to show what exactly we mean by this "also." But first we have to see clearly the question which it poses, and the basic elements in the twofold possibility of answering it.

The question raised by the fact that God's revelation has also to be regarded as a religion among other religions is basically the plain question whether theology and the Church and faith are able and willing to take themselves, or their basis, seriously. For there is an extremely good chance that they will not take themselves and their basis seriously. The problem of religion is simply a pointed expression of the problem of man in his encounter and communion with God. It is, therefore, a chance to fall into temptation. Theology and the Church and faith are invited to abandon their theme and object and to become hollow and empty, mere shadows of themselves. On the other hand, they have the chance to keep to their proper task, to become really sure in their perception of it, and therefore to protect and strengthen themselves as what they profess to be. In this decision the point at issue cannot be whether God's revelation has also to be regarded as man's religion, and therefore as a religion among other religions. We saw that to deny this statement would be to deny the human aspect of revelation, and this would be to deny revelation as such. But the question arises how the statement has to be interpreted and applied. Does it mean that what we think we know of the nature and incidence of religion must serve as a norm and principle by which to explain the revelation of God; or, *vice versa*, does it mean that we have to interpret the Christian religion and all other religions by what we are told by God's revelation? There is an obvious difference between regarding religion as *the* problem of theology and regarding it as only one problem in theology. There is an obvious difference between regarding the Church as a religious brotherhood and regarding it as a state in which even religion is "sublimated" in the most comprehensive sense of the word. There is an obvious difference between regarding faith as a form of human piety and regarding it as a form of the judgment and grace of God, which is naturally and most concretely connected with man's piety in all its forms. That is the decision which has to be made.

. . . .

It is always the sign of definite misunderstanding when an attempt is made systematically to co-ordinate revelation and religion, i.e., to treat them as comparable spheres, to mark them off from each other, to fix their mutual relationship. The intention and purpose may be to start at religion, and therefore man, and in that way to subordinate revelation to religion, ultimately perhaps even to let it merge into it. Again, the intention and purpose may be to maintain the autonomy and even the pre-eminence of the sphere of revelation by definite reservations and safeguards. But that is a purely secondary question. For all the many possible solutions, it is not decisive. The decisive thing is that we are in a position to put human religion on the same level and to treat it in the same way as divine revelation. We can regard it as in some sense an equal. We can assign it an autonomous being and status over against revelation. We can ask concerning the comparison and relationship of the two entities. And the fact that we can do this shows that our intention and purpose is to start with religion, that is, with man, and not with revelation. Anything that we say later, within this systematic framework, about the necessity and actuality of revelation, can never be more than the melancholy reminder of a war which was lost at the very outset. It can never be more than an actual veiling of the real message and content. In fact it would be better, because more instructive, if we accepted the logical consequences of our point of departure, and omitted our later efforts on behalf of revelation. For where we think that revelation can be compared or equated with religion, we have not understood it as revelation. Within the problem which now engrosses us it can be understood only where *a priori* and with no possible alternative we accept its superiority over human religion, a superiority which does not allow us even to consider religion except in the light of revelation, far less to make pronouncement as to its nature and value and in that way to treat it as an independent problem. Revelation is understood only where we expect from it, and from it alone, the first and the last word about religion. The inquiry into the problem of religion in theology involves an either-or, in which the slightest deviation, the slightest concession to religionism, at once makes the right answer absolutely impossible. . . .

If we are theologically in earnest when we speak of revelation, we shall speak after the manner of those passages in the Catechism. It is a matter of Jesus Christ the Lord. It is a matter of man, therefore, only as he is reached by revelation in order that he may live under Him and serve Him, in order that he may belong not to himself but to Jesus Christ, in order that belonging to Him he may have comfort both in life and in death. But if we deviate only a nail's breadth from this confession, we are not theologically in earnest and we do not speak about revelation at all. Revelation is God's sovereign action upon man or it is not revelation. But the concept "sovereign" – and in the context of the doctrine of the Holy Spirit we can presuppose this as "self-evident" (although not at all self-evidently) – indicates that God is not at all alone, that therefore, if revelation is to be understood, man must not be overlooked or eliminated. And the same is true of religion, whether by that we mean the Christian religion in particular or human religion in general, to which the Christian religion belongs. But one thing we are forbidden. We must not try to know and define and assess man and his religion as it were in advance and independently. We must not ascribe to him any existence except as the possession of Christ. We must not treat of him in any other sphere than that of His Kingdom, in any other relationship than that of "subordination to Him." We must not try to relate him to God's revelation only when we have first taken him seriously in this independent form. If we do, we say *a priori* that – at least in the unconditional sense of those passages of the Catechism – Jesus Christ is not his Lord, and he is not the property of Jesus Christ. We have regarded both these truths as open to discussion. We have therefore denied revelation, for revelation is denied when it is regarded as open to discussion. In relating them in that way, we have not spoken about revelation, even though we may later have tried to do so in very earnest and clear and emphatic terms. We always have to speak about revelation from the very outset if we really want to speak about it later and not about something quite different. If we only speak about it later, then we are speaking, e.g., about a postulate or an idea. What we are really and properly speaking about is not revelation, but what precedes it, man and his religion, about which we think that we know so much already which we are not ready to give up. There lies our love, there our interest, there our zeal, there our confidence, there our consolation: and where we have our consolation, there we have our God. If we only come to revelation later there is nothing that can be altered. On the other hand, if revelation is not denied but believed, if man and his religion are regarded from the standpoint of those statements in the Catechism, then to take man and his religion seriously we cannot seek them in that form which has already been fixed in advance. There can, therefore, be no question of a systematic co-ordination of God and man, of revelation and religion. For neither in its existence, nor in its relation to the first, can the second be considered, let alone defined, except in the light of the first. The only thing we can do is to recount the history of the relationships between the two: and even that takes place in such a way that whatever we have to say about the existence and nature and value of the second can only and exclusively be made plain in the light of the first, i.e., in the course of God's sovereign action on man. It is man as he is revealed in the light of revelation, and only that man, who can be seriously treated theologically. Similarly, the problem of religion in theology is not the question how the reality, religion, which has already been defined (and usually untheologically), can now be brought into an orderly and plausible relationship with the theological concepts, revelation, faith, etc. On the contrary, the question is uninterruptedly theological: What is this thing which from the standpoint of revelation and faith is revealed in the actuality of human life as religion? . . .

To sum up: we do not need to delete or retract anything from the admission that in His revelation God is present in the world of human religion. But what we have to discern is that this means that *God* is present. Our basic task is so to order the concepts revelation and religion that the connexion between the two can again be seen as identical with that event between God and man in which God is God, i.e., the Lord and Master of man, who Himself judges and alone justifies and sanctifies, and man is the man of God, i.e., man as he is adopted and received by God in His severity and goodness. It is because we remember and apply the christological doctrine of the *assumptio carnis* that we speak of revelation as the abolition of religion.

2. Religion as Unbelief

A theological evaluation of religion and religions must be characterised primarily by the great cautiousness and charity of its assessment and judgments. It will observe and understand and take man in all seriousness as the subject of religion. But it will not be man apart from God, in a human *per se*. It will be man for whom (whether he knows it or not) Jesus Christ was born, died and rose again. It will be man who (whether he has already heard it or not) is intended in the Word of God. It will be man who (whether he is aware of it or not) has in Christ his Lord. It will always understand religion as a vital utterance and activity of this man. It will not ascribe to this life-utterance and activity of his a unique "nature," the so-called "nature of religion," which it can then use as a gauge to weigh and balance one human thing against another, distinguishing the "higher" religion from the "lower," the "living" from the "decomposed," the "ponderable" from the "imponderable." It will not omit to do this from carelessness or indifference towards the manifoldness with which we have to do in this human sphere, nor because a prior definition of the "nature" of the phenomena in this sphere is either impossible or in itself irrelevant, but because what we have to know of the nature of religion from the standpoint of God's revelation does not allow us to make any but the most incidental use of an immanent definition of the nature of religion. It is not, then, that this "revealed" nature of religion is not fitted in either form or content to differentiate between the good and the bad, the true and the false in the religious world. Revelation singles out the Church as the *locus* of true religion. But this does not mean that the Christian religion as such is the fulfilled nature of human religion. It does not mean that the Christian religion is the true religion, fundamentally superior to all other religions. We can never stress too much the connexion between the truth of the Christian religion and the grace of revelation. We have to give particular emphasis to the fact that through grace the Church lives by grace, and to that extent it is the *locus* of true religion. And if this is so, the Church will as little boast of its "nature," i.e., the perfection in which it fulfils the "nature" of religion, as it can attribute that nature to other religions. We cannot differentiate and separate the Church from other religions on the basis of a general concept of the nature of religion. . . .

Revelation as the Abolition of Religion

A truly theological treatment of religion and religions, as it is demanded and possible in the Church as the *locus* of the Christian religion, will need to be distinguished from all other forms of treatment by the exercise of a very marked tolerance towards its object. Now this tolerance must not be confused with the moderation of those who actually have their own religion or religiosity, and are secretly zealous for it, but who can exercise self-control, because they have told themselves or have been told that theirs is not the only faith, that fanaticism is a bad thing, that love must always have the first and the last word. It must not be confused with the clever aloofness of the rationalistic Know-All – the typical Hegelian belongs to the same category – who thinks that he can deal comfortably and in the end successfully with all religions in the light of a concept of a perfect religion which is gradually evolving in history. But it also must not be confused with the relativism and impartiality of an historical scepticism, which does not ask about truth and untruth in the field of religious phenomena, because it thinks that truth can be known only in the form of its own doubt about all truth. That the so-called "tolerance" of this kind is unattainable is revealed by the fact that the object, religion and religions, and therefore man, are not taken seriously, but are at bottom patronised. Tolerance in the sense of moderation, or superior knowledge, or scepticism is actually the worst form of intolerance. But the religion and religions must be treated with a tolerance which is informed by the forbearance of Christ, which derives therefore from the knowledge that by grace God has reconciled to Himself godless man and his religion. It will see man carried, like an obstinate child in the arms of its mother, by what God has determined and done for his salvation in spite of his own opposition. In detail, it will neither praise nor reproach him. It will understand his situation – understand it even in the dark and terrifying perplexity of it – not because it can see any meaning in the situation as such, but because it acquires a meaning from outside, from Jesus Christ. But confronted by this object it will not display the weak or superior or weary smile of a quite inappropriate indulgence. It will see that man is caught in a way of acting that cannot be recognised as right and holy, unless it is first and at the same time recognised as thoroughly wrong and unholy. Self-evidently, this kind of tolerance, and therefore a theological consideration of religion, is possible only for those who are ready to abase themselves and their religion together with man, with every individual man, knowing that they first, and their religion, have need of tolerance, a strong forbearing tolerance.

We begin by stating that religion is unbelief. It is a concern, indeed, we must say that it is the one great concern, of godless man. . . .

In the light of what we have already said, this proposition is not in any sense a negative value-judgment. It is not a judgment of religious science or philosophy based upon some prior negative judgment concerned with the nature of religion. It does not affect only other men with their religion. Above all, it affects ourselves also as adherents of the Christian religion. It formulates the judgment of divine revelation upon all religion. It can be explained and expounded, but it cannot be derived from any higher principle than revelation, nor can it be proved by any phenomenology or history of religion. Since it aims only to repeat the judgment of God, it does not involve any human renunciation of human values, any contesting of the true and the good and the beautiful which a closer inspection will reveal in almost all religions, and which we naturally expect to find in abundant measure in our own religion, if we hold to it with any conviction. What happens is simply that man is taken by God and judged and condemned by God. That means, of course, that we are struck to the very roots, to the heart. Our whole existence is called in question. But where that is the case there can be no place for sad and pitiful laments at the non-recognition of relative human greatness. . . .

To realise that religion is really unbelief, we have to consider it from the standpoint of the revelation attested in Holy Scripture. There are two elements in that revelation which make it unmistakably clear.

1. **Revelation is God's self-offering and self-manifestation**. Revelation encounters man on the presupposition and in confirmation of the fact that man's attempts to know God from his own standpoint are wholly and entirely futile; not because of any necessity in principle, but because of a practical necessity of fact. In revelation God tells man that He is God, and that as such He is his Lord. In telling him this, revelation tells him something utterly new, something which apart from revelation he does not know and cannot tell either himself or others. It is true that he could do this, for revelation simply states the truth. If it is true that God is God and that as such He is the Lord of man, then it is also true that man is so placed towards Him, that he could know Him. But this is the very truth which is not available to man, before it is told him in revelation. If he really can know God, this capacity rests upon the fact that he really does know Him, because God has offered and manifested Himself to him. The capacity, then, does not rest upon the fact, which is true enough, that man could know Him. Between "he could" and "he can" there lies the absolutely decisive "he cannot," which can be removed and turned into its opposite only by revelation. The truth that God is God and our Lord, and the further truth that we could know Him as God and Lord, can only come to us through the truth itself. This "coming to us" of the truth is revelation. It does not reach us in a neutral condition, but in an action which stands to it, as the coming of truth, in a very definite, indeed a determinate relationship. That is to say, it reaches us as religious men; i.e., it reaches us in the attempt to know God from our standpoint. It does not reach us, therefore, in the activity which corresponds to it. The activity which corresponds to revelation would have to be faith; the recognition of the self-offering and self-manifestation of God. We need to see that in view of God all our activity is in vain even in the best life; i.e., that of ourselves we are not in a position to apprehend the truth, to let God be God and our Lord. We need to renounce all attempts even to try to apprehend this truth. We need to be ready and resolved simply to let the truth be told us and therefore to be apprehended by it. But that is the very thing for which we are not resolved and ready. The man to whom the truth has really come will concede that he was not at all ready and resolved to let it speak to him. The genuine believer will not say that he came to faith from faith, but — from unbelief, even though the attitude and activity with which he met revelation, and still meets it, is religion. For in faith, man's religion as such is shown by revelation to be resistance to it. From the standpoint of revelation religion is clearly

seen to be a human attempt to anticipate what God in His revelation wills to do and does do. It is the attempted replacement of the divine work by a human manufacture. The divine reality offered and manifested to us in revelation is replaced by a concept of God arbitrarily and wilfully evolved by man. . . .

"Arbitrarily and wilfully" means here by his own means, by his own human insight and constructiveness and energy. Many different images of God can be formed once we have engaged in this undertaking, but their significance is always the same. . . .

The image of God is always that reality of perception or thought in which man assumes and asserts something unique and ultimate and decisive either beyond or within his own existence, by which he believes himself to be posited or at least determined and conditioned. From the standpoint of revelation, man's religion is simply an assumption and assertion of this kind, and as such it is an activity which contradicts revelation – contradicts it, because it is only through truth that truth can come to man. If man tries to grasp at truth of himself, he tries to grasp at it *a priori*. But in that case he does not do what he has to do when the truth comes to him. He does not believe. If he did, he would listen; but in religion he talks. If he did, he would accept a gift; but in religion he takes something for himself. If he did, he would let God Himself intercede for God: but in religion he ventures to grasp at God. Because it is a grasping, religion is the contradiction of revelation, the concentrated expression of human unbelief, i.e., an attitude and activity which is directly opposed to faith. It is a feeble but defiant, an arrogant but hopeless, attempt to create something which man could do, but now cannot do, or can do only bcause and if God Himself creates it for him: the knowledge of the truth, the knowledge of God. We cannot, therefore interpret the attempt as a harmonious co-operating of man with the revelation of God, as though religion were a kind of outstretched hand which is filled by God in His revelation. Again, we cannot say of the evident religious capacity of man that it is, so to speak, the general form of human knowledge which acquires its true and proper content in the shape of revelation. On the contrary, we have here an exclusive contradiction. In religion man bolts and bars himself against revelation by providing a substitute, by taking away in advance the very thing which has to be given by God. . . .

He has, of course, the power to do this. But what he achieves and acquires in virtue of this power is never the knowledge of God as Lord and God. It is never the truth. It is a complete fiction, which has not only little but no relation to God. It is an anti-God who has first to be known as such and discarded when the truth comes to him. But it can be known as such, as a fiction, only as the truth does come to him. . . .

Revelation does not link up with a human religion which is already present and practised. It contradicts it, just as religion previously contradicted revelation. It displaces it, just as religion previously displaced revelation; just as faith cannot link up with a mistaken faith, but must contradict and displace it as unbelief, as an act of contradiction. . . .

2.   As the self-offering and self-manifestation of God, revelation is the act by which in grace He reconciles man to Himself by grace. As a radical teaching about God, it

is also the radical assistance of God which comes to us as those who are unrighteous and unholy, and as such damned and lost. In this respect, too, the affirmation which revelation makes and presupposes of man is that he is unable to help himself either in whole or even in part. But again, he ought not to have been so helpless. It is not inherent in the nature and concept of man that he should be unrighteous and unholy and therefore damned and lost. He was created to be the image of God, i.e., to obedience towards God and not to sin, to salvation and not to destruction. But he is not summoned to this as to a state in which he might still somehow find himself, but as one in which he no longer finds himself, from which he has fallen by his own fault. But this, too, is a truth which he cannot maintain: it is not present to him unless it comes to him in revelation, i.e., in Jesus Christ, to be declared to him in a new way – the oldest truth of all in a way which is quite new. He cannot in any sense declare to himself that he is righteous and holy, and therefore saved, for in his own mouth as his own judgment of himself it would be a lie. It is truth as the revealed knowledge of God. It is truth in Jesus Christ. Jesus Christ does not fill out and improve all the different attempts of man to think of God and to represent Him according to his own standard. But as the self-offering and self-manifestation of God He replaces and completely outbids those attempts, putting them in the shadows to which they belong. Similarly, in so far as God reconciles the world to Himself in Him, He replaces all the different attempts of man to reconcile God to the world, all our human efforts at justification and sanctification, at conversion and salvation. The revelation of God in Jesus Christ maintains that our justification and sanctification, our conversion and salvation, have been brought about and achieved once and for all in Jesus Christ. And our faith in Jesus Christ consists in our recognising and admitting and affirming and accepting the fact that everything has actually been done of us once and for all in Jesus Christ. He is the assistance that comes to us. He alone is the Word of God that is spoken to us. There is an exchange of status between him and us: His righteousness and holiness are ours, our sin is His; He is lost for us, and we for His sake are saved. By this exchange (καθααλλαθή, 2 Cor. 5:19) revelation stands or falls. It would not be the active redemptive self-offering and self-manifestation of God, if it were not centrally and decisively the *satisfactio* and *intercessio Jesu Christi*.

And now we can see a second way in which revelation contradicts religion, and conversely religion necessarily opposes revelation. For what is the purpose of the universal attempt of religions to anticipate God, to foist a human product into the place of His Word, to make our own images of the One who is known only where He gives Himself to be known, images which are first spiritual, and then religious, and then actually visible? What does the religious man want when he thinks and believes and maintains that there is a unique and ultimate and decisive being, that there is a divine being (θεΐου) a godhead, that there are gods and a single supreme God, and when he thinks that he himself is posited, determined, conditioned and overruled by this being? Is the postulate of God or gods, and the need to objectify the Ultimate spiritually or physically, conditioned by man's experience of the actual superiority and lordship of certain natural and supernatural, historical and eternal necessities, potencies and ordinances? Is this experience (or the postulate and need which correspond to it) followed by the feeling of man's impotence and failure in face of this higher world, by the urge to put himself on peaceful and friendly terms with it, to interest it on his behalf, to assure himself of its support, or, better still, to enable himself to exercise an influence on it, to participate in its power and dignity and to co-operate in its work? Does man's attempt to justify and sanctify himself follow the attempt to think of God and represent Him? Or is the relationship the direct opposite? Is the primary thing man's obscure urge to justify and sanctify himself, i.e., to confirm and strengthen himself in the awareness and exercise of his skill and strength to master life, to come to terms with the world, to make the world serviceable to him? Is religion with its dogmatics and worship and precepts the most primitive, or better perhaps, the most intimate and intensive part of the technique, by which we try to come to terms with life? Is it that the experience of that higher world, or the need to objectify it in the thought of God and the representation of God, must be regarded only as an exponent of this attempt, that is, as the ideal construction inevitable within the framework of this technique? Are the gods only reflected images and guarantees of the needs and capacities of man, who in reality is lonely and driven back upon himself and his own willing and ordering and creating? Are sacrifice and prayer and asceticism and morality more basic than God and the gods? Who is to say? In face of the two possibilities we are in a circle which we can consider from any point of view with exactly the same result. What is certain is that in respect of the practical content of religion it is still a matter of an attitude and activity which does not correspond to God's revelation, but contradicts it. At this point, too, weakness and defiance, helplessness and arrogance, folly and imagination are so close to one another that we can scarcely distinguish the one from the other. Where we want what is wanted in religion, i.e., justification and sanctification as our own work, we do not find ourselves – and it does not matter whether the thought and representation of God has a primary or only a secondary importance – on the direct way to God, who can then bring us to our goal at some higher stage on the way. On the contrary, we lock the door against God, we alienate ourselves from Him, we come into direct opposition to Him. God in His revelation will not allow man to try to come to terms with life, to justify and sanctify himself. God in His revelation, God in Jesus Christ, is the One who takes on Himself the sin of the world, who wills that all our care should be cast upon Him, because He careth for us. . . .

It is the characteristically pious element in the pious effort to reconcile Him to us which must be an abomination to God, whether idolatry is regarded as its presupposition or its result, or perhaps as both. Not by any continuing along this way, but only by radically breaking away from it, can we come, not to our own goal but to God's goal, which is the direct opposite of our goal.

. . . .

3. True Religion

The preceding expositions have established the fact that we can speak of "true" religion only in the sense in which we speak of a "justified sinner."

Religion is never true in itself and as such. The revelation of God denies that any religion is true, i.e., that it is in truth the knowledge and worship of God and the reconciliation of man with God. For as the self-offering and self-manifestation of God, as the work of peace which God Himself has concluded between Himself and man, revelation is the truth beside which there is no other truth, over against which there is only lying and wrong. If by the concept of a "true religion" we mean truth which belongs to religion in itself and as such, it is just as unattainable as a "good man," if by goodness we mean something which man can achieve on his own initiative. No religion is true. It can only become true, i.e., according to that which it purports to be and for which it is upheld. And it can become true only in the way in which man is justified, from without; i.e., not of its own nature and being, but only in virtue of a reckoning and adopting and separating which are foreign to its own nature and being, which are quite inconceivable from its own standpoint, which come to it quite apart from any qualifications or merits. Like justified man, religion is a creature of grace. But grace is the revelation of God. No religion can stand before it as true religion. No man is righteous in its presence. It subjects us all to the judgment of death. But it can also call dead men to life and sinners to repentance. And similarly in the wider sphere where it shows all religion to be false it can also create true religion. The abolishing of religion by revelation need not mean only its negation: the judgment that religion is unbelief. Religion can just as well be exalted in revelation, even though the judgment still stands. It can be upheld by it and concealed in it. It can be justified by it, and – we must at once add – sanctified. Revelation can adopt religion and mark it off as true religion. And it not only can. How do we come to assert that it can, if it has not already done so? There is a true religion: just as there are justified sinners. If we abide strictly by that analogy – and we are dealing not merely with an analogy, but in a comprehensive sense with the thing itself – we need have no hesitation in saying that the Christian religion is the true religion.

In our discussion of "religion as unbelief" we did not consider the distinction between Christian and non-Christian religion. Our intention was that whatever we said about the other religions affected the Christian similarly. In the framework of that discussion we could not speak in any special way about Christianity. We could not give it any special or assured place in face of that judgment. Therefore the discussion cannot be understood as a preliminary polemic against the non-Christian religions, with a view to the ultimate assertion that the Christian religion is the true religion. If this were the case, our task now would be to prove that, as distinct from the non-Christian religions, the Christian is not guilty of idolatry and self-righteousness, that it is not therefore unbelief but faith, and therefore true religion; or, which comes to the same thing, that it is no religion at all, but as against all religions, including their mystical and atheistical self-criticism, it is in itself the true and holy and as such the unspotted and incontestable form of fellowship between God and man. To enter on this path would be to deny the very thing we have to affirm. If the statement is to have any content, we can dare to state that the Christian religion is the true one only as we listen to the divine revelation. But a statement which we dare to make as we listen to the divine revelation can only be a statement of faith. And a statement of faith is necessarily a statement which is thought and expressed in faith and from faith, i.e., in recognition and respect of what we are told by revelation. Its explicit and implicit content is unreservedly conditioned by what we are told. But that is certainly not the case if we try to reach the statement that the Christian religion is the true religion by a road which begins by leaving behind the judgment of revelation, that religion is unbelief, as a matter which does not apply to us Christians, but only to others, the non-Christians, thus enabling us to separate and differentiate ourselves from them with the help of this judgment. On the contrary, it is our business as Christians to apply this judgment first and most acutely to ourselves: and to others, the non-Christians, only in so far as we recognise ourselves in them, i.e., only as we see in them the truth of this judgment of revelation which concerns us, in the solidarity, therefore, in which, anticipating them in both repentance and hope, we accept this judgment to participate in the promise of revelation. At the end of the road we have to tread there is, of course, the promise to those who accept God's judgment, who let themselves be led beyond their unbelief. There is faith in this promise, and, in this faith, the presence and reality of the grace of God, which, of course, differentiates our religion, the Christian, from all others as the true religion. This exalted goal cannot be reached except by this humble road. And it would not be a truly humble road if we tried to tread it except in the consciousness that any "attaining" here can consist only in the utterly humble and thankful adoption of something which we would not attain if it were not already attained in God's revelation before we set out on the road.

We must insist, therefore, that at the beginning of a knowledge of the truth of the Christian religion, there stands the recognition that this religion, too, stands under the judgment that religion is unbelief, and that it is not acquitted by any inward worthiness, but only by the grace of God, proclaimed and effectual in His revelation. But concretely, this judgment affects the whole practice of our faith: our Christian conceptions of God and the things of God, our Christian theology, our Christian worship, our forms of Christian fellowship and order, our Christian morals, poetry and art, our attempts to give individual and social form to the Christian life, our Christian strategy and tactics in the interest of our Christian cause, in short our Christianity, to the extent that it is *our* Christianity, the human work which we undertake and adjust to all kinds of near and remote aims and which as such is seen to be on the same level as the human work in other religions. This judgment means that all this Christianity of ours, and all the details of it, are not as such what they ought to be and pretend to be, a work of faith, and therefore of obedience to the divine revelation. What we have here is in its own way – a different way from that of other religions, but no less seriously – unbelief, i.e., opposition to the divine revelation, and therefore active idolatry and self-righteousness. It is the same helplessness and arbitrariness. It is the same self-exaltation of man which means his most profound abasement. But this time it is in place of and in opposition to the self-manifestation and self-offering of God, the reconciliation which God Himself has accomplished, it is in disregard of the divine consolations and admonitions that great and small Babylonian towers are erected, which cannot as such be pleasing to God, since they are definitely not set up to His glory.

. . . .

We must not allow ourselves to be confused by the fact that a history of Christianity can be written only as a story of the distress which it makes for itself. It is a story which lies completely behind the story of that which took place between Yahweh and His people, between Jesus and His apostles. It is a story whose source and meaning and goal, the fact that the Christian is strong only in his weakness, that he is really satisfied by grace, can in the strict sense nowhere be perceived directly. Not even in the history of the Reformation! What can be perceived in history is the attempt which the Christian makes in continually changing forms, to consider and vindicate his religion as a work which is in itself upright and holy. But he continually feels himself thwarted and hampered and restrained by Holy Scripture, which does not allow this, which even seems to want to criticise this Christian religion of his. He obviously cannot shut out the recollection that it is in respect of this very work of his religion that he cannot dispense with the grace of God and therefore stands under the judgment of God. At this point we are particularly reminded of the history of the Reformation. But in the very light of that history we see that the recollection has always been there, even in the pre- and post-Reformation periods. Yet the history of Christianity as a whole reveals a tendency which is quite contrary to this recollection. It would be arbitrary not to recognize this, and to claim that the history of Christianity, as distinct from that of other religions, is the story of that part of humanity, which, as distinct from others, has existed only as the part which of grace lives by grace. In the strict sense there is no evidence of this throughout the whole range of Christianity. What is evident is in the first instance a part of humanity which no less contradicts the grace and revelation of God because it claims them as its own peculiar and most sacred treasures, and its religion is to that extent a religion of revelation. Contradiction is contradiction. That it exists at this point, in respect of the religion of revelation, can be denied even less than at other points. Elsewhere we might claim in extenuation that it simply exists in fact, but not in direct contrast with revelation. But in the history of Christianity, just because it is the religion of revelation, the sin is, as it were, committed with a high hand. Yes, sin! For contradiction against grace is unbelief, and unbelief is sin, indeed it is *the* sin. It is, therefore, a fact that we can speak of the truth of the Christian religion only within the doctrine of the *iustificatio impii*. The statement that even Christianity is unbelief gives rise to a whole mass of naive and rationalising contradiction. Church history itself is a history of this contradiction. But it is this very fact which best shows us how true and right the statement is. We can as little avoid the contradiction as jump over our own shadow. . . .

Notwithstanding the contradiction and therefore our own existence, we can and must perceive that for our part we and our contradiction against grace stand under the even more powerful contradiction of grace itself. We can and must – in faith. To believe means, in the knowledge of our own sin to rely upon the righteousness of God which makes an infinite satisfaction for our sin. Concretely, it means, in the knowledge of our own contradiction against grace to cleave to the grace of God which infinitely contradicts this contradiction. In this knowledge of grace, in the knowledge that it is the justification of the ungodly, that it is grace for the enemies of grace, the Christian faith attains to its knowledge of the truth of the Christian religion. There can be no more question of any immanent rightness or holiness of this particular religion as the ground and content of the truth of it, than there can be of any other religion claiming to be the true religion in virtue of its inherent advantages. The Christian cannot avoid abandoning any such claim. He cannot avoid confessing that he is a sinner even in his best actions as a Christian. And that is not, of course, the ground, but the symptom of the truth of the Christian religion. The abandoning and confessing means that the Christian Church is the place where, confronted with the revelation and grace of God, by grace men live by grace. If this were not so, how would they believe? And if they did not believe, how would they be capable of this abandoning and confessing?

. . . .

That there is a true religion is an event in the act of the grace of God in Jesus Christ. To be more precise, it is an event in the outpouring of the Holy Spirit. To be even more precise, it is an event in the existence of the Church and the children of God. The existence of the Church of God and the children of God means that true religion exists even in the world of human religion. In other words, there is a knowledge and worship of God and a corresponding human activity. We can only say of them that they are corrupt. They are an attempt born of lying and wrong and committed to futile means. And yet we have also to say of them that (in their corruption) they do reach their goal. In spite of the lying and wrong committed, in spite of the futility of the means applied, God is really known and worshipped, there is a genuine activity of man as reconciled to God. The Church and the children of God and therefore the bearers of true religion live by the grace of God. Their knowledge and worship of God, their service of God in teaching, cultus and life, are determined by the realisation of the free kindness of God which anticipates all human thought and will and action and corrects all human corruption. For it does not leave anything for man to do except to believe and give thanks. And it teaches him to do this – not as his own work but as its own gift – which will never be denied to the man who believes and gives thanks. The Church and the children of God live under this ordinance. To that extent they live by the grace of God. But the fact that they do so is not the basis of their existence as the Church and the children of God. Nor is it the thing which makes their religion the true religion. From the standpoint of their own activity as such, they do not stand out decisively above the general level of religious history. They do not escape the divine accusation of idolatry and self-righteousness. For one thing, their life by grace hardly ever appears in history except as an occasional obstacle to the effective fulfilment even amongst them of the law of all religion. If the thought and will and action of Christians as those who live by grace were really the criterion of their existence as the Church and the children of God, with what confidence we could maintain their existence as such and the truth of their religion! But we cannot maintain it on the ground of that criterion because it is not unknown for an apparent and sometimes a very convincing life of grace, and the phenomenon of the religion of grace, to appear in other fields of religious history. And yet by biblical standards we have no authority to speak of the Church and the divine sonship or the existence of true religion in these other spheres. The decisive thing for the existence of the Church and the children of God and for the truth of their religion is something quite different. And therefore the decisive thing for their life by grace, in itself so equivocal, is also different. It is the fact that by the grace of God they live by His grace. That is what makes them what they are. That is what makes their religion true. That is what lifts it above the general level of religious history. But "by the grace of God" means by the reality of that by which they apparently but very equivocally live; by the reality of that by which men can apparently and equivocally live in other spheres of religious history. "By the reality" means by the fact that beyond all human appearance, beyond all that men can think and will and do in the sphere of their religion, even if it is a religion of grace, without any merits or deservings of their own, God acts towards them as the gracious God He is, anticipating their own thought and will and action by His own free kindness, arousing in them faith and thankfulness, and never refusing them. They are what they are, and their religion is the true religion, not because they recognise Him as such and act accordingly, not in virtue of their religion of grace, but in virtue of the fact that God has graciously intervened for them, in virtue of His mercy in spite of their apparent but equivocal religion of grace, in virtue of the good pleasure which He has in them, in virtue of His free election, of which this good pleasure is the only motive, in virtue of the Holy Spirit whom He willed to pour out upon them. It is of grace that the Church and the children of God live by His grace. It is of grace that they attain the status of the bearers of true religion. But we can see the concrete significance of this, we can see how different it is from any kind of higher principle of religion, which might be used in the assessment of all human religion, only when we are clear that "by the grace of God" means exactly the same as "through the name of Jesus Christ." He, Jesus Christ, is the eternal Son of God and as such the eternal Object of the divine good pleasure. As the eternal Son of God He became man. The result is that in Him man has also become the object of the divine good pleasure, not by his own merit or deserving, but by the grace which assumed man to itself in the Son of God. In this One, the revelation of God among men and the reconciliation of man with God has been fulfilled once and for all. And He gives the Holy Ghost. It is because of all these things and by means of them that there is in this One a Church of God and children of God. They are what they are, and they have the true religion, because He stands in their place, and therefore for His sake. They cannot for a single moment think of leaving Him with the intention and purpose of trying to be what they are in themselves, or to have the true religion in themselves. When they do in fact leave Him – as they are always doing – the result is that they become uncertain of their existence as the Church and the children of God, and therefore of the truth of their religion. But there can be no alteration in the objective content, that they are what they are, and therefore bearers of the true religion, only in Him, in the name of Jesus Christ, i.e., in the revelation and reconciliation achieved in Jesus Christ. Nowhere else, but genuinely so in Him. Therefore by the grace of God there are men who live by His grace. Or, to put it concretely, through the name of Jesus Christ there are men who believe in this name. To the extent that this is self-evident in the case of Christians and the Christian religion, we can and must say of it that it and it alone is the true religion. On this particular basis we must now expound and explain this statement under four specific aspects.

1.   In the relationship between the name of Jesus Christ and the Christian religion we have to do first with an act of divine creation. That means that its existence in historical form and individual determinations is not an autonomous or self-grounded existence. The name of Jesus Christ alone has created the Christian religion. Without Him it would never have been. And we must understand this not only in the historical but in the actual and contemporary sense. The name of Jesus Christ creates the Christian religion. Apart from Him it would not be. For if we would speak of the Christian religion as a reality, we cannot be content merely to look back at its creation and historical existence. We have to think of it in the same way as we think of our own existence and that of the world, as a reality which is to be and is created by Jesus Christ yesterday and today and tomorrow.

. . . .

2.   In the relationship between the name of Jesus Christ and the Christian religion we have to do with an act of the divine election. The Christian religion did not possess any reality of its own. Considered in and for itself it never can. It is a mere possibility among a host of others. It did not and does not bring anything of its own to the name of Jesus Christ which makes it in any way worthy to be His creation and as such the true religion. If it is real, it is so on the basis of free election, grounded in the compassion and inconceivable good pleasure of God and nothing else.

. . . .

3.   In the relationship between the name Jesus Christ and the Christian religion we have to do with an act of divine justification or forgiveness of sins. We already stated that the Christian religion as such has no worthiness of its own, to equip it specially to be the true religion. We must now aver even more clearly that in itself and as such it is absolutely unworthy to be the true religion. If it is so, it is so by election, we said. And now we must be more precise: it is so in virtue of the divine justification of sinners, of the divine forgiveness of sins.

. . . .

4.   In the relationship between the name of Jesus Christ and the Christian religion, we have to do with an act of divine sanctification. We said that to find the basis of the assertion of the truth of Christianity we must first look away from it to the fact of God which is its basis, and that we have constantly to return to this "first." When we ask concerning this truth, we can never look even incidentally to anything but this fact of God. We cannot try to find the justification of the Christian religion apart from the name of Jesus Christ in other facts, not even in the inward or outward

state of justification of the Christian religion. Yet this justification of the Christian religion only by the name of Jesus Christ obviously involves a certain positive relation between the two. Christianity is differentiated from other religions by that name. It is formed and shaped by it. It is claimed for His service. It becomes the historical manifestation and means of its revelation. We have compared the name of Jesus Christ with the sun in its relation to the earth. That must be an end of the matter. But the sun shines. And its light is not remote from the earth and alien to it. Without ceasing to be the light of the sun, it becomes the light of the earth, the light which illuminates the earth. In that light the earth which has no light of its own is bright. It is not, of course, a second sun. But it carries the reflection of the sun's light. It is, therefore, an illuminated earth. It is the same with the name of Jesus Christ in relation to the Christian religion. That name alone is its justification. But it cannot be transcendent without being immanent in it. For it is only the Christian religion which is justified by it. And that means that it is differentiated and marked off and stamped and characterised by it in a way peculiar to itself. In the light of its justification and creation and election by the name of Jesus Christ, the fact that it is the Christian religion and not another cannot possibly be neutral or indifferent or without significance. On the contrary, even though Christianity is a religion like others, it is significant and eloquent, a sign, a proclamation. There is an event on God's side – which is the side of the incarnate Word of God – God adopting man and giving Himself to him. And corresponding to it there is a very definite event on man's side. This event is determined by the Word of God. It has its being and form in the world of human religion. But it is different from everything else in this sphere and having this form. The correspondence of the two events is the relationship between the name Jesus Christ and the Christian religion from the standpoint of its sanctification. . . . That name alone is the power and mystery of the declaration which is the meaning of this particular being and form. That name alone expresses this being and form as the being and form of true religion. It is not justified because it is holy in itself – which it is not. It is made holy because it is justified. And it is not true because it is holy in itself – which it never was and never will be. But it is made holy in order to show that it is the true religion. At this point we link up with what we earlier described as the twofold subjective reality of revelation, which is the counterpart in our realm of the objective revelation in Jesus Christ. The Christian religion is the sacramental area created by the Holy Spirit, in which the God whose Word became flesh continues to speak through the sign of His revelation. And it is also the existence of men created by the same Holy Spirit, who hear this God continually speaking in His revelation. The Church and the children of God do actually exist. The actuality of their existence is quite unassuming, but it is always visible and in its visibility it is significant. It is an actuality which is called and dedicated to the declaration of the name of Jesus Christ. And that is the sanctification of the Christian religion.

15

Hendrik Kraemer, "An Attempt at an Answer"

The Dutch Reformed scholar Hendrik Kraemer (1888–1965) was a major player in twentieth-century debates about Christianity's relationship to the religions of the world. After doctoral studies in Islam at the University of Leiden, he worked as a missionary for the Dutch Bible Society in Indonesia. This work eventually launched him into international discussions about the nature and task of missions. In addition to his contributions in the area of missions, Kraemer held a professorship at the University of Leiden for some years. After the foundation of the World Council of Churches in 1948, he became the first director of its Ecumenical Institute in Switzerland and devoted much of the remainder of his life to ecumenical discussions and the emerging dialogue between the great religions of the world.

Especially influential was Kraemer's book *The Christian Message in a Non-Christian World*, which he composed for the Third International Missionary Conference held in Tambaram, India, in 1938. Well known for his conservative theological orientation and inspired by the Swiss Reformed theology of Karl Barth and Emil Brunner, in *The Christian Message* he expressed his critique of the liberal Christian attitude to the religions of the world which had long dominated Protestant thinking (the liberal position to which Kraemer was opposed is well expressed in the following essay by Joachim Wach). Convinced that the relationship between Christianity and non-Christian religions was not one of continuity but of discontinuity (that is, Christianity is *not* the fulfillment of religious striving; non-Christian religions are *not* preparations for the gospel), Kraemer clung to the conviction that all religions, Christianity included, must be judged in light of the revelation of God in Jesus Christ.

Late in his life Kraemer summarized his views in a short book entitled *Why Christianity of All Religions?*, which originated as a series of radio broadcasts given in The Netherlands. In attempting to answer the question posed in the book's title, Kraemer in the text which follows provides an accessible summary of his position, an indication of his passion for truth, and an expression of his concern about the specter of relativism.

Footnotes found in the source edition have been eliminated.

The Text

It is matter for dispute nowadays whether, in the whirligig of opinion about things religious, it is possible to live in and by the truth with any degree of honest conviction and cogency: or whether, to put it another way, one can be fair-minded and open-minded towards other beliefs which are firmly and seriously held and yet maintain a powerful conviction of one's own instead of retreating into a neutral or non-committal position.

It would not be surprising if, recalling my proposed criterion and my emphatically declared intention of giving an advisedly personal answer, people were to come up with the remark: But with your criterion do we really get out of the impasse? After all, your criterion is only one more personal affirmation of settled belief; so it still leaves us bogged down in "subjectivity". Granted that the various methods outlined by you, which claim to offer the real answer to the problem, fail in fact to do so and leave us finally out in the cold – yet do we really get any further with you? Are you not also trying to pull off a *tour de force* of the Münchhausen variety?

To comments of that sort I would reply: Let us take a calm and closer look at it all. That involves once again making clear distinctions; and above all it means being genuinely disposed to give the argument a fair hearing. As has been said already, in any discussion of the relationship of Christianity to the other religions our concern should be "to pose the problem correctly from the side or standpoint of Christianity". The emphasis here must be on the word "correctly". After all, one can have the best intentions and yet do it wrongly. If a thing is wrong, it is not by any means necessarily "worthless"; but it is still wrong, whether worthless or no. I personally am sure that it is wrong, for example, to take as a criterion any doctrine or system of doctrine, however relatively admirable an expression of Christianity it may be and however much it may contribute towards an understanding of the problem. This goes just as much for orthodox as for liberal "doctrine". I hold it to be equally wrong to adopt as a criterion this or that alleged "basic principle" of Christianity. More often than not this is taken to be the "love-principle", because people think it possible to infer from a comparison of the religions that the Christian principle of love is without any doubt qualitatively unique of its kind.

Why, despite the excellent uses which can be made of them in this connection, are these criteria – which are admittedly "Christian" – not the right ones? The reason in my view, is very simple. Doctrines, systems and principles are all things *deduced from* Christianity, and, being so deduced, they are most certainly "Christian". When they are kept in their proper place, they have their own (sometimes not inconsiderable) importance; but because they are inferences their place is a secondary one. Always in principle and frequently in practice they may be superseded and replaced. In other words: however great their value and their significance in any given set of circumstances may appear to be, they are and will always be the work of man.

Source: Hendrik Kraemer, *Why Christianity of All Religions?*, trans. H. Hoskins.

245

When theology gets to work on the basic material, on the dynamic effects and the fundamental realities of a religion and likewise when these are expressed in a number of cardinal "principles", this is an attempt to interpret that religion by *thinking about* and abstracting its peculiar, intrinsic, really vital and deepest being. As a piece of interpretative reasoning it is always an attempt to take stock, to render a proper account, which is conditioned by personal and historical circumstances. As such, it is valuable and full of significance; but for the very same reason it is not merely open to revision – it even demands it, as the ways in which men think and feel change from one historical period to another. It is not, therefore, in essence normative. One can for example, like the present writer, believe quite sincerely in God the Three-in-One and not only venerate Jesus Christ but worship Him as "my Lord and my God", or one can be deeply persuaded of the saving, keeping and reconciling power of God, disclosed before men and before the world in the Cross and Resurrection of Jesus Christ, and yet be dissatisfied with the expression of all this in terms of "classical" dogma and delighted therefore that in these days so many different approaches to fresh interpretation are being tried out which are not tied down to the idea that if something is "classical", it is also final.

Thus "to pose the problem correctly from the standpoint of Christianity" is in my view only possible when one gets back to the non-derivative, to what is original, to the primary "given" of Christianity, to that which produced Christianity and was not itself made or produced by it. Now that is neither a doctrine nor a principle. It is the Person of Jesus Christ. Here, I would say, is an objective criterion.

From what little I know of the world and of the people in it I have no doubt that not a few of my critical readers, having got as far as that short and probably most provoking sentence, will be on their feet and slamming the book shut; but I must ask them to try and restrain their feelings and to read on a little further. When I say that we have here an objective criterion, I do not of course intend this in the customary intellectual sense of "universally valid for the purpose of rational thought and so to be admitted without further question" or "removed from every possibility of subjective judgment".

What I mean by "objective" here is the precise, literal signification of the word: something "deposited in front" of us, something set, or which sets itself, before us. He, the Person of Jesus Christ, is there whether one is willing to admit it or not. The great importance which this has for our subject stems from the fact that all definitions of religion and of its capacities (fear, a feeling of dependence, the sense of the "numinous" and so forth), when thoroughly investigated, inevitably turn out to be psychological in character. That is perfectly understandable; for it is the human consciousness which gives being to religion. The study of religion, being a scientific study, has to establish the facts as conclusively as may be and then to explain them according to the best of its ability in terms of whatever coherence they may possess; it works in this plane and indeed cannot do otherwise. There you have the reason why, when people are dealing with the religions, they never get beyond the psychological and sociological aspects. That is to say, in one way or another, however concealed it may be, they keep within the "intra-human" category and never force a passage to that religious-cum-moral core which is the peculiar feature of religion and of religions.

Now explanations couched in psychological or sociological terms can certainly be meaningful and fruitful too in that a great deal of what is involved in the concrete "living out" of all religions falls within both these planes. As I have said, however, they do not penetrate to the real core. That is precisely the point at issue in the criterion I have proposed, the more so since Jesus Christ, in saying that the truth is revealed *in* Him and not just *by* Him, constitutes Himself as the criterion. On that revelation of the truth in Jesus Christ as a *given* and *effectual* quantitative reality the Christian Church is founded. Without that she is nothing. On that revelation of the truth in Him rests also the Church's claim that – to put it somewhat loosely and inaccurately – Christianity is the truth. That is her only ground for making such a claim.

It should occasion no surprise therefore that for the convinced Christian Jesus Christ, in whom God has revealed Himself and His truth, is the criterion; rather it would be astonishing if this were not so and if he were to take some other criterion. This criterion is not his discovery or choice; it chooses *him*. To apply in this instance a somewhat inappropriate figure of speech, it is his "axiom". It is his "axiom" in this sense: that when the question is raised of the *truth* and *value* of the different religions, it is there, i.e. in the Person of Jesus Christ and in whatever is comprehended in that, that he finds his standard of reference. That will determine not only his judgments and his evaluations, but above all his *discoveries*, in the positive sense of the word, of truth and value in the other religions.

The Illuminating Answer

But now a further step must be taken. Truth, in the religious sense of the word – or to put it still more broadly, truth in the existential sense – is never a "knowing" from without. It is never truth to which one's relationship is fundamentally that of a spectator – for that is the rigidly scientific conception of truth. Truth in a religious connotation is again never in the first place an intellectually demonstrable proposition. (This is indeed also true as regards philosophy.) It is even not really a proposition at all. It is a *living* in communion with a world of spiritual actuality of which God, who alone is known and therefore loved with the whole heart, with every faculty of the soul and of the spirit and of the understanding (think of the first and great Commandment) is the centre.

If someone on the outside of all this chooses to speak of subjectivity at this point, nobody can say him nay. Certainly, I shall not do so; for from his own outside standpoint he is quite right. I really did mean it when I said that the personal answer is the only answer likely to be illuminating, is in fact the only answer possible. On certain grounds which appear to him to be reasonable and irrefutable the outside observer simply dismisses this living communion as a delusion, or questions the validity of it. Of course, objections of this sort must be taken seriously; but when all is said and done they in no way alter the fact which every serious-minded person must surely allow: namely, that the truth – not just the truth which one registers on experimental and rational grounds, but the truth by which one *lives* – is a *choice* and a *decision.* This choice and decision spring from what one might call an encounter, though it is admittedly in Christian experience that the expressions "encounter" and "living communion" which I employ here arise in their most potent form. Truth encountered and perceived in *living* communion is naturally personal.

With all respect to reason and its proper uses, this is not something which can be argued out on a logical or rational basis. One can and one must *bear witness* and only then and in that context, standing always as one does so *within* that living communion, develop one's reasonable argument and give some account of the insights thus obtained into the truth and value of the religions and the relations between them. I say, witness; for the encounter with Jesus Christ is a matter of life and death, not an attempt to discover what is doing or how it goes at the moment with some item of knowledge which one has selected for objective scrutiny.

But to come back once more to the outsider: his remarks about the subjectivity of this standpoint of faith deserve to be listened to with attention, because it is undeniably true that in the forms taken by that standpoint and in the various expressions of it – and I refer here to taking one's stand within the living communion or fellowship – there are subjective elements, if only for the reason that the "believer" in Jesus Christ has his human nature in common with everyone else and cannot divest himself of it. He could as soon jump out of his own skin. When every allowance has been made for this, however, it should be said that the "outside" critic behaves unjustifiably when he gets so taken up with criticizing the subjective element that he overlooks the most salient point, which is that Jesus Christ as the criterion is there after all, in His givenness, His "deposited-ness", His "objectivity" – however one chooses to express it; unless of course one is determined to disregard Him altogether, which one is certainly at liberty to do.

By now it has become clear, I hope, that when we accept as our criterion Jesus Christ, the revelation of God, we find ourselves in a climate of thought, of judgment and of evaluation totally different from that of science and philosophy. Thus knowledge of the truth in a religious context is not an achievement on the part of man, whether enlightened and sophisticated or simple-minded and immature. It rests – and this is the whole basis of Christianity – upon God's Self-communication, upon His Self-disclosure in Jesus Christ, in whom and through whom "grace and truth" are come. The basic ground is therefore not revelation in the sense of a supernaturally communicated doctrine or a set of precepts or truths given out as infallible. That would land us back in the realm of total abstraction, would suspend or eliminate the play of intelligence and leave us enslaved to some dogmatic authority. There is nothing infallible: neither Bible nor Church nor doctrine, whether liberal or orthodox. The whole idea of infallibility is rationalistic and ignores the fact that dogmas, "sacred" books, churches and so forth, however important and valuable they may be in their proper place, are still to a manifest degree human products. God only is infallible; but in the quite different, vitalizing sense that He is utterly dependable, is solely and uniquely dependable, and that in and through Jesus Christ this is something which we may know "with all our heart, with all our mind and with all our strength".

So it is God's Self-disclosure, God's Self-communication in Jesus Christ, which reveals the truth and reveals that truth to be the criterion for every effort of ours to search out and determine where truth is to be found and where not.

Hence the reason why thinking which is centred on Jesus Christ is bound to insist on such a radical line of distinction between religion and revelation. The character of revelation being what it is, it cannot be subsumed under a general concept of religion. Revelation, if one takes the word seriously and does not muddle it up with intuition, is God acting and speaking. That is not religion at all and never could be; for religion signifies: the various ways which men have of believing, together with their consequent activities.

Even so, *Christianity* as an historical phenomenon is in many respects most certainly a religion. The normative ideas of religion with which the scientific study and the philosophy of religion always work and which are extrapolated from the various ways of believing and behaving mentioned above, although they have a great deal to tell us that is extremely valuable, are fundamentally unacceptable in the light of our criterion, as I contended earlier. Because Christianity as a phenomenon in history is a religion alongside other religions, the Christian who has thought through the implications of his own standpoint cannot hold up Christianity as his standard or criterion.

Furthermore these allegedly normative ideas are conflicting; and this suggests that the whole endeavour exhibits what I should wish to call a "strange impotence". When we start from the revelation of God in Jesus Christ, we are not called upon to speak of the "sacred mystery" in the religions as though that were the final reality in them. Should we do so (and this is a good moment to return to the matter of Symmachus) we put ourselves in line with this man who was the last considerable mouthpiece of Roman paganism on the brink of its dissolution. The heart and core of the religions is then an "It", a "Sacred Mystery" which offers a point of contact between each and all of the religions but is a mystery for ever insusceptible of definition. This method of approach proves on close examination to be philosophic and abstract and therefore not concrete. The only "sacred mystery", as one might say, is this revelation or Self-communication on God's part. Hence we can only either worship and lay ourselves open before it or reject it, either let it teach us about the true ground of things and men or shut ourselves off from it.

To come back to the point about Symmachus: I must say that the Christian who has a keen ear and a keen eye for the biblical Revelation should not need to be told that God, who dwells in light inaccessible, is a Mystery to be worshipped, a Mystery surpassing every thought and dream and definition of men. Yet the *Revelation* in Jesus Christ – and He is "Mystery" enough to meet all our requirements – means that this same God, through His Self-communication in Christ, has *made* Himself known, not indeed in relation to His total and perpetually unfathomable being, but in what concerns His purpose with regard to the world and human beings. That is why we may know Him in Jesus Christ and can speak of a pure knowledge of God; and that is also why what Symmachus propounds – and it sounds so very attractive and sincere and reverent – is in the last analysis a symptom of man's "strange impotence", that is, of his inability to frame the question of religion adequately in purely human, existential terms.

It would seem that again and again the Bible has a way of thinking, a way of putting the central issues, which is quite extraordinary and peculiarly its own and is other than the various methods conceived of by men. The Revelation in Christ hangs entirely upon God's sovereign initiative, it is an action of His in which the human element plays no part; so that viewed in the light of this, the religions and religion itself are so many documentary evidences of the struggling, questing, discovering and errant human spirit, even though the God of Revelation does not stand aside from all this. It is the fact of Revelation which involves the disclosure of that "strange impotence"; or to put it another way, the "strange impotence" points to a mysterious "something" in man which in spite of all his earnest and unremitting efforts evidently makes him incapable of finding out for himself, and in himself what true and normative religion is. *He has to be told; it has to be given* (or, in other words, *revealed*) to him. Left entirely to himself, apparently, he just cannot manage it. If we are ever to know what true and divinely willed religion is, we can do this only through God's revelation in Jesus Christ and through nothing else. That is why on the question of the truth and value of religions that revelation in the Person of Jesus Christ is *the* criterion and for the Christian the only really satisfying one.

From this it is evident that in order to arrive at a clear and stable position where this problem is concerned one must begin at the point of *profession*, of *testimony*. The great thing is to see this and to accept it realistically, as sober fact. It sounds horribly "unscientific"; for a good many of those who pursue the study of religion or of the philosophy of religion as an academic discipline are more averse to being "unscientific" than to anything else: and so they want to start off, not with some kind of "profession" or "testimony" but with a normative concept of religion, the distilled product of their researches and reflection thereon, which is taken as holding good before the bar of reason. In reality, however, as I said earlier, it is a governing principle which lies outside the scope of scientific discussion; and since it is certainly never offered as a "profession" of belief of any sort, the honours (when it comes to the point) still go to the idea of non-commitment. Can one adopt this attitude of detachment, can one be a looker-on, even a deeply interested looker-on, and still hope to get closer to the truth which this matter of the religions involves?

Now in my opinion – and I fully and readily admit how skilful and fruitful is all the honest and unremitting labour that goes into the systematic study of religion – it is just here that we find the "blind spot" of this activity, the reason for its inability to cope with the hard core of the philosophical problem. My reader may think this a rather drastic thing to say; yet I say it advisedly, not out of contempt but out of the high regard I have for this discipline and what it strives to do, and not just to get off my chest a perhaps somewhat ill-considered outburst of animosity but to do this field of study, which happens to be my own, a true and faithful service. Great matters are best served by plain speaking, if we are to get at the real problems and not just those which lie on the surface.

The Unique Element

The absolutely distinctive and peculiar and unique element in Christianity is the *fact* of Jesus Christ. I call particular attention to the word "fact" here. What, it may be asked, is so far-reaching about that? Well, of course, the proper answer to that is: because the content, the substance, of the fact is none other than Jesus Christ. It is the right answer, but hardly sufficient in itself; some further clarification is called for. Naturally enough, some people may perhaps object: one might just as well say that the absolutely distinctive, peculiar and unique element in Buddhism is the fact of Buddha, or in Islam the fact of Muhammad. That sounds quite plausible. The fact remains that one can *not* just as well say this. In order to make the point clear it is necessary to make a few comparisons which have nothing to do with setting a higher or lower value on any particular religion or with considerations of priority, but are intended to distinguish in a straightforward way what the intrinsic character is of this and that religion.

The primitive religions form a body of myths, customs (rites) and institutions by means of which primitive man sets out to strengthen and preserve the continuity of personal and communal life and so to remain in harmony with the cosmos as he understands it, at the same time combating and rendering harmless the forces hostile towards him. The Sacred Tradition is the power on which he relies. Confucianism is a code for living meant to enable man to establish and maintain a harmony between his individual and social existence within the moral order and the order of nature, so that he can become the kind of person who fulfils the lofty ideal of the "Noble One" and the "Sage". To put it in Western terms, it is a peculiar sort of humanism, albeit not in the Western sense of a full flowering and unfolding of the autonomous personality. Confucian humanism is directed towards a step-by-step process of self-realization in which the essential thing is to live in complete accord with the Heavenly Way (Tao), the Heavenly Order – and this includes one's way of living with one's fellows, that is to say, the life of society. The primary concern here is not with the Self as such, but with this harmony, with losing oneself in it and realizing oneself precisely in so doing. Confucius is held in great honour as the First Teacher; but everybody has a way to self-realization of his own. He must find it and follow it.

Buddhism is a "way" of release from life which consists essentially of suffering, change and impermanence. This way has been discovered and promulgated by the Buddha. He is, as it were, the first successful Pathfinder. His followers can learn the way from him, but the goal they must reach under their own steam. Buddha is unique in being the first Pathfinder and Promulgator of importance; but in the struggle for salvation he himself plays no direct role. When at the point of death, he himself declared in the strongest terms that since he was entering Nirvana and would thus – in the fullest sense of the word – "disappear", no further account was to be taken of him; but he enjoined upon his disciples to regard what he had taught as *the* guiding principle and means of salvation. The later development of Buddhism has, of course, paid no attention to what Buddha considered his place (or rather his lack of one) to be in Buddhism; but it remains true that with his last words Buddha gave perfectly logical expression to his own doctrine of release.

Islam is a system of teachings centred on Allah, the One, the Almighty, and enunciated in a revelational book; it summons men to penitence and conversion and to submit (=*islam*) unconditionally to Allah, the Unconditional. Further it is a Law, regulating life at every juncture and grounded in Allah's "thou shalt" and "thou shalt not", as revealed to Muhammad. Muhammad is the Envoy of Allah, the trusty Mouthpiece of the revelation contained in the Koran. Thus his status as the Envoy of Allah is affirmed in the second clause of the Confession of Faith (actually the Arabic word *sh'ahāda* means: witnessing or deposition). This is an important point; for it means that Muhammad occupies a position of prominence in Islam. He himself however always laid it down, as one may read in the Koran, that he was only a "Premonitor", a "Messenger" and "Bearer" of the revelation "sent down" to him, and not a part of the Revelation, let alone *the* Revelation itself. As in the case of Buddhism, Islam in its later developments has paid little heed in this respect to the clear and emphatic language of the Koran.

As distinct from all this, Jesus Christ is Himself the Revelation in His own Person; and He is likewise its substance. "Grace and truth came by Jesus Christ", says the Scripture (John 1:17). He thus holds a place which is quite distinctively His own; a position essentially other than that of Buddha, for example, or of Confucius or Muhammad. He presents Himself to men and to the world – places Himself, that is, in all His gentleness and lowliness before them – as the Truth, the Way and the Life. He is not what the academic experts in the study of religion call a theophany (the manifestation of a god). He is not the mediator of a Revelation, of a message imparted and entrusted to Him. As has been said already, He is Himself "God revealed", God's communication of Himself. He is the tangible, visible Revelation of God: God, revealed in His Person, His preaching, His works, His death, His resurrection; and what He asks of every man is faith in Him *as such*. It is not principles – love, for example – deduced from Him and thus isolated in the process, that He asks us to acknowledge, but Himself and the quality of the Love revealed in Him to be truly the law of life. In Him God is with and in the midst of men, of their necessities, their sufferings, expectations, errors and sins: hence the name that he bears – Emmanuel; that is, God with us.

If, when confronted with Him, men treat Him with the same seriousness with which He sets Himself before them, there are but two possibilities answering to the gravity of the situation. The Bible makes this absolutely clear. On the one hand there is the possibility of faith, of personal surrender. The other possible reaction is to take offence at Him. Every other reaction which does in fact occur, even when it is one not of ridicule or unconcern but of respect, really means that we pass by Him on the other side. It is the same when we greet Him with our quite genuine protestations of reverence or when we venerate Him as the greatest religious figure in world history. "This is eternal life, that they should know Thee, the only and true God, and Jesus Christ whom Thou hast sent"; that is how Scripture sums it all up (John 17:3).

The Truth of Revelation

This, I hope, is enough to give concrete meaning to the statement that the absolutely distinctive and absolutely unique thing about Christianity is the *fact*: the Person of Jesus Christ. I hope too that it may do something to dispel the deeply ingrained and wellnigh ineradicable notion among "believers" and "unbelievers" alike that revelation means a communication of "truths" not accessible to us through the use of our rational faculties; truths to which we are required to submit without question and to the point of abandoning, if need be, intellectual integrity itself. This falsification, this caricature, of what the Bible means by revelation is one of the biggest obstacles – manufactured to a considerable extent by the Church itself – to getting a true picture of what Christianity is. This takes added force from the fact that, as I indicated earlier, there is something peculiarly distinctive about the criterion which I have advanced: namely, that truth in the religious sense of the word cannot be known "from outside" or by some process of thought, of comparison and of analysis, but only in and through a living fellowship or communion, as is also the case with, for example, love and marriage.

The biblical, and thus the Christian, criterion of religious truth then is the Person of Jesus Christ who is the Truth; and the approach to this Truth is not by way of close reasoning and argument, whether theological, philosophical or dogmatic, but through the being in a living communion with Him. It is not a matter of choosing between Reason and Revelation as the final authority. It does mean living and thinking in the context of that communion and making it the point of reference in all those questions concerning man and the world, whatever the particular area of concern may be, where really fundamental decisions are involved. Then reason and judgment based soundly on fact take their full and proper place. Understood thus, Revelation neither fetters Reason nor lowers its status; on the contrary, Reason is *set free* to fulfil its function and is kept within its rightful sphere.

Because the criterion afforded by Revelation embraces all that I have just been describing, it plainly follows that for a convinced Christian such as the writer is, when it is his job to make a systematic study of religion, this is – nay, must be – his criterion in such cases of "fundamental decision" as are bound to arise when he comes to consider in their reciprocal relations the truth and value of Christianity and the rest of the religions. It is therefore rather astonishing that so many Christians here, there and everywhere, whose job is to make an expert, academic study of religion, when they come to these crucial questions work with the normally accepted, conventional criteria, as though no criterion existed which the Christian can call his very own. There would appear to be a sort of "pietism" in a scientific context here, or an unconscious kowtowing to the familiar nineteenth-century tenet that "religion is a private affair", held in this case to apply to the work one does within one's field of study, in so far as that work touches upon fundamental issues. Surely it is time for us to think again about this strange "one really ought to refrain" attitude. Curiously enough, a much better grasp of these matters is shown by men like Jaspers – who is a long way from accepting the revelation in Jesus Christ as his criterion –

or Menno ter Braak, who was happy to describe himself as a "Christian without God", than by a lot of the "Christians" engaged in the scientific study of religion.

It is useful to hear what the English thinker C. E. M. Joad had to say in this connection. For a great part of his life he was a "free-thinker" and was widely acclaimed as a speaker on philosophical and general questions. The list of his writings includes a book about the Hindu philosopher Radhakrishnan. In that book he commends Radhakrishnan – who of course rejects the Revelation in Jesus Christ as a criterion, but is spokesman for an authentically Indian outlook on the religions – to Westerners with enthusiasm, as meriting their greatest care and attention. Later, however, Joad became a convinced Christian and a member of the Anglican Church. In another book he offered an account of that major change in his position.

In so doing, he makes it clear on a basis of intensive philosophical argument that the idea had gradually forced itself upon him, despite his protracted refusal to accept it, that, as compared with the various types of "scientific" approach which he had followed, the Christian viewpoint still offered the most satisfactory way of looking at the actual human situation and that many of the current ways of regarding the world, although they claim to be "scientific", simply have nothing to say about the deepest and biggest problems of mankind. Because his eyes were being opened more and more to facts of this sort, he came through a process of, so to say, intellectual conversion to recognize the possibility of "revelation" and so to Christian belief. As it had been a hobby-horse of his during his pre-Christian period to dispose of the whole problem of religion with the one word "subjectivism", he devotes himself with particular skill and shrewdness to examining the proposition that religion is "a purely subjective business"; and he shows in just how slipshod and reprehensible a way that proposition can be manipulated.

The reason why I refer to him is that he demonstrates so forcefully and with the aid of an extensive training in philosophy that Revelation and faith are not concerns exclusively of the "inner man" or of the "soul", but are of the first importance chiefly because they cast a searching and a crucial light upon all the basic questions confronting mankind. That is precisely the point I have been concerned to make with the foregoing argument. The digression on Joad has, I trust, been illuminating; and the way should have been paved sufficiently by now for me to say briefly and concisely what the criterion thus explained enables us to conclude about the relation of Christianity to the other religions and about truth and value in the religions.

The Religious Mixture

The first essential thing to note follows from what has been said and it is this: having regard to Christianity as an historical phenomenon (as indeed to all other religions) one must be fair and honest about the facts; but in being fair and honest one must also be truthful and, to the best of one's ability, loyal to the criterion. For that one needs, among other things, knowledge which is accurate, though always incomplete. For making such knowledge possible we are greatly indebted to, and should be grateful for, the fruits of research in the various branches of the systematic study of religion. One can only hope that this work will continue unabated and so yield results which are evidently new and full of value.

I am fully aware – and this is the proper moment for me to say so explicitly – that the modern "scientific" study of religion, in which I am only too glad to take my share, by being free and candid in all its work of investigation and discovery and by aiming to avoid every prejudicial bias has for the first time made it really possible, in this matter of the inter-relationship of the religions where their truth and value are in question, to act with confidence in proposing Jesus Christ as one's criterion. At one time it was far more difficult to do that, because what was alleged to be the Christian way of thinking was much too inhibited in its approach to the other religions and to "Christianity". The salutary effects of modern scientific studies in breaking through this inhibitive barrier had not yet made themselves felt.

When I speak of fairness and honesty I mean that one should be not merely disposed but *eager* to recognize, in the religious as well as the moral aspects of these religions, major and minor evidences of authenticity and nobility, truth and value, whether it be in rites and practices, in institutions, ideas, experiences or people. I have had the privilege of spending a good deal of my life in the East among non-Christian peoples and of studying them; and I do not mind admitting that I am time and again carried away by the thought of how much there is which impresses me on the religious side and of the many splendid folk whom I have come to know there and to treasure as my friends.

Being fair and honest, however, means also that one has no reservations about exposing a great deal that is petty and trivial and questionable; often questionable in the extreme. The fact of the matter is that all religions – *Christianity as an historic "religion" along with the rest* – have been in the past and are still today a mixture of sublimity and perversion, of evil, falsehood and sheer absurdity. In that respect they reflect the equivocal and inwardly divided state of human nature. There is reason enough for those prophets and thinkers of integrity who have appeared from time to time in the course of history to castigate the "religion" to which they belonged or in the midst of which they had to live.

There are two sides then to this being honest and being fair; and only by having due regard to both can one be *truthful* – but even so only "truthful" in the sense of being *fair* to the facts and to the intrinsic character of the religions, for what they really are. Yet that is still not being "truthful" in the deeper sense which it is possible to realize only in the light of a specific criterion. The historical-cum-psychological judgment necessarily involved is always discriminatory, is always a process of *pre-judging* (which has nothing whatever to do with prejudice): that is to say, it remains a critical process which promises to help with the job of clarification, but which always precedes and must always precede the actual truth-judgment and value-judgment itself. From the standpoint of Christianity one can only reach a verdict of "true" or "untrue" in allegiance to the criterion which for the thinking Christian is not something he has selected but something given to him: namely, the Revelation of God in the Person of Jesus Christ.

There is another thing consequent upon this criterion which must be remarked and it is this: because it is in the nature of the criterion itself that it presupposes and implies a living communion with Jesus Christ (and not an attitude of detachment, of regarding Him from an onlooker's point of view) one can never say simply: Well, that is that. It is, in a sense, a "never, never" standpoint. Because this is something which we cannot deploy, cannot manipulate as we might, for example, manipulate an idea or a principle or a plan, but on the contrary is something to be lived with, something which is for ever forming and judging and renewing *us*, it is always open to us to see with clearer insight and to judge more profoundly, truly and honestly than before. Equally it is possible for one's vision to become less clear, one's faculty of judgment less profound, less true, less candid. Everything depends upon the quality of our communion, upon how we live it; and that means that we can never really *have done*, that in reverent response to that reality which is present to us through the Revelation of God in the Person of Jesus Christ we are always ready to expose our judgment – in this instance regarding the religions, with Christianity among them – to self-critical amendment.

The criterion further implies that in striving to see as Jesus Christ sees and by the light of that reality disclosed in God's Self-communication in Him, one is to search out, in full commitment, the evidences for revelatory activity on the part of that same God in all religions – but tracking down also the demonic and devilish forces in them. *Here again Christianity is not to be excluded.* The two sides are there and they go together. The gospels convey to us clearly enough how Nathanael's pureness and uprightness of heart, the faith of the Roman ruler (so simple and therefore so greatly commended), the potency and impotency of the demons, the satanic lapse of Peter – to mention only a few examples – are all made manifest in the confronation with Him.

Such unsparing dedication to the task of investigation and discovery is a very different thing therefore from the dilettante game of picking and choosing between various "points of contact" or, as so often happens with discussions in this area, just taking the religions lock, stock and barrel and giving them out to be revelations of the one and only God. Christianity *in toto* is itself far from being a revelation of God. But where it shows at any rate some self-understanding, it looks towards its centre in Jesus Christ who is God's Revelation. That is the essential difference between Christianity and the rest of the religions.

As the Revelation in Jesus Christ goes forth, it prompts us to single-mindeness in searching out the works of God; yet not under our own power, as it were, but rather in sensitive response to God's Revelation in Christ, who is a living reality for us and not a principle or a religious-cum-philosophical idea on which we can operate. Not even "Christianity" then is the normative or regulative religion – *that* is *revealed* solely in the Person of Jesus Christ. It is a standard given and a judgment spoken over all religions, including historic Christianity; for its own history makes it obvious enough that Christianity shares to the fullest degree the equivocal character of religions in general. That religion or Divine "service" which is normative and regulative and is revealed in Him never will be realized within the present order of things in the world in any religion, whether it be Christianity or anything else. The tremendous and liberating and renovating significance of it is that we can be prepared to let it speak its instruction and so can go on from strength to strength, but in everything bound to and by the real limitations of our contingency. Whenever Christianity permits itself to be addressed by its own primal ground and creative source, we at once find ourselves again involved in what nowadays goes by the name of "the renewal of the Church" – although we are not to imagine that this means we are at last about to pull a perfect Church out of the hat. The lesson which that primal and creative source inevitably teaches us is that "the renewal of the Church" remains with us as a permanent charge and a permanent task; it is not something which just happens to come along as an intervening period, a high-water mark, as one might say.

In the Light of Christ

Well now, we have been thinking in a fair amount of detail about what it means to put forward the Person of Jesus Christ as one's criterion, both as a means to critical self-appraisal on the part of the religion known as "Christianity" and also for reaching a verdict upon and evaluating the "other" religions; and this brings us to a point where we can and must give an answer to our question which will be clear and basic, especially with regard to those "other" religions. The best course and the most illuminating, as it appears to me, is to give the answer first in terms of general principles, without actually trying to draw any of the finer distinctions. I realize of course that in so doing I am flying in the face of an idea quite widely and strongly maintained nowadays, of what one might call "the fashionable point of view", and am thus saying something which it is not easy to swallow and which is bound to spark off a protest. However, it seems to me to be necessary in order to clarify one's thinking.

Later on, with the aid of a few examples, we shall go on to introduce those finer distinctions which, as I see it, are equally necessary.

Well now, in the light of "Jesus Christ, in whom the glory full of grace and truth" has been revealed and has entered the actual, historical world of men as a power acting and operating within it – and not therefore, let me repeat, in the light of Christianity – the first thing that has to be said, and said straight out, about the "other" religions is that considered in this light and in regard to their deepest, most essential purport they are all in error. In this light they are all noble, but misguided and abortive, attempts to take the fundamental religious questions – namely, what is the right relationship to God; who is God; who is man; in what do his Highest Good and his true vocation and destiny consist, in time and in eternity? – and to answer them in their own terms. Magnificent as they may be and often are, they represent, in this light, a "dark excursion of the mind" into what is from our standpoint as human beings the unfathomable mystery of God and into the mystery of man and the world. These are mysteries which, so far as His purpose with and attitude towards men and the world are concerned, God *makes* known in Christ.

As he is in actual fact, there is deeply rooted in the nature of man in any and every part of the world the consciousness that he needs to be released from bondage, from his condition of servitude, if he is to arrive at a state of authentic being, as

257

man. It is likewise an established fact that whether at a commonplace level or on a more elevated plane, man everywhere seeks to vindicate and justify himself, because he feels with a greater or lesser degree of subtlety that on this depends the crucial question of whether he is to preserve his self-respect and keep going or instead throw in his hand and admit defeat. Furthermore man reveals himself in all religions without exception – and indeed to no small effect – as a being who yearns and strives to impart solemnity and sacredness to life, who pines, that is to say, for some assurance that his life and he himself are subsumed within a dimension of inviolable purity and invincible power.

With these fundamental facts about man – and they are so clearly apparent in all religions – held firmly in view, and in the light of Christ who "of God was made wisdom, righteousness, sanctification and redemption" (1 Cor. 1:30), one may say that when we probe more deeply into the religions in one way or another they are shown to be religions of self-redemption, self-justification and self-sanctification and so to be, in their ultimate and essential meaning and significance, *erroneous*. Every religion, even a considerable part of the Christian religion, taking it all of a piece, is this – though each one has, of course its own characterstic accent. The Buddha's version of Buddhism is the most consistent as a religion of self-deliverance; just as the teachings of Hinduism about salvation are as such extremely consistent whilst having an emphasis all their own. Confucianism and Taoism (in its higher form), although in point of emphasis each represents a world of its own, both stress the cultivation of the Self, the realization of the self as the "Noble Man"; and so deep down they are at one, united in the powerful urge to self-sanctification and self-justification.

In saying this I do not mean to imply that the stress laid on "doing it yourself" in such a religion puts completely out of court, for instance, the vital religious concept of "grace"; far from it indeed. It is much in evidence in most of the great Asiatic religions. But one must be careful to distinguish at this point. Within the whole complex of what I termed the ultimate and essential aims of the "other" religions, the not inconsiderable sects in Hinduism and Mahayana Buddhism which base their life on a doctrine of salvation through "grace" represent one possible method, an "easier" route to the goal, as it were; but to what goal? To the goal of "self-realization". That word is invariably the key-word in these religions.

Looking at it from another angle, one might say that in virtue of their tendency to fulfil the principle of self-deliverance, self-justification and self-sanctification, from their characteristic standpoint the religions throw a totally different light on the crucial questions of God, man and the world from what is shed upon them when we start from the Person of Jesus Christ, placing Him and all that He signifies at the centre of our concern. However, this is not so much a basic cause as a momentous consequence.

In some of my more considerable published writings I have aroused a good deal of criticism and even protest by insisting that when it really comes to it, the Revelation of God in the Person of Jesus Christ is "discontinuous" even with what is normally held to be "what is best" in the "other" religions. I do not say this to make light of the "other" religions or to belittle in any way the many outstanding and impressive qualities which we find in them. I say it only in order to make a clear distinction where that is called for and, because intellectual honesty requires it, to uphold my chief contention, which is that the Person of Jesus Christ presents us with an entirely new world of facts and norms, such as "never did rise within the heart of man" and such as involves an *Umwertung aller Werte* – a total uprooting.

This something-totally-new which is disclosed in Jesus Christ is not to be discovered by "assimilating" the religions to one another according to their truth-content or value-content. It is only to be found when one lets oneself *be* found by Him and so learns by experience what it is to "have the scales fall from one's eyes". That is why "conversion" as the "way in" to this holds such a central place in the Christian message; and by the same token the call to "be converted" needs to be heard as loudly and as often within the realm of Christianity as in those of the "other" religions, because "being converted" means not "being converted" to Christianity but to Jesus Christ.

Again, this something-totally-new does not in the least mean that nothing of truth or of value is to be found in the "other" religions or that they stand, purely and simply for "God-forsakenness" or rebellion. On the contrary, the light of this entirely new world which is in Jesus Christ makes it possible to discriminate more lucidly and to detect each stirring note of authenticity and truth. That however does not materially affect my contention that in the light of Jesus Christ and of the truth realized in Him, and having regard to their deepest and most essential meaning and purpose, the religions are "in error" – an idea to which I have given more particular expression under the terms: self-redemption, self-justification, self-sanctification.

As an example of how it now becomes possible to draw much clearer and more precise distinctions, take the crucial religious idea of "grace", to which I was referring a moment ago. However considerable the part played by "grace" in such religions as Buddhism and Hinduism, as I pointed out before, it is always recommended inside Buddhism as a "soft option", an "easier" path to release, which the individual chooses as his own personal means of deliverance because he happens to represent a particular (and inferior) level of spiritual development, so that the "hard" way, the "right" way trodden by the spiritual *élite*, simply does not suit him. In those forms of Hinduism known as "bhakti" religions there is a good deal of very moving poetry and other writing on the subject of "grace"; but one must not lose sight of the fact that "grace" here refers solely to a private relationship between God and the individual soul. When we talk about the "grace" of God – speaking, that is, in the light of Jesus Christ and therefore in an authentically Christian context – we mean by it something entirely different: so that although the word in these two cases is the same, the substance of what it is meant to express is not the same at all. What grace means in the light of Jesus Christ is this: that He takes away the sins of the *world*, that the redemption and renewal of the whole *world* are involved here. As to the role of "grace" in the aforementioned "bhakti" religions, one could say that it has many features in common with Christian Pietism.

To instance another much discussed example: does "love", as it is used particularly in Buddhism, mean in that context what is meant by the Christian use of the word "love", i.e. of God and of one's neighbour (cf. John 3:16, for example; also the Sermon on the Mount, and in Matt. 22:37–40; 1 Cor. 13)? One can be really moved as one reads in the great literature of Buddhism what Buddhist monks and nuns have had to say about this, and yet feel obliged in common honesty to insist that this "love" in Buddhism – (*maitri* or *metta*) – is a wholly different affair from the "love" (*agapé*) for which Jesus Christ stands. In Buddhism it is a means by which the human being in his quest for Nirvana can loose himself from the world and its various preoccupations; it expresses itself in an outpouring of universal benevolence and in altruistic behaviour. No doubt it is an admirable thing. Its effects too have been admirable in many ways; but one can hardly say that in the end it is the same thing as the "love" disclosed in Jesus Christ. In no respect could *that* be described as a means to "self-deliverance"; it is the love of God and for God, who is the first and highest object of love; it is the love of one's neighbour for his own sake, of whatever and whoever is downtrodden and forlorn; a love of what abounds in sincerity and truth, as a cherished reflection of God, whose being *is* love.

It is useful perhaps by way of summary to say that when we particularize about the "error" in terms of self-deliverance and so forth, this is an insight which can only be brought to birth in the light of Jesus Christ. What it brings us to see is that the great religions, at their most profound and in the very fundamentals of their message, fail to give any adequate account of the sheer contrariety, the utter mysteriousness, of man, his greatness and his wretchedness, his reaching out towards the highest and his satanic devilishness, his place half-way between angel and ape; and they fail because they never give any real weight to the one basic fact which the Bible calls "sin". Though often called by a different name, it is not entirely overlooked; but it remains something essentially secondary and incidental and is never treated as the central mystery demanding solution. In what they themselves conceive to be their ultimate and fundamental aims these religions are bound therefore to be "in error", because blind to the most vital problem of man; and in that they refuse to take it really seriously, they are bound to be escapist in one way or another. In other words, the religions do not fully and realistically envisage just how serious is the problem constituted by man. This explains – and I can do no more than mention it in passing here – why it is that, quite apart from the exasperation so often and so justifiably aroused by Christianity as a religion in the concrete, the proclamation of the truth about God, the world and mankind as revealed in Jesus Christ, with its insistence on the centrality of forgiveness, propitiation and so forth, straightaway occasions so much anger and protest, and indeed will continue to do so.

That is why surrendering to Jesus Christ means in effect making a break with one's own past, religiously speaking, however impressive that past may be and often is; and the Christian Church is in duty bound to require this break, because one must *openly* confess Him.

An Attempt at an Answer

Evidence of the Seekers

The general principle of characterizing the "other" religions (and with them a good deal of what in practice passes for "Christianity") as *errors* and as the embodiment, in various forms, of the quest for self-deliverance, self-justification and self-sanctification gives offence to a lot of people. Yet this way of representing them is not to be avoided; and the best books for helping us to see why are not, in my view, the worthy manuals which deal with the "other" religions, nor those instructive books which set out to show us where the religions agree and where they differ, but books of quite another sort, which are little known, seldom read and often more or less despised. I refer to the writings of those earnest seekers after God who come from the Buddhist, Hindu or Muslim world and out of a real meeting with Jesus Christ have tried to set down an account of what they sought and what they found, of their turn about, of how they "perceived" and "took hold of" the "new world" in the Person of Jesus Christ, and of what it was that prompted them to forsake the "old world". There are not many of these writings and most of them are very hard to come by. However, their value as documentary evidence makes the trouble well worth while; for what they have to tell about is not the "passing over" from one religion to another – that is seldom an event charged with much spiritual reality – but a spiritual pilgrimage ending in a complete transformation. As documentary evidence they should belong to the scientific study of religion and be part and parcel of its literature; but we have a long way to go before that is likely to happen.

In order to illustrate this point and to help us to see more clearly that the relation between Christianity and the "other" religions, bearing as it does upon their very heart and ultimate character, is not so simply contained as is often supposed in such terms as "the stages" of a single Divine revelation, I quote here a passage from an article by the Indian Christian, Dr P. Devanandan, in which he says this:

"When the Hindu talks about a Hindu becoming a Christian ... he is thinking of accepting certain desirable elements of the Christian creed, torn out of their setting in the total creed ... Whereas from the Hindu point of view such acceptance of foreign religious elements to the original core of the Hindu creed is possible, it is not so to the Christian ... It would not be possible for instance for a Hindu, if he continues to be a Hindu, to accept the claims of the absolute lordship of Jesus Christ in his personal life, for that would be to bring everything else under the judgment of Jesus Christ ... Therefore when a Hindu claims that it is possible for a Hindu to accept the Christian faith and continue to be a Hindu he means accepting not the Christian faith as the Christian understands it, but the Christian faith as the Hindu would have it to be."

In other words, out of a spirit of broadmindedness or tolerance in his religious outlook, the Hindu is perfectly ready to draw upon certain aspects of Christianity and accept them into his Hindu system of belief, even to the extent of putting Christ on a par with Ram and Krishna and according Him the same degree of veneration. But this only goes to show that it is preceisely this typically Hindu attitude of his in religious matters – an attitude grounded in the very heart and soul of Hinduism – which prevents him from seeing that Jesus Christ demands a total surrender, a *conversion* to Himself, which is something altogether different from being "big-hearted" about religion or showing a spirit of tolerance. That is no way at all of getting to grips with the question of *truth*, not at any rate as that question is raised by Christ and Christianity. On the contrary, broadmindedness and big-heartedness in religion neither know nor wish to know of any such question; and they pass it by altogether. A generous and openminded attitude is something very much to be desired in all of us, be we Christian, Hindu or whatever else, when it comes to making a fair assessment of the other man's religion; but, as the foregoing quotation shows, it is apt to lose sight of what for the other man is the paramount and most crucial factor involved.

When one is brought face to face with Jesus Christ as the personal embodiment of the Truth and when one accepts Him as such, something quite decisive and revolutionary is bound to happen. Confronted by Him, one simply cannot get away with some harmonizing expedient, a process of thought meant to make Him fit into some religious "system" with a completely different basis and orientation; for He breaks through every such "system", Christian and non-Christian alike, whatever its origin may be.

As I said before, we talk of the religions being "erroneous"; but of course there is a good deal more to it than that. That is why I made a point of saying that this statement of a general principle requires further and finer distinctions to be drawn; and in the process of discussing it I have already indicated some of these. Indeed the very terms in which I spoke suggested as much, when I said that in the light of the Person of Jesus Christ the religions must be held to be erroneous "in their deepest and most essential meaning and purpose"; not, that is to say, in any and every aspect or direction. Again from time to time I have thrown in such qualifying expressions as: "however admirable . . ." to suggest the same thing.

Thus enunciating the general principle, as we have already seen, naturally does not imply that *everything* in the "other" religions is to be labelled "erroneous"; but neither must one be so naïve as to think it possible to draw up a simple inventory, with all the phenomena and all the utterances associated with these religions neatly marshalled under the two heads of "erroneous" and "not erroneous". That would be quite wrong. Our verdict on the religions – that "in their deepest and most essential meaning and purpose" they are *in error* – must be firmly maintained, as I see it; but to be fair (and even to be correct) we must, I think, balance that by saying with equal emphasis and conviction that despite that fundamental failing the religions constitute a field of human endeavour in which, yes, even at the very heart of "error" itself, we are to discover and to recognize that "God has passed this way"; and that will be at the precise moment when in the light of Jesus Christ, which does not quench the smoking flax but "discovers" whatever has an affinity with Him, we have brought home to us the nature of such a religion.

There is another thing, equally important. It is that, if we set aside the familiar fact that all religions, Christianity included, bear the marks not only of all that is human but of all that is base in human nature too, still in their nobler aspects they aspire to

Jesus Christ; and in many if not in all respects they point to Him who is "full of grace and truth".

One cannot study any religion at close quarters and with an open mind and not be moved at what one discovers there: the great potentialities of man which appear in every religion – his striking insights, the depth and nobility of his thinking, the way in which he builds a culture upon the basis of his religion, his zealous determination, his often heroic readiness to make any sacrifice in order to gain his pearl of great price, to find the "Truth" or "The Highest Good". And along with this will go the no less affecting discovery of how, notwithstanding these noble aspirations and achievements, man with these religions of his – such as Christianity! – can go on committing blunders, perverting this and that and going right off the rails, so that what he makes of it all is very often a degrading caricature of man and of what it means to be human.

A fundamental "being in error"; a field in which we can trace God's own footmarks; noble aspiration and a tremendous capacity for creative action; and, in the light of Jesus Christ, humiliating aberration: these form the main outline of what I have been trying to say; and it would require several volumes to work them out in any detail. Still it seems to me that for the wise and understanding they are sufficient index to my views on the whole question with which we are here concerned.

I hope I have made it clear in what I have said that when Christianity is reproached for being exclusive, that is something which, when it comes to the point, it just has to accept. A better way of putting it would be to say that, as emerged earlier, Jesus Christ as *the* Revelation of God is at once exclusive and inclusive. That meets us clearly enough in the gospels, where it is summed up, for instance, in the two sayings: "whoever is not against me is for me" and "whoever is not for me is against me".

Even if it is perhaps labouring a point, just so that there should be no possibility of misunderstanding, let it be said once more that Christianity as an historical religion has no right to put itself forward as exclusive, without any qualification.

Some Observations on Islam and Israel

In my estimation of the facts and my comments so far I have paid more especial attention to the great religions of Asia, religions concerned with deliverance or salvation through mysticism; and I have not taken so very much account of Islam and the Jewish religion. I must therefore make one or two observations about them in particular.

There are two reasons for this. In the first place, it is bound to occur to quite a lot of people, when they come across words like "self-deliverance" and so forth, to ask: "But can you say that about Islam, anyway?"; and they might very well add: "or of the Jewish religion?" – by which I have in mind not so much "Israel" as one particular later phase of Jewish religion, to wit, Judaism. These questions are fair enough; for the situation is not the same with Islam and Judaism as with the Asiatic religions.

With Islam it is different because whether the Highest Good is made accessible to a man or not depends entirely upon the ultimate decision of Allah, the Almighty, the Merciful, whose actions are incalculable. Yet that in no way cancels out the preponderant fact that Islam is above all a legalistic religion in which everything hangs upon the efforts of the believer and on whether he fulfils the requirements of the Divine Law. Thus it is, so to say, a religion permeated by a form – a somewhat inflected form – of self-deliverance, self-justification and self-sanctification with, in the end, no firm and settled basis for it. Islam is certainly no religion of deliverance or redemption; nor indeed could it be so, because the revelation which it brings is not a self-communication on the part of Allah but a Law, informing men of Allah's commands and interdicts. The strong and decided monotheism which is Islam's boast – in the best sense of that word – and shows, apart from other things that one could mention, what a close kinship there is between Islam and the prophetic proclamation of God in the Bible, none the less differs profoundly from biblical monotheism, precisely because Islam is not a religion of redemption and knows nothing of the central biblical idea of the Kingdom of God. That is why, although both represent a kind of "monotheism" or "theism", it is not possible to equate Allah with the God and Father of Jesus Christ.

Where Judaism is concerned, there is always in it, clearly and actively present, an element of the Holy and Merciful God of Israel; but this again is of a quality unlike anything we find in Islam, for God is conceived of in a very different way. All the same, as a religion of "keeping the law", Judaism is in actual fact a religion of self-deliverance and all the rest. It is because of this that Paul takes issue with it, as in the celebrated words: By the fulfilling of the Law, or by faith in Christ; our own work or Christ's? His whole argument is centred on showing that the way of self-deliverance through self-justification is inherently beyond the bounds of possibility. That is something which anyone can read for himself in the New Testament.

Another reason for saying something more particularly under this head is that Islam and Israel (which is something with a reference wider than Judaism) stand in their own ways in a special relationship to Christianity or to the Church; or to put it the other way round, which is better: Christianity or the Christian Church has a relationship to Islam and Israel which it does not have in the same way to the other religions.

In the case of Islam the reason is in the first place an historical one. Islam came into existence as a new word of Revelation and a religion in its own right *after* Christianity, in the seventh century of our era. Moreover Islam appeared and grew into an independent religion within an environment strongly infused with "Christian" and "Jewish" ideas and institutions, along with a knowledge of the Old and New Testaments which was fragmentary and often distorted and inaccurate, like the knowlege of the ideas and institutions themselves. But the main point is that Islam, on the strength of the Revelation evidenced in the Koran, sets itself above Christianity and Judaism as the final, concluding Revelation and religion. It is part of Islam's fundamental position to reject Christianity and Judaism and to say so openly. The Asiatic religions in their "doctrine" and their Sacred Books know nothing of Christianity. Islam expresses its own conception of its relationship to Christianity and Jewry by laying down the principle that Christians and Jews in particular – as distinct from the "heathen" – need not embrace Islam, in that they are "Peoples of the Book" – are in possession, that is to say, of a book of Revelation. The Muslim Empire which came into being after Muhammad for that reason allowed Christians and Jews to continue to exist within its society as second-class citizens, whom it termed "the protected ones".

Lastly, one ought to mention as a special factor in the relationship between Islam and Christianity the fact that from the early Middle Ages the Muslim Empire and Christendom existed together in the area of the Mediterranean Sea, where they were time after time engaged in armed conflict (the crusades) as well as a warfare of the spirit. The latter was indeed only to be expected in that Islam, taking its cue from the Koran, was severely critical of certain ideas central to Christianity (and to Judaism). Nevertheless that "spiritual conflict" constitutes one of the most shameful chapters in the history of the Church. If there is to be any real understanding and any fair assessment of the one by the other, both Christianity and Islam will need to clear away whole mountains of misapprehension; a task which on both sides calls for much patience and no less a degree of candour.

With Israel however the relationship is of a quite different and much more fundamental character. Israel, according to the Bible, is part and parcel of God's revelational activity, through His Covenant with that people. Jesus Christ comes from out of the Jewish people, from out of Israel; and it is as the Messiah of Israel – though rejected by the Jews of His own day – that He is also Messiah for the whole world. Israel is still held by the God who has revealed Himself in Jesus Christ, is still retained within His Covenant; and so the "Old" and the "New" Covenants remain intimately bound up together in the Divine Revelation. The Church has not superseded Israel or usurped her place. The Church, as Paul says in Romans 11:17, is a branch grafted on to God's ancient "tree of the Covenant". She is to be the Church of the "nations" (the heathen); but in proclaiming the gospel of Jesus, as it is her duty to do, she has as part of her vocation to address herself to the Jews of every age, including the present.

This altogether unique connection of the Church with Israel, this intimate bond which she has with Israel in the revelational activity of one and the same God, is part of her very nature. Just as she has done with Islam, so too in her dealings with Israel the Christian Church has nearly always been forgetful of this connection and, what is more, has regarded Israel and behaved towards her in an inhuman way, calculated to bring disgrace upon the Church herself. Only in the last quarter of a century have matters really begun to take a better turn in this respect.

The Church's very special relationship to Israel, and again to Islam, does not preclude her in any way, therefore, from proclaiming the gospel of Jesus Christ in and to those "religions" and their adherents. The gospel is universal: that is, it is intended for and is addressed to the entire world. If anyone should want to exclude Israel and Islam from this, he would very soon discover that the rest of the world would have to be left out of it too, seeing that *every* religion can plead its determination and desire to find its own way to God, or to whatever "it" may be, and to preserve its own typical form of religion and culture.

However, as the Christian Church has laid upon herself such a heavy burden of guilt, historically speaking, with respect to Israel and the Islamic world, one must realize that deep-rooted and perfectly understandable feelings of aversion and of hostility towards the preaching of Jesus Christ (feelings stirred up by the behaviour of the Christian Church herself) are still very much alive in those quarters. One might take as a guide in this matter, so far as both Israel and the Muslim world are concerned, the revealing suggestion contained in some words of the American Rabbi Stephen S. Wise: "There is but one influence, one power, in the world which can ever succeed in persuading Jews to claim Jesus as their own (and he is their own): namely, a real devotion to brotherliness on the part of Christians in their daily lives."

16

Joachim Wach, "General Revelation and the Religions of the World"

Friedrich Schleiermacher's impact on Protestant thought in the nine-teenth and early twentieth centuries was enormous. For those inspired by his exemplary work and approach, this impact was translated by some into a strong interest in the religious feeling, consciousness, or experience of non-Christians. Those who studied the history of religion under the canopy of Protestant liberalism could not but come to theological conclusions about their historical investigations. One scholar who fits this general liberal Protestant description was the twentieth-century scholar Joachim Wach (1898–1955).

Wach was of Jewish descent, but his family had become Protestant. He was trained as a historian of religion and became a professor at the University of Leipzig, but under the threat of Nazism in the 1930s he became one of many émigrés to the United States, where he became a professor of history of religion first at Brown University and then at the University of Chicago.

In his essay "General Revelation and the Religions of the World," which he composed relatively late in his life, Wach reflected on his work as a historian of religion and as a Christian. He saw a relation between the study of religion and Christian theology and a parallel relation between general revelation and special revelation. In fact, Wach understood the history of religion as a kind of experiential response to general revelation, to the powerful and various manifes-tations of the Holy – or God. The world's religions, he thought, were preparations for Christianity; and the fulfillment of all general revel-ation is the special and final revelation of God in Jesus Christ. While remaining Christocentric, thus, Wach's position includes non-Christians in God's plan for the cosmos: knowledge of God, truth, and even salvation are included as possibilities or even as realities.

In the text which follows, the footnotes in the source edition have been omitted.

267

The Text

"At the heart of the theological issue today lies the problem of revelation."
(L. S. Thornton, *Revelation and the Modern World*, p. 129)

We shall proceed in this discussion upon a topic central to the field of the history of religions and of the comparative study of religions, on the assumption that we are all familiar, in broad outline, with recent developments in the study of religion which have tended to concentrate our attention on the problems of the nature of general revelation and its relation to special revelation. Such developments have taken place both in the last twenty-five or thirty years in *theology* and in the field of the *history of religions*. The best general statement on the problem in theology, it seems to me, has been given by Alan Richardson in his *Christian Apologetics* (1947). He has shown that, instead of contrasting natural (non-Christian) and revealed knowledge of God as had been done previously, the theology of liberalism eschewed the notion of revelation while neo-orthodox theology has been inclined to acknowledge only *one* special revelation. The famous controversies between Barth and Brunner, and between Hocking and Kraemer, illustrate this phase of theological discussion. Meanwhile, a highly important attempt at a constructive statement concerning the nature of general and of special revelation had been made by William Temple in his great work *Nature, Man and God* and in a briefer article in *Revelation*, edited by John Baillie. Here, you will remember, in Lecture XII of his book, entitled "Revelation and its Modes," Temple rejects an all too sharp distinction between the different works of God, "so as to regard some of these as constituting His self-revelation and the others as offering no such revelation." Here the famous passage occurs which may serve as a motto for our discussion:

> We affirm then, that unless all existence is a medium of Revelation, no particular revelation is possible ... If there is no ultimate Reality which is the ground of all else, then there is no God to be revealed ... Either all occurrences are in some degree revelations of God or else there is no such revelation at all ... Only if God is revealed in the rising of the sun in the sky can he be revealed in the rising of a son of man from the dead, only if he is revealed in the history of the Syrians and Philistines can he be revealed in the history of Israel.

Not only in theology but also in the history of religions the concept of general revelation has been stressed by those who have helped to overcome the era of historicism. We shall name here especially Nathan Soederblom, Rudolf Otto and G. van der Leeuw. Though all three men are theologians, the better part of their life work was dedicated to the history of religions, and that is why we feel that we are justified in claiming them for our field. Just a half-century ago, in 1903, very shortly after Troeltsch's *Die Absolutheit des Christentums* (1900), Soederblom published his

Source: *Understanding and Believing: Essays by Joachim Wach*, ed. Joseph Kitagawa.

booklet, *The Nature of Revelation*. "A revelation of God," he says there, "is present wherever a real religion is found. When God is known, it may be imperfectly and through a distorting medium, there he has in some degree allowed himself to become known, yes, made himself known." He does expressly reject the two theories proffered to explain "the existence of religious faith and truth outside the Biblical revelation through the interference of demons or the activity of man's reason." "No religion is a product of culture, all religion depends on revelation," says Soederblom with special reference to Troeltsch's thesis. And in a passage very similar to Temple's previously quoted statement, he refers to the elevated and powerful elements found in the "Babylonian and Assyrian expressions of piety" and claims that in "this age of world missions, it is high time that the church acquainted itself with the thought of the general revelation of God." Yet, "in Israel a new content of revelation comes in through new revealers," and in Jesus Christ we see the "fulfillment of revelation" – Soederblom uses this term which is so objectionable to Dr Kraemer – "the fullness of the Godhead bodily." "So Christianity," he says, "may be called revealed religion in a special sense," a "unique species of revelation."

Rudolf Otto, who may have been influenced by Soederblom's use of the term "the Holy," has, as the first among modern historians of religions, given real content to the notion of general revelation by his analysis of religious experience as a communion with the holy, and his demonstration of the ubiquity of the "*sensus numinis*." It is well-known that he indicates the relationship between special and general revelation, as he sees it, by the sharp contrast into which he places "the Son" as over against other charismatic men of God. But it has to be admitted that this powerful expression of a religious conviction by the author of *The Idea of the Holy* is not matched by an articulate statement of the methodological aspect of the problem.

A similar criticism, it seems, has to be levelled against the great modern historian of religions to whom we owe *Religion In Essence and Manifestation*, Gerardus van der Leeuw. And yet we feel that he is as much concerned with illumining the fact of general revelation as with pointing up the meaning and significance of the special revelation in Christ. It is characteristic that in his magnum opus he treats revelation in the section on "The World." When man will enter into contact with the world, he needs, according to van der Leeuw, revelation in order to be able to "follow God." Yet the Dutch scholar expressly rejects the distinction between general revelation which everyone could have and a special one which "was accessible only to one of a particular faith" ("*die einzig dem in bestimmter Weise Gläubigen geschenkt wäre*"). Rightly he stresses that revelation is never general in the sense that it would not be addressed to someone in particular; *all* revelation is, he says, particular in that it is given to *me* ("*Insofern sie immer mir ursprünglich gegeben ist*" – agreeing here with Christian existentialism). *Qua* phenomenologists – in the peculiar sense in which van der Leeuw uses this term – we have to regard as revelation "whatever offers itself as such." We can distinguish, though, between a genuine and a non-genuine revelatory experience ("*Offenbarungserlebnis?*"). G. van der Leeuw, who has contributed the article on "revelation" in RGG, believes that the historian of religions has to regard as revelation all that which claims to be such. I think it would be fair to say that the Dutch scholar assumes general revelation though he denies that the "*Elementarge-*

269

danke" or the notion of a religious a priori could do justice to the content of actual revelation. He wants to distinguish between *intuition* as it occurs in the arts and the sciences, and *revelation*; he assumes grades and gives a detailed account of the media of revelation at various stages of the development of religion. Revelation, according to van der Leeuw, may be experienced first in mana (that is: "powerful objects"); then in the Word; then in an inner voice; then in mediators and, finally in the incarnation of the Logos – a development toward the more personal modes.

With these teachings we have arrived at a juncture where it becomes evident that the *separatism* which characterizes much of the work in history of religions and in theology is in the process of being overcome. The *historian of religions* is ready to admit that he needs to transcend the purely empirical approach which since the end of the nineteenth century has limited him to description and cataloguing, and quite a few of the *theologians* are ready to see that they have to take note of and include in their constructive work the new material which the historians of religions have put at their disposal. The viewpoint from which this interpretation is to be undertaken, will for the Christian theologian be Christian principles. For the Jewish theologian it will be the Torah, and for the Mohammedan, the Islamic faith. It goes without saying that the great achievements of the preceding era in critical methods and historical research should be safeguarded, but that is not the same thing as treating them as aims in themselves. The last fifty years have witnessed a resurgence of a normative interest, the desire for an *articulation of our own faith*, an articulation which takes cognizance of the widening of the horizon which has taken place in the nineteenth century and which, above all, is firmly rooted in the tradition of our Christian faith. I am convinced that we have a great potential treasure-house in the writings of the Christian Fathers who were at their time facing the same basic problems in apologetics as we have to cope with. In his very stimulating lectures on *Revelation and the Modern Mind*, L. S. Thornton has illustrated from the writings of Irenaeus how singularly illuminating the concept of primordial revelation is for the interpretation of non-Christian religions in the light of general revelation. And the same Father has been quoted amply by Jean Daniélou in his *Salvation of the Nations*.

It remains for us to summarize now briefly the statement of one eminent modern thinker who has recently devoted an important work to our problem. I have in mind Paul Tillich's statement in the first volume of his *Systematic Theology*. There seems to be some ambiguity in the rather detailed section which deals with the "Reality of Revelation." He says that "there is no revelation in general," but what he means is that revelation is always had in a concrete situation, that there is, as he puts it, no "*Offenbarung überhaupt*." He definitely thinks of revelation in a pluralistic sense as he recognizes various fields and *media* which may become revelatory (nature, history, groups, individuals, the word – the latter not a medium in addition to other mediums but "a necessary element in all forms of revelation"). So Tillich stipulates on the history of religions a three-fold *preparation* for what he calls the *final revelation*, namely conservation, criticism, and anticipation. The second, the critical preparation, can be divided again into a mystical, a rational and a prophetic type. Though Tillich mentions only the history of Israel, the New Testament, and Church history in which this process takes place, we are, I think, not wrong in assuming that the history of religions generally shows us examples of such preparation. Tillich sees the center of the history of revelation dividing the whole process into preparing for and receiving of revelation. The bearer of the receiving revelation is the Christian Church. Religions and cultures outside it and ("even more") nations and churches within it, are in the stage of "preparation." But the Christian Church is based on the final revelation and is, as Tillich says, "supposed to receive it in a continuous process of reception, interpretation, and actualization." Definitely then, Tillich rejects both contentions that there is only *one* revelation (that in Jesus Christ), and that there are such everywhere and that none of them is ultimate. "The history of revelation is a necessary correlate of final revelation." A distinction is made rightly by Tillich between universal and general revelation, the former meaning "a special event with an all-embracing claim" while he identifies, as we saw, general revelation with "revelation in general." Because of the intimacy of the unity with the Father and because of the totality of his sacrifice, Jesus Christ is the universally valid, final revelation.

Thus, we have found some agreement between some theologians and historians of religions as to *the fact of general revelation* or revelation outside of Christianity. From here on, then, we will not be further concerned in this lecture with the argument of those who deny this fact, in the traditional black and white fashion or otherwise with or without an acquaintance with non-Christian religions. We shall rather discuss *the nature of general revelation*, and further, the form which it takes in other religions.

We agree with Rudolf Otto that the *sensus numinis* is universal. All men possess potentially a sense of the Divine. How can we account for that theologically? Some have pointed to the Holy Spirit who comes into the world to enlighten every man. Thus, according to L. S. Thornton, "as all religion presupposes revelation, so all genuine response to revelation is made under the influence of God's spirit." Therefore J. Daniélou is right when he says: "The task of the missionary is rather one of *redirecting* the *religious sense* so that it may attain its true object. He is not faced with a *religious vacuum* which he must fill, as it were, from zero." Important implications for the theory and practice of missions follow, but this is not the place to develop them.

We cannot agree with a definition which the Indian theologian Dr Moses suggests in his thesis on *Religious Truth and the Relation Between Religions* when, following A. Richardson, he calls general revelation "revelation in the world of nature, in the conscience and reason of man," and "special revelation" revelation in the events of history and in prophetic individuals. We rather hold that genuine religious experience is the apprehension of the *revelatum wherever it occurs*, that is, within whatever ethnic, cultural, social or religious context. That would mean that there could be revelation in Judaism, Islam, Hinduism, and Buddhism and many other religious communities besides Christianity. This may sound like an endorsement of the *relativism* of some representative of the *Religionsgeschichtliche Schule* past and present who refuse to go beyond the acknowledgment of general revelation. Over against this view we agree with its critics who claim that this is not enough and insist that there is particular revelation. We part ways with them when they insist that there can only be *one* particular revelation. There are Christians but also Jews, Mohammedans, Hindus, and Buddhists who do so insist. Actually, every instance of general revelation is a particular one as we have previously implied. It is arrogance to subsume all non-Christian expression of religious experience under the heading of "human self-enfolding." Does this recognition of a plurality of particular revelation reduce God's revelation in Jesus Christ to *one* other *among many*? No, its uniqueness is not only not obscured, but actually rendered more credible by lesser revelations. I will not respect and love my friend less because I know other people whom I respect, but more so. Canon Richardson has rightly said that we do not need to denigrate other religions because we are Christians. We agree with Dr Kraemer when he answers the question: "Who owns revelation?" Neither Christians, nor Jews, nor non-Christians can pretend or boast to be in possession of it: "Revelation," he says, is *eo ipso* an act of divine condescension. The real Christian contention is not: "We have the revelation and not you," but pointing gratefully and humbly to Christ: "It has pleased God to reveal himself fully and decisively in Christ; repent, believe, adore." This is exactly right. It is also true that the special revelation in Christ "contradicts and upsets all human religious aspiration," that the Cross is in a sense "antagonistic to all human aspirations," that is, Christian and non-Christian aspirations, Many faiths, *one* Cross!

The problem of general revelation is not identical with that of the so-called points of contact, which is really a question of missionary approach, nor with that of spontaneity and receptivity, divine and humane. As all revelation must be acknowledged to depend on divine *grace* for its reception, as well as its occurrence, there is no difference between general and special revelation in this point. J. Daniélou errs when he says, "In other religions grace is not present." As Rudolf Otto has shown, in his study of *Christianity and the Indian Religion of Grace*, there is a tremendously strong awareness of divine grace in theistic Hinduism. The same is true of Mahayana Buddhism, as L. de la Vallée-Poussin has proved. There are two other aspects which have to be considered in a discussion of general revelation: In which sense are we to speak of it if we wish to conceive of general revelation as *"preparation*," and what about the problem of *truth*? There is good reason to refer to the religion of ancient Israel as preparatory. "It appears," says H. R. Niebuhr, "that we have religious knowledge apart from revelation in our history since we can speak about God with members of non-Christian communities, not only with Jews whose memories we largely have made our own but with Mohammedans and Hindus, using words which appear to have some common meaning." Among most Christian scholars there will be agreement that the apprehensions of the Hebrew faith are preparatory for the Gospel in a sense in which no other particular revelation is. This is recognized in the old Messianic scheme of promise and fulfillment ("*Weissagung und Erfüllung*") and in the conception of a "*Heilsgeschichte.*" I might remind you in this connection of Will Herberg's interesting address on "Judaism and Christianity: Their Unity and Difference." In his *Salvation of the Nations*, J. Daniélou has enumerated three points which mark the advance of the Hebrew over other "revelation," namely the understanding that God, as the living God, intervenes directly in the life of the people, the understanding of and stress upon the fundamental unity of God, and, finally the understanding that God reveals himself as the God of holiness.

We do not share Wilhelm Herrmann's scepticism. In *The Communion of the Christian with God*, he doubts that we could understand even the religious life of a pious

Israelite because the facts which he interpreted as revelation do not have this power for us anymore. Recent attempts to dissolve the close relationship between the two Testaments have only renewed our conviction of their indissoluble unity which we have to uphold also against distinguished non-Western Christian theologians.

We still remain within the *chronological* order when we attribute a modicum of preparatory character to the religions of ancient Iran, Greece, and Rome, including the so-called mystery cults, and perhaps those of Egypt and the ancient Near East. This is not only to claim historical connections, a pursuit with which the scholars of the *Religionsgeschichtliche Schule* were preeminently engaged, but rather to recognize, *phenomenologically* speaking, a type of religious experience which, because it was characterized by a strong sense of the awesome mystery of the nature of ultimate Reality, may be called *preparatory*, notwithstanding profound differences. Now what shall we say with regard to religions which, antedating Christianity, show no historical or causal relations or none which could be documented? That would include the so-called primitive religions, lower and higher; those of the middle type, dead and alive, such as the religions of the Aztecs, Teutons, Japanese, and finally world religions such as Hinduism, Buddhism, Confucianism. (Islam, dependent upon Christianity, and the faiths derived from it are in a special category.) Here only a *phenomenological* approach can help.

The first, and most important of all questions, to ask – and here we have an unexpected ally in Karl Barth – is: how is Ultimate Reality, how is *God apprehended?* As Christians we know of the supreme manifestation of God in Christ Jesus that is and must remain our standard, but that cannot mean that the apprehensions of the Divine which occur in these religions is to be seen as nothing and treated on a par with the claims of cults of *finite* values such as blood, soil, class, etc., as Barth suggests. It is not that we wish to play up the intimations which we find in an analysis of the religious experience of these religious communities to compete with the claim that the Christian kerygma has upon us, but rather to illumine the latter in the light of these experiences and their expression. And it is not necessary that we examine the non-Christian expressions of the experience of God, by viewing them under catgories borrowed from Christian dogmatics and the Christian doctrine of God. We should also seriously consider what implications these non-Christian apprehensions have for thought, life, and conduct in those communities. But there is more to general revelation even than that. There is no doubt in my mind that it is significant if in some religions, e.g., in primitive religions a very incisive *preparation* has to precede any attempt to enter into contact with the supreme reality – vigils, fasting, purifications, meditations. It is also significant that some religions seem to stress heavily what R. Otto has designated as the *mysterium tremendum*: the religions of Melanesia, of Western and equatorial Africa, of the Mayas, Aztecs, Assyrians, Japanese, and Islam and the Lamaistic form of Buddhism. In others, especially the so-called mystical, the aspect of the *mysterium fascinosum* prevails. Let us consider one more important instance where it is justified to speak of preparation for the Gospel in non-Christian religions. F. Thomas Ohm, the outstanding German Catholic missionary expert, has gathered in a large volume the evidence for the many expressions for the *love of God* found in the various religions of the world.

Finally – as a third example – there is the degree to which the basic apprehension of the Divine includes a *moral* element. I think that R. Otto was rightly criticized by Dr Oman, Streeter, and others for failing to demonstrate adequately the interrelationship between the Holy and the Good in *The Idea of the Holy*. Recent studies in anthropology have provided theologians and philosophers with very much important material. There can be no question but that religions such as the Egyptian, Sumerian, Vedic-Brahmanic, and more especially Judaism, Islam, Buddhism, and Confucianism are far from prescribing indistinguishable or purely negative solutions to this problem. Max Mueller was not altogether wrong when he jotted down in his *Chips*: "An intuition of God, a sense of human weakness and dependence, a belief in a Divine government of the World, a distinction between good and evil and a hope of a better life, these are some of the radical elements of all religions."

All this goes to show that we have no right to treat non-Christian religions indiscriminately as a *massa perditionis*. The early Fathers of the Christian Church, especially the Alexandrians, were quite right in allowing for the notion of general revelation, and the Medieval Church was right to follow this lead. "The great pillars of the Catholic faith," says Otto Karrer in his *Religions of Mankind*, "from St Paul, Clement of Alexandria, St Augustine and St Gregory the Great, to Gorres, Mohler and Newman were no less convinced champions of Christian truth, because they combined their faith in the one holy Catholic Church with an open eye for all that was noble and worthy of reverence in the non-Christian world...." As late as the seventeenth century, Karrer has shown, Cardinal John de Lugo upheld this notion. (In Protestant theology this view still has to wait for recognition.) Thus he can say "that the adherents of religions and philosophies outside the Church or Christianity have saved their souls within their respective creeds, and have done so by the grace of God" attaching it to their good faith and teaching them "to cherish and put in practice those features of their worship, doctrine, philosophy and religious community which are true and good and from God."

We have indicated above some criteria by which to evaluate the apprehensions of the Divine in other religions. Another criterion is the degree of *awareness* and *articulation* of these apprehensions. The Australian native (or the Bushman or Hottentot) is aware of a numinous presence as his behaviour at the sound of the bull-roarer shows. He would not behave this way at the sight of any other finite object. But this awareness does not match that expressed by Iranian or Hindu men of God of the types of Arda Viraf or Manikka Vasaga. The highly sophisticated theological statements of a Moses Ibn Maimun, an al Ghazali or a Ramanuja, exhibit the highest degree of awareness as well as articulation of their vision and notion of God. Indeed it will surprise even those somewhat acquainted with non-Christian religions to what degree the differentiation of theological views is carried and how fine the distinctions which have been made. I should like to refer to Gardet and Anawati's *Introduction à la theologie musulmane*, recent studies in the Shaiva Siddhanta and Lamotte's commentary on the *Prajnaparamita-Sutra*, to name just these inquiries into and expositions of the development of doctrine in some major non-Christian religions.

We may also call "preparation" *worship* as it has been and is practiced outside of

Christianity. First of all is the very fact *that* in acts of *reverence* man seeks God, waits for him and is aware of his own numinous unworth vis-à-vis ultimate reality, as R. Otto calls this feeling. We find that many a non-Christian act of worship has a closer resemblance to our own attitude of life if we be religious than to the indifferent one of the sceptic or the contemptuous one of the modern atheist. The laudable attempt to do away with all idolatry and idolatrous forms of worship may lead to the creation of a deplorable vacuum such as exists among many preliterate peoples who have been led to abandon their traditional ways, without having something better to replace them. The cultivation of a genuine sense of *awe* I should consider a very important *praeparatio evangelica*. Though it would be wrong to measure the nearness of religion to true worship by the complexity of its cultus – just as it would be wrong to measure it by the absence of any and all, it is true that certain genuine and meaningful ways by which communion with the Divine may be facilitated and preserved and which have been lost or are not shared in other religious communities, could well be regarded as "preparatory." Prayer, fasting, meditation, certain forms of discipline are some of these forms. History shows us that a purely *spiritualistic* interpretation of worship is difficult to maintain and easily leads to its evaporation. It is well and good to spiritualize the notion of *sacrifice*, but it may be asked if a sacrifice with the right intuition might not be more acceptable in the eyes of God than the complete absence of all sacrificial intention so often found in modern Western man. If the author of one of the finest books on worship, Evelyn Underhill, is right in stating that worship is the heart of religion, then, it seems to me, its presence, its degree of intensity, its nature and form would be of the utmost importance in evaluating cultus where we find it. Here too we may see a *praeparatio evangelica*.

There is, finally, wherever religion is found some form of *togetherness*. The Christian knows his fellowship to be unique as the Body of Christ. But here also we feel obliged to ask: is all other associating and covenanting just one *massa perditionis* or may we regard as "preparation" religious communities, communities of believers in the non-Christian world? It is easy to point out the heterogeneity of all natural religious groupings among men, be it on a basis of consanguinity, locality or any other such principle. But what do we have to say in view of the fact that the religious community which is legitimately referred to as the forerunner of the ecclesia, namely, the Hebrew *Qahal*, is of the type of natural grouping based on ties of blood whereas the Buddhist Sangha resembles much more closely the ecclesia by being a *specifically* religious association? This latter type actually occurs already on the level of so-called preliterate societies in the form of the secret – and even more the mystery – societies. This does not imply equating the Christian notion of the church with that of the mystery association of the ancient Greco-Roman-Oriental world – as has been done frequently in the past – if we see in the principle of *spiritual relationship and brotherhood* a *praeparatio* for the profoundest notion of the communion of saints. Or again we may find that the respect paid to the spiritual father, teacher, *guru* in various parts of the world, contrasts favorably with the lack of reverence or understanding of what charisma means in our own supposedly Christian civilization. May not a true follower of Christ feel more at home in a *gurukula* in the midst of earnest disciples rather than in the typical bourgeois congregation or in any stereotyped cult-group?

All of this implies a criticism of Kraemer's stress in his *Christian Message in a non-Christian World*, upon the *monolithic* character of religious structures and institutions. These are, of course, in a sense, unified wholes: Judaism, Zoroastrianism, Hinduism, Buddhism, Confucianism, and the so-called primitive religions.

Nobody will regard these colossal institutions *in toto* as a "preparation for Christ." But Kraemer dispenses himself too easily this way from the task of carefully scrutinizing the *composing elements*.

The historian of religions will study them and, because he must be more than a registrar of facts and phenomena, he will attempt to *evaluate* them. Just as the Christian theologian will evaluate elements in the Hebrew religion differently according to their affinity to the Christian kerygma, so he will be impressed by various apprehensions, notions, or attitudes in Islam, Hinduism, or Buddhism in differing ways. Last year's *Journal of Bible and Religion* carried two interesting articles on "Reason and Experience" and on "Mutual Love" in Mahayana Buddhism. Once more we wish to take issue with Dr Kraemer who criticizes sharply in his Madras paper the term *"fulfillment."* "It is," he says, "mistaken ... To describe the religious pilgrimage of mankind as a preparation or a leading up to a so-called consummation or fulfillment in Christ." We agree with his designation of Christ as the *crisis* of all religion and with his statement that "God as he is revealed in Jesus Christ is contrary to the sublimest pictures we made of him before we knew of him in Jesus Christ," but we reject his formula: *continuity* or *discontinuity* – the title he gave characteristically to his contribution in the *Madras* volume. Of course, "the Veda, the Koran, and the Gospel do not make a coherent scheme" (as Chenciah admits to Kraemer), of course they do not answer the same questions. We would never claim that. Even Bultmann says rightly: "The Christian faith does not criticize from its standpoint the quest for God in non-Christian religions, which it can only perceive and clarify, but rather the *answer* which is given by non-Christian religions." Dr Kraemer disavows any right to see in the Persian religion, which even Brunner declares comes the closest of the non-Christian faiths to Christianity, anything related, because "the Mazdean believer is the courageous and self-confident fighter for God whereas the man who lives by the faith of Christ is a pardoned sinner." This is right but does not prove that in other ways (insistence on truthfulness, purity, sincerity) Zoroastrianism would not represent a "preparation," compared to some of the crude and ethically insensitive notions of certain primitive religions or the questionable sensuousness of certain Hindu and Buddhist cults (Sahajiya, Tantrism).

Dr David G. Moses suggests in his previously mentioned book that *fulfillment* need not signify *continuation*. Quite rightly he speaks of "fulfillment by repudiation." In the words of Alan Richardson, "Special revelation is not a concrete illustration of general revelation but a correction and transvaluation of it."

What we are advocating here is not some sort of *syncretism*, nor are we *relativists*. Our allegiance is to *Christ* and we do deem him the crisis of religions, Christian and non-Christian. But we feel that in the physical and spiritual struggle which is going on in the world today, we simply cannot afford and should not even want to deny that general revelation of God includes the other faiths. In the words of a Catholic author (P. de Montcheuil): "Christianity need not adapt itself to successive philosophies but it must take into account the spiritual experiences from which those philosophies are born." Dr Kraemer says, "the problem whether and if so where, and in how far God, i.e., the God and Father of Jesus Christ, the only God we Christians know – has been and is working in the religious history of the world and in man – is a baffling and awful problem." Indeed it is. We should therefore give it the most painstaking attention. Though we cannot anticipate the result of labors which will occupy scholars for perhaps the rest of this century at least, we should think that, to stay with Kraemer's two examples, we should side with Clement rather than with Karl Barth here. "General revelation," to quote him again, "does not mean to the Alexandrian father that all religious men have the true knowledge of God, but that all mankind is instructed and prepared for Christ when he comes, the religious history of mankind being a unity in which the Incarnation of Christ is the culmination point." For Barth all religions are – we add: only – "*Unglaube*" because "they do not constitute a real response to God's self-manifestation in Jesus Christ." The history which for Schopenhauer was a "*semper eadem sed aliter*," is for the Swiss theologian and for his Dutch followers, the endless and manifold repetition of endeavors at self-justification. We think that it is not impossible to reconcile both the belief in general revelation and belief in the Incarnation.

In the last chapter of his book on *The Meaning of Revelation*, Prof. H. R. Niebuhr says, "Revelation means God, God who discloses himself to us through our history. As our knower, our author, our judge and our only Savior." The way which man is traveling toward a realization of this insight is identical with the history of religions. In this sense all history is potentially "*Heilsgeschichte*," or as Dr D. Moses puts it, "all religions are 'continuous' in the sense that they are all attempts to meet the fundamental religious needs and aspirations of men everywhere." More accurate still is Dr Farquhar's statement in his classic, *The Crown of Hinduism*, which Friedrich von Hügel quotes in the first volume of his Essays: "Neither is any one religion alone true in the sense that all others are merely so much sheer error; nor, again, are they all equally true; but while all contain some truth, they not only differ each from the other in the points on which they are true but also in the amount of importance of the truth and power possessed."

One last word. An era in the history of our studies was marked when the attempts at construing a *unilineal* development in non-Christian religion, such as the eighteenth and nineteenth centuries had indulged in, came to a close at approximately the time of the First World War. It was followed by a period of resolute refraining from all tracing of progress, development or even growth. Where a registration of fact was deemed insufficient, typological schemes were suggested. We have mentioned G. van der Leeuw's *Religion in Essence and Manifestation* already as a highwater mark of these endeavors. Now the tide is turning again. Living in one world we wish to comprehend something of the religious history of man after having amassed so much material which concerns it, seeing it in its unity – without failing in our loyalty to Christ, our Savior and Redeemer. The Christian answer to the non-Christian religions cannot be disregard or contempt, it must be understanding. That is, as Christians, we are convinced that man is created by God and thus that man may seek and find him, the same God who revealed himself in Christ and is Redeemer as well as Creator. Because in the Incarnation and in the Crucifixion the supreme love of God is revealed unambiguously, as nowhere else, we have to see in this particular disclosure God's final revelation. Because God created not only Europeans and Americans but Africans and Indians, Chinese and Japanese, it will also take Africans and Indians, Chinese and Japanese to apprehend this truth fully. Much misunderstanding and scandal could have been avoided if that could always have been understood by Western Christians. Some Westerners and many Easterners had seen this, but many of the former thought that Christianity as such had failed. So they were ready to abandon it in favor of an Eastern cult or a so-called world-faith. Many and not the least gifted among the latter, after shedding their traditional beliefs are driven into scepticism, thinly disguised as "scientific world-view," because they are not made to feel that they too are called to help in the appropriation of the meaning of the Christian kerygma. "Christianity," Baron von Hügel has written, "can, never ought to, satisfy just simply what men of this or that particular race desire, that and nothing else; Christianity is extant chiefly to make us grow, and not simply to suit us with clothes fitting exactly to the growth already attained." The great text of the historian of religions thus becomes the Epistle to the Hebrews (Chap. II), "So the God who revealed himself continues to reveal Himself – the one God of all times and places." Or, to quote Godfrey Phillips, "The universal religious life of mankind is the context in which Christian affirmations reveal their fullest meaning. The general revelation of God, partial and many-sided, which has given rise to multitudinous forms of religion on the earth, is the best preface to the special revelation in history of which Jesus Christ is the center."

17

Paul Tillich, "Christianity Judging Itself in the Light of Its Encounter with the World Religions"

The German Protestant theologian Paul Tillich (1886–1965) became interested in the problem of religious pluralism late in his life. An émigré from Nazi Germany in the 1930s, Tillich taught at Union Theological Seminary, Harvard Divinity School, and the University of Chicago. In his last years, he became convinced that Christian theology's attempt since the Enlightenment to engage modern atheism was an insufficient strategy, for just as pressing for Christian thought is the need to enter into conversation with the religions of the world. After his famous and determinative visit to Japan, Tillich delivered a series of lectures at Columbia University which were published under the title *Christianity and the Encounter of the World Religions*. In the last of the lectures (reproduced here), he raised the question of the criteria for Christianity's judgment of itself in the light of its encounter with the world religions. He argued that the key criterion is participation in the spiritual power of the Christ-event, the power which makes Christianity dynamic. Rather than seeking to convert non-Christians, Tillich argued, Christians should seek to penetrate to the depth of their own tradition and see how it bursts the bonds of its own particularity. So doing reveals a spiritual freedom which in turn unveils a vision of spiritual presence in non-Christian expressions of the ultimate meaning of human existence.

The Text

Under the general title, "Christianity and the Encounter of the World Religions," we gave first a view of the present situation, distinguishing between religions proper and secular quasi-religions. In drawing a map of their encounters all over the world we emphasized the fact that the most conspicuous encounters are those of the quasi-religions – Fascism, Communism, liberal humanism – with the primitive as well as the high religions, and that in consequence of this situation all religions have the common problem: how to encounter secularism and the quasi-religions based on it.

In the second chapter, under the title, "Christian Principles of Judging Non-Christian Religions," we tried to show a long line of Christian universalism affirming revelatory experiences in non-Christian religions, a line starting in the prophets and Jesus, carried on by the Church Fathers, interrupted for centuries by the rise of Islam and of Christian anti-Judaism, and taken up again in the Renaissance and the Enlightenment. This principle of universalism has been under continual attack by the opposite principle, that of particularity with the claim to exclusive validity, which has led to the unsettled and contradictory attitude of present-day Christianity towards the world religions. The same ambiguous attitude, we pointed out, is prevalent in the judgments of contemporary Christian leaders with respect to the quasi-religions and secularism generally.

In the third chapter, entitled "A Christian-Buddhist Conversation," we discussed, first, the problem of a typology of religions and suggested the use of a dynamic typology, based on polarities instead of antitheses, as a way of understanding the seemingly chaotic history of religions. As a most important example of such polarity Christianity and Buddhism were confronted, points of convergence and divergence shown, and the whole summed up in the two contrasting symbols, Kingdom of God and Nirvana. The chapter ended with the question: How can a community of democratic nations be created without the religions out of which liberal democracy in the Western world originally arose?

The last question leads us to the subject of this chapter, "Christianity Judging Itself in the Light of Its Encounter with the World Religions," meaning both religions proper and quasi-religions.

I

Let us consider first the basis of such self-judgment. Where does Christianity find its criteria? There is only one point from which the criteria can be derived and only one way to approach this point. The point is the event on which Christianity is based, and the way is the participation in the continuing spiritual power of this event, which is the appearance and reception of Jesus of Nazareth as the Christ, a symbol which

Source: Paul Tillich, *Christianity and the Encounter of the World Religions*.

stands for the decisive self-manifestation in human history of the source and aim of all being. This is the point from which the criteria of judging Christianity in the name of Christianity must be taken.

The way to this point is through participation, but how can one participate in an event of the past? Certainly not by historical knowledge, although we must listen to the witnesses to what happened; certainly not by acceptance of a tradition, although only through tradition can one be in living contact with the past; certainly not by subjecting oneself to authorities past or present, although there is no spiritual life without an actual (but not principal) dependence on authorities. Participation in an event of the past is only possible if one is grasped by the spiritual power of this event and through it is enabled to evaluate the witnesses, the traditions and the authorities in which the same spiritual power was and is effective.

It is possible, through participation, to discover in the appearance of the Christ in history the criteria by which Christianity must judge itself, but it is also possible to miss them. I am conscious of the fact that there is a risk involved, but where there is spirit, and not letter and law, there is always risk. This risk is unavoidable if one tries to judge Christianity in the name of its own foundation, but *if* it is done, it gives an answer to the question implied in the general subject of these lectures, "Christianity and the Encounter of the World Religions."

In the second chapter we discussed two tensions in the Christian self-interpretation, the first decisive for the relation of Christianity to the religions proper, and the second decisive for the relation of Christianity to the quasi-religions. The first is the tension between the particular and the universal character of the Christian claim; the second is the tension between Christianity as a religion and Christianity as the negation of religion. Both of these tensions follow from the nature of the event on which Christianity is based. The meaning of this event shows not in its providing a foundation for a new religion with a particular character (though this followed, unavoidably, with consequences partly creative and partly destructive, ambiguously mixed in church history), but it shows in the event itself, which preceded and judges these consequences. It is a personal life, the image of which, as it impressed itself on his followers, shows no break in his relation to God and no claim for himself in his particularity. What is particular in him is that he crucified the particular in himself for the sake of the universal. This liberates his image from bondage both to a particular religion – the religion to which he belonged has thrown him out – and to the religious sphere as such; the principle of love in him embraces the cosmos, including both the religions and the secular spheres. With this image, particular yet free from particularity, religious yet free from religion, the criteria are given under which Christianity must judge itself and, by judging itself, judge also the other religions and the quasi-religions.

II

On this basis Christianity has developed into a specific religion through a process of perpetuating the tradition of the Old Testament and, at the same time, of receiving elements from all the other confronted religions. As Harnack has said, Christianity in itself is a compendium of the history of religion. Although the first formative centuries were the most important in the whole development, the process has continued up to the present day. In it Christianity judged, was judged, and accepted judgment. The dynamic life it showed was nourished by the tension between judging the encountered religions in the strength of its foundation, and accepting judgment from them in the freedom its foundation gives. Christianity has in its very nature an openness in all directions, and for centuries this openness and receptivity was its glory. But there were two factors which limited more and more the freedom of Christianity to accept judgment: the hierarchical and the polemical. With the strengthening of the hierarchical authority it became increasingly difficult for it to recant or to alter decisions made by bishops, councils and, finally, Popes. The tradition ceased to be a living stream; it became an ever-augmented sum of immovably valid statements and institutions. But even more effective in this development was the polemical factor. Every important decision in the history of the church is the solution of a problem raised by conflicts in history, and a decision, once made, cuts off other possibilities. It closes doors, it narrows down. It increases the proclivity to judge, and it decreases the willingness to accept judgment. The worst consequence of this tendency was the split of the church in the period of the Reformation and the Counter Reformation. After that the glory of openness was lost to both sides. The church of the Counter Reformation was incomparably less able to encounter the other religions or quasi-religions than the early church had been, and in the Protestant churches, in spite of the freedom the Protestant principle gives, it was only the influence of secularism which again opened them to a creative encounter with other religions. One sometimes points to the skill with which missionaries, especially in Catholic orders, adapt their message and their demands to the pagan substance of a superficially converted group. But adaptation is not reception and does not lead to self-judgment. In the light of this consideration we must acknowledge the degree to which Christianity has become a religion instead of remaining a center of crystallization for all positive religious elements after they have been subjected to the criteria implied in this center. Much of the criticism directed against Christianity is due to this failure.

With this general view in mind I want now to give examples of the way in which Christianity both judged other religions and accepted judgment from them, and finally to show the inner-Christian struggle against itself as a religion, and the new vistas which open up in consequence of these struggles for the future encounters of Christianity with the world religions.

Strictly in the Jewish tradition, the early Christians judged polytheism as idolatry, or the service of demonic powers. This judgment was accompanied by anxiety and horror. Polytheism was felt to be a direct attack on the divinity of the divine, an attempt to elevate finite realities, however great and beautiful, to ultimacy in being and meaning. The glory of the Greek gods impressed the Christians as little as did the animal-shaped divinities of the "barbaric" nations. But there arose a counter-judgment: the cultivated adherents of polytheistic symbolism accused the Jews and Christians of atheism, because they denied the divine presence in every realm of being. They were accused of profanizing the world. Somehow they were themselves aware of this fact. They did not moderate their abhorrence of polytheism, but they found many concrete manifestations of the divine in the world, for instance, hypostatized qualities or functions of God like His "Wisdom" or His "Word" or His "Glory." They saw in nature and history traces of angelic and demonic powers. Further – and in this Christianity parted ways with Judaism – they affirmed a divine mediator between God and man, and through him a host of saints and martyrs – mediators between the mediator and man, so to speak. In this respect Christianity has accepted influences from the polytheistic element of religion. In a secular form the conflict is alive even today as the conflict between a romantic philosophy of nature and its religious-artistic expressions, on the one hand, and the total profanization of nature and its moral and technical subjection to man's purposes, on the other.

I have chosen this example of a most radical judgment of another religious type by Christianity, which yet did not prevent the Christians from accepting judgment from it in turn.

Although it is itself based on the Old Testament, Christianity judged and still judges Judaism, but because of its dependence upon it, is most inhibited from accepting judgment from it. Nevertheless, Christians have done so since the removal of the barriers of medieval suppression which was born of anxiety and fanaticism. For almost two hundred years Christianity, by way of liberal humanism, has received Jewish judgment indirectly and has transformed the critique into self-judgment. It was partly the resurgence of pagan elements in the national and territorial churches, and partly the suppression of the self-critical spirit in all churches, which called forth a prophetic reaction in democratic and socialist Christians.

I would like to be able to say more about judgment and the acceptance of judgment in relation to Islam, but there is little to say. The early encounter resulted only in mutual rejection. Are there possibilities for Christian self-judgment in these encounters? There are at two points – in the solution of the racial problem in Islam and in its wisdom in dealing with the primitive peoples. But this is probably all.

Another example of a radical rejection in connection with elements of acceptance was the dualistic religion of Persia, introduced into Christianity by Gnostic groups and supported by the Greek doctrine of matter resisting the spirit. The fight against dualism and the rejection of a God of darkness with creative powers of his own were consequences of the Old Testament doctrine of creation. For this Christianity fought, but the Christians were, at the same time, impressed by the seriousness with which dualism took the problem of evil; Augustine was for this reason a Manichean for ten years. There are also many Christians today who, with Augustine and his Protestant followers up to Karl Barth, accept the "total depravity" of man, a dualistic concept which was judged and accepted at the same time, and is being judged and accepted in present discussions for and against the existentialist view of man's predicament.

Christianity had encountered mysticism long before the modern opening up of India. A decisive struggle was made against Julian the Apostate's ideas of a restitution of paganism with the help of Neoplatonic mysticism. When we look at this struggle we find, on both sides, arguments similar to those used in our contemporary encounters with Indian mysticism. The Christian theologians were and are right in criticizing the nonpersonal, nonsocial and nonhistorical attitude of the mystical religions, but they had to accept the countercriticism of the mystical groups that their own personalism is primitive and needs interpretation in transpersonal terms. This has been at least partly accepted by Christian theologians who, in agreement with the long line of Christian mystics, have asserted that without a mystical element – namely, an experience of the immediate presence of the divine – there is no religion at all.

The examples could be multiplied, but these may suffice to illustrate the rhythm of criticism, countercriticism and self-criticism throughout the history of Christianity. They show that Christianity is not imprisoned in itself and that in all its radical judgments about other religions some degree of acceptance of counterjudgments took place.

III

We have discussed the judgment of Christianity against itself on the basis of the judgment it received from outside. But receiving external criticism means transforming it into self-criticism. If Christianity rejects the idea that it is a religion, it must fight in itself everything by which it becomes a religion. With some justificiation one can say that the two essential expressions of religion in the narrower sense are myth and cult. If Christianity fights against itself as a religion it must fight against myth and cult, and this it has done. It did so in the Bible, which, one should not forget, is not only a religious but also an antireligious book. The Bible fights for God against religion. This fight is rather strong in the Old Testament, where it is most powerful in the attack of the prophets against the cult and the polytheistic implications of the popular religion. In harsh criticism the whole Israelitic cult is rejected by some early prophets, and so is the mythology which gives the national gods ultimate validity. The God of Israel has been "demythologized" into the God of the universe, and the gods of the nations are "nothings." The God of Israel rejects even Israel in the moment when she claims Him as a national god. God denies His being *a* god.

The same fight against cult and myth is evident in the New Testament. The early records of the New Testament are full of stories in which Jesus violates ritual laws in order to exercise love, and in Paul the whole ritual law is dispossessed by the appearance of the Christ. John adds demythologization to deritualization: the eternal life is here and now, the divine judgment is identical with the acceptance or rejection of the light which shines for everybody. The early church tried to demythologize the idea of God and the meaning of the Christ by concepts taken from the Platonic-Stoic tradition. In all periods theologians tried hard to show the transcendence of the divine over the finite symbols expressing him. The idea of "God above God" (the phrase I used in *The Courage To Be*) can be found implicitly in all patristic theology. Their encounter with pagan polytheism, i.e., with gods on a finite basis, made the Church Fathers extremely sensitive to any concept which would present

God as being analogous to the gods of those against whom they were fighting. Today this particular encounter, namely with polytheism, no longer has manifest reality; therefore the theologians have become careless in safeguarding their idea of a personal God from slipping into "henotheistic" mythology (the belief in *one* god who, however, remains particular and bound to a particular group).

The early theologians were supported by the mystical element which in the fifth century became a powerful force in Christianity. The main concept of mysticism is immediacy: immediate participation in the divine Ground by elevation into unity with it, transcending all finite realities and all finite symbols of the divine, leaving the sacramental activities far below and sinking cult and myth into the experienced abyss of the Ultimate. Like the prophetical and the theological critique, this is an attack against religion for the sake of religion.

The ritual element was devaluated by the Reformation, in the theology of both the great reformers and of the evangelical radicals. One of the most cutting attacks of Luther was direted against the *vita religiosa*, the life of the *homini religiosi*, the monks. God is present in the secular realm; in this view Renaissance and Reformation agree. It was an important victory in the fight of God against religion.

The Enlightenment brought a radical elimination of myth and cult. What was left was a philosophical concept of God as the bearer of the moral imperative. Prayer was described by Kant as something of which a reasonable man is ashamed if surprised in it. Cult and myth disappear in the philosophy of the eighteenth century, and the Church is redefined by Kant as a society with moral purposes.

All this is an expression of the religious or quasi-religious fight against religion. But the forces which were fighting to preserve Christianity as a religion were ultimately stronger, in defense and counterattack. The main argument used in the counterattacks is the observation that the loss of cult and myth is the loss of the revelatory experience on which every religion is based. Such experience needs self-expression to continue, and that means it needs mythical and ritual elements. Actually they are never lacking. They are present in every religion and quasi-religion, even in their most secularized forms. An existential protest against myth and cult is possible only in the power of myth and cult. All attacks against them have a religious background, which they try to conceal, but without success. We know today what a secular myth is. We know what a secular cult is. The totalitarian movements have provided us with both. Their great strength was that they transformed ordinary concepts, events, and persons into myths, and ordinary performances into rituals; therefore they had to be fought with other myths and rituals – religious and secular. You cannot escape them, however you demythologize and deritualize. They always return and you must always judge them again. In the fight of God against religion the fighter for God is in the paradoxical situation that he has to use religion in order to fight religion.

It is a testimony to present-day Christianity that it is aware of this situation. We have mentioned the opposition to the concept of religion in the philosophy of religion as one of the symptoms of this fight. We have used the word demythologize. We have used the term quasi-religion to indicate that man's ultimate concern can express itself in secular terms. We find contemporary theologians (like Bonhöffer martyred by the Nazis) maintaining that Christianity must become secular, and that God is present in what we do as citizens, as creative artists, as friends, as lovers of nature, as workers in a profession, so that it may have eternal meaning. Christianity for these men has become an expression of the ultimate meaning in the actions of our daily life. And this is what it should be.

And now we have to ask: What is the consequence of this judgment of Christianity of itself for its dealing with the world religions? We have seen, first of all, that it is a mutual judging which opens the way for a fair valuation of the encountered religions and quasi-religions.

Such an attitude prevents contemporary Christianity from attempting to "convert" in the traditional and depreciated sense of this word. Many Christians feel that it is a questionable thing, for instance, to try to convert Jews. They have lived and spoken with their Jewish friends for decades. They have not converted them, but they have created a community of conversation which has changed both sides of the dialogue. Some day this ought to happen also with people of Islamic faith. Most attempts to convert them have failed, but we may try to teach them on the basis of their growing insecurity in face of the secular world, and they may come to self-criticism in analogy to our own self-criticism.

Finally, in relation to Hinduism, Buddhism, and Taoism, we should continue the dialogue which has already started and of which I tried to give an example in the third chapter. Not conversion, but dialogue. It would be a tremendous step forward if Christianity were to accept this! It would mean that Christianity would judge itself when it judges the others in the present encounter of the world religions.

But it would do even more. It would give a new valuation to secularism. The attack of secularism on all present-day religions would not appear as something merely negative. If Christianity denies itself as a religion, the secular development could be understood in a new sense, namely as the indirect way which historical destiny takes to unite mankind religiously, and this would mean, if we include the quasi-religions, also politically. When we look at the formerly pagan, now Communist, peoples, we may venture the idea that the secularization of the main groups of present-day mankind may be the way to their religious transformation.

This leads to the last and most universal problem of our subject: Does our analysis demand either a mixture of religions or the victory of one religion, or the end of the religious age altogether? We answer: None of these alternatives! A mixture of religions destroys in each of them the concreteness which gives it its dynamic power. The victory of *one* religion would impose a particular religious answer on all other particular answers. The end of the religious age – one has already spoken of the end of the Christian or the Protestant age – is an impossible concept. The religious principle cannot come to an end. For the question of the ultimate meaning of life cannot be silenced as long as men are men. Religion cannot come to an end, and a particular religion will be lasting to the degree in which it negates itself as a religion. Thus Christianity will be a bearer of the religious answer as long as it breaks through its own particularity.

The way to achieve this is not to relinquish one's religious tradition for the sake of a universal concept which would be nothing but a concept. The way is to penetrate into the depth of one's own religion, in devotion, thought and action. In the depth of every living religion there is a point at which the religion itself loses its importance, and that to which it points breaks through its particularity, elevating it to spiritual freedom and with it to a vision of the spiritual presence in other expressions of the ultimate meaning of man's existence.

This is what Christianity must see in the present encounter of the world religions.

18

Karl Rahner, "Christianity and the Non-Christian Religions"

The German theologian Karl Rahner (1904–84) was one of the most important Catholic theologians of the twentieth century. In the spirit of newness in the mid-twentieth-century Catholic Church, Rahner in his multivolume work *Theological Investigations* turned his attention, among a host of other theological issues, to the question of Christianity's relationship to non-Christian religions.

In the essay "Christianity and the Non-Christian Religions" Rahner argues that Christianity is the absolute religion and necessary for salvation but with an important qualification. Christianity, he says, comes to people as the true religion; and this encounter with Christianity occurs at different times. Until the time of such encounter, other religions, which contain elements of grace and faith, are valid means to salvation. After such encounter, however, such religions are no longer valid or lawful. In encountering members of such religions, Rahner argues, Christianity confronts not non-Christians but anonymous Christians, people already touched by truth, revelation, grace, and faith – and already on the way to salvation. The task for the Church is to transform such anonymous Christians into conscious, confessional Christians. The matter of the anonymous Christian is one to which Rahner returned in the *Theological Investigations* several times.

The Text

"Open Catholicism" involves two things. It signifies the fact that the Catholic Church is opposed by historical forces which she herself cannot disregard as if they were purely "worldly" forces and a matter of indifference to her but which, on the contrary, although they do not stand in a positive relationship of peace and mutual recognition to the Church, do have a significance for her. "Open Catholicism" means also the task of becoming related to these forces in order to understand their existence (since this cannot be simply acknowledged), in order to bear with and overcome the annoyance of their opposition and in order to form the Church in such a way that she will be able to overcome as much of this pluralism as should not exist, by understanding herself as the higher unity of this opposition. Open Catholicism means therefore a certain attitude towards the present-day pluralism of powers with different outlooks on the world. We do not, of course, refer to pluralism merely as a fact which one simply acknowledges without explaining it. Pluralism is meant here as a fact which ought to be thought about and one which, without denying that – in part at least – it should not exist at all, should be incorporated once more from a more elevated viewpoint into the totality and unity of the Christian understanding of human existence. For Christianity, one of the gravest elements of this pluralism in which we live and with which we must come to terms, and indeed the element most difficult to incorporate, is the pluralism of religions. We do not refer by this to the pluralism of Christian denominations. This pluralism too is a fact, and a challenge and task for Christians. But we are not concerned with it here. Our subject is the, at least in its ultimate and basic form, more serious problem of the different religions which still exist even in Christian times, and this after a history and mission of Christianity which has already lasted two thousand years. It is true, certainly, that all these religions together, including Christianity, are faced today with an enemy which did not exist for them in the past. We refer to the decided lack of religion and the denial of religion in general. This denial, in a sense, takes the stage with the ardour of a religion and of an absolute and sacred system which is the basis and the yard-stick of all further thought. This denial, organized on the basis of a State, represents itself as *the* religion of the future – as the decided, absolute secularization of human existence excluding all mystery. No matter how paradoxical this may sound, it does remain true that precisely this state of siege in which religion in general finds itself, finds one of its most important weapons and opportunities for success in the fact that humanity is so torn in its religious adherence. But quite apart from this, this pluralism is a greater threat and a reason for greater unrest for Christianity than for any other religion. For no other religion – not even Islam – maintains so absolutely that it is *the* religion, the one and only valid revelation of the one living God, as does the Christian religion. The fact of the pluralism of religions, which endures and still from time to time becomes virulent anew even after a history

Source: Karl Rahner, *Theological Investigations*, vol. 5, trans. K.-H. Kruger.

of two thousand years, must therefore be the greatest scandal and the greatest vexation for Christianity. And the threat of this vexation is also greater for the individual Christian today than ever before. For in the past, the other religion was in practice the religion of a completely different cultural environment. It belonged to a history with which the individual only communicated very much on the periphery of his own history; it was the religion of those who were even in every other respect alien to oneself. It is not surprising, therefore, that people did not wonder at the fact that these "others" and "strangers" had also a different religion. No wonder that in general people could not seriously consider these other religions as a challenge posed to themselves or even as a possibility for themselves. Today things have changed. The West is no longer shut up in itself; it can no longer regard itself simply as the centre of the history of this world and as the centre of culture, with a religion which even from this point of view (i.e. from a point of view which has really nothing to do with a decision of faith but which simply carries the weight of something quite self-evident) could appear as the obvious and indeed sole way of honouring God to be thought of for a European. Today everybody is the next-door neighbour and spiritual neighbour of every one else in the world. And so everybody today is determined by the intercommunication of all those situations of life which affect the whole world. Every religion which exists in the world is – just like all cultural possibilities and actualities of other people – a question posed, and a possibility offered, to every person. And just as one experiences someone else's culture in practice as something relative to one's own and as something existentially demanding, so it is also involuntarily with alien religions. They have become part of one's own existential situation – no longer merely theoretically but in the concrete – and we experience them therefore as something which puts the absolute claim of our own Christian faith into question. Hence, the question about the understanding of and the continuing existence of religious pluralism as a factor of our immediate Christian existence is an urgent one and part of the question as to how we are to deal with today's pluralism. This problem could be tackled from different angles. In the present context we simply wish to try to describe a few of those basic traits of a Catholic dogmatic interpretation of the non-Christian religions which may help us to come closer to a solution of the question about the Christian position in regard to the religious pluralism in the world of today. Since it cannot be said, unfortunately, that Catholic theology – as practised in more recent times – has really paid sufficient attention to the questions to be posed here, it will also be impossible to maintain that what we will have to say here can be taken as the common thought of Catholic theology. What we have to say carries, therefore, only as much weight as the reasons we can adduce, which reasons can again only be briefly indicated. Whenever the propositions to be mentioned carry a greater weight than this in theology, anyone trained in theology will realize it quite clearly from what is said. When we say that it is a question here of a *Catholic* dogmatic interpretation of the non-Christian religions, this is not meant to indicate that it is necessarily a question also of theories controverted among Christians themselves. It simply means that we will not be able to enter explicitly into the question as to whether the theses to be stated here can also hope to prove acceptable to Protestant theology. We say too that we are going to give a dogmatic interpretation, since we will pose our question not as empirical historians of religion but out of the self-understanding of Christianity itself, i.e. as dogmatic theologians.

1st Thesis: We must begin with the thesis which follows, because it certainly represents the basis in the Christian faith of the theological understanding of other religions. This thesis states that Christianity understands itself as the absolute religion, intended for all men, which cannot recognize any other religion beside itself as of equal right. This proposition is self-evident and basic for Christianity's understanding of itself. There is no need here to prove it or to develop its meaning. After all, Christianity does not take valid and lawful religion to mean primarily that relationship of man to God which man himself institutes on his own authority. Valid and lawful religion does not mean man's own interpretation of human existence. It is not the reflection and objectification of the experience which man has of himself and by himself. Valid and lawful religion for Christianity is rather God's action on men, God's free self-revelation by communicating himself to man. It is God's relationship to men, freely instituted by God himself and revealed by God in this institution. *This* relationship of God to man is basically the same for all men, because it rests of the Incarnation, death and resurrection of the one Word of God become flesh. Christianity is God's own interpretation in his Word of this relationship of God to man founded in Christ by God himself. And so Christianity can recognize itself as the true and lawful religion for all men only where and when it enters with existential power and demanding force into the realm of another religion and – judging it by itself – puts it in question. Since the time of Christ's coming – ever since he came in the flesh as the Word of God in absoluteness and reconciled, i.e. united the world with God by his death and resurrection, not merely theoretically but really – Christ and his continuing historical presence in the world (which we call "Church") is *the* religion which binds man to God. Already we must, however, make one point clear as regards this first thesis (which cannot be further developed and proved here). It is true that the Christian religion itself has its own pre-history which traces this religion back to the beginning of the history of humanity – even though it does this by many basic steps. It is also true that this fact of having a pre-history is of much greater importance, according to the evidence of the New Testament, for the theoretical and practical proof of the claim to absolute truth made by the Christian religion than our current fundamental theology is aware of. Nevertheless, the Christian religion as such has a beginning in history; it did not always exist but began at some point in time. It has not always and everywhere been *the* way of salvation for men – at least not in its historically tangible ecclesio-sociological constitution and in the reflex fruition of God's saving activity in, and in view of, Christ. As a historical quantity Christianity has, therefore, a temporal and spatial starting point in Jesus of Nazareth and in the saving event of the unique Cross and the empty tomb in Jerusalem. It follows from this, however, that this absolute religion – even when it begins to be this for practically all men – must come in a historical way to men, facing them as the only legitimate and demanding religion for them. It is therefore a question of whether this moment, when the existentially real demand is made by the absolute religion in its historically tangible form, takes place really at the same chronological moment for all men, or whether the occurrence of this moment has itself a history and thus is not chronologically simultaneous for all men, cultures and spaces of history. (This is a question which up until now Catholic theology has not thought through with sufficient clarity and reflection by really confronting it with the length and intricacy of real human time and history.) Normally the beginning of the objective obligation of the Christian message for all men – in other words, the abolition of the validity of the Mosaic religion *and* of all other religions which (as we will see later) may also have a period of validity and of being-willed-by-God – is thought to occur in the apostolic age. Normally, therefore, one regards the time between this beginning and the actual acceptance or the personally guilty refusal of Christianity in a non-Jewish world and history as the span between the already given promulgation of the law and the moment when the one to whom the law refers takes cognizance of it. It is not just an idle academic question to ask whether such a conception is correct or whether, as we maintain, there could be a different opinion in this matter, i.e. whether one could hold that the beginning of Christianity for actual periods of history, for cultures and religions, could be postponed to those moments in time when Christianity became a real historical factor in an individual history and culture – a real historical moment in a particular culture. For instance, one concludes from the first, usual answer that *everywhere* in the world, since the first Pentecost, baptism of children dying before reaching the use of reason is necessary for their supernatural salvation, although this was not necessary before that time. For other questions, too, a correct and considered solution of the present question could be of great importance, as for instance for the avoidance of immature conversions, for the justification and importance of "indirect" missionary work, etc. One will have to ask oneself whether one can still agree today with the first opinion mentioned above, in view of the history of the missions which has already lasted two thousand years and yet is still to a great extent in its beginnings – for even Suarez himself, for instance, had already seen (at least with regard to the *Jews*) that the *promulgatio* and *obligatio* of the Christian religion, and not merely the *divulgatio* and *notitia promulgationis*, take place in historical sequence. We cannot really answer this question here, but it may at least be pointed out as an open question; in practice, the correctness of the second theory may be presupposed since it alone corresponds to the real historicity of Christianity and salvation-history. From this there follows a delicately differentiated understanding of our first thesis: we maintain positively only that, as regards destination, Christianity is the absolute and hence the only religion for all men. We leave it, however, an open question (at least in principle) at what exact point in time the absolute obligation of the Christian religion has in fact come into effect for every man and culture, even in the sense of the *objective* obligation of such a demand. Nevertheless – and this leaves the thesis formulated still sufficiently exciting – wherever in practice Christianity reaches man in the real urgency and rigour of his actual existence, Christianity – once understood – presents itself as the only still valid religion for this man, a necessary means for his salvation and not merely an obligation with the necessity of a precept. It should be noted that this is a question of the necessity of a *social* form for salvation. Even though this is Christianity and not some other religion, it may surely still be said without hesitation that this thesis contains implicitly another thesis which states that in concrete human existence as such, the nature of religion itself must include a social constitution – which means that religion can exist only in a social form. This means, therefore, that man, who is commanded to have a religion, is also commanded to seek and accept a social form of religion. It will soon become clear what this reflection implies for the estimation of non-Christian religions.

Finally, we may mention one further point in this connection. What is vital in the *notion* of *paganism* and hence also of the non-Christian pagan religions (taking "pagan" here as a theological concept without any disparaging intent) is not the actual refusal to accept the Christian religion but the absence of any sufficient historical encounter with Christianity which would have enough historical power to render the Christian religion really present in this pagan society and in the history of the people concerned. If this is so, then paganism ceases to exist in this sense by reason of what is happening today. For the Western world is opening out into a universal world-history in which every people and every cultural sector becomes an inner factor of every other people and every other cultural sector. Or rather, paganism is slowly entering a new phase: there is *one* history of the world, and in this *one* history both the Christians and the non-Christians (i.e. the old and new pagans together) live in one and the same situation and face each other in dialogue, and thus the question of the theological meaning of the other religions arises once more and with even greater urgency.

2nd Thesis: Until the moment when the gospel really enters into the historical situation of an individual, a non-Christian religion (even outside the Mosaic religion) does not merely contain elements of a natural knowledge of God, elements, moreover, mixed up with human depravity which is the result of original sin and later aberrations. It contains also supernatural elements arising out of the grace which is given to men as a gratuitous gift on account of Christ. For this reason a non-Christian religion can be recognized as a *lawful* religion (although only in different degrees) without thereby denying the error and depravity contained in it. This thesis requires a more extensive explanation.

We must first of all note the point up to which this evaluation of the non-Christian religions is valid. This is the point in time when the Christian religion becomes a historically real factor for those who are of this religion. Whether this point is the same, theologically speaking, as the first Pentecost, or whether it is different in chronological time for individual peoples and religions, is something which even at this point will have to be left to a certain extent an open question. We have, however, chosen our formulation in such a way that it points more in the direction of the opinion which seems to us the more correct one in the matter although the *criteria* for a more exact determination of this moment in time must again be left an open question.

The thesis itself is divided into two parts. It means first of all that it is *a priori* quite possible to suppose that there are supernatural, grace-filled elements in non-Christian religions. Let us first of all deal with this statement. It does not mean, of course, that all the elements of a polytheistic conception of the divine, and all the other religious, ethical and metaphysical aberrations contained in the non-Christian religions, are to be or may be treated as harmless either in theory or in practice. There have been constant protests against such elements throughout the history of Christianity and throughout the history of the Christian interpretation of the non-Christian religions, starting with the Epistle to the Romans and following on the Old Testament polemics against the religion of the "heathens". Every one of these protests is still valid in what was really meant and expressed by them. Every such protest remains a part of the message which Christianity and the Church has to give to the peoples who profess such religions. Furthermore, we are not concerned here with an *a-posteriori* history of religions. Consequently, we also cannot describe empirically what should not exist and what is opposed to God's will in these non-Christian religions, nor can we represent these things in their many forms and degrees. We are here concerned with dogmatic theology and so can merely repeat the universal and unqualified verdict as to the unlawfulness of the non-Christian religions right from the moment when they came into real and historically powerful contact with Christianity (and at first only thus!).It is clear, however, that this condemnation does not mean to deny the very basic differences within the non-Christian religions especially since the pious, God-pleasing pagan was already a theme of the Old Testament, and especially since this God-pleasing pagan cannot simply be thought of as living absolutely outside the concrete socially constituted religion and construcing his own religion on his native foundation – just as St Paul in his speech on the Areopagus did not simply exclude a positive and basic view of the pagan religion. The decisive reason for the first part of our thesis is basically a theological consideration. This consideration (prescinding from certain more precise qualifications) rests ultimately on the fact that, if we wish to be Christians, we must profess belief in the universal and serious salvific purpose of God towards all men which is true even within the post-paradisean phase of salvation dominated by original sin. We know, to be sure, that this proposition of faith does not say anything certain about the *individual* salvation of man understood as something which has in fact been reached. But God desires the salvation of everyone. And this salvation willed by God is the salvation won by Christ, the salvation of supernatural grace which divinizes man, the salvation of the beatific vision. It is a salvation really intended for all those millions upon millions of men who lived perhaps a million years before Christ – and also for those who have lived after Christ – in nations, cultures and epochs of a very wide range which were still completely shut off from the viewpoint of those living in the light of the New Testament. If, on the one hand, we conceive salvation as something specifically *Christian*, if there is no salvation apart from Christ, if according to Catholic teaching the supernatural divinization of man can never be replaced merely by good will on the part of man but is necessary as something itself given in this earthly life; and if, on the other hand, God has really, truly and seriously intended this salvation for all men – then these two aspects cannot be reconciled in any other way than by stating that every human being is really and truly exposed to the influence of divine, supernatural grace which offers an interior union with God and by means of which God communicates himself whether the individual takes up an attitude of acceptance or of refusal towards this grace. It is senseless to suppose cruelly – and without any hope of acceptance by the man of today, in view of the enormous extent of the extra-Christian history of salvation and damnation – that nearly all men living outside the official and public Christianity are so evil and stubborn that the offer of supernatural grace ought not even to be made in fact in most cases, since these individuals have already rendered themselves unworthy of such an offer by previous, subjectively grave offences against the natural moral law. If one gives more exact theological thought to his matter, then one cannot regard nature and grace as two phases in the life of the individual which follow each other in time. It is furthermore impossible to think that this offer of supernatural, divinizing grace made to all men on account of the universal salvific purpose of God, should in general (prescinding from the relatively few exceptions) remain ineffective in most cases on account of the personal guilt of the individual. For, as far as the gospel is concerned, we have no really conclusive reason for thinking so pessimistically of men. On the other hand, and contrary to every merely human experience, we do have every reason for thinking optimistically of God and his salvific will which is more powerful than the extremely limited stupidity and evil-mindedness of men. However little we can say with certitude about the final lot of an individual inside or outside the officially constituted Christian religion, we have every reason to think optimistically – i.e. truly hopefully and confidently in a Christian sense – of God who has certainly the last word and who has revealed to us that he has spoken his powerful word of reconciliation and forgiveness into the world. If it is true that the eternal Word of God has become flesh and has died the death of sin for the sake of our salvation and in spite of our guilt, then the Christian has no right to suppose that the fate of the world – having regard to the whole of the world – takes the same course on account of man's refusal as it would have taken if Christ had not come. Christ and his salvation are not simply one of two possibilities offering themselves to man's free choice; they are the deed of God which bursts open and redeems the false choice of man by overtaking it. In Christ God not only gives the *possibility* of salvation, which in that case would still have to be effected by man himself, but the actual salvation itself, however much this includes also the right decision of human freedom which is itself a gift from God. Where sin already existed, grace came in superabundance. And hence we have every right to suppose that grace has not only been offered even outside the Christian Church (to deny this would be the error of Jansenism) but also that, in a great many cases at least, grace gains the victory in man's free acceptance of it, this being again the result of grace. Of course, we would have to show more explicitly than the shortness of time permits that the empirical picture of human beings, their life, their religion and their individual and universal history does not disprove this optimism of a faith which knows the whole world to be subjected to the salvation won by Christ. But we must remember that the theoretical and ritualistic factors in good and evil are only a very inadequate expression of what man actually accomplishes in practice. We must remember that the same transcendence of man (even the transcendence elevated and liberated by God's grace) can be exercised in many different ways and under the most varied labels. We must take into consideration that whenever the religious person acts really religiously, he makes use of, or omits unthinkingly, the manifold forms of religious institutions by making a consciously critical choice among and between them. We must consider the immeasurable difference – which it seems right to suppose to exist even in the Christian sphere – between what is objectively wrong in moral life and the extent to which this is really realized with subjectively grave guilt. Once we take all this into consideration, we will not hold it to be impossible that grace is at work, and is even being accepted, in the spiritual, personal life of the individual, no matter how primitive, unenlightened, apathetic and earth-bound such a life may at first sight appear to be. We can say quite simply that wherever, and in so far as, the individual makes a moral decision in his life (and where could this be declared to be in any way absolutely impossible – except in precisely "pathological" cases?), this moral decision can also be thought to measure up to the character of a supernaturally elevated, believing and thus saving act, and hence to be more in actual fact than merely "natural morality". Hence, if one believes seriously in the universal salvific purpose of God towards all men in Christ, it need not and cannot really be doubted that gratuitous influences of properly Christian supernatural grace are conceivable in the life of all men (provided they are first of all regarded as individuals) and that these influences can be presumed to be accepted in spite of the sinful state of men and in spite of their apparent estrangement from God.

Our second thesis goes even further than this, however, and states in its second part that, from what has been said, the actual religions of "pre-Christian" humanity too must not be regarded as simply illegitimate from the very start, but must be seen as quite capable of having a positive significance. This statement must naturally be taken in a very difference sense which we cannot examine here for the various particular religions. This means that the different religions will be able to lay claim to being lawful religions only in very different senses and to very different degrees. But precisely this variability is not at all excluded by the notion of a "lawful religion", as we will have to show in a moment. A lawful religion means here an institutional religion whose "use" by man at a certain period can be regarded on the whole as a positive means of gaining the right relationship to God and thus for the attaining of salvation, a means which is therefore positively included in God's plan of salvation. That such a notion and the reality to which it refers can exist even where such a religion shows many theoretical and practical errors in its concrete form becomes clear in a theological analysis of the structure of the Old Covenant. We must first of all remember in this connection that only in the New Testament – in the Church of Christ understood as something which is eschatologically final and *hence* (and only for this reason) "indefectible" and infallible – is there realized the notion of a Church which, because it is instituted by God in some way or other, already contains the permanent norm of differentiation between what is right (i.e. willed by God) and what is wrong in the religious sphere, and contains it both as a permanent institution and as an intrinsic element of this religion. There was nothing like this in the Old Testament, although it must undoubtedly be recognized as a lawful religion. The Old Covenant – understood as a concrete, historical and religious manifestation – contained what is right, willed by God, *and* what is false, erroneous, wrongly developed and depraved. But there was no permanent, continuing and institutional court of appeal in the Old Covenant which could have differentiated authoritatively, always and with certainty for the conscience of the individual between what was willed by God and what was due to human corruption in the actual religion. Of course, there were the prophets. They were not a permanent institution, however, but a conscience which had always to assert itself anew on behalf of the people in order to protest against the corruption of the religion as it existed at the time, thus – incidentally – confirming the existence of this corruption. The official, institutional forms known as the "kingdom" and the priesthood were so little proof against this God-offending corruption that they could bring about the ruin of the Israelitic religion itself. And since there were also pseudo-prophets, and no infallible "institutional" court of appeal for distinguishing genuine and false prophecy, it was – in the last analysis – left to the conscience of the individual Israelite himself to differentiate between what in the concrete appearance of the Israelitic religion was the true covenant with God and what was a humanly free, and so in certain cases falsifying, interpretation and corruption of this God-instituted religion. There might have been objective criteria for such a distinction of spirits, but their application could not simply be left to an "ecclesiastical" court – not even in the most decisive questions – since official judgements could be wrong even about these questions and in fact were completely wrong about them. This and nothing more – complete with its distinction between what was willed by God and what was human, all too human, a distinction which was ultimately left to be decided by the individual – was the concrete Israelitic religion. The Holy Scriptures do indeed give us the official and valid deposit to help us differentiate among the spirits which moved the history of the Old Testament religion. But since the infallible delimitation of the canon of the Old Testament is again to be found only in the New Testament, the exact and final differentiation between the lawful and the unlawful in the Old Testament religion is again possible only by making use of the New Testament as something eschatologically final. The unity of the concrete religion of the Old Testament, which (ultimately) could be distinguished only gropingly and at one's own risk, was however the unity willed by God, providential for the Israelites in the order of salvation and indeed the lawful religion for them. In this connection it must furthermore be taken into consideration that it was meant to be this only for the Israelites and for no one else; the institution of those belonging to the Jewish religion without being of the Jewish race, (i.e., of the proselytes) was a very much later phenomenon. Hence it cannot be a part of the notion of a lawful religion in the above sense that it should be free from corruption, error and objective moral wrong in the concrete form of its appearance, or that it should contain a clear objective and permanent final court of appeal for the conscience of the individual to enable the individual to differentiate clearly and with certainty between the elements willed and instituted by God and those which are merely human and corrupt. We must therefore rid ourselves of the prejudice that we can face a non-Christian religion with the dilemma that it must either come from God in everything it contains and thus correspond to God's will and positive providence, or be simply a purely human construction. If man is under God's grace even in these religions – and to deny this is certainly absolutely wrong –

then the possession of this supernatural grace cannot but show itself, and cannot but become a formative factor of life in the concrete, even where (though not only where) this life turns the relationship to the absolute into an explicit theme, viz. in religion. It would perhaps be possible to say in theory that where a certain religion is not only accompanied in its concrete appearance by something false and humanly corrupted but also makes this an explicitly and consciously adopted element – an explicitly declared condition of its *nature* – this religion is wrong in its deepest and most specific being and hence can no longer be regarded as a lawful religion – not even in the widest sense of the word. This may be quite correct in theory. But we must surely go on to ask whether there is any religion apart from the Christian religion (meaning here even only the Catholic religion) with an authority which could elevate falsehood into one of its really essential parts and which could thus face man with an alternative of either accepting this falsehood as the most real and decisive factor of the religion or leaving this religion. Even if one could perhaps say something like this of Islam as such, it would have to be denied of the majority of religions. It would have to be asked in every case to what extent the followers of such religions would actually agree with such an interpretation of their particular religion. It one considers furthermore how easily a concrete, originally religious act can be always directed in its intention towards one and the same absolute, even when it manifests itself in the most varied forms, then it will not even be possible to say that theoretical polytheism, however deplorable and objectionable it may be objectively, must always and everywhere be an absolute obstacle to the performance in such a religion of genuinely religious acts directed to the one true God. This is particularly true since it cannot be proved that the practical religious life of the ancient Israelites, in so far as it manifested itself in popular theory, was always more than mere henotheism.

Furthermore, it must be borne in mind that the individual ought to and must have the possibility in his life of partaking in a genuine saving relationship to God, and this at all times and in all situations of the history of the human race. Otherwise there could be no question of a serious and also actually effective salvific design of God for all men, in all ages and places. In view of the social nature of man and the previously even more radical social solidarity of men, however, it is quite unthinkable that man being what he is, could actually achieve this relationship to God – which he must have and which if he is to be saved, is and must be made possible for him by God – in an absolutely private interior reality and this outside of the actual religious bodies which offer themselves to him in the environment in which he lives. If man had to be and could always and everywhere be a *homo religiosus* in order to be able to save himself as such, then he was this *homo religiosus* in the concrete religion in which "people" lived and had to live at that time. He could not escape this religion, however much he may have and did take up a critical and selective attitude towards this religion on individual matters, and however much he may have and did put different stresses in practice on certain things which were at variance with the official theory of this religion. If, however, man can always have a positive, saving relationship to God, and if he always had to have it, then he has always had it within *that* religion which in practice was at his disposal by being a factor in his sphere of existence. As already stated above, the inherence of the individual exercise of religion in a social religious order is one of the essential traits of true religion as it exists in practice. Hence, if one were to expect from someone who lives outside the Christian religion that he should have exercised his genuine, saving relationship to God absolutely outside the religion which society offered him, then such a conception would turn religion into something intangibly interior, into something which is always and everywhere performed only indirectly, a merely transcendental religion without anything which could become tangible in categories. Such a conception would annul the above-mentioned principle regarding the necessarily social nature of all religion in the concrete, so that even the Christian Church would then no longer have the necessary presupposition of general human and natural law as proof of her necessity. And since it does not at all belong to the notion of a lawful religion intended by God for man as something positively salvific that it should be pure and positively willed by God in all its elements, such a religion can be called an absolutely legitimate religion for the person concerned. That which God has intended as salvation for him reached him, in accordance with God's will and by his permission (no longer adequately separable in practice), in the *concrete* religion of his actual realm of existence and historical condition, but this fact did not deprive him of the right and the limited possibility to criticize and to heed impulses of religious reform which by God's providence kept on recurring within such a religion. For a still better and simpler understanding of this, one has only to think of the natural and socially constituted morality of a people and culture. Such a morality is never pure but is always also corrupted, as Jesus confirmed even in the case of the Old Testament. It can always be disputed and corrected, therefore, by the individual in accordance with his conscience. Yet, taken in its totality, it is *the* way in which the individual encounters the natural divine law according to God's will, and the way in which the natural law is given real, actual power in the life of the individual who cannot reconstruct these tablets of the divine law anew on his own responsibility and as a private metaphysician. The morality of a people and of an age, taken in its totality, is therefore the legitimate and concrete form of the divine law (even though, of course, it can and may have to be corrected), so that it was not until the New Testament that the institution guaranteeing the purity of this form became (with the necessary reservations) an element of this form itself. Hence, if there existed a divine moral law and religion in the life of man *before* this moment, then its absolute purity (i.e. its constitution by divinely willed elements alone) must not be made the condition of the lawfulness of its existence. In fact, if every man who comes into the world is pursued by God's grace — and if one of the effects of this grace, even in its supernatural and salvifically elevating form, is to cause changes in consciousness (as is mantained by the better theory in Catholic theology) even though it cannot be simply *as* such a direct object of certain reflection — then it cannot be true that the actually existing religions do not bear any trace of the fact that all men are in some way affected by grace. These traces may be difficult to distinguish even to the enlightened eye of the Christian. But they must be there. And perhaps we may only have looked too superficially and with too little love at the non-Christian religions and so have not really seen them. In any case it is certainly not right to regard them as new conglomerates of natural theistic metaphysics and as a humanly incorrect interpretation and institutionalization of this "natural religion". The religions existing in the concrete must contain supernatural, gratuitous elements, and in using *these* elements the pre-Christian was able to attain God's grace: presumably, too, the pre-Christian exists even to this day, even though the possibility is gradually disappearing *today*. If we say that there were lawful religions in pre-Christian ages even outside the realm of the Old Testament, this does not mean that these religions were lawful in *all* their elements – to maintain this would be absurd. Nor does it mean that *every* religion was lawful; for in certain cases several forms, systems and institutions of a religious kind offered themselves within the historically concrete situation of the particular member of a certain people, culture, period of history, etc., so that the person concerned had to decide as to *which* of them was here and now, and on the whole, the more correct way (and hence for him *in concreto* the only correct way) of finding God. This thesis is not meant to imply that the lawfulness of the Old Testament religion was of exactly the same kind as that which we are prepared to grant in a certain measure to the extra-Christian religions. For in the Old Testament the prophets saw to it (even though not by way of a permanent institution) that there existed a possibility of distinguishing in public salvation-history between what was lawful and what was unlawful in the history of the religion of the Israelites. This cannot be held to be true to the same extent outside this history, although this again does not mean that outside the Old Testament there could be no question of any kind of divinely guided salvation-history in the realm of public history and institutions. The main difference between such a salvation-history and that of the Old Testament will presumably lie in the fact that the historical, factual nature of the New Testament has *its* immediate pre-history in the *Old Testament* (which pre-history, in parenthesis, is insignificantly brief in comparison with the general salvation-history which counts perhaps a millions years – for the former can be known with any certainly only from the time of Abraham or of Moses). Hence, the New Testament unveils *this* short span of salvation-history distinguishng its divinely willed elements and those which are contrary to God's will. It does this by a distinction which we cannot make in the same way in the history of any other religion. The second part of this second thesis, however, states two things positively. It states that even religions other than the Christian and the Old Testament religions contain quite certainly elements of a supernatural influence by grace which must make itself felt even in these objectifications. And it also states that by the fact that in practice man as he really is can live his proffered relationship to God only in society, man must have had the right and indeed the duty to live this his relationship to God within the religious and social realities offered to him in his particular historical situation.

3rd Thesis: If the second thesis is correct, then Christianity does not simply confront the member of an extra-Christian religion as a mere non-Christian but as someone who can and must already be regarded in this or that respect as an anonymous Christian. It would be wrong to regard the pagan as someone who has not yet been touched in any way by God's grace and truth. If, however, he has experienced the grace of God – if, in certain circumstances, he has already accepted this grace as the ultimate, unfathomable entelechy of his existence by accepting the immeasurableness of his dying existence as opening out into infinity – then he has already been given revelation in a true sense even before he has been affected by missionary preaching from without. For this grace, understood as the *a priori* horizon of all his spiritual acts, accompanies his consciousness subjectively, even though it is not known objectively. And the revelation which comes to him from without is not in such a case the proclamation of something as yet absolutely unknown, in the sense in which one tells a child here in Bavaria, for the first time in school, that there is a continent called Australia. Such a revelation is then the expression in objective concepts of something which this person has already attained or could already have attained in the depth of his rational existence. It is not possible here to prove more exactly that this *fides implicita* is something which dogmatically speaking can occur in a so-called pagan. We can do no more here than to state our thesis and to indicate the direction in which the proof of this thesis might be found. But if it is true that a person who becomes the object of the Church's missionary efforts is or may be already someone on the way towards his salvation, and someone who in certain circumstances finds it, without being reached by the proclamation of the Church's message – and if it is at the same time true that this salvation which reaches him in this way is Christ's salvation, since there is no other salvation – then it must be possible to be not only an anonymous theist but also an anonymous Christian. And then it is quite true that in the last analysis, the proclamation of the gospel does not simply turn someone absolutely abandoned by God and Christ into a Christian, but turns an anonymous Christian into someone who now also knows about his Christian belief in the depths of his grace-endowed being by objective reflection and in the profession of faith which is given a social form in the Church. It is not thereby denied, but on the contrary implied, that this explicit self-realization of his previously anonymous Christianity is itself part of the development of this Christianity itself – a higher stage of development of this Christianity demanded by his being – and that it is therefore intended by God in the same way as everything else about salvation. Hence, it will not be possible in any way to draw the conclusion from this conception that, since man is already an anonymous Christian even without it, this explicit preaching of Christianity is superfluous. Such a conclusion would be just as false (and for the same reasons) as to conclude that the sacraments of baptism and penance could be dispensed with because a person can be justified by his subjective acts of faith and contrition even before the reception of these sacraments. The reflex self-realization of a previously anonymous Christianity is demanded (1) by the incarnational and social structure of grace and of Christianity, and (2) because the individual who grasps Christianity in a clearer, purer and more reflective way has, other things being equal, a still greater chance of salvation than someone who is merely an anonymous Christian. If, however, the message of the Church is directed to someone who is a "non-Christian" only in the sense of living by an anonymous Christianity not as yet fully conscious of itself, then her missionary work must take this fact into account and must draw the necessary conclusions when deciding on its missionary strategy and tactics. We may say at a guess that this is still not the case in sufficient measure. The exact meaning of all this, however, cannot be developed further here.

4th Thesis: It is possibly too much to hope, on the one hand, that the religious pluralism which exists in the concrete situation of Christians will disappear in the foreseeable future. On the other hand, it is nevertheless absolutely permissible for the Christian himself to interpret this non-Christianity as Christianity of an anonymous kind which he does always still go out to meet as a missionary, seeing it as a world which is to be brought to the explicit consciousness of what already belongs to it as a divine offer or already pertains to it also over and above this as a divine gift of grace accepted unreflectedly and implicitly. If both these statements are true, then the Church will not so much regard herself today as the exclusive community of those who have a claim to salvation but rather as the historically tangible vanguard and the historically and socially constituted explicit expression of what the Christian hopes is present as a hidden reality even outside the visible Church. To begin with, however much we must always work, suffer and pray anew and indefatigably for the unification of the whole human race, in the one Church of Christ, we must nevertheless expect, for theological reasons and not merely by reason of a profane historical analysis, that the religious pluralism existing in the world and in our own historical sphere of existence will not disappear in the foreseeable future. We know from the gospel that the opposition to Christ and to the Church will not disappear until the end of time. If anything, we must even be prepared for a heightening of this antagonism to Christian existence. If, however, this opposition to the Church cannot confine itself merely to the purely private sphere of the individual but must also be of a public, historical character, and if this opposition is said to be present in a history which today, in contrast to previous ages, possesses a world-wide unity, then the continuing opposition to the Church can no longer exist merely locally and outside a certain limited sector of history such as that of the West. It must be found in our vicinity and everywhere else. And this is part of what the Christian must expect and must learn to endure. The Church which is at the same time the homogeneous characterization of an in itself homogeneous culture (i.e. the medieval Church) will no longer exist if history can no longer find any way to escape from or go back on the period of its planetary unity. In a unified world-history in which everything enters into the life of everyone, the "necessary" public opposition to Christianity is a factor in the existential sphere of all Christianity. If this Christianity, thus always faced with opposition and unable to expect seriously that this will ever cease, nevertheless believes in God's universal salvific will – in other words, believes that God can be victorious by his secret grace even where the Church does not win the victory but is contradicted – then this Church cannot feel herself to be just *one* dialectic moment in the whole of history but has already overcome this opposition by her faith, hope and charity. In other words, the others who oppose her are merely those who have not yet recognized what they nevertheless really already are (or can be) even when, on the surface of existence, they are in opposition; they are already anonymous Christians, and the Church is not the communion of those who possess God's grace as opposed to those who lack it, but is the communion of those who can explicitly confess what they *and* the others hope to be. Non-Christians may think it presumption for the Christian to judge everything which is sound or restored (by being sanctified) to be the fruit in every man of the grace of his Christ, and to interpret it as anonymous Christianity; they may think it presumption for the Christian to regard the non-Christian as a Christian who has not yet come to himself reflectively. But the Christian cannot renounce this "presumption" which is really the source of the greatest humility both for himself and for the Church. For it is a profound admission of the fact that God is greater than man and the Church. The Church will go out to meet the non-Christian of tomorrow with the attitude expressed by St Paul when he said: What therefore you do not know and yet worship (and yet *worship!*) that I proclaim to you (Ac 17.23). On such a basis one can be tolerant, humble and yet firm towards all non-Christian religions.

19

The Second Vatican Council, "Declaration on the Relationship of the Church to Non-Christian Religions"

Roman Catholicism in the last two centuries has undergone many changes. To bolster its authority over against the challenges of secularism and modernism in the nineteenth century, the Church declared at the First Vatican Council in 1870 that when the pope speaks *ex cathedra* in regard to faith and morals, he speaks infallibly. Its desire in the mid-twentieth century to throw open the windows of the Church in order to allow some fresh air to blow through, expressed by the Italian term *aggiornamento* (meaning "update"), prompted Pope John XXIII to call the Second Vatican Council. Pope John XXIII, however, was not to see the Council through to completion; after his death in 1963, Pope Paul VI assumed the leadership of the Church. Vatican II met from 1962 through 1965. It introduced many reforms into the Roman Catholic Church and made official Catholic pronouncements on a wide variety of issues.

The Council's "Declaration on the Relationship of the Church to Non-Christian Religions" indicates that it clearly understands the encounter with the great traditions of the world as an important contemporary challenge for the Church. The "Declaration" expresses a remarkable spirit of openness and reconciliation. It therefore highlights the unity that exists among all religions: their common origin in God, their common struggle with the problems of human existence, and their common end in God. While recognizing truth in non-Christian religions as well as the universal scope of God's plan of salvation, the Council nonetheless declares her duty to proclaim the fulfilment of religious striving in Christ, who is the way, the truth, and the life.

In the text which follows, the footnotes in the source edition have been eliminated.

The Text

PAUL, BISHOP
SERVANT OF THE SERVANTS OF GOD
TOGETHER WITH THE FATHERS OF THE SACRED COUNCIL
FOR EVERLASTING MEMORY

1. In our times, when every day men are being drawn closer together and the ties between various peoples are being multiplied, the Church is giving deeper study to her relationship with non-Christian religions. In her task of fostering unity and love among men, and even among nations, she gives primary consideration in this document to what human beings have in common and to what promotes fellowship among them.

For all peoples comprise a single community, and have a single origin, since God made the whole race of men dwell over the entire face of the earth (cf. Acts 17:26). One also is their final goal: God. His providence, His manifestations of goodness, and His saving designs extend to all men (cf. Wis. 8:1; Acts 14:17; Rom. 2:6–7; 1 Tim. 2:4) against the day when the elect will be united in that Holy City ablaze with the splendor of God, where the nations will walk in His light (cf. Apoc. 21:23 f.).

Men look to the various religions for answers to those profound mysteries of the human condition which, today even as in olden times, deeply stir the human heart: What is a man? What is the meaning and the purpose of our life? What is goodness and what is sin? What gives rise to our sorrows and to what intent? Where lies the path to true happiness? What is the truth about death, judgment, and retribution beyond the grave? What, finally, is that ultimate and unutterable mystery which engulfs our being, and whence we take our rise, and whither our journey leads us?

2. From ancient times down to the present, there has existed among diverse peoples a certain perception of that hidden power which hovers over the course of things and over the events of human life; at times, indeed, recognition can be found of a Supreme Divinity and of a Supreme Father too. Such a perception and such a recognition instill the lives of these peoples with a profound religious sense. Religions bound up with cultural advancement have struggled to reply to these same questions with more refined concepts and in more highly developed language.

Thus in Hinduism men contemplate the divine mystery and express it through an unspent fruitfulness of myths and through searching philosophical inquiry. They seek release from the anguish of our condition through ascetical practices or deep meditation or a loving, trusting flight toward God.

Buddhism in its multiple forms acknowledges the radical insufficiency of this

Source: *The Documents of Vatican II.*

shifting world. It teaches a path by which men, in a devout and confident spirit, can either reach a state of absolute freedom or attain supreme enlightenment by their own efforts or by higher assistance.

Likewise, other religions to be found everywhere strive variously to answer the restless searchings of the human heart by proposing "ways," which consist of teachings, rules of life, and sacred ceremonies.

The Catholic Church rejects nothing which is true and holy in these religions. She looks with sincere respect upon those ways of conduct and of life, those rules and teachings which, though differing in many particulars from what she holds and sets forth, nevertheless often reflect a ray of that Truth which enlightens all men. Indeed, she proclaims and must ever proclaim Christ, "the way, the truth, and the life" (John 14:6), in whom men find the fullness of religious life, and in whom God has reconciled all things to Himself (cf. 2 Cor. 5:18–19).

The Church therefore has this exhortation for her sons: prudently and lovingly, through dialogue and collaboration with the followers of other religions, and in witness of Christian faith and life, acknowledge, preserve, and promote the spiritual and moral goods found among these men, as well as the values in their society and culture.

3. Upon the Moslems, too, the Church looks with esteem. They adore one God, living and enduring, merciful and all-powerful, Maker of heaven and earth and Speaker to men. They strive to submit wholeheartedly even to His inscrutable decrees, just as did Abraham, with whom the Islamic faith is pleased to associate itself. Though they do not acknowledge Jesus as God, they revere Him as a prophet. They also honor Mary, His virgin mother; at times they call on her, too, with devotion. In addition they await the day of judgment when God will give each man his due after raising him up. Consequently, they prize the moral life, and give worship to God especially through prayer, almsgiving and fasting.

Although in the course of the centuries many quarrels and hostilities have arisen between Christians and Moslems, this most sacred Synod urges all to forget the past and to strive sincerely for mutual understanding. On behalf of all mankind, let them make common cause of safeguarding and fostering social justice, moral values, peace, and freedom.

4. As this sacred Synod searches into the mystery of the Church, it recalls the spiritual bond linking the people of the New Covenant with Abraham's stock.

For the Church of Christ acknowledges that, according to the mystery of God's saving design, the beginnings of her faith and her election are already found among the patriarchs, Moses, and the prophets. She professes that all who believe in Christ, Abraham's sons according to faith (cf. Gal. 3:7), are included in the same patriarch's call, and likewise that the salvation of the Church was mystically foreshadowed by the chosen people's exodus from the land of bondage.

The Church, therefore, cannot forget that she received the revelation of the Old Testament through the people with whom God in his inexpressible mercy deigned to establish the Ancient Covenant. Nor can she forget that she draws sustenance from the root of that good olive tree onto which have been grafted the wild olive branches of the Gentiles (cf. Rom. 11:17–24). Indeed, the Church believes that by His cross Christ, our Peace, reconciled Jew and Gentile, making them both one in Himself (cf. Eph. 2:14–16).

Also, the Church ever keeps in mind the words of the Apostle about his kinsmen, "who have the adoption as sons, and the glory and the covenant and the legislation and the worship and the promises; who have the fathers, and from whom is Christ according to the flesh" (Rom. 9:4–5), the son of the Virgin Mary. The Church recalls too that from the Jewish people sprang the apostles, her foundation stones and pillars, as well as most of the early disciples who proclaimed Christ to the world.

As holy Scripture testifies, Jerusalem did not recognize the time of her visitation (cf. Lk. 19:44), nor did the Jews in large number accept the gospel; indeed, not a few opposed the spreading of it (cf. Rom. 11:28). Nevertheless, according to the Apostle, the Jews still remain most dear to God because of their fathers, for He does not repent of the gifts He makes nor of the calls He issues (cf. Rom. 11:28–29). In company with the prophets and the same Apostle, the Church awaits that day, known to God alone, on which all peoples will address the Lord in a single voice and "serve him with one accord" (Soph. 3:9; cf. Is. 66:23; Ps. 65:4; Rom. 11:11–32).

Since the spiritual patrimony common to Christians and Jews is thus so great, this sacred Synod wishes to foster and recommend that mutual understanding and respect which is the fruit above all of biblical and theological studies, and of brotherly dialogues.

True, authorities of the Jews and those who followed their lead pressed for the death of Christ (cf. Jn. 19:6); still, what happened in His passion cannot be blamed upon all the Jews then living, without distinction, nor upon the Jews of today. Although the Church is the new people of God, the Jews should not be presented as repudiated or cursed by God, as if such views followed from the holy Scriptures. All should take pains, then, lest in catechetical instruction and in the preaching of God's Word they teach anything out of harmony with the truth of the gospel and the spirit of Christ.

The Church repudiates all persecutions against any man. Moreover, mindful of her common patrimony with the Jews, and motivated by the gospel's spiritual love and by no political considerations, she deplores the hatred, persecutions, and displays of anti-Semitism directed against the Jews at any time and from any source.

Besides, as the Church has always held and continues to hold, Christ in His boundless love freely underwent His passion and death because of the sins of all men, so that all might attain salvation. It is, therefore, the duty of the Church's preaching to proclaim the cross of Christ as the sign of God's all-embracing love and as the fountain from which every grace flows.

5. We cannot in truthfulness call upon that God who is the Father of all if we refuse to act in a brotherly way toward certain men, created though they be to

God's image. A man's relationship with God the Father and his relationship with his brother men are so linked together that Scripture says: "He who does not love does not know God" (1 Jn. 4:8).

The ground is therefore removed from every theory or practice which leads to a distinction between men or peoples in the matter of human dignity and the rights which flow from it.

As a consequence, the Church rejects, as foreign to the mind of Christ, any discrimination against men or harassment of them because of their race, color, condition of life, or religion.

Accordingly, following in the footsteps of the holy Apostles Peter and Paul, this sacred Synod ardently implores the Christian faithful to "maintain good fellowship among the nations" (1 Pet. 2:12), and, if possible, as far as in them lies, to keep peace with all men (cf. Rom. 12:18), so that they may truly be sons of the Father who is in heaven (cf. Mt. 5:45).

Each and every one of the things set forth in this Declaration has won the consent of the Fathers of this most sacred Council. We too, by the apostolic authority conferred on us by Christ, join with the Venerable Fathers in approving, decreeing, and establishing these things in the Holy Spirit, and we direct that what has thus been enacted in synod be published to God's glory.

Rome, at St. Peter's, October 28, 1965

I, Paul, Bishop of the Catholic Church

There follow the signatures of the Fathers.

20

Wilfred Cantwell Smith, "The Church in a Religiously Plural World"

The Canadian historian of religion Wilfred Cantwell Smith (b. 1916) is an internationally recognized expert in the history of the Islamic religious tradition. He is also one of the most influential figures of his generation when it comes to the theory and practice of the study of the world religions – or what Smith would prefer to call the study of the faith and cumulative traditions of religious persons and communities. Smith has taught at McGill University, Harvard University, and Dalhousie University. Although most of his publications deal with the history and study of religion, he has also written on the subject of Christianity's relationship to the religious traditions of the world.

In his essay "The Church in a Religiously Plural World," Smith tries to convince the reader of the significance of the fact of religious pluralism. He notes in this essay, the original edition of which dates from the 1960s, that we are living in a time of transition in which humanity's religious history is taking a monumental turn. Christians need to recognize the changes taking place in the current Copernican revolution, for the time of religious proselytization is over. Christian theologians can no longer in good conscience work out their positions in ignorance of other religious traditions. In a religiously plural world, Christians must learn to approach the members of the world's great traditions in a spirit of humility – and not in the spirit of arrogance based on the notion of Christian exclusivity, which has been the historical pattern.

Footnotes in the source edition have been omitted.

The Text

It has long been a platitude to insist that we live in a time of transition. There is excitement and at times almost terror in the new world in which even the cherished aspects of our past are giving way. Some Christians have hardly recognized that this dynamic, however commonplace in general, applies also to the Church's theology; and they may thereby include themselves among those for whom it means terror. Excitement comes rather when we become conscious that in fact the Church, existing as it does within history, has throughout been an institution in change and development; has always, consciously or unwittingly, spent each day on its way between what it was yesterday and what it would become tomorrow. We may rejoice in the new awareness that we, and indeed all other religious groups on earth, are and always have been participants in a process, not carriers of a pattern.

Such awareness involves also responsiblity, particularly of course for those who are in any way leaders, fashioners for good or ill of the next phase of the on-going process: the clergy, theologians, biblical scholars, thinking laity, and so on.

I wish here to attempt to discern and to delineate something, at least, of a momentous current that has begun to flow around and through the Christian Church. It is a current that is about to become a flood, one that could sweep us quite away unless we can through greatly increased consciousness of its force and direction learn to swim in its mighty surge.

One of the transformations that we all face is the recent emergence of a new cosmopolitanism, permeating more and more areas of modern life. Widely noticed, thought about, and acted on, have been the political and economic aspects of our "one world." For Christians specifically this broadening means, according to the wording of my title, the Christian Church in a religiously plural world – which of course is the only world there is. To come to terms with living in it, however, especially with living in it gracefully, means for the Church a transformation.

Wrestling with the issues began at the frontier, on the "mission field", the active confrontation of the Church with humanity's other forms of faith, other religious traditions. It was not long before it became evident that the concerns raised could not be left "out there" in the distance. Participants in those traditions, living by those forms of faith, have been increasingly present in the West, within "Christendom"; and the issues penetrate back into the scholar's study, pursuing us into what we were brought up to think of as the most intimate and most sanctified recesses of our theological traditions.

Regarding the missionary movement itself, except for fundamentalists who want no transition beyond what they know from the recent past, it is manifestly in profound crisis. Even the one-time acknowledged leader of the conservative wing of Christian missionary thinking, Hendrik Kraemer, closely familiar especially with missions to Muslims, affirmed that all attitudes on this matter "in so far as they

Source: Wilfred Cantwell Smith, *Patterns of Faith Around the World.*

derived from the past, are therefore necessarily outmoded," and "betray . . . deafness to the voice of the sweeping turn in world-history and blindness to . . . the new situation." The religious history of humankind is indeed taking as monumental a turn in our century as is the political or economic history, if only we could see it. The upsurge of a vibrant and self-assertive new religious orientation among Buddhists, Hindus, Muslims, and others evinces a new phase not merely in the history of those particular traditions, but in the history of the whole complex of human religiousness, of which the Christian is a part, and an increasingly participant part.

A traditional relation of the Christian Church to the world's other religious traditions has been that of proselytizing evangelism, at least in theory. The end of that phase is the beginning of a new period, in which the relation of the Church to those of other forms of faith will be new. But what it will be, in theory or practice, has yet to be worked out – not by the Church alone, but by the Church in its involvement with these others.

The most vivid and most masterly summing up of the missionary crisis was perhaps the brief remark of Canon Max Warren, sensitive and responsible recent General Secretary in London of the Church Missionary Society. His obituary on traditional mission policy and practice was summed up in three sentences: "We have marched around alien Jerichos the requisite number of times. We have sounded the trumpets. And the walls have not collapsed."

We turn from these matters to present-day theology, this chapter's central concern. Traditional missions are the extrapolation of an earlier theology of the Church. The passing of traditional missions is a supersession of one phase of that theology. The so-called "ecumenical" movements in the Western Church have been in part the result of pressures from the mission field because there, to sensitive missionaries, the problem of a divided Christendom "at home" came most starkly to light. It was from the mission field also that a fundamental fallacy in traditional theology has been shown up, though more recently as we have said it has been made the more vivid by the new pluralist situation in the West itself. The rise of science in the nineteenth century induced a revision in Christian theology – what has sometimes been called the second Reformation. Some may think that Canon Warren exaggerated, but at least he called attention to the seriousness of the new challenge, when he said that the impact of agnostic science will turn out to have been as child's play compared to the challenge to Christian theology of the faith of others.

The woeful thing is that the meeting of that challenge has hardly seriously begun.

The matter is illustrated by the career of probably the most widely respected Protestant theologian of the twentieth century, Paul Tillich. Towards the end of his life, in his late seventies, Tillich was invited to Japan, where his eyes were opened to a new horizon, and after his return he published shortly before his death a booklet comprising four lectures on *Christianity and the Encounter of the World Religions*. Previously, however, during practically his entire productive and highly influential life, he had taught, and written works on, theology – understood as Christian theology, and as seen in its Western ambience.

A year or so before the end of that pre-Japan period, an illuminating story was told me by a friend from Harvard, where Tillich was teaching at the time. Apparently a letter in the student paper, *The Harvard Crimson*, was able to show up as superficial in a particular case this eminent theologian's understanding of religious traditions in Asia. Some perhaps found it not notably surprising that an undergraduate in the second half of this century should know more on this matter than a major Christian thinker. Until recently, certainly, it was not particularly expected that a man (it normally was) should know much, or indeed anything, about the religious life of other communities before undertaking to become a spokesman for his own.

To me, however, the incident raised a significant issue. Looking at the matter historically, one might perhaps put it thus: probably Tillich belonged throughout most of his life to the last generation of theologians who could formulate their conceptual system as religiously isolationist. The era of religious isolationism is about to be as much at an end as that of political and economic isolationism already is. A major theme of Tillich's exposition had to do with a theology's deliberate aptness for the intellectual context in which it appears: the correlation technique, of question and answer. Yet that context as he saw it was the mental climate of the Western world; and he was speaking to it just at the end of its separatist tradition, just before it was being superseded by a new context, a climate modified radically by new breezes, or new storms, blowing in from the other parts of the planet. The new generation of the Church, unless it is content with a ghetto, will live in a cosmopolitan environment, which will make the work of even a Tillich appear parochial.

Ever since the impact of Greek philosophy on the Church – or shall we say the forced discovery of Greek philosophy by the Church – in the early centuries, every Christian theology has been written in the light of it. Whether various Christian thinkers rejected or accepted it, modified or enriched it, they formulated their expositions aware of it, and aware that their readers would read them in the light of it. No serious intellectual statement of Christian faith since that time has ignored this conceptual context.

Similarly, ever since the rise of science and the forced discovery of science by the Church, Christian doctrine has been written in the light of it. Formulator and reader are aware of this context, and no intellectual statement that ignores it can be fully serious.

I suggest that we have entered a comparable situation with regard to other religious traditions. The time will soon be with us when theologians who attempt to work out their position unaware that they do so as members of a world society in which other theologians, who are equally intelligent, equally devout, equally moral, are Hindus, Buddhists, Muslims, and others; unaware that their readers are likely perhaps to be Buddhists or to have Muslim husbands or Hindu colleagues – such theologians will be as out of date as is one who attempts to construct an intellectual position unaware that Aristotle and Kant have thought about the world, or unaware that the earth is a minor planet in a galaxy that is vast only by terrestrial standards. Philosophy and science have impinged so far on theological thought more effectively than has comparative religion, but this will not last.

It is not my purpose in this essay to suggest the new theological systems that the Church will in the new situation bring forth. My task here is to delineate the problems that such a system must answer, to try to analyze the context within which future theological thought will inescapably be set.

One of my theme songs in comparative-religion study has been that human religious diversity poses an intellectual problem, a moral problem, and a theological problem. In the rest of this essay I will consider the situation under these three headings – with emphasis on the last two. By "intellectual" I mean at the academic level: the sheer challenge to the human mind to understand, when confronted as it is today with what appears at first to be the bewildering variety of our religious life. At this level we have had or are having our Copernican Revolution, but we have not yet met our Newton. By this I mean that we have discovered the facts of our earth's being one of the planets, but have not yet explained them. The pew, if not yet the pulpit, the undergraduate, if not yet the seminary professor, have begun to recognize not only that the Christian answers on humanity's ultimate quality and purpose are not the only answers, but even that the Christian questions are not the only questions. The awareness of multiformity is becoming vivid, and compelling.

Before Newton's day it was thought that we lived in a radically dichotomous universe: there was our earth, where things fell to the ground, and there were the heavens, where things went round in circles. These were two quite different realms, and one did not think of confusing or even much relating the two. A profoundly significant step was taken when people recognized that the apple and the moon are in much the same kind of motion. Newton's mind was able to conceive an interpretation – accepted now by all of us, but revolutionary at the time – that, without altering the fact that on earth things do fall to the ground and in the heavens things do go round in circles, saw both these facts as instances of a single kind of behavior. In the comparative-religion field, a comparable dichotomy is seen, but has as yet not been satisfactorily interpreted theoretically. It is observed that many groups have in the past seen "our" tradition (whichever it be) as faith, others' behavior as superstition, the two realms to be interpreted in quite unrelated ways, understood on separate principles. The Christian's faith has come down from God, the Buddhist's goes round in the circles of purely human aspiration; and so on. The intellectual challenge here is to make coherent sense, in a rational, integrated manner, of a wide range of apparently comparable and yet conspicuously diverse phenomena. And the academic world is closer to meeting this challenge than some theologians have noticed (though at first it turned to the simplistic solution that all religious views were false).

Certain Christians have even made the rather vigorous assertion that Christian faith is not one of "the religions of the world," that one misunderstands it if one attempts to see it in those terms. Most students of comparative religion have tended to pooh-pooh such a claim as unacceptable. I, perhaps surprisingly, take it very seriously indeed; but I discovered that the same applies to the other traditions also. Christian faith is not to be seen as a religion, one of the religions. But neither is the faith of Buddhists, Hindus, Muslims, or Andaman Islanders; and to think of it so is seriously to misunderstand and distort it. However, this is a large issue that I am currently writing a book about; forgive me for introducing it here, though it seemed perhaps that the point might be illustrative. I believe there is no question but that modern inquiry is showing that the faith of others is not so different from ours as we were brought up to suppose. (Their "beliefs" may be; but that is a subsidiary matter.)

The intellectual problem, however, because of its essentially academic nature, we may leave aside now to pass on to the two issues from religious pluralism that are of moment to us professionally: to all Christians as Christians, and saliently to those of us who are charged to perceive conceptually and to formulate intellectually Christian faith as we ought to have it. These issues are what I have called the moral problem and the theological problem that religious diversity raises.

Religious diversity poses a moral problem because it disrupts community. It does so with new force in the modern world because divergent traditions that in the past did and could develop separately and insouciant of each other are today face to face; and, perhaps even more important and radical, are for the first time side by side. Different civilizations have in the past either ignored each other or fought each other; very occasionally in tiny ways perhaps they met each other. Today they not only meet but interpenetrate; they meet not only each other, but jointly meet joint problems, and must jointly try to solve them. They must collaborate. Perhaps the single most important challenge that humankind faces in our day is the need to turn our nascent world society into a world community.

This is not easy. In fact, the first effect of bringing diverse groups together, and particularly religiously diverse groups, is often conflict. This may be overt, or hidden. On the whole, as I have already remarked, I think that few Westerners, including Christians, have any inkling of how profound and bitter and massive, and also how much on the increase, is anti-Western feeling throughout the world; and in Africa and in Asia this is in many ways anti-Christian. Christian antagonism to outsiders is evident mostly in the realm of color – though in more subtle ways it vitiates many other relations. There is also plenty of religious strife among the non-Christian traditions – as was explosively demonstrated in the Hindu–Muslim massacres around the partition of India.

Humanity has yet to learn our new task of living together as partners in a world of religious and cultural plurality. The technological and economic aspects of "one world," of a humanity in process of global integration, are proceeding apace, and at the least are receiving the attention of many minds and influential groups (though too often with an eye to power or profit for the influential). The political aspects also are under active and constant consideration, even though success here is not as evident as one would wish. The ideological and cultural question of human cohesion, on the other hand, has received little attention, and relatively little progress can be reported; even though in the long run it may prove crucial, and is already basic to much else. Unless we can learn to understand and to be loyal to each other across religious frontiers, unless we can build a world in which people of markedly differing forms of faith can live together and work together, then the prospects for our planet's future are not bright.

My own view is that the task of constructing even that minimum degree of world fellowship that will be necessary for humanity to survive at all is far too great to be accomplished on any other than a religious basis. From no other source than faith, I believe, can human beings muster the energy, devotion, vision, resolve, the capacity to survive disappointment, that will be necessary – that *are* necessary – for this challenge. Cooperation among persons of diverse forms of religion is a moral imperative, even at the lowest level of social and political life. Some would agree that the world community must have a religious basis, conceding that a lasting and peaceful society cannot be built by a group of men and women who are ultimately divided religiously, who have come to no mutual appreciation and understanding; but would go on to hold that this is possible only if their own one tradition prevails. No doubt to some it would seem nice if all throughout the world were Roman Catholics, or Communists, or Muslims, or liberal universalists; or if all would agree that religion does not really matter, or that it should be kept a private affair. Apart, however, from those who find such a vision inherently less appealing, if not downright frightening, many others will agree that for the moment it seems in any case hardly likely. Coexistence, if not a final truth of human diversity, would seem at least an immediate necessity, and indeed, an immediate virtue.

If we must have rivalry among the religious communities of earth, might we not for the moment at least, as we remarked in our chapter on the Chinese above, rival each other in our determination and capacity to promote reconciliation? Christians, Muslims, Buddhists, secularists, each believe that only they are able to do this. Rather than arguing this point ideologically, let us strive in a friendly race to see which can implement it most effectively and vigorously in practice – each recognizing that any success of the other is to be applauded, not decried.

There is, then, this general moral level of the imperative towards community, which is some sense all people of goodwill share. We may move from that to the specifically Christian level. Here I have something very special to adduce. It is a thesis that I have been trying to develop for a couple of years now. The thesis essentially is this: that the emergence of the new world situation has brought to light a lack of integration in one area of Christian awareness, namely between the moral and the intellectual facets of our relations with others.

I begin with the affirmation that there are moral as well as conceptual implications of revealed truth. If Christians take seriously the revelation of God in Christ – if we really mean what we say when we affirm that his life, and his death on the cross, and his final triumph out of the very midst of self-sacrifice, embody the ultimate truth and power and glory of the universe – then two kinds of consequence follow, two orders of inference. On the moral level, there follows an imperative towards reconciliation, unity, harmony, and fellowship. At this level, all humanity is included: we strive to break down barriers, to bridge gulfs; we recognize all people everywhere as neighbors, as friends, as loved of God as we are. At this level, we do not become truly Christian until we have reached out towards a community that turns all humankind into one total "we."

On the other hand, there is another level, the intellectual, the order of ideas, where it is the business of those of us who are theologians to draw out concepts, to construct doctrines. At this level, the doctrines that most Christians have traditionally derived have tended to affirm a Christian exclusivism, a separation between those who believe and those who do not, a division of humanity into a "we" and a "they," a gulf between Christendom and the rest of the world: a gulf profound, ultimate, cosmic.

I shall come to the theological consideration of these theological ideas later. At the moment, I wish to consider the moral consequences of our theological ideas. Here my submission is that on this front the traditional doctrinal position of the Church has in fact militated against its traditional moral position, and has in fact encouraged Christians to approach others immorally. Christ has taught us humility, but we have approached them with arrogance.

I do not say this lightly. This charge of arrogance is a serious one. It is my observation over more than twenty years of study of the Orient, and a little now of Africa, that the fundamental flaw of Western civilization in its role in world history is arrogance, and that this has infected also the Christian Church. If you think that I am being reckless or unwarranted here, ask any Jew, or read between the lines of the works of modern African or Asian thinkers.

May I take for illustration a phrase, not unrepresentative, which was under discussion a few years ago by the United Church of Canada's commission on faith, and which ran as follows: "Without the particular knowledge of God in Jesus Christ, men do not really know God at all." Let us leave aside for the moment any question of whether or not this is true. We shall return to that presently. My point here is simply that, in any case, it is arrogant. At least, it becomes arrogant when one carries it out to the non-Western or non-Christian world. In the quiet of the study, it may be possible for the speculative mind to produce this kind of doctrine, provided that one keeps it purely bookish. But except at the cost of insensitivity or delinquency, it is morally not possible actually to go out into the world and say to devout, intelligent, fellow human beings: "We are saved and you are damned"; or, "We believe that we know God, and we are right; you believe that you know God, and you are altogether wrong."

This is deplorable from merely human standards. It is doubly so from Christian ones. Any position that antagonizes and alienates rather than reconciles, that is arrogant rather than humble, that promotes segregation rather than fellowship, that is unlovely, is *ipso facto* un-Christian.

There is a further point at which the traditional position seems to me morally un-Christian. From the notion that if Christianity is true, then other religions must be false (a notion whose logic I shall challenge later), it is possible to go on to the converse proposition: that if anyone else's faith turns out to be valid or adequate or divinely given, then it would follow that Christianity must be false – a form of logic that has, in fact, driven many from their own faith, and indeed from any faith at all. If one's chances of getting to Heaven – or to use a nowadays more acceptable metaphor, of coming into God's presence – are dependent upon other people's not getting there, then one becomes walled up within the quite intolerable position that the Christian has a vested interest in other people's damnation. It is shocking to admit it, but this actually takes place. When an observer comes back from Asia, or from a study of Asian religious traditions, and reports that, contrary to accepted theory, some Hindus and Buddhists and some Muslims lead a pious and moral life, and seem very near to God by any possible standard, so that, so far as one can see, in these particular cases at least, faith is as genuine as Christian faith, then presumably a Christian should be overjoyed, enthusiastically hopeful that this be true, even though he or she might be permitted a fear lest it might not be so. Instead, I have sometimes witnessed just the opposite: an emotional resistance to the news, persons hoping firmly that it is not so, though perhaps with a covert fear that it might be. Whatever the rights and wrongs of the situation theoretically, I submit that in practice this is just not Christian, and indeed is not tolerable. It will not do, to have a faith that can be undermined by God's saving one's neighbor; or to be afraid lest other persons turn out to be closer to God than one had been led to suppose.

Let us turn, finally, to the theological problem that the existence of the other religious communities of humankind poses for the Christian (and that today's new immediate and face-to-face awareness of their presence poses urgently). This problem began, in a compelling form, with the discovery of America by Europeans, and the concomitant discovery of people on this continent who therefore had been "out of reach of the Gospel." In theory the peoples of Africa and Asia could have heard the gospel story and could have believed it and "been saved." If they had not become Christian, this could be interpreted as due to their stubborness, or to Christian lethargy in not evangelizing them, and so on. But with the discovery of North and South American peoples who had lived for fifteen centuries since Christ died, unable to be saved through faith in Him, some sensitive theologians were bewildered.

In our day a comparable problem is presented, and may be viewed in two ways. First, how does one account, theologically, for the fact of humanity's religious diversity? It seems not to cohere with Christians' traditional sense of a world under divine aegis. It seemed comparable, in a certain light, with another relentlessly nagging Christian question, that of how one accounts theologically for the imperfection, at times devastating imperfection, of a world supposedly under divine providence. Why is the world not closer to good than it observably is; or at least more tolerably close? This question has never, some would say, found a satisfying answer, even though Christian theologians have been much more conscious of the "problem of evil" (theodicy) than of that of religious pluralism.

Another way of viewing the latter difficulty is to phrase a question as to whether, or how far, or how, non-Christians are "saved," or know God. This has of late found a considerable number of attempted answers, though to my taste none of these is at all satisfactory.

I would simply like to suggest that from now on any serious intellectual statement of Christian faith must include, if it is to serve its purpose in the Church, some sort of doctrine of other religious ways. We explain the fact that the Milky Way is there by the doctrine of creation, but how do we explain the fact that the Bhagavad Gita is there?

One may venture to comment on one of the answers that have in fact been elicited by the issue of pluralism. It is the one that we have already mentioned: "Without the particular knowledge of God in Jesus Christ, men do not really know God at all." First, of course, one must recognize the point that this intellectualization stems from and attempts to affirm, in however skewed a fashion, the positive conviction of the Church that "in Christ God died for us men and our salvation," that "through faith in Him we are saved." In the new formulations to which we may look forward, this positive apprehension must be preserved. Yet in the negative proposition as framed in the sentence that we are considering, one may see a number of inescapable difficulties, and one may suppose that the force of these will come to be increasingly felt in coming decades. First, there is an epistemological difficulty. How could one possibly know?

If one asks how we know the Christian form of faith to be true, there are perhaps two kinds of answer. First, we ourselves have found in our lives, by accepting and interiorizing it and attempting to live in accordance with it, that Christian faith proves itself. We know it to be true because we have lived it. Secondly, one may answer that for now almost two thousand years the Church has proven it and found it so; hundreds of millions of people, of all kinds and in all circumstances and in many ages and many places, have staked their lives upon it, and have found it right. On the other hand, if one is asked how one knows the faith of people in other traditions to be false, one is rather stumped.

Most people who make this kind of statement do not in fact know much about the matter. Actually the only basis on which their position can and does rest is a logical inference. It seems to them a theoretical implication of what they themselves consider to be true, that other peoples' faith must be illusory. Personally, I think that this is to put far too much weight on logical implication. There have been innumerable illustrations of the human capacity for starting from some cogent theoretical position and then inferring from it logically something else that at the time seems persuasive but that in fact turns out on practical investigation not to hold. It is far too sweeping to condemn the great majority of humankind to lives of utter meaninglessness and perhaps to Hell, simply on the basis of what seems to some individuals the force of logic. Part of what the Western world has been doing for the last four or so centuries (since that alleged affair in Pisa) has been learning to get away from this kind of reliance on purely logical structures, totally untested by experience or by any other consideration. The damnation of my neighbor is too weighty a matter to rest on a syllogism.

Secondly, there is the problem of empirical observation. One cannot be anything but tentative here, of course, and inferential. Yet so far as actual observation goes, the evidence would seem overwhelming that in fact individual Buddhists, Hindus, Muslims, and others have known, and do know, God. I personally have friends from these communities whom it seems to me preposterous to think about in any other way. (If we do not have friends among these "other" communities, we should surely refrain from generalizations about them.)

This point, however, presumably need not be labored. The position set forth has obviously not been based, and does not claim to be based, upon empirical observation. If one insists on holding it, it must be held against the evidence of empirical observation. This can be done, as one writer earlier this century formulated it:

> The Gospel of Jesus Christ comes to us with a built-in prejudgment of all other faiths
> so that we know in advance of our study what we must ultimately conclude about

them. They give meanings to life apart from that which God has given in the biblical story culminating with Jesus Christ, and they organize life outside the covenant community of Jesus Christ. Therefore, devoid of this saving knowledge and power of God, these faiths not only are unable to bring men to God, they actually lead men away from God and hold them captive from God. This definitive and blanket judgment . . . is not derived from our investigation of the religions but is given in the structure and content of Gospel faith itself.

Again, a careful study by a neo-orthodox trainer of missionaries in Basel said that Islam, like other "foreign religions," is a "human attempt to win God for oneself . . . to catch Him and confine Him on the plane of one's own spiritual life . . . and for oneself to hold Him fast." He knows this, he says explicitly, not from a study of Islam but before he begins that study, from his Christian premises; he knows it by revelation, and therefore he can disdain all human argument against it. The position seems thoroughly logical, and once one has walled oneself up within it, impregnable. Those of us who, after our study of Islam or of Indian or Chinese religion, and after our fellowship with Muslims and other personal friends, have come to know that these religious traditions are, rather, channels through which God does indeed come into touch with these men, women, children – what answer can we give?

One possible answer is that empirical knowledge does in the end have to be reckoned with, does in the end win out even over conviction that claims for itself the self-certification of revelation. We do not deny that upholders of this sort of position are recipients of revelation, genuinely; but we would maintain that the revelation itself is not propositional, and that their interpretation of whatever revelation they have received is their own, is human and fallible, is partial, and in this case in in some ways wrong. (God reveals Him/Her/It-self, and we may again cast this in Archbishop Temple's words, that theology is to revelation what programme notes are to music.) In fact, we have been through all this before. A hundred years ago Christians argued that they knew by divine revelation that the earth was but six thousand years old and that evolution did not happen, and therefore any evidence that geologists or biologists might adduce to the contrary need not be taken seriously. A repentant Church still claims revelation but now admits that its former theology needed revision. In the twentieth century the evidence has been increasing that the faith of those in other religious communities is not so different from our own as we have often asserted it to be. It has forced some to abandon any faith in revelation at all, and will in general, I predict, force us rather to revise our theological formulations.

Finally, even on the level of internal Christian doctrine itself this "exclusivist" position, as it is called – excluding non-Christians from salvation – is theoretically problematic. For according to traditional Christian doctrine, there is not only one person in the Trinity, namely Christ, but three persons: God the Father, God the Son, and God the Holy Spirit. Is God not Creator? If so, then is "He" not "Father" of all, not to be known – however partially, inaccurately – in creation, nor in people's lives? Is the Holy Spirit totally absent from any history, including even the history of others' faith?

It has been contended that outside the Christian tradition people may know God in part, but cannot know God fully. This is undoubtedly valid, but the apparent implications are precarious. For one may well ask: Is is possible for Christians to know God fully? I personally do not see what it might mean to say that anyone, Christian or other, has a complete knowledge of God. This would certainly be untenable this side of the grave, at the very least. The finite cannot comprehend the infinite. (Moreover, Church history makes the argument's fallacy all too apparent.)

(In asking what one actually means when one speaks of knowledge of God, we may recall here the aphorism about the only true atheist being he or she who loves no one and whom no one loves. To know God, to use that theistic language, is not an ability to pass an examination in theology.)

Christians know God only in part. Yet one part of their knowing has been, surely, the recognition that God does not leave any of us utterly outside the knowledge.

It is easier, of course, to demolish a theological position than to construct a better alternative one. The fallacy of relentless exclusivism is becoming more obvious than is the right way of reconciling a truly Christian charity and perceptivity with doctrinal adequacy. On this matter I personally have a number of views, but the one about which I feel most strongly is that this matter is important – while the rest of my particular views on it are not necessarily so. In other words, I am much more concerned to stress the fact that the Church must work, and work vigorously, and work on a large scale, in order to construct an adequate doctrine in this realm, than I am concerned to push my own particular suggestions. Most of all I would emphasize that whether or not my particular construction seems inadequate, the position formulated above from which I strongly dissent must in any case be seen to be inadequate also.

Having expressed this caution, I may nonetheless make one or two suggestions. First, I rather feel that the final doctrine on this matter might run along the lines of Christians' affirming that a Buddhist who is "saved," or a Hindu or a Muslim or whoever, is saved, and is saved only, because God is (in part) the kind of God that Jesus Christ has revealed. This is not exclusivist; indeed, it coheres, I feel, with the points that I have made above in dissenting from exclusivism. If Christian revelation were not true, then it might be possible to imagine that God would allow Hindus to worship Him/Her/It, or Muslims to obey the One whom they perceive God to be, or Buddhists to act compassionately towards other "sentient beings," without responding, without reaching out to embrace them. Even, however, in traditional Christian language, because God is what He is, because He is what Christ has shown Him to be, therefore others do live in His presence. Also, therefore we (as Christians) know this to be so.

I rather wonder whether the fundamental difficulty in the formulated position here criticized, and in all similar statements, does not arise somehow from an anthropocentric emphasis that it surreptitiously implies. To focus on persons' knowing of God is to be in danger of moving in the realm of thinking of religion as a human quest, and of knowledge of God as if it were a human attainment, or even a human achievement. Of course it does not state it thus, but it skirts close to implying somehow that we are saved by *our* doings (or knowings). Must one not rather take the Christian doctrine of grace more seriously? The question must be more adequately phrased – in traditional language: Does God let Himself be known only to those to whom He has let Himself be known explicitly through Christ? Does God love only those who respond to Him in this tradition?

We are not saved by our knowledge; we are not saved by our being members of the Church; we are not saved by anything of *our* doing. We are saved rather by what alone could possibly save us, the anguish and the love of God. While we have no final way of knowing with assurance how God deals or acts in other people's lives (nor indeed in our own), and therefore cannot make any final pronouncement (such as the formulator of the position stated has attempted to make), nonetheless we must perhaps at least be hesitant in setting boundaries to that anguish and that love.

The God whom we have come to know, so far as we can sense the divine action, reaches out after all persons everywhere, and speaks to all who will listen. Both within and without the Church we listen all too dimly. Yet both within and without the Church, so far as we can see, God does somehow enter human hearts.

21

John Hick, "Whatever Path Men Choose Is Mine" and "A Philosophy of Religious Pluralism"

The British philosopher of religion John Hick was born in 1922. One of the most important theorists of religious pluralism in the second half of the twentieth century, Hick has taught in both the United Kingdom and the United States. In addition to the numerous articles and books that he has written on Christianity's encounter with and response to the religious traditions of the world, Hick has also contributed significantly to the field of philosophy of religion in the difficult area of theodicy as well as in theories concerning death and eternal life. Clearly, he has not been a thinker inclined to the avoidance of complex and perplexing questions.

In his essay "Whatever Path Men Choose Is Mine" (the title is taken from the Hindu sacred text, *The Bhagavad Gita*), Hick seeks to offer a Christian response to the problem of religious pluralism. In so doing, he first describes the changing world situation regarding humanity's awareness of unity within religious plurality. Next, he explores the theological implications of this changing situation, marshaling a critique of both Christocentric exclusivism and inclusivism *en route* to his own theocentric and pluralistic position. Central to his Copernican revolution is an assumption, which owes much to the philosopher Immanuel Kant, about the unknowability of divine reality and the inability of human language to name this reality in any definitive way. God, Hick argues, answers to many names; and although the various world religions name and conceive the one God differently, each of these names serves as a saving point of contact with the divine. To make his position palatable to fellow Christians, finally, Hick substantially revises the Christian Church's doctrine of Christ by arguing that the incarnation is not literal-historical but metaphorical-mythological.

Hick's "A Philosophy of Religious Pluralism" clarifies and expands the view articulated in "Whatever Path Men Choose Is Mine." Most significant, perhaps, is Hick's specification of the conception of salvation operative in his own pluralist position. Over against exclusivism's restrictive and Christocentric conception of salvation, he propounds a nonrestrictive and theocentric conception of salvation which involves a transformation from self-centeredness to Reality-centeredness, in which "Reality" is taken as an expression for the divine or the ultimate – that is, the end toward which all religions are understood to move. In so doing, Hick seeks to offer fellow Christians a plausible way of embracing his position and so forsaking what he takes to be the instability of the currently dominant Christian position – namely, inclusivism.

In the texts which follow, the footnotes in the source editions have been omitted.

"Whatever Path Men Choose Is Mine"

For many of us in the West the relation between Christianity and the other world religions has until recently been a rather theoretical issue to which rather theoretical responses have seemed sufficient. We have lived within the cultural borders of Christendom and – many of us – within the ecclesiastical borders of the Church. From this centre we – that is, our forebears, and still the church today – have been sending out missionaries into all the continents of the earth, and have enjoyed a vague sense that the world is, however tardily, in process of becoming Christianized. And so we have in the past generally thought of the non-Christian world in negative terms, as the unfortunate not-yet-Christianized portion of humanity and as potential recipients of the divine grace which is coming through the evangelists whom we send out to them.

However, several things have happened to shatter this attitude of religious imperialism.

One has been the growing awareness, produced by the news media and by travel, of the sheer size and religious variety of mankind outside our own Anglo-Saxon tribe. The estimated Christian population of the world is 983.6 million, constituting just under a quarter of the world's total population of 4123.9 million (*Encyclopedia Britannica 1978 Book of the Year*, p. 616). But whilst the total number of Christians is slowly rising, the proportion of Christians is slowly declining, because the explosion in the human population (the number of which will have roughly doubled between 1970 and about 2005) is taking place more rapidly outside Christendom than within it. Thus the Christian faith is held today, as in the past, only by a minority of the human race; and it looks as though this minority may well be smaller rather than larger in the future. This thought casts a massive shadow over any assumption that it is God's will that all mankind shall be converted to the Christian faith.

Again, it is a fact evident to ordinary people (even though not always taken into account by theologians) that in the great majority of cases – say, 98 or 99 per cent – the religion in which a person believes and to which he adheres depends upon where he was born. That is to say, if someone is born to Muslim parents in Egypt or Pakistan, that person is very likely to be a Muslim; if to Buddhist parents in Sri Lanka or Burma, that person is very likely to be a Buddhist; if to Hindu parents in India, that person is very likely to be a Hindu; if to Christian parents in Europe or the Americas, that person is very likely to be a Christian. Of course in each case he may be a fully committed or a merely nominal adherent of his religion. But whether one is a Christian, a Jew, a Muslim, a Buddhist, a Sikh, a Hindu – or for that matter a Marxist or a Maoist – depends nearly always on the part of the world in which one happens to have been born. Any credible religious faith must be able to make sense of this circumstance. And a credible Christian faith must make sense of it by relating it to the universal sovereignty and fatherhood of God. This is rather conspicuously

Source: *Christianity and Other Religions: Selected Readings*, eds J. Hick and B. Hebblethwaite.

not done by the older theology which held that God's saving activity is confined within a single narrow thread of human life, namely that recorded in our own scriptures.

Another factor making for change is that the old unflattering caricatures of other religions are now being replaced by knowledge based on serious objective study. Our bookshops now carry shelves of good popular as well as technical works on the history of religion, the phenomenology of religion, and the comparative study of religions; and only one who prefers to be ignorant can any longer complacently congratulate himself upon knowing nothing about other faiths. It is no longer acceptable to plead ignorance concerning the wider religious life of mankind as an excuse for parochial theological prejudices. Times have changed and today no one wishes to present the eighteenth-century image of Fielding's Parson Thwackum who said, "When I mention religion, I mean the Christian religion; and not only the Christian religion, but the Protestant religion; and not only the Protestant religion, but the Church of England."

And, perhaps most importantly of all, since the 1950s Asian immigration from India, Pakistan and (as it now is) Bangladesh has brought sizeable Muslim, Hindu and Sikh communities to many of our cities, adding three more non-Christian groups to the Jews who had already been there for more than two centuries. By their very existence these non-Christian communities presented the Church with a number of new questions, which it has generally chosen to see as difficult problems. Should we try to help the Muslims, Sikhs and Hindus to find suitable premises in which to worship? Should we be willing to sell them redundant church buildings? Should local religious broadcasting include or exclude them? Should we try to insist that all children in the state schools shall receive Christian religious instruction, regardless of the religion which they or their parents profess? And so on. These questions all have theological implications, and have helped to turn the attention of Christians to the problem of the relation of Christianity to the other world religions.

When you visit the various non-Christian places of worship in one of our big cities you discover – possibly with a shock of surprise – that phenomenologically (or in other words, to human observation) the same kind of thing is taking place in them as in a Christian church. That is to say, human beings are coming together to open their minds to a higher reality, which is thought of as the personal creator and Lord of the universe, and as making vital moral demands upon the lives of men and women. Of course the trappings are very different – in a church men wear shoes and no hat; in mosque, gurdwara and temple, a hat and no shoes; in a synagogue, both. In some you sit on a pew, in others on the floor. In some there is singing, in others there is not. Different musical instruments or none are used. More importantly, the supreme being is referred to as God in a Christian church, as Adonai in a Jewish synagogue, as Allah in a Muslim mosque, as Param Atma in a Sikh gurdwara, as Rama or as Krishna in a Hindu temple. And yet there is an important sense in which what is being done in the several forms of worship is essentially the same.

In the Jewish synagogue God is worshipped as maker of heaven and earth and the God of Abraham and Isaac and Jacob, who led the children of Israel out of Egypt into the promised land and who has called them to live as a light to lighten the world. Worship is very close in form and ethos to Christian worship in the Protestant traditions. Here is a passage of typical Jewish prayer:

> With a great love have You loved us, O Lord our God, and with exceeding compassion have You pitied us. Our Father and King, our fathers trusted in You, and You taught them the laws of life: be gracious also to us, and teach us. Have compassion upon us, and guide us, our Merciful Father, that we may grasp and understand, learn and teach, observe and uphold with love all the words of Your law.

In Muslim mosques God is worshipped as the maker of heaven and earth, and as the sovereign Lord of the Universe, omnipotent, holy and merciful, before whom men bow in absolute submission. Here is a typical passage of Muslim prayer:

> Praise be to God, Lord of creation,
> Source of all livelihood, who orders the morning.
> Lord of majesty and honour, of grace and beneficence.
> He who is so far that he may not be seen and so near
>   that he witnesses the secret things.
> Blessed be He and for ever exalted.

Or again:

> To God belongs the praise, Lord of the heavens and Lord of the earth, the Lord of all being. His is the dominion in the heavens and in the earth: he is the Almighty, the All-wise.

In Sikh gurdwaras God is worshipped as the maker of heaven and earth, the gracious lord of time and eternity, who demands righteousness and seeks peace and goodwill between men. Here is the Sikh morning prayer which is at the same time a creed:

> There is but one God. He is all that is.
> He is the Creator of all things and He is all-Pervasive.
> He is without fear and without enmity.
> He is timeless, unborn and self-existent.
> He is the Enlightener
> And can be realized by grace of Himself alone.
> He was in the beginning; He was in all ages.
> The True One is, was, [O Nanak,] and shall forever be.

The Hindu temples which have been established in Britain represent the *bhakti* or theistic-devotional form of Hinduism. In them God is worshipped as the ultimate Lord of all, the infinite divine Life known under many aspects and names. Against the background of throbbing music the name of God is chanted again and again by ecstatic worshippers. The language of *bhakti* devotion is emotional and personal. Here is a typical Vaishnavite hymn:

O save me, save me, Mightiest,
  Save me and set me free.
O let the love that fills my breast
  Cling to thee lovingly.

Grant me to taste how sweet thou art;
  Grant me but this, I pray,
And never shall my love depart
  Or turn from thee away.

Then I thy name shall magnify
  And tell thy praise abroad,
For very love and gladness I
  Shall dance before my God.

And here is a verse expressing the Hindu idea of the many incarnations of God:

Seers and sages, saints and hermits, fix on Him their reverent gaze,
And in faint and trembling accents, holy scripture hymns His praise.
He the omnipresent spirit, Lord of heaven and earth and hell,
To redeem His people, freely has vouchsafed with men to dwell.

In the light of the phenomenological similarity of worship in these different traditions we have to ask whether people in church, synagogue, mosque, gurdwara and temple are worshipping different Gods or are worshipping the same God? Are Adonai and God, Allah and Param Atma, Rama and Krishna different Gods, or are these different names for the same ultimate Being?

There would seem to be three possibilities. One is that there exist, ontologically, many gods. But this conflicts with the belief concerning each that he is the creator or the source of the world. A second possibility is that one faith-community, let us say our own, worships God whilst the others vainly worship images which exist only in their imaginations. But even within Christianity itself, is there not a variety of overlapping mental images of God — for example, as stern judge and predestinating power, and as gracious and loving heavenly Father — so that different Christian groups, and even different Christian individuals, are worshipping the divine Being through their different images of him? And do not the glimpses which I have just offered of worship within the various religious traditions suggest that our Christian images overlap with many non-Christian images of God? If so, a third possibility must seem the most probable, namely that there is but one God, who is maker and lord of all; that in his infinite fullness and richness of being he exceeds all our human attempts to grasp him in thought; and that the devout in the various great world religions are in fact worshipping that one God, but through different, overlapping concepts or mental images of him.

If this is so, the older Christian view of other faiths as areas of spiritual darkness within which there is no salvation, no knowledge of God, and no acceptable worship must be mistaken. This older view, which few still entertain in practice today, was enshrined in the traditional Roman Catholic dogma, *extra ecclesiam nulla salus* (outside the Church no salvation). To quote a classic utterance from this point of view, the Council of Florence in 1438–45 declared that "no one remaining outside the Catholic Church, not just pagans, but also Jews or heretics or schismatics, can become partakers of eternal life; but they will go to the everlasting fire which was prepared for the devil and his angels, unless before the end of life they are joined to the church". The Protestant missionary equivalent, which likewise is entertained by few today, is the doctrine that outside Christianity there is no salvation. As a fairly recent expression of this, the Congress on World Mission at Chicago in 1960 declared, "In the years since the war, more than one billion souls have passed into eternity and more than half of these went to the torment of hell fire without even hearing of Jesus Christ, who He was, or why He died on the cross of Calvary."

This older view has come to seem increasingly implausible and unrealistic in the light of growing knowledge of other faiths and as a result of better contacts with their adherents. Consequently Christian theologians, perhaps most notably within the Roman communion, have been making strenuous efforts to escape from the unacceptable implications of the older view, though usually without feeling entitled explicitly to renounce it. This is, of course, in accordance with the established ecclesiastical method of developing and changing doctrine. One cannot say that a formerly proclaimed dogma was wrong, but one can reinterpret it to mean something very different from what it was originally understood to mean. Such exercises often display a high level of ingenuity; though no amount of intellectual sophistication can save them from seeming slightly ridiculous or slightly dishonest to the outsider. At any rate, in the attempt to retain the dogma of no salvation outside the Church, or outside Christianity, we have the ideas of implicit, as distinguished from explicit, faith; of baptism by desire, as distinguished from literal baptism; and as a Protestant equivalent, the idea of the latent Church as distinguished from the manifest Church; and, again, the suggestion that men can only come to God through Jesus Christ but that those who have not encountered him in this life will encounter him in the life to come.

Or again there is Karl Rahner's notion of the anonymous Christian. The devout Muslim, or Hindu, or Sikh, or Jew can be regarded as an anonymous Christian, this being an honorary status granted unilaterally to people who have not expressed any desire for it. Or again there is the claim that Christianity, properly understood, is not a religion but is a revelation which judges and supersedes all religions. Or finally there is Hans Küng's distinction between the ordinary way of salvation in the world religions and the extraordinary way in the Church. Küng says, "A man is to be saved within the religion that is made available to him in his historical situation. Hence it is his right and duty to seek God within that religion in which the hidden God has already found him." Thus the world religions are, he says, "the way of salvation in universal salvation history; the general way of salvation, we can even say, for the people of the world religions: the more common, the 'ordinary' way of salvation, as against which the way of salvation in the Church appears as something very special and extraordinary". This sounds at first extremely promising. However, Küng goes on to take away with one hand what he has given with the other. The ordinary way of salvation for the majority of mankind in the world religions turns out to be only an interim way until, sooner or later, they come to an explicit Christian faith. The people of the world religions are, he says, "pre-Christian, directed towards Christ . . . The men of the world religions are not professing Christians but, by the grace of God, they are called and marked out to be Christians." One is reminded of the British amnesty for illegal immigrants. Although they are unauthorized entrants into the Kingdom of Heaven, the Indian and Pakistani and other foreign worshippers of God will be accepted if sooner or later they come forward to be legally registered by Christian baptism!

Thus all of these thinkers, who are trying so hard to find room for their non-Christian brethren in the sphere of salvation, are still working within the presuppositions of the old dogma. Only Christians can be saved; so we have to say that devout and godly non-Christians are really, in some metaphysical sense, Christians or Christians-to-be without knowing it. Although to the ordinary non-ecclesiastical mind this borders upon double-talk, yet in intention it is a charitable extension of the sphere of grace to people who had formerly been regarded as beyond the pale. As such it can function as a psychological bridge between the no longer acceptable older view and the new view which is emerging. But sooner or later we have to get off the bridge on to the other side. We have to make what might be called a Copernican revolution in our theology of religions. You will remember that the old Ptolemaic astronomy held that the earth is the centre of the solar system and that all the other heavenly bodies revolve around it. And when it was realized that this theory did not fit the observed facts, particularly the wandering movements of the planets, epicycles were added, circles revolving on circles to complicate the theory and bring it nearer to the facts. By analogy the "no salvation outside Christianity" doctrine is theologically Ptolemaic. Christianity is seen as the centre of the universe of faiths, and all the other religions are regarded as revolving round it and as being graded in value according to their distance from it. And the theories of implicit faith, baptism by desire, anonymous Christianity, the latent Church, the "ordinary" and "extraordinary" ways of salvation, and the claim that the Christian religion is not a religion whereas all the others are, are so many epicycles added to this Ptolemaic theology to try to accommodate our growing knowledge of other faiths and our awareness of the true piety and devotion which they sustain.

It is worth noting that just as a Ptolemaic astronomy could be developed, not only from the standpoint of this earth, but from any of the other planets, so also a Ptolemaic theology can be developed not only from a Christian standpoint but equally from the standpoint of any other faith. From, let us say, a Hindu centre one could say that devout Christians are implicit Hindus in virtue of their sincere desire for the truth even though they do not yet know what the truth is; that other faiths provide the "ordinary way" of salvation whilst Hinduism is the "extraordinary" way, in which the truth is manifest which in the others is latent; that Hinduism is not a religion but the eternal truth judging and superseding all religions. The Ptolemaic stance can be taken by anyone. But it can only serve as an interim position whilst we prepare our minds for a Copernican revolution. Copernicus realized that it is the sun, and not the earth, that is at the centre, and that all the heavenly bodies, including our own earth, revolve around it. And we have to realize that the universe of faiths centres upon *God*, and not upon Christianity or upon any other religion. He is the sun, the originative source of light and life, whom all the religions reflect in their own different ways.

This must mean that the different world religions have each served as God's means of revelation to and point of contact with a different stream of human life. Such a conclusion makes sense of the history of religions. The first period was one in which the innate religiousness of the human mind expressed itself in the different forms of what we can call natural religion – the worship of spirits, ancestors, nature gods, and often bloodthirsty national deities. But about 900 or 800 B.C. there began what Karl Jaspers has called the axial period in which seminal moments of religious experience occurred in each of the four principal centres of civilization – Greece, the Near East, India, and China – out of which the higher religions have come. In this immensely rich and important band of time the great Hebrew prophets lived; in Persia, Zoroaster; in China, Confucius and the author (or authors) of the Taoist Scriptures; in India, the Buddha, and Mahavira, and the writers of the Upanishads and of the Bhagavad Gita; in Greece, Pythagoras, Socrates and Plato. And then later, out of the stream of prophetic religion established by the Hebrew prophets there came Jesus and the rise of Christianity, and Mohammad and the rise of Islam.

Now in this axial period, some two and a half thousand years ago, communication between the continents and civilizations of the earth was so slow that for all practical purposes men lived in different cultural worlds. There could not be a divine revelation, through any human means, to mankind as a whole, but only separate revelations within the different streams of human history. And so it is a natural and indeed an inevitable hypothesis that God, the ultimate divine reality, was in this axial period revealing his presence and his will to mankind through a number of specially sensitive and responsive spirits. In each case the revelatory experiences, and the religious traditions to which they gave rise, were conditioned by the history, culture, language, climate, and indeed all the concrete circumstances of human life at that particular time and place. Thus the cultural and philosophical form of the revelation of the divine is characteristically different in each case, although we may believe that everywhere the one divine Spirit has been at work, pressing in upon the human spirit.

I shall return presently to this historical view of the different religious traditions to ask what difference it makes that the world has now become a communicational unity. But let me first ask the question that is so important to us as Christians, namely, what does all this imply concerning the person of our Lord? What about the uniqueness of Christ, the belief that Jesus was God Incarnate, the second Person of the Holy Trinity become man, the eternal Logos made flesh? Did he not say, "I and the Father are one", and "No one comes to the Father, but by me"? Here, unfortunately, we have to enter the realm of New Testament criticism: and I say "unfortunately" because of the notorious uncertainties of this realm. There are powerful schools of thought, following fashions which tend to change from generation to generation, but no consensus either across the years or across the schools. But this at least can be said: that whereas until some three or four generations ago it was generally accepted among biblical scholars that Jesus claimed to be the Son of God, with a unique consciousness of oneness with the Heavenly Father, so that the doctrine of the Incarnation was believed to be firmly based in the consciousness and teaching of Jesus himself, today this is no longer generally held and is indeed very widely thought not to be the case. I am not going to enter into a detailed discussion of the New Testament evidence: I am neither competent to do this, nor is there time. I will only quote some summarizing words of Wolfhart Pannenberg in his massive work, *Jesus: God and Man* (SCM Press, London, 1968), where he says that "After D. F. Strauss and F. C. Bauer, John's Gospel could no longer be claimed uncritically as a historical source of authentic words of Jesus. Consequently, other concepts and titles that were more indirectly connected with Jesus's relation to God came into the foreground of the question of Jesus's 'Messianic self-consciousness'. However, the transfer of these titles to Jesus ... has been demonstrated with growing certainty by critial study of the Gospels to be the work of the post-Easter community. Today it must be taken as all but certain that the pre-Easter Jesus neither designated himself as Messiah (or Son of God) nor accepted such a confession to him from others" (p. 327). Not all New Testament scholars would endorse Pannenberg's words. But certainly one can no longer regard it as a fact proved out of the New Testament that Jesus thought of himself as God Incarnate. On the contrary, this now seems to be very unlikely. And certainly we cannot rest anything on the assumption that the great Christological sayings of the Fourth Gospel (such as "I and my Father are one") were ever spoken, in sober historical fact, by the Jesus who walked the hills and villages of Galilee. It seems altogether more probable that they reflect the developing theology of the Church at about the end of the first century.

Now if Jesus himself did not think of himself as God Incarnate, one might well ask whether his disciples ought to do so. But instead of pursuing that question directly it seems more profitable to accept that the Son-of-God and God-Incarnate language has become deeply entrenched in the discourse of Christian thought and piety, and to ask what *kind* of language it is. Is the statement that Jesus was God Incarnate, or the Son of God, or God the Son, a statement of literal fact?; and if so, what precisely is the fact? Or is it a poetic, or symbolic, or mythological statement? It can, I think, only be the latter. It can hardly be a literal factual statement, since after nearly 2000 years of Christian reflection no factual content has been discerned in it. Unless, that is, we give it factual content in terms of the idea of Jesus's Virgin Birth. We could then say that his being the Son of God means that the Holy Spirit fulfilled the role of the male parent in his conception. But he would then be a divine-human figure such as is familiar from Greek mythology; for example, Hercules, whose father was the god Jupiter and whose mother was a human woman. However, this has never seriously been regarded as the real meaning of the doctrine of the Incarnation. What then is its real meaning? Whenever in the history of Christian thought theologians have tried to spell out its meaning in literal, factual terms the result has been heretical. A classic example would be Apollinarius's theory that Jesus's body and soul were human but that his spirit was the eternal divine Logos. This was rejected as heresy because it implied that Jesus was not genuinely human. And all attempts to treat the Incarnation as a factual hypothesis have likewise been rejected by the Church because they have failed to do justice either to Jesus's full humanity or to his full deity. Indeed, one may say that the fundamental heresy is precisely to treat the Incarnation as a factual hypothesis! For the reason why it has never been possible to state a literal meaning for the idea of Incarnation is simply that it has no literal meaning. It is a mythological idea, a figure of speech, a piece of poetic imagery. It is a way of saying that Jesus is our living contact with the transcendent God. In his presence we find that we are brought into the presence of God. We believe that he is so truly God's servant that in living as his disciples we are living according to the divine purpose. And as our sufficient and saving point of contact with God there is for us something absolute about him which justifies the absolute language which Christianity has developed. Thus reality is being expressed mythologically when we say that he is the Son of God, God Incarnate, the Logos made flesh.

When we see the Incarnation as a mythological idea applied to Jesus to express the experienced fact that he is our sufficient, effective and saving point of contact with God, we no longer have to draw the negative conclusion that he is man's one and only effective point of contact with God. We can revere Christ as the one through whom we have found salvation, without having to deny other points of reported saving contact between God and man. We can commend the way of Christian faith without having to discommend other ways of faith. We can say that there is salvation in Christ without having to say that there is no salvation other than in Christ.

Let us return, finally, to the historical situation. We have seen that the great world religions arose within different streams of human life and have in the past flowed down the centuries within different cultural channels. They have until recently interacted with one another only spasmodically, and nearly always in hostile clashes rather than in mutual dialogue and friendly interpenetration. But latterly this situation has been changing radically. Since the late nineteenth century there has been a positive influence of Christianity upon Hinduism, bearing fruit in a new social concern in India; and an influence of both Hinduism and Buddhism upon Christianity, bearing fruit in the new Western appreciation of meditation and the arts of spiritual self-development. And today the world religions are increasingly in contact with one another in conscious dialogue and in deliberate attempts to learn about and to learn from one another. These mutual influences can only increase in the future. It is I think very important to notice that each of the world religions is in practice an on-going history of change. Each likes to think of itself as immutable, the same yesterday, today and for ever. But the historian can see that this is not so. Each of the major world faiths has gone through immense historical developments, revolutions and transformations. Each has experienced both times of rapid change, in sudden expansions, schisms, reformations and renaissances, and also periods of relative stability. Islam has perhaps changed less than the others; but even within Islam there have been immense evolutionary developments and also the growth of important divisions. Hinduism has always been able to change, and to absorb new influences into its own life. Christianity and Buddhism have both developed through the centuries almost out of recognition. And in each case there is in principle no limit to the further developments that may take place in the future. In the next period these will occur in a context of interaction. The future of Christianity will be formed partly by influences stemming from Hinduism, Buddhism, and Islam; and so also, in a mutually interactive system, with the other world faiths. And all partly also by influences stemming from the secular civilization within which they will all exist.

Can we peer into the future and anticipate the pattern of development? Obviously, in trying to do so we are guessing. However, such guessing is today dignified by the name of Futurology and large books are written about the state of the planet in, say, the year 2000. These speculations are not random guesses, but are based on the projection of present trends, together with the foreseeable emergence of new trends. If secular seers can speculate in these ways about the future of man, why should we not try to consider the forms which the religious life of mankind will take in, say, a hundred years' time if the present basic trends continue? I am making the very major assumption, which there is no time here to defend, that man's religiousness is innate and that religion will continue in some form so long as human nature remains essentially the same. But what forms will it take? The broad trend of the present century is ecumenical. Old divisions are being transcended. The deeper essentials in which people agree are tending to seem more important than the matters on which they differ. Projecting this trend into the future we may suppose that the ecumenical spirit which has already so largely transformed Christianity will increasingly affect the relations between the world faiths. There may well be a growing world ecumenism, in which the common commitment of faith in a higher spiritual reality which demands brotherhood on earth will seem more and more significant, whilst the differences between the religious traditions will seem proportionately less significant. The relation between them may thus become somewhat like that between the Christian denominations in Britain – that is to say, they are on increasingly friendly speaking terms; they freely visit one another's worship and are beginning to be able to share places of worship; they co-operate in all sorts of service to the community; their clergy are accustomed to meet together for discussion, and there is even a degree of interchange of ministries; and so on.

What we are picturing here as a future possibility is not a single world religion, but a situation in which the different traditions no longer see themselves and each other as rival ideological communities. A single world religion is, I would think, never likely, and not a consummation to be desired. For so long as there is a variety of human types there will be a variety of kinds of worship and a variety of theological emphases and approaches. There will always be the more mystical and the more prophetic types of faith, with their corresponding awareness of the ultimate Reality as non-personal and as personal. There will always be the more spontaneous, warm and Spirit-filled forms of devotion, and the more liturgical, orderly and rationally controlled forms. There will always be the more vivid consciousness of the divine as gracious love, and as infinite demand and judgement, and so on. But it is not necessary, and it may in a more ecumenical age not be felt to be necessary, to assume that if God is being truly worshipped by Christians he cannot also be being truly worshipped by Jews and Muslims and Sikhs and by theistic Hindus and Amida Buddhists; or even that if the Ultimate Divine Reality is being validly experienced within the theistic streams of religious life as a personal presence, that Reality may not also be validly experienced within other streams of religious life as the infinite Being-Consciousness-Bliss (*Satchitananda*) of some forms of Hinduism, or as the ineffable cosmic Buddha-nature (the *Dharmakaya*) of some forms of Buddhism.

Let me then end with a quotation from one of the great revelatory scriptures of the world: "Howsoever man may approach me, even so do I accept them; for, on all sides, whatever path they may choose is mine."

A Philosophy of Religious Pluralism

Wilfred Cantwell Smith in his work on the concepts of religion and of religions has been responsible, more than any other one individual, for the change which has taken place within a single generation in the way in which many of us perceive the religious life of mankind.

Seen through pre-Cantwell Smith eyes there are a number of vast, long-lived historical entities or organisms known as Christianity, Hinduism, Islam, Buddhism, and so on. Each has an inner skeletal framework of beliefs, giving shape to a distinctive form of religious life, wrapped in a thick institutional skin which divides it from other religions and from the secular world within which they exist. Thus Buddhism, Islam, Christianity, and the rest, are seen as contraposed socio-religious entities which are the bearers of distinctive creeds; and every religious individual is a member of one or other of these mutually exclusive groups.

This way of seeing the religious life of humanity, as organised in a number of communities based upon rival sets of religious beliefs, leads to the posing of questions about religion in a certain way. For the beliefs which a religion professes are beliefs about God, or the Ultimate, and as such they define a way of human salvation or liberation and are accordingly a matter of spiritual life and death. Looking at the religions of the world, then, in the plural we are presented with competing claims to possess the saving truth. For each community believes that its own gospel is true and that other gospels are false in so far as they differ from it. Each believes that the way of salvation to which it witnesses is the authentic way, the only sure path to eternal blessedness. And so the proper question in face of this plurality of claims is, which is the true religion?

In practice, those who are concerned to raise this question are normally fully convinced that theirs is the true religion; so that for them the task is to show the spiritual superiority of their own creed and the consequent moral superiority of the community which embodies it. A great deal of the mutal criticism of religions, and of the derogatory assessment of one by another, has been in fulfilment of this task.

This view of mankind's religious life as divided into great contraposed entities, each claiming to be the true religion, is not however the only possible way of seeing the religious situation. Cantwell Smith has offered an alternative vision.

He shows first that the presently dominant conceptuality has a history that can be traced back to the European Renaissance. It was then that the different streams of religious life began to be reified in Western thought as solid structures called Christianity, Judaism, and so forth. And having reified their own faith in this way Westerners have then exported the notion of "a religion" to the rest of the world, causing others to think of themselves as belonging to the Hindu, or the Confucian, or the Buddhist religion, and so on, over against others. But an alternative perception can divide the scene differently. It sees something of vital religious significance taking

Source: *A John Hick Reader*, ed. Paul Badham.

different forms all over the world within the contexts of the different historical traditions. This "something of vital religious significance" Cantwell Smith calls faith. I would agree with some of his critics that this is not the ideal word for it; for "faith" is a term that is more at home in the Semitic than in the Indian family of traditions and which has, as his own historical researches have shown, become badly over-intellectualised. But I take it that he uses the term to refer to the spiritual state, or existential condition, constituted by a person's present response to the ultimate divine Reality. This ranges from the negative response of a self-enclosed consciousness which is blind to the divine presence, whether beyond us or in the depths of our own being, to a positive openness to the Divine which gradually transforms us and which is called salvation or liberation or enlightenment. This transformation is essentially the same within the different religious contexts within which it occurs: I would define it formally as the transformation of human existence from self-centredness to Reality-centredness. This is the event or process of vital significance which one can see to be occurring in individuals all over the world, taking different forms within the contexts of the different perceptions of the Ultimate made available by the various religious traditions.

These cumulative traditions themselves are the other thing that one sees with the aid of the new conceptuality suggested by Cantwell Smith. They are distinguishable strands of human history in each of which a multitude of religious and cultural elements interact to form a distinctive pattern, constituting, say, the Hindu, Buddhist, Confucian, Jewish, Christian or Muslim tradition. These traditions are not static entities but living movements; and they are not tightly homogeneous but have each become in the course of time internally highly various. Thus there are large differences between, for example, Buddhism in the time of Gautama and Buddhism after the development of the Mahāyāna and its expansion northwards into China; or between the Christian movement in Roman Palestine and that in medieval Europe. And there are large differences today between, say, Zen and Amida Buddhism in Japan, or between Southern Baptist and Northern Episcopalian Christianity in the United States. Indeed, since we cannot always avoid using the substantives, we might do well to speak of Buddhisms, Christianities, and so on, in the plural. A usage consonant with Cantwell Smith's analysis has however already become widespread, and many of us now often prefer to speak not of Christianity but of the Christian tradition, the Hindu tradition, and so on, when referring to these historically identifiable strands of history.

These cumulative traditions are composed of a rich complex of inner and outer elements cohering in a distinctive living pattern which includes structures of belief, life-styles, scriptures and their interpretations, liturgies, cultic celebrations, myths, music, poetry, architecture, literature, remembered history and its heroes. Thus the traditions constitute religious cultures, each with its own unique history and ethos. And each such tradition creates human beings in its own image. For we are not human in general, participating in an eternal Platonic essence of humanity. We are human in one or other of the various concrete ways of being human which constitute the cultures of the earth. There is a Chinese way of being human, an African way, an Arab way, a European way, or ways, and so on. These are not fixed moulds but living organisms which develop and interact over the centuries, so that the patterns of human life change, usually very slowly but sometimes with startling rapidity. But we are all formed in a hundred ways of which we are not normally aware by the culture into which we were born, by which we are fed, and with which we interact.

Let us then enter, with Cantwell Smith, into the experiment of thinking, on the one hand, of "faith", or human response to the divine, which in its positive and negative forms is salvation and non-salvation and, on the other hand, of the cumulative religious traditions within which this occurs; and let us ask what the relation is between these two realities – on the one hand salvation/liberation and on the other the cumulative traditions.

In various different forms this question has been much discussed within the Christian world, particularly during the last hundred and fifty years or so, as Christians have become increasingly conscious of the continuing reality of the other great religious traditions. For this period has seen renaissances within the Hindu and Buddhist worlds – to an important extent, it would seem, in reaction to eighteenth- and nineteenth-century Christian imperialism – and a resurgence of Islam is currently taking place. These developments have precipitated intense debate among Christian thinkers in which many different options have been and are being canvassed. Both because of the fullness of this discussion within Christianity, and because I am myself a Christian and am concerned with the problem from a Christian point of view, I propose to describe the main options in Christian terms. They are three in number.

The first, which we may call "exclusivism", relates salvation/liberation exclusively to one particular tradition, so that it is an article of faith that salvation is restricted to this one group, the rest of mankind being either left out of account or explicitly excluded from the sphere of salvation. The most emphatic and influential expression of such a faith occurred in the Catholic dogma *Extra ecclesiam nulla salus* (outside the Church, no salvation) and the corresponding assumption of the nineteenth-century Protestant missionary movement: outside Christianity, no salvation. In these developments Christian thought went beyond a mere overlooking of non-Christian humanity – which might perhaps simply be attributed to restricted vision – to a positive doctrine of the unsaved status of that wider human majority. Exclusiveness of this strong kind was supported by a juridical conception of salvation. If salvation consists in a change of status in the eyes of God from the guilt of participation in Adam's original sin to a forgiveness made possible by Christ's sacrifice on the cross, the appropriation of which is conditional upon a personal response of faith in Christ, this salvation can very naturally be seen as restricted to the Christian faith community. If on the other hand salvation is understood as the actual transformation of human life from self-centredness to Reality-centredness, this is not necessarily restricted within the boundaries of any one historical tradition. One cannot know *a priori* where or to what extent it occurs; one can only look at the living of human life in its endlessly varied circumstances and try to discern the signs of this transformation. Except in those whom we call saints, in whom the transformation is sufficiently advanced to be publicly evident, such discernment is often extremely difficult; for salvation/liberation, understood in this way, is to be found in many stages and degrees in the varying qualities of true humanity, often realised more in some areas of life than in others, and with advances and regressions, efforts and lapses in all the respects in which human beings develop and change through the experience of life in time. There may of course – as the Hindu and Buddhist traditions generally teach – be a final moment of enlightenment in which the transformation is completed and Reality-centredness definitively supersedes the last remnants of self-centredness. But, even if this should be a universal pattern, the journey leading towards that final moment must be long and slow; and progress on the journey can to some extent be humanly discerned as the process of salvation gradually taking place. This understanding of salvation/liberation as the actual transformation of human beings is more easily open than is the juridical understanding of it to the possibility that the salvific process may be taking place not only within one tradition but within a number of traditions.

Christian exclusivism has now largely faded out from the "mainline" churches, but is still powerful in many of the "marginal" fundamentalistic sects; and it should be added that the "margins" of Christianity are probably more extensive today than ever before.

However, we may now turn to a second Christian answer to our question, which can be labelled "inclusivism". This can be expressed in terms either of a juridical or of a transformation-of-human-existence conception of salvation. In the former terms it is the view that God's forgiveness and acceptance of humanity have been made possible by Christ's death, but that the benefits of this sacrifice are not confined to those who respond to it with an explicit act of faith. The juridical transaction of Christ's atonement covered *all* human sin, so that all human beings are now open to God's mercy, even though they may never have heard of Jesus Christ and why he died on the cross of Calvary. I take it that it is this form of inclusivism that the present Pope was endorsing in his first encyclical when he said that "man – ever man without any exception whatever – has been redeemed by Christ, and because with man – with each man without any exception whatever – Christ is in a way united, even when man is unaware of it". This statement could however also be an expression of the other form of Christian inclusivism, which accepts the understanding of salvation as the gradual transformation of human life and sees this as taking place not only within Christian history but also within the contexts of all the other great world traditions. It regards this however, wherever it happens, as the work of Christ – the universal divine Logos, the Second Person of the divine Trinity, who became incarnate in Jesus of Nazareth. Thus we can speak of "the unknown Christ of Hinduism" and of the other traditions, and indeed the unknown Christ within all creative transformations of individuals and societies. And, if we ask how this differs from simply saying that within all these different streams of human life there is a creative and re-creative response to the divine Reality, the answer of this kind of Christian inclusivism is that Christians are those, uniquely, who are able to identify the source of salvation because they have encountered that source as personally incarnate in Jesus Christ.

Both forms of inclusivism do however involve certain inner strains and certain awkward implications. How are they to be combined with the traditional *Extra ecclesiam* dogma? The best known attempt is that of Karl Rahner, with his concept of the "anonymous Christian". Those who do not have an explicit Christian faith but who nevertheless seek, consciously or unconsciously, to do God's will can be regarded as, so to speak, honorary Christians – and this even though they do not so regard themselves and even though they may insist that they are not Christians but Muslims, Jews, Hindus, or whatever. Rahner's is a brave attempt to attain an inclusivist position which is in principle universal but which does not thereby renounce the old exclusivist dogma. But the question is whether in this new context the old dogma has not been so emptied of content as no longer to be worth affirming. When salvation is acknowledged to be taking place without any connection with the Christian Church or Gospel, in people who are living on the basis of quite other faiths, is it not a somewhat empty gesture to insist upon affixing a Christian label to them? Further, having thus labelled them, why persist in the aim of gathering all humankind into the Christian Church? Once it is accepted that salvation does not depend upon this, the conversion of the people of the other great world faiths to Christianity hardly seems the best way of spending one's energies.

The third possible answer to the question of the relation between salvation/ liberation and the cumulative religious traditions can best be called pluralism. As a Christian position this can be seen as an acceptance of the further conclusion to which inclusivism points. If we accept that salvation/liberation is taking place within all the great religious traditions, why not frankly acknowledge that there is a plurality of saving human responses to the ultimate divine Reality? Pluralism, then, is the view that the transformation of human existence from self-centredness to Reality-centredness is taking place in different ways within the contexts of all the great religious traditions. There is not merely one way but a plurality of ways of salvation or liberation. In Christian theological terms, there is a plurality of divine revelations, making possible a plurality of forms of saving human response.

What however makes it difficult for Christians to move from inclusivism to pluralism, holding the majority of Christian theologians today in the inclusivist position despite its evident logical instability, is of course the traditional doctrine of the incarnation, together with its protective envelope, the doctrine of the Trinity. For in its orthodox form, as classically expressed at the Councils of Nicaea and Chalcedon, the incarnational doctrine claims that Jesus was God incarnate, the Second Person of the Triune God living a human life. It is integral to this faith that there has been (and will be) no other divine incarnation. This makes Christianity unique in that it, alone among the religions of the world, was founded by God in person. Such a uniqueness would seem to demand Christian exclusivism – for must God not want all human beings to enter the way of salvation which he has provided for them? However, since such exclusivism seems so unrealistic in the light of our knowledge of the wider religious life of mankind, many theologians have moved to some form of inclusivism, but now feel unable to go further and follow the argument to its conclusion in the frank acceptance of pluralism. The break with traditional missionary attitudes and long-established ecclesiastical and liturgical language would, for many, be so great as to be prohibitive.

There is however the possibility of an acceptable Christian route to religious pluralism in work which has already been done, and which is being done, in the field of Christology with motivations quite other than to facilitate pluralism, and on grounds which are internal to the intellectual development of Christianity. For there is a decisive watershed between what might be called all-or-nothing Christologies and degree Christologies. The all-or-nothing principle is classically expressed in the Chalcedonian Definition, according to which Christ is "to be acknowledged in Two Natures", "Consubstantial with the Father according to his Deity, Consubstantial with us according to his Humanity". Substance is an all-or-nothing notion, in that A either is or is not composed of the same substance, either has or does not have the same essential nature, as B. Using this all-or-nothing conceptuality Chalcedon attributed to Christ two complete natures, one divine and the other human, being in his divine nature of one substance with God the Father. Degree Christologies, on the other hand, apply the term "incarnation" to the activity of God's Spirit or of God's grace in human lives, so that the divine will is done on earth. This kind of reinterpretation has been represented in recent years by, for example, the "paradox of grace" Christology of Donald Baillie (in *God was in Christ*, 1948) and the "inspiration Christology" of Geoffrey Lampe (in *God as Spirit*, 1977). In so far as a human being is open and responsive to God, so that God is able to act in and through that individual, we can speak of the embodiment in human life of God's redemptive activity. And in Jesus this "paradox of grace" – the paradox expressed by St Paul when he wrote "it was not I, but the grace of God which is in me" (1 Corinthians 15:10) – or the inspiration of God's Spirit, occurred to a startling extent. The paradox, or the inspiration, are not however confined to the life of Jesus; they are found, in varying degrees, in all free human response to God. Christologies of the same broad family occur in the work of Norman Pittenger (*The Word Incarnate*, 1957), John Knox (*The Humanity and Divinity of Christ*, 1967), and earlier in John Baillie (*The Place of Jesus Christ in Modern Christianity*, 1929), and more recently in the authors of *The Myth of God Incarnate* (1977).

These modern degree Christologies were not in fact for the most part developed in order to facilitate a Christian acceptance of religious pluralism. They were developed as alternatives to the old substance Christology, in which so many difficulties, both historical and philosophical, had become apparent. They claim to be compatible with the teachings of Jesus and of the very early Church, and to avoid the intractable problem, generated by a substance Christology, of the relation between Jesus' two natures. But, as an unintended consequence, degree Christologies open up the possibility of seeing God's activity in Jesus as being of the same kind as God's activity in other great human mediators of the divine. The traditional Christian claim to the unique superiority of Christ and of the Christian tradition is not of course precluded by a degree Christology; for it may be argued (as it was, for example, by both Baillie and Lampe) that Christ was the *supreme* instance of the paradox of grace or of the inspiration of the Spirit, so that Christianity is still assumed to be the *best* context of salvation/liberation. But, whereas, starting from the substance Christology, the unique superiority of Christ and the Christian Church are guaranteed *a priori*, starting from a degree Christology they have to be established by historical evidence. Whether this can in fact be done is, clearly, an open question. It would indeed be an uphill task today to establish that we know enough about the inner and outer life of the historical Jesus, and of the other founders of great religious traditions, to be able to make any such claim; and perhaps an even more uphill task to establish from the morally ambiguous histories of each of the great traditions, complex mixtures of good and evil as each has been, that one's own tradition stands out as manifestly superior to all others.

I think, then, that a path exists along which Christians can, if they feel so drawn, move to an acceptance of religious pluralism. Stated philosophically such a pluralism is the view that the great world faiths embody different perceptions and conceptions of, and correspondingly different responses to, the Real or the Ultimate from within the major variant cultural ways of being human; and that within each of them the transformation of human existence from self-centredness to Reality-centredness is manifestly taking place – and taking place, so far as human observations can tell, to much the same extent. Thus the great religious traditions are to be regarded as alternative soteriological "spaces" within which, or "ways" along which, men and women can find salvation/liberation/enlightenment/fulfilment.

But how can such a view be arrived at? Are we not proposing a picture reminiscent of the ancient allegory of the blind men and the elephant, in which each runs his hands over a different part of the animal, and identifies it differently, a leg as a tree, the trunk as a snake, the tail as a rope, and so on? Clearly, in the story the situation is being described from the point of view of someone who can observe both elephant and blind men. But where is the vantage-point from which one can observe both the divine Reality and the different limited human standpoints from which that Reality is being variously perceived? The advocate of the pluralist understanding cannot pretend to any such cosmic vision. How then does he profess to know that the situation is indeed as he depicts it? The answer is that he does not profess to *know* this, if by knowledge we mean infallible cognition. Nor indeed can anyone else properly claim to have knowledge, in this sense, of either the exclusivist or the inclusivist picture. All of them are, strictly speaking, hypotheses. The pluralist hypothesis is arrived at inductively. One starts from the fact that many human beings experience life in relation to a limitlessly greater transcendent Reality – whether the direction of transcendence be beyond our present existence or within its hidden depths. In theory such religious experience is capable of a purely naturalistic analysis which does not involve reference to any reality other than the human and the natural. But to participate by faith in one of the actual streams of religious experience – in my case, the Christian stream – is to participate in it as an experience of transcendent Reality. I think that there is in fact a good argument for the rationality of trusting one's own religious experience, together with that of the larger tradition within which it occurs, so as both to believe and to live on the basis of it; but I cannot develop that argument here. Treating one's own form of religious experience, then, as veridical – as an experience (however dim, like "seeing through a glass, darkly") of transcendent divine Reality – one then has to take account of the fact that there are other great streams of religious experience which take different forms, are shaped by different conceptualities, and embodied in different institutions, art forms, and life-styles. In other words, besides one's own religion, sustained by its distinctive form of religious experience, there are also other religions, through each of which flows the life blood of a different form of religious experience. What account is one to give of this plurality?

At this point the three answers that we discussed above become available again: exclusivism, inclusivism and pluralism. The exclusivist answer is that only one's own form of religious experience is an authentic contact with the Transcendent, other forms being delusory: the naturalistic interpretation applies to those other forms, but not to ours. This is a logically possible position; but clearly it is painfully vulnerable to the charge of being entirely arbitrary. It thus serves the cause of general scepticism, as David Hume noted with regard to claims that the miracles of one's own religion are genuine whilst those of others are spurious.

Moving to the inclusivist answer, this would suggest that religious experience in general does indeed constitute a contact with the Transcendent, but that this contact occurs in its purest and most salvifically effective form within one's own tradition, other forms having value to the varying extents to which they approximate to ours. This is a more viable position than the previous one, and less damaging to the claim that religion is not a human projection but a genuine human response to transcendent Reality. There is however a range of facts which do not fit easily into the inclusivist theory, namely the changed and elevated lives, moving from self-centredness towards Reality-centredness, within the other great religious traditions. Presumably there must be a strong correlation between the authenticity of the forms of religious experience and their spiritual and moral fruits. It would then follow from the inclusivist position that there should be a far higher incidence and quality of saintliness in one tradition – namely, that in which contact with the Transcendent occurs in "its purest and most salvifically effective form" – than in the others. But this does not seem to be the case. There is of course no reliable census of saints! Nor indeed is the concept of a saint by any means clear and unproblematic; very different profiles of saintliness have operated at different times and in different places. But if we look for the transcendence of egoism and a recentring in God or in the transcendent Real, then I venture the proposition that, so far as human observation and historical memory can tell, this occurs to about the same extent within each of the great world traditions.

If this is so, it prompts us to go beyond inclusivism to a pluralism which recognises a variety of human religious contexts within which salvation/liberation takes place.

But such a pluralistic hypothesis raises many questions. What is this divine Reality to which all the great traditions are said to be oriented? Can we really equate the personal Yahweh with the non-personal Brahman, Shiva with the Tao, the Holy Trinity with the Buddhist *Trikāya*, and all with one another? Indeed, do not the Eastern and Western faiths deal incommensurably with different problems?

As these questions indicate, we need a pluralistic theory which enables us to recognise and be fascinated by the manifold differences between the religious traditions, with their different conceptualisations, their different modes of religious experience, and their different forms of individual and social response to the divine. I should like in these final pages to suggest the ground plan of such a theory – a theory which is, I venture to think, fully compatible with the central themes of Cantwell Smith's thought.

Each of the great religious traditions affirms that in addition to the social and natural world of our ordinary human experience there is a limitlessly greater and higher Reality beyond or within us, in relation to which or to whom is our highest good. The ultimately real and the ultimately valuable are one, and to give oneself freely and totally to this One is our final salvation/liberation/enlightenment/ fulfilment. Further, each tradition is conscious that the divine Reality exceeds the reach of our earthly speech and thought. It cannot be encompassed in human concepts. It is infinite, eternal, limitlessly rich beyond the scope of our finite conceiving or experiencing. Let us then both avoid the particular names used within the particular traditions and yet use a term which is consonant with the faith of each of them – Ultimate Reality, or the Real.

Let us next adopt a distinction that is to be found in different forms and with different emphases within each of the great traditions, the distinction between the Real *an sich* (in him/her/itself) and the Real as humanly experienced and thought. In Christian terms this is the distinction between God in God's infinite and eternal self-existent being, "prior" to and independent of creation, and God as related to and known by us as creator, redeemer and sanctifier. In Hindu thought it is the distinction between *nirguna* Brahman, the Ultimate in itself, beyond all human categories, and *saguna* Brahman, the Ultimate as known to finite consciousness as a personal deity, Iśvara. In Taoist thought, "The Tao that can be expressed is not the eternal Tao" (*Tao-Te Ching*, 1). There are also analogous distinctions in Jewish and Muslim mystical thought in which the Real *an sich* is called *en Soph* and *al Haqq*. In Mahāyāna Buddhism there is the distinction between the *dharmakāya*, the eternal cosmic Buddha-nature, which is also the infinite Void (*śūnyatā*), and on the other hand the realm of heavenly Buddha figures (*sambhogakāya*) and their incarnation in the earthly Buddhas (*nirmānakāya*). This varied family of distinctions suggests the perhaps daring thought that the Real *an sich* is one but is nevertheless capable of being humanly experienced in a variety of ways. This thought lies at the heart of the pluralistic hypothesis which I am suggesting.

The next point of which we need to take account is the creative part that thought, and the range of concepts in terms of which it functions, plays in the formation of conscious experience. It was above all Immanuel Kant who brought this realisation into the stream of modern reflection, and it has since been confirmed and amplified by innumerable studies, not only in general epistemology but also in cognitive psychology, in the sociology of knowledge, and in the philosophy of science. The central fact, of which the epistemology of religion also has to take account, is that our environment is not reflected in our consciousness in a simple and straightforward way, just as it is, independently of our perceiving it. At the physical level, out of the immense richness of structure and detail around us, only that minute selection that is relevant to our biological survival and flourishing affects our senses; and these inputs are interpreted in the mind/brain to produce our conscious experience of the familiar world in which we live. Its character as an environment within which we can learn to behave appropriately can be called its *meaning* for us. This all-important dimension of meaning, which begins at the physical level as the habitability of the material world, continues at the personal, or social, level of awareness as the moral significance of the situations of our life, and at the religious level as a consciousness of the ultimate meaning of each situation and of our situation as a whole in relation to the divine Reality. This latter consciousness is not however a general consciousness of the divine, but always takes specific forms; and, as in the case of the awareness of the physical and of the ethical meaning of our environment, such consciousness has an essential dispositional aspect. To experience in this way rather than in that involves being in a state of readiness to behave in a particular range of ways, namely that which is appropriate to our environment having the particular character that we perceive (or of course misperceive) it to have. Thus to be aware of the divine as "the God and Father of our Lord Jesus Christ", in so far as this is the operative awareness which determines our dispositional state, is to live in the kind of way described by Jesus in his religious and moral teaching – in trust towards God and in love towards our neighbours.

How are these various specific forms of religious awareness formed? Our hypothesis is that they are formed by the presence of the divine Reality, this presence coming to consciousness in terms of the different sets of religious concepts and structures of religious meaning that operate within the different religious traditions of the world. If we look at the range of actual human religious experience and ask ourselves what basic concepts and what concrete images have operated in its genesis, I would suggest that we arrive at something like the following answer. There are, first, the two basic religious concepts which between them dominate the entire range of the forms of religious experience. One is the concept of Deity, or God, i.e. the Real as personal; and the other is the concept of the Absolute, i.e. the Real as non-personal. (The term "Absolute" is by no means ideal for the purpose, but is perhaps the nearest that we have.) We do not however, in actual religious experience, encounter either Deity in general or the Absolute in general, but always in specific forms. In Kantian language, each general concept is schematised, or made concrete. In Kant's own analysis of sense-experience the schematisation of the basic categories is in terms of time; but religious experience occurs at a much higher level of meaning, presupposing and going beyond physical meaning and involving much more complex and variable modes of dispositional response. Schematisation or concretisation here is in terms of "filled" human time, or history, as diversified into the different cultures and civilisations of the earth. For there are different concrete ways of being human and of participating in human history, and within these different ways the presence of the divine Reality is experienced in characteristically different ways.

To take the concept of God first, this becomes concrete as the range of specific deities to which the history of religion bears witness. Thus the Real as personal is known in the Christian tradition as God the Father; in Judaism as Adonai; in Islam as Allah, the Qur'ānic Revealer; in the Indian traditions as Shiva, or Vishnu, or Paramātmā, and under the many other lesser images of deity which in different regions of India concretise different aspects of the divine nature. This range of personal deities who are the foci of worship within the theistic traditions constitutes the range of the divine *personae* in relation to mankind. Each *persona*, in his or her historical concreteness, lives within the corporate experience of a particular faith-community. Thus the Yahweh *persona* exists and has developed in interaction with the Jewish people. He is a part of their history, and they are a part of his; and he cannot be extracted from this historical context. Shiva, on the other hand, is a quite different divine *persona*, existing in the experience of hundreds of millions of people in the Shaivite stream of Indian religious life. These two *personae*, Yahweh and Shiva, live within different worlds of faith, partly creating and partly created by the features of different human cultures, being responded to in different patterns of life, and being integral to different strands of historical experience. Within each of these worlds of faith great numbers of people find the ultimate meaning of their existence, and are carried through the crises of life and death; and within this process many are, in varying degrees, challenged and empowered to move forward on the way of salvation/liberation from self-centredness to Reality-centredness. From the pluralist point of view Yahweh and Shiva are not rival gods, or rival claimants to be the one and only God, but rather two different concrete historical *personae* in terms of which the ultimate divine Reality is present and responded to by different large historical communities within different strands of the human story.

This conception of divine *personae*, constituting (in Kantian language) different divine phenomena in terms of which the one divine noumenon is humanly experienced, enables us to acknowledge the degree of truth within the various projection theories of religion from Feuerbach through Freud to the present day. An element of human projection colours our mental images of God, accounting for their anthropomorphic features – for example, as male or female. But human projection does not – on this view – bring God into existence; rather it affects the ways in which the independently existing divine Reality is experienced.

Does this epistemological pattern of the schematisation of a basic religious concept into a range of particular correlates of religious experience apply also to the non-theistic traditions? I suggest that it does. Here the general concept, the Absolute, is schematised in actual religious experience to form the range of divine *impersonae* – Brahman, the Dharma, the Tao, *nirvāna*, *śūnyāta*, and so on – which are experienced within the Eastern traditions. The structure of these *impersonae* is however importantly different from that of the *personae*. A divine *persona* is concrete, implicitly finite, sometimes visualisable and even capable to being pictured. A divine *impersona*, on the other hand, is not a "thing" in contrast to a person. It is the infinite being-consciousness-bliss (*saccidānanda*) of Brahman; or the beginningless and endless process of cosmic change (*pratītya samutpāda*) of Buddhist teaching; or again the ineffable "further shore" of *nirvāna* or the eternal Buddha-nature (*dharmakāya*); or the ultimate Emptiness (*śūnyāta*) which is also the fullness or suchness of the world; or the eternal principle of the Tao. It is thus not so much an entity as a field of spiritual force, or the ultimate reality of everything, that which gives final meaning and joy. These non-personal conceptions of the Ultimate inform modes of consciousness varying from the advaitic experience of becoming one with the Infinite, to the Zen experience of finding a total reality in the present concrete moment of existence in the ordinary world. And according to the pluralistic hypothesis these different modes of experience constitute different experiences of the Real as non- or trans-personal. As in the case of the divine *personae*, they are formed by different religious conceptualities which have developed in interaction with different spiritual disciplines and methods of meditation. The evidence that a range of *impersonae* of the one Ultimate Reality are involved in the non-theistic forms of religious experience, rather than the direct unmediated awareness of Reality itself, consists precisely in the differences between the experiences reported within the different traditions. How is it that a "direct experience" of the Real can take such different forms? One could of course at this point revert to the exclusivism or the inclusivism whose limitations we have already noted. But the pluralist answer will be that even the most advanced form of mystical experience, as an experience undergone by an embodied consciousness whose mind/brain has been conditioned by a particular religious tradition, must be affected by the conceptual framework and spiritual training provided by that tradition, and accordingly takes these different forms. In other words the Real is experienced not *an sich*, but in terms of the various non-personal images or concepts that have been generated at the interface between the Real and different patterns of human consciousness.

These many different perceptions of the Real, both theistic and non-theistic, can only establish themselves as authentic by their soteriological efficacy. The great world traditions have in fact all proved to be realms within which or routes along which people are enabled to advance in the transition from self-centredness to Reality-centredness. And, since they reveal the Real in such different lights, we must conclude that they are independently valid. Accordingly, by attending to other traditions than one's own one may become aware of other aspects or dimensions of the Real, and of other possibilities of response to the Real, which had not been made effectively available by one's own tradition. Thus a mutual mission of the sharing of experiences and insights can proceed through the growing network of inter-faith dialogue and the interactions of the faith-communities. Such mutual mission does not aim at conversion – although occasionally individual conversions, in all directions, will continue to occur – but at mutual enrichment and at co-operation in face of the urgent problems of human survival in a just and sustainable world society.

There are many topics which I have not had space to take up in this chapter. I have spoken of "the great world traditions"; but what about the other smaller ones, including the many new religious movements which are springing up around us today? And what about the great secular faiths of Marxism and Maoism and humanism? Again, I have spoken of salvation/liberation as the transformation of human existence from self-centredness to Reality-centredness; but what about the social and political dimensions of this transformation? These are among the many important questions which any complete philosophy of religious pluralism must answer. But I hope that in this paper I may have said enough to indicate the possible fruitfulness of this general standpoint, a standpoint to which Wilfred Cantwell Smith's work has contributed so centrally and so notably.

22

Lesslie Newbigin,
"The Gospel and the Religions"

The British missionary and churchman Lesslie Newbigin (1909–98)
wrote extensively on Christianity and its relationship to the religions
of the world. In his book *The Gospel in a Pluralist Society*, he analyzes
the contours of the modern and postmodern problem of religious
pluralism from a Christian and theological point of view. In the chapter
entitled "The Gospel and the Religions," Newbigin suggests that
exclusivism, inclusivism, and pluralism – as represented by Hendrik
Kraemer, Karl Rahner, and John Hick, respectively – are all in some
way flawed as theological positions. Accordingly, he espouses a view
which is in some ways exclusivist, inclusivist, and pluralist – although
closer on the whole to the first two views than to the last one. However
one might seek to characterize Newbigin's own position, central to it
is his conviction about the Christian contribution to interreligious
dialogue – namely, the telling and retelling of the biblical and Christian
story.

The Text

1. If, as I have affirmed, we are to reject religious pluralism and acknowledge Jesus Christ as the unique and decisive revelation of God for the salvation of the world, what is the proper attitude which believers in that revelation ought to take towards the adherents of the great world religions? Perhaps one should begin by making the elementary point that the word "religion" covers an extremely wide and varied range of entities, and the way in which we relate to them as Christians will vary accordingly. One might divide the religions, as Nicol Macnicol does in his fine book *Is Christianity Unique?*, into those which understand God's self-revelation in historical terms – Judaism, Christianity, Islam – and those for whom the essential religious experience is a-historical – Hinduism, Jainism, Sikhism, Buddhism. Within the first group one would again have to distinguish between Judaism, which looks for a Messiah still to come, Christianity, which confesses Jesus as the Messiah who has come and is to come, and Islam, which affirms not a Messiah but a succession of messengers culminating in the Prophet. One should perhaps also include in this list Marxism, which functions in some respects as a religion in which the proletariat is the messianic people whose victory will inaugurate the final removal of human alienation from the sources of being. Clearly the gospel is related to each of these in differing ways.

    One could also classify the religions in a different way which takes account of the very important group of religions which are known as primal religions. Dr Harold Turner, well known as a student and interpreter of new religious movements in primal societies, says that there are only three possible ways of understanding the world: the atomic, the oceanic, and the relational – symoblized respectively by billiard balls, the ocean, and the net. This is a classification of worldviews rather than of religions, but all religions embody some kind of worldview. The atomic, which is characteristic of contemporary Western society and has deep roots in Greek philosophy, sees reality in terms of its individual units. The atom, conceived as a minute piece of matter, is the ultimate constituent of the visible world. The human individual, conceived as an autonomous center of knowing and willing, is the ultimate constituent of society. The oceanic view, on the other hand, sees all things ultimately merged into one entity which is both the soul and all that exists. Atma is Brahma. The third view sees everything as constituted by relationships, whether it is the material world or human society. This view, characteristic of what we are accustomed to call primitive societies and primal religions, is also the view of the Bible. That is probably why the gospel is more readily accepted by so-called primitive peoples than by those who inhabit atomic or oceanic worldviews. It also calls into question the conventional use of the term "higher religions" to denote the other world faiths.

2. These preliminary remarks about classifications of religions and worldviews

Source: Lesslie Newbigin, *The Gospel in a Pluralist Society*.

should serve to remind us that in using the word "religion" we are already making assumptions which need to be examined. In most human cultures religion is not a separate activity set apart from the rest of life. Neither in practice nor in thought is religion separate from the rest of life. In practice all the life of society is permeated by beliefs which Western Europeans would call religious, and in thought what we call religion is a whole worldview, a way of understanding the whole of human experience. The sharp line which modern Western culture has drawn between religious affairs and secular affairs is itself one of the most significant peculiarities of our culture and would be incomprehensible to the vast majority of people who have not been brought into contact with this culture. It follows that in thinking about the implications of the claim that Jesus is God's unique self-revelation for our relation to the world religions, we must take into view more than what we call religion. The contemporary debate about Christianity and the world's religions is generally conducted with the unspoken assumption that "religion" is the primary medium of human contact with the divine. But this assumption has to be questioned. When the New Testament affirms that God has nowhere left himself without witness, there is no suggestion that this witness is necessarily to be found in the sphere of what we call religion. The parables of Jesus are notable for the fact that they speak of secular experiences. When the Fourth Gospel affirms that the light of the Logos who came into the world in Jesus shines on every human being, there is no suggestion that this light is identified with human religion. The text goes on to say that this light shines in the darkness, and the ensuing story constantly suggests that it is religion which is the primary area of darkness, while the common people, unlearned in religious matters, are the ones who respond to the light. And it is significant that Justin Martyr, one of the earliest apologists to use this Johannine teaching in making contact with the unbelieving world, affirms that the true light did indeed shine on the great philosophers like Socrates, but that the contemporary religion was the work of devils. Our thought must therefore be directed not just to the religions so called; we must ask about the relation of the gospel to all who live by other commitments, whether they are called religious or secular.

3.   We must look first at the strictly exclusivist view which holds that all who do not accept Jesus as Lord and Savior are eternally lost. We shall look later at the question whether this is in fact what fidelity to Scripture requires us to hold. There are several reasons which make it difficult for me to believe this. If it were true, then it would be not only permissible but obligatory to use any means available, all the modern techniques of brainwashing included, to rescue others from this appalling fate. And since it is God alone who knows the heart of every person, how are we to judge whether or not another person truly has that faith which is acceptable to him? If we hold this view, it is absolutely necessary to know who is saved and who is not, and we are then led into making the kind of judgments against which Scripture warns us. We are in the business of erecting barriers: Has she been baptized? Has he been confirmed by a bishop in the historic succession? Or has she had a recognizable conversion and can she name the day and the hour when it happened? We are bound to become judges of that which God alone knows. Moreover, every missionary

knows that it is impossible to communicate the gospel without acknowledging in practice that there is some continuity between the gospel and the experience of the hearer outside the Christian Church. One cannot preach the gospel without using the word "God." If one is talking to a person of a non-Christian religion, one is bound to use one of the words in her language which is used to denote God. But the content of that word has necessarily been formed by his experience outside the church. By using the word, the preacher is taking the non-Christian experience of the hearer as the starting point. Without this there is no way of communicating. This fact by itself does not refute the position we are considering, but it makes it impossible to affirm a total discontinuity between Christian faith and the religions. And anyone who has had intimate friendship with a devout Hindu or Muslim would find it impossible to believe that the experience of God of which his friend speaks is simply illusion or fraud.

4.   An important group of writers who reject both this exclusivism on the one hand and a total pluralism on the other, take an inclusivist position which acknowledges Christ as the only Savior but affirm that his saving work extends beyond the bounds of the visible church. Probably the most influential exponent of this view has been Karl Rahner with his conception of anonymous Christianity. It is important to note here that Rahner is not merely affirming that individual non-Christians can be saved – certainly no new doctrine – but that the non-Christian religions as such have a salvific role. Rahner (*Theological Investigations*, vol. 5) set out his position in four theses:

a. Christianity is the absolute religion, being founded on the unique event of the incarnation of the Son of God. But, since this event occurred at a certain point in history, we have to ask about God's relation to those who lived before it occurred or before it was brought to their knowledge. This question will not be just about individuals but about the religions to which they adhered. To quote Rahner, "Man who is required to have a religion is also commanded to seek and accept a social form of religion" (p.120).

b. It follows that non-Christian religions, even if they contain error (as they do), are lawful and salvific up to the time at which the gospel is brought to the attention of their adherents. The gospel requires us to assume that God's grace is offered to all, and that "in a great many cases at least" it is accepted (p. 124). But after the time when the gospel has been preached and heard, the non-Christian religion is no longer lawful.

c. The faithful adherent of a non-Christian religion must therefore be regarded as an "anonymous Christian." He can be saved through his faithful practice of his religion. But the one who accepts Christ "has a greater chance of salvation than the anonymous Christian" (p. 132).

d. The other religions will not be displaced by Christianity. Religious pluralism will continue and conflict will become sharper.

5.   While Rahner's idea of "anonymous Christianity" has not proved widely acceptable, the idea that the non-Christian religions as such are to be understood as vehicles of salvation is widely accepted. It has indeed become a sort of orthodoxy and those who are not willing to accept it are dismissed as simply out-of-date (as by

Wesley Ariarajah – see *International Review of Mission*, July 1988, pp. 419–20). He attacks the position of those who are not willing to make this judgment but wish to leave it in God's hands as "theological neutrality," and says that we cannot now afford this neutrality because we urgently need to have a basis for praying together with people of other faiths for world peace. An alleged practical need overrides the question of truth. What are we to say, on the basis of a scriptural faith, about the status and role of the great world religions?

6.   I believe that we must begin with the great reality made known to us in Jesus Christ, that God – the creator and sustainer of all that exists – is in his own triune being an ocean of infinite love overflowing to all his works in all creation and to all human beings. I believe that when we see Jesus eagerly welcoming the signs of faith among men and women outside the house of Israel; when we see him lovingly welcoming those whom others cast out; when we see him on the cross with arms outstretched to embrace the whole world and when we hear his whispered words, "Father, forgive them; they know not what they do"; we are seeing the most fundamental of all realities, namely a grace and mercy and loving-kindness which reaches out to every creature. I believe that no person, of whatever kind or creed, is without some witness of God's grace in heart and conscience and reason, and none in whom that grace does not evoke some response – however feeble, fitful, and flawed.

7.   The same revelation in Jesus Christ, with its burning center in the agony and death of Calvary, compels me to acknowledge that this world which God made and loves is in a state of alienation, rejection, and rebellion against him. Calvary is the central unveiling of the infinite love of God and at the same time the unmasking of the dark horror of sin. Here not the dregs of humanity, not the scoundrels whom all good people condemn, but the revered leaders in church, state, and culture, combine in one murderous intent to destroy the holy one by whose mercy they exist and were created.

8.   All true thinking about this, as about every matter, must be held within the magnetic field set up between these two poles: the amazing grace of God and the appalling sin of the world. To live in this magnetic field is to live in an atmosphere which is charged with power, tingling, as it were, with electricity. One is always in the (humanly speaking) impossible position of knowing that one is – along with all others – at the same time the enemy of God and the beloved child of God. To live in this charged field of force is always at the same time supremely demanding and supremely affirming. But we are always tempted to slacken the tension by drawing away from one or other of the two poles. Nowhere is this more clear than in the attitude we take to people outside the household of faith. We can opt for a solution which relies wholly on the universality and omnipotence of grace and move toward some form of universalism. Here the sharpness of the issue which God's action in Christ raises for every human soul is blunted. There is no life-or-death decision to be made. We can relax and be assured that everything will be all right for everybody in the end. Over much theological writing about the gospel and the world's religions

one is tempted to write the famous words of Anselm: "Nondum considerasti quanti ponderis sit peccatum" – "You have not yet taken full account of sin." Or, on the other hand, the Christian may be so conscious of the abyss of sin from which only the grace of God in Jesus Christ could rescue him that he is unwilling to believe that the same grace can operate in ways beyond his own experience and understanding. His relation to the man or woman outside the Church, or outside the particular embodiment of Christianity to which he adheres, can only be that of the saved to the lost. In both cases genuine dialogue is impossible. In the first case there is no real dialogue because nothing vital is at stake; it is merely a sharing of varied experiences of the same reality. In the second case dialogue is simply inappropriate. The person in the lifeboat and the person drowning in the sea do not have a dialogue. The one rescues the other; the time to share their experiences will come only afterward.

9. If we are to avoid these two dangers, if we are to live faithfully in this spiritual magnetic field between the amazing grace of God and the appalling sin of the world, how are we to regard the other commitments, faiths, worldviews to which the people around us and with whom we live and move adhere? I believe that the debate about this question has been fatally flawed by the fact that it has been conducted around the question, "Who can be saved?" It has been taken for granted that the only question was, "Can the good non-Christian be saved?" and by that question what was meant was not, "Can the non-Christian live a good and useful life and play a good and useful role in the life of society?" The question was, "Where will she go when she dies?" I am putting this crudely because I want to make the issue as clear as possible. The quest for truth always requires that we ask the right questions. If we ask the wrong questions we shall get only silence or confusion. In the debate about Christianity and the world's religions it is fair to say that there has been an almost unquestioned assumption that the only question is, "What happens to the non-Christian after death?" I want to affirm that this is the wrong question and that as long as it remains the central question we shall never come to the truth. And this for three reasons:

a. First, and simply, it is the wrong question because it is a question to which God alone has the right to give the answer. I confess that I am astounded at the arrogance of theologians who seem to think that we are authorized, in our capacity as Christians, to inform the rest of the world about who is to be vindicated and who is to be condemned at the last judgment. There has been an odd reversal of roles here. There was a time when Protestants accused Catholics of lacking assurance of salvation, and Catholics accused Protestants of being too sure. Today Roman Catholic theologians accuse Protestants of a failure in responsibility when they say that God alone knows the ultimate fate of unbelievers. Hans Küng (*On Being a Christian*, p. 99) is scathing in his contempt for Protestant theologians who say that we must leave the question of the ultimate fate of non-Christians in the hands of God. Rahner is equally sure that it is the duty of Christian theologians to tell the faithful adherent of a non-Christian religion that he can be saved but that he will have a better chance of salvation if he becomes a Christian and no chance at all if he refuses this invitation. And Wesley Ariarajah rebukes Visser 't Hooft for what he calls a "theology of neutrality" because the latter said, "I don't know whether a Hindu is saved: I only know that salvation comes in Jesus Christ" (*International Review of Mission*, pp. 419–20). I find this way of thinking among Christians astonishing in view of the emphatic warnings of Jesus against these kinds of judgments which claim to preempt the final judgment of God. Nothing could be more remote from the whole thrust of Jesus' teaching than the idea that we are in a position to know in advance the final judgment of God. It would be tedious to repeat again the innumerable warnings of Jesus in this matter, his repeated statements that the last day will be a day of surprises, of reversals, of astonishment. In his most developed parable of the last judgment, the parable of the sheep and the goats, both the saved and the lost are astonished. Surely theologians at least should know that the judge on the last day is God and no one else. Perhaps the "feel" of Jesus' teaching is best captured in the brief story of the rich young ruler who had kept all God's commandments but turned away from the call to surrender his wealth, prompting Jesus' famous statement that for a rich man to enter the kingdom of God was harder than for a camel to go through the eye of a needle. When Peter protests, "Then who can be saved?" Jesus answers, "With men it is impossible, but with God all things are possible." I repeat that I find it astonishing that a theologian of the stature of Küng can so contemptuously reject the position of writers like Barth and Kraemer who refuse to pronounce on the final salvation of the non-Christian. If a theologian is really serious he must learn to understand the impossible possibility of salvation.

In St Paul we find this same tension of confidence and awareness of the abyss that lies beneath. Paul, who is certain that nothing can separate him from the love of God in Christ Jesus, also tells his friends that he has to exercise severe self-discipline "lest having preached to others I myself should be disqualified" (1 Cor. 9:27). The Christian life, lived in the magnetic field between the two poles of the amazing grace of God and the appalling sin in which I share, has a corresponding synthesis of a godly confidence and a godly fear. The fear is lest I should put my trust in anything other than God's grace in Jesus Christ; the confidence is in the infinite abundance of his grace to me and to every one of his creatures.

b. The second reason for rejecting this way of putting the question is that it is based on an abstraction. By concentrating on the fate of the individual soul after death, it abstracts the soul from the full reality of the human person as an actor and sufferer in the ongoing history of the world. Once again we have to insist that the human person is not, essentially, a soul which can be understood in abstraction from the whole story of the person's life. This reductionist move is as misleading as the corresponding move of the materialists and behaviorists who want to explain the human person simply as a bundle of physical activities. If we refuse both these forms of reductionism, then the question we have to ask is not, "What will happen to this person's soul after death?" but "What is the end which gives meaning to this person's story as part of God's whole story?" It has often been pointed out that the verb "to save" is used in the New Testament in three tenses – past, present, and future. We were saved, we are being saved, and we look for salvation. By common consent it is agreed that to understand the word we must begin from its eschatological sense, from the end to which it all looks. Salvation in this sense is the completion of God's whole work in creation and redemption, the summing up of all things with Christ as head (Eph. 1:10), the reconciling of all things in heaven and earth through the blood of the cross (Col. 1:20), the subjecting of all hostile powers under the feet of Christ (1 Cor. 15:24–28). The other uses of the verb (we have been saved, we are being saved) must be understood in the light of the end to which they look. The question of salvation is wrongly posed if it is posed in respect of the human soul abstracted from God's history of salvation, abstracted therefore from the question, "How do we understand the human story?" Being saved has to do with the part we are playing now in God's story and therefore with the question whether we have understood the story rightly. If follows that our dialogue with people of other faiths must be about what is happening in the world now and about how we understand it and take our part in it. It cannot be only, or even mainly, about our destiny as individual souls after death. Insofar as the debate has concentrated on this latter question, it has been flawed.

c. The third reason for rejecting this way of putting the question is the most fundamental: it is that the question starts with the individual and his or her need to be assured of ultimate happiness, and not with God and his glory. All human beings have a longing for ultimate happiness, and the many worldviews, religious or otherwise, have as part of their power some promise of satisfying that longing. We must believe that this longing is something implanted in us by God. He has so made us that we have infinite desires beyond the satisfaction of our biological necessities, desires which only God himself can satisfy. Our hearts are restless till they find rest in him. On our journey he gives us good things which whet our appetite but do not finally satisfy, for they are always corrupted by the selfishness that desires to have them as our own possession. The gospel, the story of the astonishing act of God himself in coming down to be part of our alienated world, to endure the full horror of our rebellion against love, to take the whole burden of our guilt and shame, and to lift us up into communion and fellowship with himself, breaks into this self-centred search for our own happiness, shifts the center from the self and its desires to God and his glory. It is true, God forgive us, that Christians have turned even this into something that they thought they could possess for themselves; that they have privatized this mighty work of grace and talked as if the whole cosmic drama of salvation culminated in the words "For me; for me"; as if the one question is "How can I be saved?" leading inevitably to the question, "How can anyone be saved?" But this is a perversion of the gospel. For anyone who has understood what God did for us all in Jesus Christ, the one question is: "How shall God be glorified? How shall his amazing grace be known and celebrated and adored? How shall he see of the travail of his soul and be satisfied?" The whole discussion of the role of the world religions and secular ideologies from the point of view of the Christian faith is skewed if it begins with the question, Who is going to be saved at the end? That is a question which God alone will answer, and it is arrogant presumption on the part of theologians to suppose that it is their business to answer it. We have to begin with the mighty work of grace in Jesus Christ and ask, How is he to be honored and glorified? The goal of missions is the glory of God.

*

The Gospel and the Religions

What are the practical consequences of taking this as the starting point in our relation to people of other faiths? I suggest four immediate implications.

1. The first is this: we shall expect, look for, and welcome all the signs of the grace of God at work in the lives of those who do not know Jesus as Lord. In this, of course, we shall be following the example of Jesus, who was so eager to welcome the evidences of faith in those outside the household of Israel. This kind of expectancy and welcome is an implication of the greatness of God's grace as it has been shown to us in Jesus. For Jesus is the personal presence of that creative word by which all that exists was made and is sustained in being. He comes to the world as no stranger but as the source of the world's life. He is the true light of the world, and that light shines into every corner of the world in spite of all that seeks to shut it out. In our contact with people who do not acknowledge Jesus as Lord, our first business, our first privilege, is to seek out and to welcome all the reflections of that one true light in the lives of those we meet. There is something deeply repulsive in the attitude, sometimes found among Christians, which makes only grudging acknowledgment of the faith, the godliness, and the nobility to be found in the lives of non-Christians. Even more repulsive is the idea that in order to communicate the gospel to them one must, as it were, ferret out their hidden sins, show that their goodness is not so good after all, as a precondition for presenting the offer of grace in Christ. It is indeed true that in the presence of the cross we come to know that, whoever we are, we are sinners before the grace of God. But that knowledge is the result, not the precondition of grace. It is in the light of the amazing grace of God in Jesus Christ that I am compelled to say, "God, be merciful to me a sinner." Indeed, as the Fourth Gospel teaches us, it is only the presence of the living Holy Spirit that can convict the world in respect of sin and righteousness and judgment. The preacher of the gospel may well be mistaken in regard to these matters; he may see sin where no sin is, and may be blind to the sins of which he himself is a party. As a fellow human being and a fellow sinner, his relation to the man or woman of another faith must be modeled on that of Jesus to all who came to him.

2. The second consequence of the approach I suggest is that the Christian will be eager to cooperate with people of all faiths and ideologies in all projects which are in line with the Christian's understanding of God's purpose in history. I have repeatedly made the point that the heart of the faith of a Christian is the belief that the true meaning of the story of which our lives are a part is that which is made known in the biblical narrative. The human story is one which we share with all other human beings – past, present, and to come. We cannot opt out of the story. We cannot take control of the story. It is under the control of the infinitely patient God and Father of our Lord Jesus Christ. Every day of our lives we have to make decisions about the part we will play in the story, decisions which we cannot take without regard to the others who share the story. They may be Christians, Muslims, Hindus, secular humanists, Marxists, or of some other persuasion. They will have different understandings of the meaning and end of the story, but along the way there will be many issues in which we can agree about what should be done. There are struggles for justice and for freedom in which we can and should join hands with

those of other faiths and ideologies to achieve specific goals, even though we know that the ultimate goal is Christ and his coming in glory and not what our collaborators imagine.

3. Third, it is precisely in this kind of shared commitment to the business of the world that the context for true dialogue is provided. As we work together with people of other commitments, we shall discover the places where our ways must separate. Here is where real dialogue may begin. It is a real dialogue about real issues. It is not just a sharing of religious experience, though it may include this. At heart it will be a dialogue about the meaning and goal of the human story. If we are doing what we ought to be doing as Christians, the dialogue will be initiated by our partners, not by ourselves. They will be aware of the fact that, while we share with them in commitment to some immediate project, our action is set in a different context from theirs. It has a different motivation. It looks to a different goal. Specifically – and here I am thinking of the dialogue with secular ideologies – our partners will discover that we do not invest our ultimate confidence in the intrahistorical goal of our labors, but that for us the horizon is one that is both nearer and farther away than theirs. They will discover that we are guided by something both more ultimate and more immediate than the success of the project in hand. And they will discover that we have resources for coping with failure, defeat, and humiliation, because we understand human history from this side of the resurrection of the crucified Lord. It is – or it ought to be – the presence of these realities which prompts the questions and begins the dialogue. And, once again, the dialogue will not be about who is going to be saved. It will be about the question, "What is the meaning and goal of this common human story in which we are all, Christians and others together, participants?"

4. Therefore, the essential contribution of the Christian to the dialogue will simply be the telling of the story, the story of Jesus, the story of the Bible. The story is itself, as Paul says, the power of God for salvation. The Christian must tell it, not because she lacks respect for the many excellencies of her companions – many of whom may be better, more godly, more worthy of respect than she is. She tells it simply as one who has been chosen and called by God to be part of the company which is entrusted with the story. It is not her business to convert the others. She will indeed – out of love for them – long that they may come to share the joy that she knows and pray that they may indeed do so. But it is only the Holy Spirit of God who can so touch the hearts and consciences of the others that they are brought to accept the story as true and to put their trust in Jesus. This will always be a mysterious work of the Spirit, often in ways which no third party will ever understand. The Christian will pray that it may be so, and she will seek faithfully both to tell the story and – as part of a Christian congregation – so conduct her life as to embody the truth of the story. But she will not imagine that it is her responsibility to insure that the other is persuaded. That is in God's hands.

It has become customary to classify views on the relation of Christianity to the world religions as either pluralist, exclusivist, or inclusivist, the three positions being typically represented by John Hick, Hendrik Kraemer, and Karl Rahner. The position which I have outlined is exclusivist in the sense that it affirms the unique truth of the revelation in Jesus Christ, but it is not exclusivist in the sense of denying the possibility of the salvation of the non-Christian. It is inclusivist in the sense that it refuses to limit the saving grace of God to the members of the Christian Church, but it rejects the inclusivism which regards the non-Christian religions as vehicles of salvation. It is pluralist in the sense of acknowledging the gracious work of God in the lives of all human beings, but it rejects a pluralism which denies the uniqueness and decisiveness of what God has done in Jesus Christ. Arguments for pluralism and inclusivism usually begin from the paramount need for human unity, a need hugely increased by the threats of nuclear and ecological disaster. We must surely recognize that need. But the recognition of the need provides no clue as to how it is to be met, and certainly does not justify the assertion that religion is the means by which human unity is to be achieved. The question of truth must be faced. C. S. Song is one of those who wishes to play down the role of truth because, as he says, truth judges, polarizes, divides. Truth, he says, cannot unite the ununitable; only love can. So the Christian mission must be an affair of love, not an affair of truth (*Tell Us Our Names*, Orbis Books, 1984, p. 114). But it is not love which encourages people to believe a lie. As a human race we are on a journey and we need to know the road. It is not true that all roads lead to the top of the same mountain. There are roads which lead over the precipice. In Christ we have been shown the road. We cannot treat that knowledge as a private matter for ourselves. It concerns the whole human family. We do not presume to limit the might and the mercy of God for the ultimate salvation of all people, but the same costly act of revelation and reconciliation which gives us that assurance also requires us to share with our fellow pilgrims the vision that God has given us the route we must follow and the goal to which we must press forward.

23

John Paul II, from
Crossing the Threshold of Hope

The challenge of religious pluralism has not escaped the eye of Pope
John Paul II (b. 1920). In his book *Crossing the Threshold of Hope*, in
which the Holy Father responded in writing to questions posed by lay
religious writer Vittorio Messori, the Pope attempts to address the
matter of the centrality of Christ in a world which is religiously plural.
Drawing on the thinking of the Second Vatican Council (i.e. the
"Declaration on the Relationship of the Church to Non-Christian Religions," which is referred to in what follows by its Latin title and first
words: "*Nostra Aetate*" – "In our time"), he argues that there is unity
among and truth in all religions, which the Church respects. However,
he continues, the Church also is bound to proclaim that Christ is the
way and the truth and the life. More particularly, the Pope goes on to
note that there are *semina verbi* (seeds of the word – the parallel to
Justin Martyr's *logos spermatikos* seems clear) in all religions, which
the Church recognizes in affirmation of God's universal manifestation
and salvific will. In this way, through Jesus Christ, salvation is made
available to all.

Why So Many Religions?

But if God who is in heaven – and who saved and continues to save the world – is One and only One and is He who has revealed Himself in Jesus Christ, why has He allowed so many religions to exist?

Why did He make the search for the truth so arduous, in the midst of a forest of rituals, of beliefs, of revelations, of faiths which have always thrived – and still do today – throughout the world?

You speak of many religions. Instead I will attempt to show the *common fundamental element* and the *common root* of these religions.

The Council defined the relationship of the Church to non-Christian religions in a specific document that begins with the words "*Nostra aetate*" ("*In our time*"). It is a concise and yet very rich document that authentically hands on the Tradition, faithful to the thought of the earliest Fathers of the Church.

From the beginning, Christian Revelation has viewed the spiritual history of man as including, in some way, all religions, thereby demonstrating *the unity of humankind with regard to the eternal and ultimate destiny of man.* The Council document speaks of this unity and links it with the current trend to bring humanity closer together through the resources available to our civilization. The Church sees the promotion of this unity as one of its duties: "*There is only one community and it consists of all peoples.* They have only one origin, since God inhabited the entire earth with the whole human race. And they have one ultimate destiny, God, whose providence, goodness, and plan for salvation extend to all ... Men *turn to various religions to solve mysteries of the human condition,* which today, as in earlier times, burden people's hearts: the nature of man; the meaning and purpose of life; good and evil; the origin and purpose of suffering; the way to true happiness; death; judgment and retribution after death; and finally, the ultimate ineffable mystery which is the origin and destiny of our existence. From ancient times up to today all the various peoples have shared and continue to share an awareness of that enigmatic power that is present throughout the course of things and throughout the events of human life, and, in which, at times, even the Supreme Divinity or the Father is recognizable. This awareness and recognition imbue life with an intimate religious sense. Religions that are tied up with cultural progress strive to solve these issues with more refined concepts and a more precise language" (*Nostra Aetate* 1–2).

Here the Council document brings us to the *Far East* – first of all to Asia, a continent where the Church's missionary activity, carried out since the times of the apostles, has borne, we must recognize, very modest fruit. It is well known that only a small percentage of the population on what is the largest continent believes in Christ.

Source: John Paul II, *Crossing the Threshold of Hope,* trans. J. and M. McPhee, ed. V. Messori.

This does not mean that the Church's missionary effort has lapsed – quite the opposite: that effort has been and still remains intense. And yet *the tradition of very ancient cultures*, antedating Christianity, *remains very strong in the East*. Even if faith in Christ reaches hearts and minds, the negative connotations associated with the image of life in Western society (the so-called Christian society) present a considerable obstacle to the acceptance of the Gospel. Mahatma Gandhi, Indian and Hindu, pointed this out many times, in his deeply evangelical manner. He was disillusioned with the ways in which Christianity was expressed in the political and social life of nations. Could a man who fought for the liberation of his great nation from colonial dependence accept Christianity in the same form as it had been imposed on his country by those same colonial powers?

The Second Vatican Council realized this difficulty. This is why the document on the relations between the Church and *Hinduism* and other religions of the Far East is so important. We read: "In *Hinduism* men explore the divine mystery and express it through an endless bounty of myths and through penetrating philosophical insight. They seek freedom from the anguish of our human condition, either by way of the ascetic life, profound meditation, or by taking refuge in God with love and trust. The various schools of *Buddhism* recognize the radical inadequacy of this malleable world and teach a way by which men, with devout and trusting hearts, can become capable either of reaching a state of perfect liberation, or of attaining, by their own efforts or through higher help, supreme illumination" (*Nostra Aetate* 2).

Further along, the Council remarks that *"The Catholic Church rejects nothing that is true and holy in these religions.* The Church has a high regard for their conduct and way of life, for those precepts and doctrines which, although differing on many points from that which the Church believes and propounds, often *reflect a ray of that truth which enlightens all men.* However, the Church proclaims, and is bound to proclaim that *Christ is 'the way and the truth and the life'* [Jn 14:6], in whom men must find the fullness of religious life and in whom God has reconciled everything to Himself" (*Nostra Aetate* 2).

The words of the Council recall the conviction, long rooted in the Tradition, of the existence of the so-called *semina Verbi* (seeds of the Word), present in all religions. In the light of this conviction, the Church seeks to identify the *semina Verbi* present in the great traditions of the Far East, in order to trace a common path against the backdrop of the needs of the contemporary world. We can affirm that here the position of the Council is inspired by a *truly universal concern.* The Church is guided by the faith that *God the Creator wants to save all humankind in Jesus Christ,* the only mediator between God and man, inasmuch as He is the Redeemer of all humankind. The Paschal Mystery is equally available to all, and, through it, the way to eternal salvation is also open to all.

In another passage the Council says that the Holy Spirit works effectively even outside the visible structure of the Church (cf. *Lumen Gentium* 13), making use of these very *semina Verbi*, that constitute a kind of *common soteriological root present in all religions.*

*

I have been convinced of this on numerous occasions, both while *visiting the countries of the Far East* and while meeting representatives of those religions, especially during the historic *meeting at Assisi*, where we found ourselves gathered together praying for peace.

Thus, instead of marveling at the fact that Providence allows such a great variety of religions, we should be amazed at the number of common elements found within them.

At this point it would be helpful to recall all the *primitive religions*, the *animistic religions* which stress ancestor worship. It seems that those who practice them are particularly close to Christianity, and among them, the Church's missionaries also find it easier to speak a common language. Is there, perhaps, in this veneration of ancestors a kind of preparation for the Christian faith in the Communion of Saints, in which all believers – whether living or dead – form a single community, a single body? And faith in the Communion of Saints is, ultimately, faith in Christ, who alone is the source of life and of holiness for all. There is nothing strange, then, that the African and Asian animists would become believers in Christ more easily than followers of the great *religions of the Far East*.

As the Council also noted, these last religions possess the *characteristics of a system*. They are *systems of worship* and also *ethical systems*, with a strong emphasis on good and evil. Certainly among these belong Chinese Confucianism and Taoism: Tao means eternal truth – something similar to the "Word" – which is reflected in the action of man by means of truth and moral good. The religions of the Far East have contributed greatly to the history of morality and culture, forming a national identity in the Chinese, Indians, Japanese, and Tibetans, and also in the peoples of Southeast Asia and the archipelagoes of the Pacific Ocean.

Some of these peoples come from age-old cultures. The indigenous peoples of Australia boast a history tens of thousands of years old, and their ethnic and religious tradition is older than that of Abraham and Moses.

Christ came into the world for all these peoples. He redeemed them all and has His own ways of reaching each of them in the present eschatological phase of salvation history. In fact, in those regions, many accept Him and many more have an implicit faith in Him (cf. Heb 11:6).

Buddha?

Before moving on to monotheism, to the two other religions (Judaism and Islam) which worship one God, I would like to ask you to speak more fully on the subject of Buddhism. Essentially – as you well know – it offers a "doctrine of salvation" that seems increasingly to fascinate many Westerners as an "alternative" to Christianity or as a sort of "complement" to it, at least in terms of certain ascetic and mystical techniques.

Yes, you are right and I am grateful to you for this question. Among the religions mentioned in the Council document *Nostra Aetate*, it is necessary to pay special attention to *Buddhism*, which from a certain point of view, like Christianity, is a religion of salvation. Nevertheless, it needs to be said right away that the doctrines of salvation in Buddhism and Christianity are opposed.

The *Dalai Lama*, spiritual leader of the Tibetans, is a well-known figure in the West. I have met him a few times. He brings Buddhism to people of the Christian West, stirring up interest both in Buddhist spirituality and in its methods of praying. I also had the chance to meet the Buddhist "patriarch" in Bangkok, Thailand, and among the monks that surrounded him there were several, for example, who came from the United States. Today we are seeing a certain *diffusion of Buddhism in the West*.

The *Buddhist doctrine of salvation* constitutes the central point, or rather the only point, of this system. Nevertheless, both the Buddhist tradition and the methods deriving from it have an almost exclusively *negative soteriology*.

The "enlightenment" experienced by Buddha comes down to the conviction that the world is bad, that it is the source of evil and of suffering for man. To liberate oneself from this evil, one must free oneself from this world, necessitating a break with the ties that join us to external reality – ties existing in our human nature, in our psyche, in our bodies. The more we are liberated from these ties, the more we become indifferent to what is in the world, and the more we are freed from suffering, from the evil that has its source in the world.

Do we draw near to God in this way? This is not mentioned in the "enlightenment" conveyed by Buddha. Buddhism is in large measure an *"atheistic" system*. We do not free ourselves from evil through the good which comes from God; we liberate ourselves only through detachment from the world, which is bad. The fullness of such a detachment is not union with God, but what is called nirvana, a state of perfect indifference with regard to the world. *To save oneself* means, above all, to free oneself from evil by becoming *indifferent to the world, which is the source of evil*. This is the culmination of the spiritual process.

At various times, attempts to link this method with the Christian mystics have been made – whether it is with those from northern Europe (Eckhart, Tauler, Suso, Ruysbroeck) or the later Spanish mystics (Saint Teresa of Avila, Saint John of the Cross). But when Saint John of the Cross, in the *Ascent of Mount Carmel* and in the *Dark Night of the Soul*, speaks of the need for purification, for detachment from the world of the senses, he does not conceive of that detachment as an end in itself. "To arrive at what now you do not enjoy, you must go where you do not enjoy. To reach what you do not know, you must go where you do not know. To come into possession of what you do not have, you must go where now you have nothing" (*Ascent of Mount Carmel*, I. 13. II). In Eastern Asia these classic texts of Saint John of the Cross have been, at times, interpreted as a confirmation of Eastern ascetic methods. But this Doctor of the Church does not merely propose detachment from the world. He proposes detachment from the world in order to unite oneself to that which is outside of the world – by this I do not mean nirvana, but a personal God. Union with Him comes about not only through purification, but through love.

Carmelite mysticism begins at the point where the reflections of Buddha end, together with his instructions for the spiritual life. In the active and passive purification of the human soul, in those specific nights of the senses and the spirit, Saint John of the Cross sees, above all, the preparation necessary for the human soul to be permeated with the living flame of love. And this is also the title of his major work – *The Living Flame of Love*.

Therefore, despite similar aspects, there is a fundamental difference. *Christian mysticism* from every period – beginning with the era of the Fathers of the Eastern and Western Church, to the great theologians of Scholasticism (such as Saint Thomas Aquinas), to the northern European mystics, to the Carmelite mystics – is not born of a purely negative "enlightenment." It is not born of an awareness of the evil which exists in man's attachment to the world through the senses, the intellect, and the spirit. Instead, Christian mysticism is born of the *Revelation of the living God*. This God opens Himself to union with man, arousing in him the capacity to be united with Him, especially by means of the theological virtues – faith, hope, and, above all, love.

Christian mysticism in every age up to our own – including the mysticism of marvelous men of action like Vincent de Paul, John Bosco, Maximilian Kolbe – has built up and continues to build up Christianity in its most essential element. It also builds up the Church as a community of faith, hope, and charity. It builds up civilization, particularly "Western civilization," which is marked by a *positive approach to the world*, and which developed thanks to the achievements of science and technology, two branches of knowledge rooted both in the ancient Greek philosophical tradition and in Judeo-Christian Revelation. The truth about God the Creator of the world and about Christ the Redeemer is a powerful force which inspires a positive attitude toward creation and provides a constant impetus to strive for its transformation and perfection.

The Second Vatican Council has amply confirmed this truth. To indulge in a negative attitude toward the world, in the conviction that it is only a source of suffering for man and that he therefore must break away from it, is negative not only because it is unilateral but also because it is fundamentally contrary to the development of both man himself and the world, which the Creator has given and entrusted to man as his task.

We read in *Gaudium et Spes*: "Therefore, the *world* which [the Council] has in mind is the world *of men, of the entire human family* considered in the context of all realities; the world which is the theater of human history and which bears the marks of humanity's struggles, its defeats, and its victories; the world which the Christians believe has been created and is sustained by the Creator's love, a world enslaved by sin but liberated by the crucified and resurrected Christ in order to defeat evil, and destined, *according to the divine plan, to be transformed and to reach its fulfillment*" (*Gaudium et Spes* 2).

These words indicate how between Christianity and the religions of the Far East, in particular Buddhism, there is an essentially different way of perceiving the world. For Christians, the world is God's creation, redeemed by Christ. It is in the world that man meets God. Therefore he does not need to attain such an absolute detachment in order to find himself in the mystery of his deepest self. For Christianity, it does not make sense to speak of the world as a "radical" evil, since at the beginning of the world we find God the Creator who loves His creation, a God who "gave his only Son, so that everyone who believes in him might not perish but might have eternal life" (Jn 3:16).

For this reason it is not inappropriate to *caution* those Christians who enthusiastically *welcome certain ideas originating in the religious traditions of the Far East* – for example, techniques and methods of meditation and ascetical practice. In some quarters these have become fashionable, and are accepted rather uncritically. First one should know one's own spiritual heritage well and consider whether it is right to set it aside lightly. Here we need to recall, if only in passing, the brief but important document of the Congregation for the Doctrine of the Faith "on certain aspects of Christian meditation" (10/15/1989). Here we find a clear answer to the question "whether and how [Christian prayer] can be enriched by methods of meditation originating in different religions and cultures" (n.3).

A separate issue is the *return of ancient gnostic ideas under the guise of the so-called New Age*. We cannot delude ourselves that this will lead toward a renewal of religion. It is only a new way of practicing gnosticism – that attitude of the spirit that, in the name of a profound knowledge of God, results in distorting His Word and replacing it with purely human words. Gnosticism never completely abandoned the realm of Christianity. Instead, it has always existed side by side with Christianity, sometimes taking the shape of a philosophical movement, but more often assuming the characteristics of a religion or para-religion in distinct, if not declared, conflict with all that is essentially Christian.

Muhammad?

A very different discussion, obviously, is the one that leads us to the synagogues and mosques, where those who worship the One God assemble.

Yes, certainly it is a different case when we come to these *great monotheistic* religions, beginning with *Islam*. In the Declaration *Nostra Aetate* we read: "The Church also has a high regard for the Muslims, who worship one God, living and subsistent, merciful and omnipotent, the Creator of heaven and earth" (*Nostra Aetate* 3). As a result of their monotheism, believers in Allah are particularly close to us.

. . .

I remember an event from my youth. In the convent of the Church of Saint Mark in Florence, we were looking at the frescoes by Fra Angelico. At a certain point a man joined us who, after sharing his admiration for the work of this great religious artist, immediately added: "But nothing can compare to our magnificent Muslim monotheism." His statement did not prevent us from continuing the visit and the conversation in a friendly tone. It was on that occasion that I got a kind of first taste of the dialogue between Christianity and Islam, which we have tried to develop systematically in the post-conciliar period.

Whoever knows the Old and New Testaments, and then reads the Koran, clearly sees the *process by which it completely reduces Divine Revelation*. It is impossible not to note the movement away from what God said about Himself, first in the Old Testament through the Prophets, and then finally in the New Testament through His Son. In Islam all the richness of God's self-revelation, which constitutes the heritage of the Old and New Testaments, has definitely been set aside.

Some of the most beautiful names in the human language are given to the God of the Koran, but He is ultimately a God outside of the world, a God who is *only Majesty, never Emmanuel*, God-with-us. *Islam is not a religion of redemption*. There is no room for the Cross and the Resurrection. Jesus is mentioned, but only as a prophet who prepares for the last prophet, Muhammad. There is also mention of Mary, His Virgin Mother, but the tragedy of redemption is completely absent. For this reason not only the theology but also the anthropology of Islam is very distant from Christianity.

Nevertheless, *the religiosity of Muslims deserves respect*. It is impossible not to admire, for example, their *fidelity to prayer*. The image of believers in Allah who, without caring about time or place, fall to their knees and immerse themselves in prayer remains a model for all *those who invoke* the true God, in particular for those Christians who, having deserted their magnificent cathedrals, pray only a little or not at all.

The Council has also called for the Church to have a *dialogue* with followers of the "Prophet," and the Church has proceeded to do so. We read in *Nostra Aetate*: "Even if over the course of centuries Christians and Muslims have had more than a few dissensions and quarrels, this sacred Council now urges all to forget the past and to work toward mutual understanding as well as toward the preservation and promotion of social justice, moral welfare, peace, and freedom for the benefit of all mankind" (*Nostra Aetate* 3).

From this point of view, as I have already mentioned, the meetings for prayer held at Assisi (especially that for peace in Bosnia, in 1993), certainly played a significant role. Also worthwhile were my meetings with the followers of Islam during my numerous apostolic trips to Africa and Asia, where sometimes, in a given country, the majority of the citizens were Muslims. Despite this, the Pope was welcomed with great hospitality and was listened to with similar graciousness.

The trip I made to Morocco at the invitation of King Hassan II can certainly be defined as a historic event. It was not simply a courtesy visit, but an event of a truly pastoral nature. The encounter with the young people at Casablanca Stadium (1985) was unforgettable. The openness of the young people to the Pope's words was striking when he spoke of faith in the one God. It was certainly an unprecedented event.

Nevertheless, concrete difficulties are not lacking. In countries where *fundamentalist* movements come to power, human rights and the principle of religious freedom are unfortunately interpreted in a very one-sided way – religious freedom comes to mean freedom to impose on all citizens the "true religion." In these countries the situation of Christians is sometimes terribly disturbing. Fundamentalist attitudes of this nature make reciprocal contacts very difficult. All the same, the Church remains always open to dialogue and cooperation.

Judaism?

At this point it is natural to assume that Your Holiness intends to speak of Judaism.

That is right. Through the amazing plurality of religions, arranged as it were in concentric circles, we come to the religion that is closest to our own – that of the people of God of the Old Testament.

The words from the Declaration *Nostra Aetate* represent a turning point. The Council says: "The Church of Christ, in fact, recognizes that according to the divine mystery of salvation the origins of the Church's faith and election are already found in the Patriarchs, Moses, and the Prophets. . . . The Church, then, can forget neither that it received the revelation of the Old Testament through that people with whom God, in his ineffable mercy, made the Ancient Covenant, nor can the Church forget that it draws sustenance from the root of that good olive tree onto which have been grafted the wild shoots, the Gentiles. . . . Therefore, since the spiritual patrimony common to Christians and Jews is so great, this Sacred Council recommends and promotes a mutual understanding and respect, which can be obtained above all through biblical study and fraternal discussion" (*Nostra Aetate* 4).

The words of the Council's Declaration reflect the experience of many people, both Jews and Christians. They reflect *my personal experience* as well, from the very first years of my life in my hometown. I remember, above all, the Wadowice elementary school, where at least a fourth of the pupils in my class were Jewish. I should mention my friendship at school with one of them, Jerzy Kluger – a friendship that has lasted from my school days to the present. I can vividly remember the Jews who gathered every Saturday at the synagogue behind our school. Both religious groups, Catholics and Jews, were united, I presume, by the awareness that they prayed to the same God. Despite their different languages, prayers in the church and in the synagogue were based to a considerable degree on the same texts.

. . .

Then came the Second World War, with its concentration camps and systematic extermination. First and foremost, the sons and daughters of the Jewish nation were condemned for no other reason than that they were Jewish. Even if only indirectly, whoever lived in Poland at that time came into contact with this reality.

Therefore, this was also a personal experience of mine, an experience I carry with me even today. Auschwitz, perhaps the most meaningful symbol of the *Holocaust of the Jewish people*, shows to what lengths a system constructed on principles of racial hatred and greed for power can go. To this day, Auschwitz does not cease to admonish, reminding us that *anti-Semitism is a great sin against humanity*, that all racial hatred inevitably leads to the trampling of human dignity.

I would like to return to the synagogue at Wadowice. It was destroyed by the Germans and no longer exists today. A few years ago Jerzy came to me to say that the place where the synagogue had stood should be honored with a special commemorative plaque. I must admit that in that moment we both felt a deep emotion. We saw faces of people we knew and cared for, and we recalled those Saturdays of our childhood and adolescence when the Jewish community of Wadowice gathered for prayer. I promised him I would gladly send a personal note as a sign of my solidarity and spiritual union on the occasion of such an important event. And so I did. It was Jerzy himself who brought that letter to my fellow citizens in Wadowice. That trip was not easy for him. All the members of his family who had remained in that small town had died at Auschwitz. His visit to Wadowice for the unveiling of the plaque in commemoration of the local synagogue was his first in fifty years. . . .

The words of *Nostra Aetate*, as I have said, reflect the experience of many. I think back to *the time of my pastoral work in Kraków*. Kraków, and especially the Kazimierz neighborhood, retain many traces of Jewish culture and tradition. In Kazimierz, before the war, there were several dozen synagogues which were in some sense great cultural monuments as well. As Archbishop of Kraków, I was in close contact with the city's Jewish community. I enjoyed very cordial relations with the head of that community, which continued even after I came to Rome.

After my election to the See of Saint Peter, I have continued to cherish these deeply significant ties. On my pastoral journeys around the world I always try to meet representatives of the Jewish community. But a truly exceptional experience for me was certainly my *visit to the synagogue of Rome*. The history of the Jews in Rome is a unique chapter in the history of the Jewish people, a chapter closely linked for that matter to The Acts of the Apostles. During that memorable visit, I spoke of the Jews as our *elder brothers in the faith*. These words were an expression both of the Council's teaching, and a profound conviction on the part of the Church. The Second Vatican Council did not dwell on this subject at length, but what it did affirm embraces an immense reality which is not only religious but also cultural.

This extraordinary people continues to bear signs of its divine election. I said this to an Israeli politician once and he readily agreed, but was quick to add: "*If only it could cost less!* . . ." Israel has truly paid a high price for its "election." Perhaps because of this, Israel has become more similar to the Son of man, who, according to the flesh, was also a son of Israel. The two thousandth anniversary of His coming to the world will be a celebration for Jews as well.

I am pleased that my ministry in the See of Saint Peter has taken place during the period following the Second Vatican Council, when the insights which inspired the Declaration *Nostra Aetate* are finding concrete expression in various ways. Thus the way two great moments of divine election – the Old and the New Covenants – are drawing closer together.

The New Covenant has its roots in the Old. The time when the people of the Old Covenant will be able to see themselves as part of the New is, naturally, a question to be left to the Holy Spirit. We, as human beings, try only not to put obstacles in the way. The form this "not putting obstacles" takes is certainly dialogue between Christians and Jews, which, on the Church's part, is being carried forward by the Pontifical Council for Promoting Christian Unity.

I am also pleased that as a result of the peace process currently taking place, despite setbacks and obstacles, in the Middle East, and thanks also to the initiative of the State of Israel, it became possible to *establish diplomatic relations between the Apostolic See and Israel.* As for the recognition of the State of Israel, it is important to reaffirm that I myself never had any doubts in this regard.

Once, after the conclusion of one of my meetings with the Jewish community, someone present said: "I want to thank the Pope for all that the Catholic Church has done over the last two thousand years to make the true God known."

These words indirectly indicate how the New Covenant serves to fulfill all that is rooted in the vocation of Abraham, in God's covenant with Israel at Sinai, and in the whole rich heritage of the inspired Prophets who, hundreds of years before that fulfillment, pointed in the Sacred Scriptures to the One whom God would send in the "fullness of time" (cf. Gal 4:4).

A Minority by the Year 2000

Pardon me, Your Holiness, but my role (which gives me great honor but also a certain responsibility) is also that of a respectful "provocateur" with regard to questions – even troubling ones – which are also present among Catholics.

I will continue, then, by observing how you have frequently recalled – with an awareness of the symbolic importance of the event – the approach of the third millennium of the Redemption. According to statistical projections, by the year 2000, for the first time in history, Muslims will outnumber Catholics. Already Hindus alone are more numerous than Protestants and Orthodox Greeks and Slavs combined. In your pastoral journeys around the world, you have often visited places where believers in Christ, and Catholics in particular, are a small and even shrinking minority.

How do you feel when faced with this reality, after twenty centuries of evangelization? What divine plan do you see at work here?

I think that such a view of the problem arises from a somewhat simplistic interpretation of the matter. In reality, the essence goes far deeper, as I have already tried to explain in my response to the preceding question. Here statistics are not useful – we are speaking of *values which are not quantifiable*.

To tell the truth, the sociology of religion – although useful in other areas – does not help much here. As a basis for assessment, the criteria for measurement which it provides do not help when considering people's interior attitude. *No statistic* aiming at a quantitative measurement of faith (for example, the number of people who participate in religious ceremonies) will get to the heart of the matter. *Here numbers alone are not enough.*

The question you ask – albeit "provocatively," as you say – amounts to this: let us count the number of Muslims in the world, or the number of Hindus, *let us count the number of Catholics*, or Christians in general, and we can determine which religion is in the majority, *which has a future ahead of it*, and which instead seems to belong only to the past, or is undergoing a systematic process of decomposition and decline.

From the point of view of the Gospel the issue is completely different. Christ says: "*Do not be afraid any longer, little flock*, for your Father is pleased to give you the kingdom" (Lk 12:32). I think that in these words Christ best responds to this problem that some find troubling and that is raised in your question. Jesus goes even further when He asks: "When the Son of Man comes, will he find faith on earth?" (cf. Lk 18:8).

Both this question and the earlier saying about the little flock indicate the profound realism which inspired Jesus in dealing with His apostles. *He did not prepare them for easy success*. He spoke clearly. He spoke of the persecutions that awaited those who would believe in Him. At the same time, *He established a solid foundation for the faith*. "The Father was pleased to give the Kingdom" to those twelve men from Galilee, and through them to all humanity. He forewarned them that the mission He sent them on would involve opposition and persecution because He Himself had been persecuted: "If they persecuted me, they will also persecute you." But He hastened to add: "If they kept my word, they will also keep yours" (cf. Jn 15:20).

Since my youth I have felt that the heart of the Gospel is contained in these words. *The Gospel is not a promise of easy success*. It does not promise a comfortable life to anyone. It makes demands and, at the same time, it is *a great promise* – the promise of eternal life for man, who is subject to the law of death, and the promise of victory through faith for man, who is subject to many trials and setbacks.

The Gospel contains a *fundamental paradox*: to find life, one must lose life; to be born, one must die; to save oneself, one must take up the cross. This is the essential truth of the Gospel, which always and everywhere is bound to meet with man's protest.

Always and everywhere the Gospel will be a challenge to human weakness. But precisely in this challenge lies all its power. Man, perhaps, subconsciously waits for such a challenge; *indeed, man feels the inner need to transcend himself*. Only in transcending himself does man become fully human (cf. Blaise Pascal, *Pensées*, ed. Brunschvicg, 434: "Apprenez que l'homme passe infiniment l'homme").

This is the most profound truth about man. *Christ is the first to know this truth*. He truly knows "that which is in every man" (cf. Jn 2:25). With His Gospel He has touched the intimate truth of man. He has touched it first of all with His Cross. Pilate, who, pointing to the Nazarene crowned with thorns after His scourging, said, "Behold, the man!" (Jn 19:5), did not realize that he was proclaiming an essential truth, expressing that which always and everywhere remains the heart of evangelization.

Further Reading

General Works on the Bible, Theology, and the Christian Tradition

Childs, Brevard. *Biblical Theology of the Old and New Testaments: Theological Reflection on the Christian Bible*. Minneapolis: Fortress Press, 1992.

Hauer, Christian E., and William A. Young. *An Introduction to the Bible: A Journey into Three Worlds*. 3rd edn. Englewood Cliffs, NJ: Prentice-Hall, 1994.

McGrath, Alister. *Christian Theology: An Introduction*. 2nd edn. Oxford: Blackwell Publishers, 1997.

Pelikan, Jaroslav. *The Christian Tradition: A History of the Development of Doctrine*. 5 vols. Chicago: University of Chicago Press, 1971–89.

The Ancient and Patristic Period

St Augustine. *Of True Religion*. Trans. J. H. S. Burleigh. South Bend, Ind.: Regnery/Gateway, Inc., 1959.

—. "On the Profit of Believing." In *The Nicene and Post-Nicene Fathers of the Christian Church*, vol. 3. Trans C. L. Cornish. Ed. P. Schaff. Grand Rapids, Mich.: W. B. Eerdmans, 1993, 347–66.

Cicero. *The Nature of the Gods*. Trans Horace C. P. McGregor. Harmondsworth: Penguin, 1972.

Clement of Alexandria. "The Stromata, or Miscellanies." In *The Ante-Nicene Fathers: Translations of the Writings of the Fathers down to A.D. 325*, vol. 2. Arranged and rev. A. C. Coxe. Ed. A. Roberts and J. Donaldson. Grand Rapids, Mich.: W. B. Eerdmans, 1951, 299–568.

Justin Martyr. "The Second Apology of Justin to the Roman Senate in Behalf of the Christians." In *Writings of Saint Justin Martyr. The Fathers of the Church*, vol. 6. Trans. T. B. Falls. New York: Christian Heritage, 1948, 119–35.

Origen. "De Principiis". In *The Ante-Nicene Fathers: Translations of the Writings of the Fathers down to A.D. 325*, vol. 4. Trans. F. Crombie. Ed. A. Roberts and J. Donaldson. Grand Rapids, Mich.: W. B. Eerdmans, 1956, 260–2, 344–8.

Tertullian. "The Prescriptions Against the Heretics." In *Early Latin Theology*. Library of Christian Classics, 5. Trans. and ed. S. L. Greenslade. Philadelphia: Westminster Press, 1953, 31–64.

Further Reading

The Medieval Period

Anselm. "Proslogion." In *The Prayers and Meditations of Saint Anselm*. Trans. Sister Benedicta Ward. Harmondsworth: Penguin, 1973, 238–67.

Aquinas, Thomas. *On the Truth of the Catholic Faith: Summa Contra Gentiles*. 4 vols. Trans. Anton C. Pegis et al. Garden City, NY: Doubleday/Image Books, 1955–6.

——. *Summa Theologica*. 5 vols. Trans. Fathers of the English Dominican Province. Westminster, Md.: Christian Classics, 1948.

Gilson, Etienne. *Reason and Revelation in the Middle Ages*. New York: Charles Scribner's Sons, 1938.

The Renaissance and Reformation Period

Bodin, Jean. *Colloquium of the Seven about Secrets of the Sublime*. Trans. Marion L. D. Kuntz. Princeton, NJ: Princeton University Press, 1975.

Calvin, John. *Institutes of the Christian Religion*. Library of Christian Classics, 20. Trans. F. L. Battles. Ed. J. T. McNeill. Philadelphia: Westminster Press, 1960, 270–89.

Luther, Martin. "The Freedom of a Christian." In *Martin Luther: Selections from His Writings*. Ed. John Dillenberger. Garden City, NY: Doubleday/Anchor Books, 1961, 42–85.

Nicholas of Cusa. "De Pace Fidei." In *Nicholas of Cusa's De Pace Fidei and Cribratio Alkorani*. Trans. J. Hopkins. Minneapolis: Arthur J. Banning Press, 1990, 33–71.

The Modern and Postmodern Period

Bavinck, J. H. *The Church between Temple and Mosque*. Grand Rapids, Mich.: W. B. Eerdmans, n.d.

Berger, Peter. "God in a World of Gods." *First Things* 35 (August/September 1993): 25–31.

——. *The Sacred Canopy: Elements of a Sociological Theory of Religion*. Garden City, NY: Doubleday/Anchor Books, 1967.

Bouquet, A. C. *The Christian Faith and Non-Christian Religions*. New York: Harper and Brothers, 1958.

Braaten, Carl. *No Other Gospel! Christianity among the World's Religions*. Minneapolis: Fortress Press, 1992.

Brunner, Emil, and Karl Barth. *Natural Theology: Comprising "Nature and Grace" by Professor Dr Emil Brunner and the Reply "No!" by Dr Karl Barth*. Trans. Peter Fraenkel. Introduction by John Baillie. London: Geoffrey Bles and The Centenary Press, 1946.

Camps, Arnulf. *Partners in Dialogue: Christianity and Other World Religions*. Trans. John Drury. Maryknoll, NY: Orbis Books, 1983.

The Christian Life and Message in Relation to Non-Christian Systems. Report of the Jerusalem Meeting of the International Missionary Council March 24th–April 8th 1928. Vol 1. London: Humphrey Milford/Oxford University Press, 1928.

Dawe, Donald G., and John B. Carman. *Christian Faith in a Religiously Plural World*. Maryknoll, NY: Orbis Books, 1978.

Descartes, René. *Meditations on First Philosophy with Selections from the Objections and Replies*. Trans. John Cottingham. Cambridge: Cambridge University Press, 1986.

Hallencreutz, Carl. *Kraemer towards Tambaram: A Study in Hendrik Kraemer's Missionary Approach*. Studia Missionalia Upsaliensia, 7. Lund: C. W. K. Gleerup, 1966.

Further Reading

—. *New Approaches to Men of Other Faiths*. Research Pamphlet, 18. Geneva: World Council of Churches, 1970.

Heim, S. Mark. "Pluralism and the Otherness of World Religions". *First Things* 25 (August/ September 1992): 29–35.

Hick, John. *A Christian Theology of Religions: The Rainbow of Faiths*. Louisville, Ky.: Westminster/ John Knox Press, 1995.

—. *God and the Universe of Faiths: Essays in the Philosophy of Religion*. London: Macmillan, 1973.

—. *God Has Many Names: Britain's New Religious Pluralism*. London: Macmillan, 1980.

—. *Problems of Religious Pluralism*. New York: St Martin's Press, 1985.

—. *The Rainbow of Faiths: Critical Dialogues on Religious Pluralism*. London: SCM Press, 1995.

Hocking, William Ernest, et al. *Re-Thinking Missions: A Laymen's Inquiry after One Hundred Years*. New York: Harper and Brothers, 1932.

Hume, David. *Dialogues Concerning Natural Religion*. Ed. Norman Kemp Smith. Indianapolis: Bobbs-Merrill, 1947.

—. "Of Miracles." In *Enquiries Concerning Human Understanding and Concerning the Principles of Morals*. 3rd edn. Ed. L. A. Selby-Bigge. Rev. P. H. Nidditch. Oxford: Clarendon Press, 1975, 109–31.

Kant, Immanuel. *Prolegomena to Any Future Metaphysics*. Ed. Lewis White Beck. Indianapolis: Bobbs-Merrill, 1950.

—. *Religion within the Limits of Reason Alone*. Trans. T. M. Green and H. H. Hudson. New York: Harper and Row, 1960.

Knitter, Paul. *No Other Name? A Critical Survey of Christian Attitudes toward the World Religions*. American Society of Missiology Series, 7. Maryknoll, NY: Orbis Books, 1985.

Kraemer, Hendrik. *The Christian Message in a Non-Christian World*. 3rd edn. Grand Rapids, Mich.: Kregel Publications, 1956.

—. *Religion and the Christian Faith*. London: Lutterworth Press, 1956.

—. *World Cultures and World Religions: The Coming Dialogue*. Philadelphia: Westminster Press, 1960.

Küng, Hans. *On Being a Christian*. Trans. E. Quinn. Garden City, NY: Doubleday, 1976, 89–116.

Küng, Hans, et al. *Christianity and the World Religions: Paths of Dialogue with Islam, Hinduism, and Buddhism*. New York: Doubleday, 1986.

Locke, John. "The Reasonableness of Christianity." In *Locke on Politics, Religion, and Education*. Ed. Maurice Cranston. New York: Collier Books, 1965, 207–31.

Newbigin, Lesslie. *Foolishness to the Greeks: The Gospel and Western Culture*. Grand Rapids, Mich.: W. B. Eerdmans, 1986.

Otto, Rudolf. *The Idea of the Holy: An Inquiry into the Non-Rational Factor in the Idea of the Divine and its Relation to the Rational*. 2nd edn. Trans. J. W. Harvey. London: Oxford University Press, 1950.

Oxtoby, Willard G. *The Meaning of Other Faiths*. Library of Living Faith, 10. Ed. John M. Mulder. Philadelphia: Westminster Press, 1983.

Paley, William. *Natural Theology*. Ed. Frederick Ferré. Indianapolis: Library of Liberal Arts, 1963.

Panikkar, Raimundo. *The Unknown Christ of Hinduism: Towards an Ecumenical Christophany*. Rev. enl. edn. Maryknoll, NY: Orbis Books, 1981.

Pannenberg, Wolfhart. *Theology and the Philosophy of Science*. Trans. Francis McDonagh. London: Darton, Longman, and Todd, 1976.

—. "Toward a Theology of the History of Religions." In *Basic Questions in Theology: Collected Essays*, vol. 2. Trans. George H. Kehm. Philadelphia: Fortress Press, 1971, 65–118.

Paton, Wm., ed. *The Authority of the Faith.* Tambaram Madras Series, 1. London: Humphrey Milford/Oxford University Press, 1939.

Pinnock, Clark. *A Wideness in God's Mercy: The Finality of Jesus Christ in a World of Religions.* Grand Rapids, Mich.: Zondervan, 1992.

Race, Alan. *Christians and Religious Pluralism: Patterns in the Christian Theology of Religions.* London: SCM Press, 1983.

Rahner, Karl. "Anonymous and Explicit Faith." In *Theological Investigations,* vol. 16. Trans. David Morland. New York: Crossroad, 1983, 52–9.

——. "Anonymous Christianity and the Missionary Task of the Church." In *Theological Investigations,* vol. 12. Trans. David Bourke. New York: Seabury, 1974, 161–78.

——. "History of the World and Salvation-History." In *Theological Investigations,* vol. 5. Trans. Karl-H. Kruger. New York: Crossroad, 1983, 97–114.

——. "Observations on the Problem of the 'Anonymous Christian.'" In *Theological Investigations,* vol. 14. Trans. David Bourke. New York: Seabury, 1976, 280–94.

Rousseau, Jean Jacques. *The Social Contract.* Trans. Willmoore Kendall. South Bend, Ind.: Gateway Editions, Ltd., 1954.

Samartha, Stanley. "Dialogue as a Continuing Christian Concern." In *Christianity and Other Religions: Selected Readings.* Ed. J. Hick and B. Hebblethwaite. Philadelphia: Fortress Press, 1980, 151–70.

Schleiermacher, Friedrich. *On Religion: Speeches to its Cultured Despisers.* Trans. John Oman. New York: Harper and Row, 1958.

Schlette, H. R. *Towards a Theology of Religions.* Montreal: Palm Publishers, 1966.

Sharpe, Eric. *Faith Meets Faith: Some Christian Attitudes to Hinduism in the Nineteenth and Twentieth Centuries.* London: SCM Press, 1977.

Smith, Wilfred Cantwell. *The Meaning and End of Religion.* New York: Harper and Row, 1978.

——. *Towards a World Theology: Faith and the Comparative History of Religion.* Philadelphia: Westminster Press, 1981.

Söderblom, Nathan. *The Living God: Basal Forms of Personal Religion.* Boston: Beacon Press, 1962.

Tillich, Paul. "The Significance of the History of Religions for the Systematic Theologian." In *The Future of Religions.* Ed. J. C. Brauer. New York: Harper and Row, 1966, 80–94.

Toynbee, Arnold. *Christianity among the Religions of the World.* New York: Charles Scribner's Sons, 1957.

Troeltsch, Ernst. *The Absoluteness of Christianity.* Trans. David Reid. Richmond, Va.: John Knox Press, 1971.

Vallée, Gérard. *Mouvement oecuménique et religions non chrétiennes: un débat oecuménique sur la rencontre interreligieuse de Tambaram à Uppsala (1938–1968).* Recherches, 14. Montreal: Bellarmin, 1975.

Van Lin, J. J. E. *Protestantse theologie der godsdiensten: Van Edinburgh naar Tambaram (1910–1938).* Assen: Van Gorcum, 1974.

Voegelin, Eric. "Theology Confronting World Religions." In *Conversations with Eric Voegelin.* Ed. R. E. O'Connor. Thomas More Institute Papers, 76, Montreal: Thomas More Institute, 1980, 37–74.

Index

Note: boldface type refers to chapters of this book.

CPSIA information can be obtained at www.ICGtesting.com
Printed in the USA
LVOW03s0945080814

397895LV00005B/12/P